Praise for Joyce Maynard

At Home in the World

"*At Home in the World* is not a sleazy tell-all memoir about the author's affair with a famous (and famously reclusive) man. It's actually an earnest autobiography that, in the course of tracing the author's coming of age, delineates her first serious love affair, one that happened to be with the author of *Catcher in the Rye*. Unsparing self-scrutiny, maturity, and emotional candor."

—Michiko Kakutani, *The New York Times*

"I see [Maynard] as one of America's literary pioneers."

—Barbara Raskin, *The Washington Post Book World*

"A wry, painful, engaging book."

—Frank McCourt, author of *Angela's Ashes*

"Riveting and disturbing."

—Katha Pollitt, *The New York Times Book Review*

To Die For

"A seductive page-turner . . . psychologically penetrating."

—*The New York Times*

"Brilliant, deft . . . Maynard gets the psychopathic personality exactly right."

—*Entertainment Weekly*

"Shocking, mesmerizing . . . impossible to put down."

—Judy Blume

Other Books by Joyce Maynard

Looking Back: A Chronicle of Growing Up Old in the Sixties
Baby Love *(a novel)*
Domestic Affairs
To Die For *(a novel)*
Where Love Goes *(a novel)*
At Home in the World *(memoir)*
The Usual Rules *(a novel)*
The Cloud Chamber *(for young adults)*

Joyce Maynard

Internal Combustion

The True Story of a Marriage
and a Murder in the Motor City

JOSSEY-BASS
A Wiley Imprint
www.josseybass.com

Published by Jossey-Bass
A Wiley Imprint
989 Market Street, San Francisco, CA 94103-1741   www.josseybass.com

Jossey-Bass books and products are available through most bookstores. To contact Jossey-Bass directly call our Customer Care Department within the U.S. at 800-956-7739, outside the U.S. at 317-572-3986, or fax 317-572-4002.

Jossey-Bass also publishes its books in a variety of electronic formats. Some content that appears in print may not be available in electronic books.

Library of Congress Cataloging-in-Publication Data

Maynard, Joyce, date.
  Internal combustion : the true story of a marriage and a murder in the Motor City / Joyce Maynard.
     p. cm.
  Includes bibliographical references and index.
  ISBN-13: 978-0-7879-8226-3 (alk. paper)
  ISBN-10: 0-7879-8226-1 (alk. paper)
  1. Seaman, Nancy. 2. Seaman, Nancy—Trials, litigation, etc. 3. Seaman, Robert, d. 2004.
4. Murder—Michigan—Farmington Hills. 5. Murder—Investigation—Michigan—
Farmington Hills. 6. Trials (Murder)—Michigan—Farmington Hills. 7. Problem families—
Michigan—Farmington Hills. I. Title.
  HV6534.F37M39 2006
  364.152'3092—dc22

                                                                                        2006017098

Printed in the United States of America
FIRST EDITION
HB Printing   10 9 8 7 6 5 4 3 2 1

Internal Combustion
An explosion in a confined space, ignited by
compressed heat or a high-voltage electrical spark

—⟳— **Contents**

For my family

How I Wrote This Book

T he story told in these pages is the result of fourteen months of research into the lives of Robert and Nancy Seaman, their families, and their world.

To gain as full an understanding as I could of what took place in this family, I made a series of short trips to Michigan, beginning in early December of 2004, when I attended the final day of Nancy Seaman's trial for the murder of her husband. I went back again to Michigan in February, March, and April of 2005. At the beginning of July 2005, I went back again, but this time I took up residence there for most of what remained of that summer. I made my final trip to Detroit in September of 2005.

During this period, I interviewed more than fifty individuals who had known the Seamans or had been connected in some way to their lives or to the events described in this book. Wherever possible, these interviews were conducted in person, though in a few cases, individuals I hoped to speak with refused to see me, and when this was so, the conversations I describe with them—which tended to be brief—occurred on the telephone. I also communicated with several individuals—most particularly Julie Dumbleton—by e-mail as well as in frequent personal encounters.

I have never been a fan of the tape recorder as an interview tool. Although the tape recorder definitely ensures accuracy, it has been my experience over the course of more than thirty-five years as a journalist that the presence of the machine frequently alters the nature of the communication it records. So the dialogue reported here was transcribed by me onto a laptop, nearly always as it was taking place, though in a few instances (when I was engaging in a fastpitch softball lesson, or at church, or powerwalking with Julie) I took notes by hand at the time or immediately after. I stand by the authenticity of my transcriptions.

Other sources I relied on for the writing of this book were the transcript of the entire trial of Nancy Seaman (close to a thousand pages long) and videotapes of the highlights of testimony, from Court TV. I studied news reports from the *Detroit News* and the *Detroit Free Press,* from both the trial itself and the months leading up to it. I was also fortunate to have access to the entire investigative report of Detective Al Patterson of the Farmington Hills Police Department, and the evidence submitted during trial. Particularly indispensable were the tapes and transcripts of Nancy Seaman's conversations from jail with her son Greg and her father, Eugene D'Onofrio.

One aspect of the way in which I have chosen to tell this story requires particular explanation. Because I did not begin my exploration of the Seaman case until the last day of the trial, I was not present for any of the testimony when it was presented in court. Although I studied the transcripts and tapes extensively, an additional and invaluable resource was the observations of family, friends, witnesses, officials, and reporters with whom I've spoken at length who were actually present in the courtroom.

There is no one to whom I owe a greater debt in the telling of this story than Lori Brasier, Oakland County Courthouse correspondent for the *Detroit Free Press,* who became, over the course of the many months of my work on this project, a treasured friend. The story that unfolds in these pages will fully document Lori Brasier's role in supporting my work in Michigan, and the indispensable contribution she made to my understanding not only of this case but of the workings of Oakland County. It is not an overstatement when I say that this book could not have been written without her.

Because I wanted to present the story in the most comprehensible and, certainly, the most readable fashion, I took a few liberties, but, particularly in light of recent events in the world of so-called nonfiction publication, I want to spell them out clearly here and to confirm that no facts of the story were altered in any way.

What I have done here, on occasion, is to rearrange the order in which certain interviews and visits took place. In a couple of instances (chiefly, softball games), I have created a kind of composite of a game or a softball practice. Now and then a conversation that actually took place over several visits has been condensed into a single session.

Two young journalists—Leia Menlove and Jon Irwin—assisted me in research and reporting. Leia is responsible for coverage, here, of the 2005 Woodward Avenue Dream Cruise. Jon tracked down numerous jurors, classmates of Greg Seaman, yearbooks, and the mother of one of Nancy Seaman's fourth-grade students.

Nothing reported on these pages was invented. In rare instances, dialogue was reconstructed in a manner extremely close to what was originally said. What I describe here is what I saw and heard, or (in the case of the events leading up to the crime, the crime itself, and the trial) what I learned from dozens of personal interviews, the transcripts, tapes, and Lori Brasier's observations as a reporter in the courtroom, during those early days when I was not yet on the scene myself.

A number of important voices are missing here. Chief among those of course is that of Bob Seaman himself, and because of the circumstances that made it impossible for him to tell his story, I spent a vast amount of time in conversation with his brother, sister, parents, sons, colleagues, and especially a single individual, Julie Dumbleton, whose reports and observations I relied on extensively though by no means exclusively. I recognized, as I did so, that Julie Dumbleton could in no way be regarded as an objective observer, and because of that, I took great pains to corroborate her reports. In every instance in which this was possible, what she told me was later confirmed by others, but there were also instances (and some of these were not insignificant) in which the only source I had was Julie herself. Nevertheless, over the many months we spent talking and writing to each other, I came to regard Julie Dumbleton as an unassailably honest and reliable woman, whose word I trust. I would say the same of her husband and two children, all of whom experienced extreme pain and humiliation in the weeks and months following the murder, and in the media coverage it received.

A number of centrally important principals in this story refused to speak with me—chief among them, Nancy Seaman and her son Greg. Because of Nancy Seaman's decision not to participate in this book, others in her circle—her brother, John; Bob's former business partner Rick Cox; numerous teachers at Longacre Elementary School; and friends of Nancy Seaman—also chose not to speak with me.

Although at first I believed it might be impossible to tell this story without their participation, I came to believe otherwise. In the end, the questions surrounding my pursuit of Nancy Seaman's version of what happened, and her ongoing silence, became a part of the story I tell here. This would certainly be a different book had she chosen to speak with me, and I have no doubt she has her tale to tell. I can only say that I provided ample opportunity for her and her son to meet with me. She chose not to, and her younger son aligned himself with his mother.

The list is long, of individuals who were kind enough to give me their time. There are a few whom I want to single out in particular: Lisa Ortlieb, Michelle Cernits, Larry Kaluzny, John Pallas, Dennis Seaman, Eugene D'Onofrio, Heidi Frank, Scott Gardner, Don Shim, Margie Palmer, Ward and Helen Seaman, Jill Fleming, Michelle Siskowski, Detective Al Patterson, Chief Bill Dwyer (Farmington Hills Police), Mary De Paolo, Brent Hunt, Jenna Dumbleton, Jake Dumbleton, Michael Benczik, Dr. Ljubisa Dragovic, Elbert Hatchett, Russ McClure, Susan Whitall, Rebecca Vlasic, Bill Vlasic, Charlie Greene, Dr. Candis Cousins Kerns, and Dr. Arthur Raisman. On the home front, I was unwaveringly supported by my friends, in particular Susan and Jeffrey Rudsten, Elizabeth Mooney, Graf Mouen, and T. Beller. And always, by my children, Audrey, Charlie, and Wilson Bethel.

Several books were hugely important to me: *Understanding the Borderline Mother,* by Dr. Christine Lawson; *The Battered Woman Syndrome,* by Dr. Lenore Walker; *Ford Tough,* by TK; *Mustang,* by David Magee; *Made in Detroit,* by Paul Clemens; and *The Autobiography of Malcolm X.*

As a writer, I drew guidance, as I have for years, from the writings of Joan Didion, most particularly in *Slouching Toward Bethlehem* and *The White Album.* Other crucial readings that informed the writing of this book were *The Journalist and the Murderer,* by Janet Malcolm; *Too Brief a Treat (The Letters of Truman Capote)*; and the book that remains, for me, the standard by which all other reporting on crime should be measured, *In Cold Blood,* by Truman Capote.

Two individuals provided me with a constant source of encouragement, guidance, and wisdom. They are my agent, Randi Murray, and my editor, Alan Rinzler. Theirs were the voices I counted on most during the many months I spent immersed in what proved to be the most disturbing story I ever encountered as a writer. Many times, I might have abandoned this project, had they not reminded me that the best way out of a dark forest is sometimes to make one's way through it.

Introduction

In early December of 2004, *Good Morning America* aired a four-minute segment on the case of a woman named Nancy Seaman, accused of murdering her husband with a hatchet, but claiming self-defense. Married for thirty-two years and the mother of two grown sons, Nancy Seaman was a fourth-grade teacher who had been honored —only two years earlier—with an award for excellence, presented to her by the governor of Michigan.

At the time of the murder, the couple was living in a Tudor-style home in a gated community in suburban Detroit, purchased with the proceeds of Bob Seaman's successful career as an executive and engineer in the automotive industry from which he had retired some years earlier. For the eight years preceding his death, he had been—somewhat improbably—the proprietor of a batting-cage operation housed in a renovated Ford plant, coaching a girls' fastpitch softball team, and pursuing his lifelong passion of restoring classic Ford Mustangs. If his wife was to be believed, he had also been engaging in an affair with the mother of his star player.

So there you had it: cars, baseball, the suburbs, money, and midlife marriage trouble. It was hard to imagine a more American story. There was even a big box store in the picture: the murder weapon—whose purchase, on Mother's Day of that year, had been recorded on store surveillance cameras—came from Home Depot.

I was sipping coffee and eating a grapefruit at my kitchen counter at the time I heard the news report. There was plenty of interest there, but what caught my attention more than anything else was the reference to the sons of Nancy Seaman, two brothers who had taken opposing sides in a murder in which one of their parents had been the victim, the other the accused.

As it happens, I am a mother of two sons close to the ages of Jeff and Greg Seaman. Mine were also children of a troubled marriage— trouble taking many forms, as it does—but unlike Bob and Nancy Seaman, who had stayed so long entangled, with neither one willing to let go of the rope, my children's father and I had parted when they were small. For them—unlike the Seaman brothers—there had been no source of comfort or strength more sustaining than each other's presence. The idea of two brothers, two years apart like my sons but divided so deeply and with so much bitterness that they might never find their way back to each other, struck me as a particularly poignant and terrible situation, all the more so because the very events that divided them (their father's murder, their mother's incarceration and trial) should have driven them to find solace with each other.

So here was this woman almost exactly my age (fifty-one), on trial for murder in the state of Michigan (just a few miles, I noted, from the equally privileged suburb where my children's father had grown up, though I told myself this was not a factor in my interest). To look at us—Nancy Seaman and me—you would not have identified any particular source of common ground or kinship, but there was this: her marriage, like mine, had broken down irretrievably, leaving two sons (also a daughter, in my case) to witness the sad spectacle.

The part about the breakdown of a marriage I knew, and sixteen years after my divorce, I continued to carry it around with me—a wound that still gave me trouble, like an injury from a car wreck that causes the once-broken bone to ache on rainy days, or a piece of music you hear on the radio for the first time in a decade that brings tears to your eyes.

Irreconcilable differences. The phrase trips lightly enough off the tongue, but living through them nearly killed me, and it had killed Nancy Seaman's husband. I wanted to know how, and why.

I also wanted to know how it was that this couple's sons had taken sides as they did. Long ago, when they were still small, my children had figured out a way of continuing to love two parents who didn't love each other anymore, and now, almost twenty years later, it was a fact of their lives and ours that this would be so forever.

The Seaman brothers had apparently felt the need to ally themselves squarely and unwaveringly with one side or another—with any sign of affection for the other parent viewed as a betrayal of the one whose side they had taken, or so it seemed. It was an excruciating place for a child of any age to find himself.

I learned from the television report that day that Nancy Seaman had struck her husband with a hatchet sixteen times, then took out a knife and started stabbing him. The violence in my family took the more familiar and bloodless course: our story featured custody issues, guardian ad litem assessments, property disputes, and many years of slowly cooling bitterness and anger, all of which had brought my children's father and me to the closest we may ever know to a state of armistice. By the time the whole thing was over (and years passed before that day arrived), we had become like two continents, once part of a single land mass, each now surrounded by a vast and chilly body of water virtually impassable except by the three brave figures who paddled their little boats between the shores of the two territories we'd staked out, where virtually nothing (not the language spoken, or the weather, native dress, or the terrain) bore any similarity to the place they'd left to get there.

Greg and Jeff Seaman, on the other hand, lived as exiles, from the sound of it: each unable to cross what were perceived as enemy lines, to enter the land of the forbidden parent. Even the death of their father had not ended the war. Far from it.

I looked up from my breakfast that morning to study the television screen because I saw a shred of connection between my life and that of the woman now on trial for her husband's murder, as well as a crucial difference between us. I too had inhabited the dark territory of a relationship in ruins and lived, too many years, in a state of anger and bitterness toward a man I once loved.

As much similarity as I perceived between myself and the woman whose face I saw on my TV screen now, on trial for murder, I was also reassured by the fundamental difference between us. She chose murder.

I chose divorce. Her children didn't speak to each other. Mine, I sometimes thought, would die for each other. In some deep way, she had
taken a disastrous turn, when I had taken the right one.

I was thirty-five years old in 1989, when my marriage ended—the
same year that my mother died. (This, too, strangely mirrored the experience of Nancy Seaman, whose mother had died unexpectedly only
a few months before the murder.)

My children were five, seven, and eleven when their father and I
parted, but my sons, like Nancy Seaman's, were in their early twenties
by this point.

From the moment I heard about this particular crime, I said (with
a certain air of self-congratulation, probably), "I can't imagine my sons
ever turning against each other. I can't imagine murdering anyone,
but even if I could, I can't imagine using a hatchet to do it."

Still, I was open minded. I believed that if I knew enough about
what this family had experienced, what this marriage had been like, I
would come to understand, and I wanted to. I believed that perhaps if
I knew Nancy Seaman's story, I might find it comprehensible and
therefore forgivable.

I thought, when I looked up at the television screen that morning,
that I was hearing the story of a battered woman and the man who
abused her. I thought that what fascinated me about the story was the
prospect of two people unwilling to disentangle—however much
damage they did to one another. As a woman who had carried for
close to two decades a large measure of guilt over having inflicted on
her own children the pain of a particularly hard divorce, I could tell
myself now that their father and I had been smart enough, at least, to
put some distance between each other when they were still young.
We'd stayed out of hatchet range, you might say.

As angry as I'd felt toward my former husband at a few hundred
different moments over the years (more, no doubt), I had never, for
an instant even, wanted to see him dead, let alone imagined myself
taking a hatchet to his skull. I was unacquainted with that brand of
violence. But I was not unacquainted with rage.

I entered into an exploration of the Seamans' story out of a belief
that the seemingly unimaginable and inexplicable behavior that had
decimated their family could be explained if I only looked deep
enough into the lives of the people who had lived or died through it.

I embarked on a journey that morning, into the origins of an act of violence so bizarre I could only imagine that it had grown out of equally violent acts inflicted against its perpetrator.

For Nancy Seaman to do what she did to her husband, I believed, he must have done something unimaginably terrible to her first. For Greg Seaman to disown his father as he had, his father must have done something monstrous. For Jeff Seaman to turn away from his mother, he must have been so fearful of knowing the truth that he constructed a whole other story to substitute for it.

We make up the stories we can stand to live with. I wanted to find out the real one. So I got on a plane to Michigan.

PART ONE

Missing Man

CHAPTER 1

Something Is Terribly Wrong

The first one to file a missing person report on Robert Leroy Seaman was Julie Dumbleton. Monday afternoons, Bob always met Julie's daughter, Jenna, age thirteen, at the Put One in the Upper Deck batting cage in Northville, Michigan, a few miles from his home in Farmington Hills, an affluent suburb about fifteen miles from Detroit. Since leaving his highly paid job as a vice president of engineering at Borg Warner, Bob had bought a part share —with his longtime acquaintance Rick Cox—in an old Ford factory known as the Waterwheel Building in Northville, which housed the Upper Deck.

The Upper Deck was a kind of fantasy business for Bob: not your usual run-down batting-cage operation with a couple of rusty old machines cranking out balls. This one boasted state-of-the-art machines set to shoot out seven different kinds of pitches, forming a semicircle around the batter. Bob had hired a mural painter to recreate the stands at Tiger Stadium on the walls surrounding the batting area—right down to the faces on the fans and a score on the scoreboard meant to recreate the 1968 World Series game indicating that the St. Louis Cardinals, his beloved home team, were leading the Detroit Tigers by four runs.

The Upper Deck was at best only marginally profitable, but the business had never been about making a lot of money for Bob, and his 3 P.M. after-school get-togethers with Jenna Dumbleton were off the clock. Although at thirteen Jenna was younger than most of the other players on the elite Compuware team Bob coached, she was a star pitcher, and as Bob's particular favorite, she got to work with him, solo, three times a week. Afternoons, when he pitched for her, they'd talk about baseball and sometimes not about baseball. He told her corny jokes, or they'd count the pitches he threw in Spanish. If she'd had a bad day at school, she'd tell him about it.

"Bob loved Jenna. He never missed catching for her," said her mother, Julie. "So when he didn't show up that day, I knew something was wrong."

There were a few more reasons why Julie felt anxious. In the seven years since Julie's husband, Dick, had first shown up at the Upper Deck with their son, Jake, for a round of batting practice, Bob had become like a member of her family. For a while there, Julie had helped out in the office; on weekends Bob and Dick tackled home improvement projects together and Bob tinkered, with Jake, on Bob's precious old cars.

"Mr. Seaman knew everything there was about engines," Jake said. "Before I met him, I didn't even know what torque was."

Bob had a fleet of vehicles in varying states of repair, but the pride of his collection were a red Ferrari and two classic Mustangs: an orange 1969 Boss and a blue '69 Shelby, whose value, now that he'd fixed it up, stood at well over $100,000. Every August he took it out for an event that represented a high point of the year for car collectors in the Detroit area and beyond: the Woodward Avenue Dream Cruise. All up and down Woodward Avenue, from 8 Mile Road to 14 Mile Road, crowds gathered for an entire weekend to watch the finest vehicles Detroit ever produced glide past, as the men who'd restored them (they were always men) waved and took in the respect of their fellow automobile lovers. Few cars in the Dream Cruise, if any, were more coveted than a Shelby.

For Bob, though, nothing was as important as baseball and, now, softball. In those early days when Dick used to bring the kids down to the Upper Deck after work, Bob had coached Jake only, but after six-year-old Jenna demanded a chance at bat, he'd gotten interested in working with her too, particularly after it became clear she had a lot of talent, a powerful arm, a passion for softball equal to that of her brother, and the kind of nerve essential for a pitcher.

Her father bought her a batting-cage discount card, as he had for Jake; that was the beginning. Pretty soon, Bob was suggesting that the Dumbletons put Jenna on the Northville girls' fastpitch softball team, the eleven and unders. Dick, ever protective, was worried she wouldn't be good enough and might get hurt or feel rejected. Bob—always the more aggressive of the two men, the brash, risk-taking cowboy—said Jenna was as good as any of those girls and better than most. Pretty soon he was coaching the team himself, with Jenna pitching, and she was a star.

All his life Bob had been a baseball man, but now, with his own sons grown and his days on the Little League bench over, he'd discovered an affection for fastpitch, and to his surprise, though he still worked out with Jake and tried never to miss his games, Bob found he liked coaching the girls. They listened to you. They played their hearts out. They were a little more emotional than the boys, for sure, but Bob was not one to be thrown by tears and outbursts. Nothing the Dumbletons ever saw, on the field or off, had ever shaken Bob's calm demeanor much, they said, and the other parents on the team agreed.

Girls' softball was not a passion Bob Seaman shared with his wife of thirty-two years, Nancy—and in fact, the opposite was true. Where the Dumbletons were pretty much inseparable, Bob and Nancy seldom spent time together. Now and then she'd go to a Tigers game with Bob, but she took no interest in a team of young girls. In the early days of the friendship, Dick and Julie had taken in a Tigers game with Bob and Nancy, and once or twice they'd had dinner together. For a long time now, the friendship had been about just the three of them. Nancy Seaman didn't like the Dumbletons, and they knew it.

Many nights, after practice, Bob and the Dumbletons shared pizza, and after games or tournaments Bob could spend hours going over the fine points of the game, analyzing the performance of his players.

"You've never seen a person that could go on so long about a single play," said Dick, "and make it interesting. He cared about every single one of those girls and noticed every single little thing."

One thing Bob didn't dwell on was his marriage to Nancy, the mother of his sons, Jeff and Greg. But Julie and Dick both knew that it wasn't good.

"He never wanted to go home," said Julie. "When he did, he tried to keep out of Nancy's way. That last year, he'd been living in the basement."

In fact, Bob had told Julie he'd been thinking about getting a divorce, and had recently consulted with an attorney. For a long time, what kept him from doing it, he said, was his reluctance to shake up his son Greg's world, but Greg was off at college now—Purdue—and about to graduate. And anyway, Bob's relationship with Greg had become so bad over the last year that the only words his son spoke to him now were angry ones. Although he'd paid for the expensive Purdue tuition, Bob wasn't invited to his son's graduation.

All in all, Bob told Julie that the only reasons to stay in the marriage now were his substantial assets (cars, house, boat, retirement funds) and the knowledge that a divorce from Nancy would mean losing half of them. For a long time, that prospect had been sufficiently compelling to keep Bob from moving forward with a divorce, but circumstances were changing. Not only was Greg graduating, but the situation with Nancy had become increasingly intolerable, to the point where the two communicated now almost exclusively through the exchange of angry notes—Nancy's, on school stationery left on the kitchen counter, Bob's written on Post-its he stuck on cabinets and appliances around the house. And they communicated with actions—or inaction—too. For months, a standoff had been going on in which neither one had carried out the trash, which had accumulated to the point of covering an entire wall of their three-car garage, a stinking mountain.

Things had to change, and it seemed finally that they would. Sometime in the winter of that year, a couple of events had occurred that were bringing Bob and Nancy closer to the edge. First had come the sudden death, in late December, of Nancy's mother, Lenore, with whom she'd always been close. Sometime in January, she had made a confession to her son Jeff and his wife, Becka: Bob was beating her, she said. She rolled up the sleeve of her blouse and showed them a bruise.

Becka, whose own parents had an abusive relationship, up until their divorce, urged Nancy to get out of the marriage. Not long after this, she and Jeff (along with Greg and his girlfriend, Kristin, and Nancy's father, Eugene) had accompanied Nancy on an inspection of condos in the area, with the thought that she might buy one for herself; sometime in late January, she had put down $10,000 on a unit in the King's Crossing development a few miles from where both Nancy's father and Jeff and Becka lived.

At the time she signed the papers, Nancy had instructed them all to keep the condo purchase secret from Bob, on the theory that if he found out what she'd done "he'd kill me." Although Nancy's father, Eugene D'Onofrio, was hardly a man of means, he'd given her money for the down payment, and she arranged to have the condo papers sent to her at school.

In February, Bob Seaman had received a call from the Compuware Softball Association, saying that it had received an anonymous complaint about him, suggesting improprieties with players. Believing that the letter must have been written by his wife, Bob had confronted Nancy about it, but she had denied authorship of the letter. The softball association, after studying the complaint, had determined it to be baseless and had not pursued any action against Bob.

In March, papers had arrived at the Seaman home from the condominium association, concerning Nancy's purchase of the unit at King's Crossing. Bob had chosen not to reveal to Nancy that he knew about the condo purchase, though he and Julie Dumbleton had driven downriver, to King's Crossing to see the place. He had received the discovery of the purchase with a certain sense of relief, Julie said, having been told by Nancy in the past that she would never divorce him.

Around this same time—and largely in response to the secret condo purchase and the anonymous letter to the softball association—Bob had stopped paying the mortgage on their home.

"He didn't see the point anymore of paying for a house, when he was living in the basement and she was putting all the bills on his charge card," said Julie.

In early April, Bob had flown to St. Louis to spend time with his father, Ward, who was having surgery. In early May—telling nobody but the Dumbletons—he took off again, this time for Arizona, to see his brother Dennis. This was the first such visit he had ever made, and it was over the course of the week the two spent together, with Dennis's wife, Robin, that Bob disclosed for the first time the extent of his alienation from Nancy and the trouble that had been going on with Greg.

"It really hurt Bob that Greg didn't invite him to his Purdue graduation," Dennis said. "But he was still hoping Greg might change his mind at the last minute. He had some hope he could repair that relationship. Where with Nancy, he knew it was over."

Bob told Dennis about his discovery that Nancy had secretly put a down payment on a condominium, and about the anonymous letter to the softball association. He told Dennis what Nancy had said, after he raised the subject of divorce not long before: "You'll never get the Shelby."

To a man like Bob Seaman, who loved his Mustangs more than almost anything in the world, those words had been devastating.

That week in Arizona, Dennis told his brother some important information. Nancy didn't have the kind of assets Bob did, but ever since she'd gone back to school and gotten her teaching certificate seven or eight years earlier, she'd been pulling in around $48,000 a year as a fourth-grade teacher.

"So I mentioned to him how, if they got a divorce, he'd be entitled to half of everything she had," Dennis said. "Same as she'd be entitled to half of what was his. That was news to him. He was planning to tell her that when he got home. Not because the money or the condo was such a big value to him, but for the principle of the thing. It would have made her crazy, hearing that."

Bob told Dennis and Robin another story that week: of a night not long before when Nancy had come down to the basement with a bowl of ice cream for him—a highly unusual event in the lives of a couple who barely spoke to one another. According to Dennis, Bob told him (as he had told Julie and several other friends) that the ice cream had tasted funny and burned his throat, so he'd stopped eating it, and that the next morning, when he went upstairs to the kitchen, he'd looked for the container and had been surprised to discover that despite the longtime standoff regarding trash at their household, the ice cream container had been disposed of.

In Bob's view, his wife had been trying to poison him. Somewhat surprisingly, to Dennis, Bob had dealt with the situation simply by making the decision to eat no more meals at his house, except for take-out food he had bought himself.

It was over the course of this visit with Dennis, Robin, and their two teenage children that Bob had finally come to a point of resolution, Dennis said. To some people it might have seemed the conclusion was long overdue: assets or no assets, it was time to divorce Nancy.

Dennis and Robin took Bob to the airport on Saturday evening, May 8, the night before Mother's Day.

"He wasn't usually the type for a lot of hugging, but that day he kept holding on to me even after I started to let go," said Robin.

"I lost you once," he said, referring to the many years in which the brothers had barely seen each other, as part of Bob's effort not to rock the boat with Nancy. "I'm not letting it happen anymore."

"I kept telling Bob, 'Why are you going back?'" Dennis said. "'Don't go back to your house. Go get a motel room, or go stay at the Dumbletons while you look for an apartment.' He told us could take care of himself."

Robin had a bad feeling about the idea of Bob returning to his house on Briarwood Court, but she still joked with him. "Now that you're going to be single, you'd better stop wearing those white socks and black shoes."

Nancy wasn't home that Saturday night, when Bob returned from Arizona. She'd been celebrating Mother's Day weekend with Jeff and Becka, and had stayed over at their house.

Julie saw Bob briefly that Sunday—Mother's Day—at a ball game in which Jenna was serving as umpire. They had parted with the understanding that the next day, Monday, Bob would see Jenna at the Upper Deck for pitching practice, as always.

When Bob didn't show up that Monday, Julie's anxiety about her friend intensified. Later that day, when Dick got home from work, the two of them drove past Bob and Nancy's house on Briarwood. Bob's Explorer was in the driveway, but he still wasn't answering his cell phone.

"So I called the police," said Julie. "Then I called Dennis."

Back at the Dumbletons' house, Dick and Julie's son, Jake, was upset about Bob. A quiet boy for whom teenage rebelliousness never went past coming home a few minutes after curfew on Saturday nights, Jake looked up to Bob and viewed him as a second father. Jake worshipped Bob, in part perhaps because Bob offered a somewhat looser, more free-spirited style compared to that of his parents. For example, Bob had told Jake that for his eighteenth birthday, he was taking him to a strip club—and though that was not the kind of thing his parents would ever do, and not really something Jake would have felt comfortable with either, there was something great about having an adult in his life who'd make an offer like that.

That Bob had gone a whole day without calling his family felt to Jake like a really bad sign.

"I'm going over there," he told his parents on Monday afternoon.

"Not alone, you aren't," they said. Julie and Dick Dumbleton were more protective of their children than most parents. They were not about to let their son go alone to the Seaman home. So Dick said he'd accompany his son.

As the two approached the house on Briarwood Court, they saw lights on in the garage and the basement. No longer welcome guests when Nancy was around, they knocked on the front door. She answered. She told Dick she had no idea where Bob was, and closed the door. As Dick and Jake drove away, they saw the lights go out in the garage.

The next morning, with Jake increasingly disturbed and no word from Bob, Julie let Jake stay home from school. The two drove to the Longacre Elementary School, where they observed Nancy Seaman's Ford Explorer in the parking lot. Then they drove again to the Seaman residence, where Bob's Explorer remained in the driveway. They walked the property for a few minutes, but finding nothing, left. Julie called Rick Cox, who told her she should get on with her life and let Jeff Seaman handle the matter.

Believing now that something was terribly wrong, Julie went to the office at the Upper Deck, where she'd helped out for the last couple of years.

"I just knew I needed to get some things out of there," she said.

She packed up a bunch of framed photographs she'd kept there of her daughter, Jenna. The thought came to her—in her state of building anxiety over her friend's whereabouts—that she should also retrieve, from the office safe, copies of several letters Nancy had written to Bob in the last couple of years, which he had shown to Julie and kept in a folder labeled "Nancy Crap File."

Now Julie, who had been given the combination by Bob, removed the file from the office and brought it home. "I just had this feeling that if I left it there," she said, "someone might come and take it."

CHAPTER 2

Tardy for School

On Monday, May 10, Nancy Seaman showed up for work at Longacre Elementary School as usual, but she arrived almost an hour late, whereas typically she was often the first one in the building, besides the custodian. Christine Brueck, one of the two other fourth-grade teachers at the school, had finally moved Nancy's students into her own classroom until somewhere between 8:47 and 9:00 A.M., when Nancy finally arrived.

When she did, Brueck said she could tell immediately that something was wrong. Where some teachers at Longacre dressed in casual slacks and sweaters, Nancy was known at the school for her impeccable grooming and a put-together appearance. This particular morning, however, Nancy's clothes looked rumpled, and she seemed to be preoccupied, Brueck said, which led Brueck to look for Nancy at lunch. Usually the teachers ate together, but on this particular day, Brueck couldn't locate Nancy Seaman anywhere in the building.

Another teacher, Barb "Lovee" Mikel, also noted Nancy's absence at lunch—highly unusual for her. When she spotted Nancy at the end of school, the two women walked out to the parking lot together. She commented to Nancy on the many boxes in the back of her friend's

Explorer—saying "More boxes?" or something along those lines—and Nancy came back, Mikel said, with "some witty remark."

The next day, Nancy's other fellow fourth-grade teacher, Jeff Rehbine (who, like Brueck, had noted Nancy's lateness the day before and her uncharacteristically rumpled clothing), once again observed that Nancy seemed not to be herself. She was very distant, he said, and seemed "to have been through something." He did not ask her about it, or inquire about the weekend just past or Mother's Day, he said, "because I didn't want to upset her any further."

Like Brueck—who didn't come to work that Tuesday, but was sufficiently concerned to try reaching Nancy at home that day, without success—Rehbine had come to the conclusion that Nancy's relationship with her husband was probably not very good, though she didn't talk about him much. Over the years, she had made comments like "I wish I had a husband like you" and "Do you have a brother?" Lately, in particular, Rehbine had seen a marked change in her demeanor, which, like Brueck and Mikel, he attributed to the unexpected death of her mother the previous December.

Wednesday morning, Christine Brueck returned to school, but this time Nancy Seaman was absent, having called in for a substitute early that morning. Brueck was sufficiently concerned now that she spoke to the school principal, William Smith, to say that Nancy was not herself. She told him that Nancy had confided in her recently that she was afraid of her husband. Principal Smith then called Nancy's home, leaving a message inquiring about lesson plans for the substitute teacher. He didn't really need those, but chose to leave that message, he said, because he didn't know who would pick it up. Nancy didn't call back.

On May 12, when two-and-a-half days had passed with no sign of Bob Seaman, Dick Dumbleton filed a missing person report with the Farmington Hills Police Department. This time both he and Julie made statements to the police that Nancy did not like them and that they believed she had lied to them in the past.

Julie told the officer on duty about a police report Nancy had filed against her in fall 2003, accusing Julie of having assaulted her at the Upper Deck—a charge not corroborated by any witnesses and refuted by Bob Seaman, who had been present. At the time, Nancy Seaman had made an extensive statement to the police and insisted that they photograph the knuckle on her hand, which she claimed to have been bruised by Julie. The other photograph she requested was of a torn fingernail. Evidently the police had not been sufficiently impressed with these claims to pursue any charges against Julie Dumbleton. The matter had been dropped.

At age twenty-six, Jeff Seaman—the older of the two Seaman sons, and an engineer who worked, as his father had early in his career, for the Ford Motor Company—maintained a close relationship with both of his parents, despite how little they had to do with each other. He stopped by the Upper Deck regularly to work on his baseball swing or just to talk with his dad, and often at night the two of them would go down to the basement in the Waterwheel Building, where Bob kept his fleet of vintage cars, to work on them.

Like his father (whom he resembled strongly, with his compact, stocky build and his confident manner that left some people viewing him as a know-it-all), Jeff could make his way around any engine and maintained a set of tools as extensive as that of many professional mechanics, as well as his own hydraulic lift. He and his father attended Tigers games or watched them together on TV, and hung out on Bob's boat, the *Liberty*, moored in Grosse Pointe.

But Jeff spent time with his mother too. he and his wife of two years, Becka (also trained as an engineer), had lunch with Nancy almost every Saturday, and Becka and Nancy would often go shopping together afterward.

"My mom wasn't the kind to have a lot of friends," said Jeff. "But she and Becka hung out a lot."

Because of Mother's Day, Jeff and Becka's time with his mother the previous weekend had extended beyond the usual. On Saturday, May 8, the three attended a game of the Toledo Mud Hens Triple A baseball team. Nancy had spent the night at Jeff and Becka's apartment in Troy, and the next day—Mother's Day—Jeff and Becka took his mother out to dinner at Applebee's restaurant. When they brought Nancy home to Farmington Hills at around 6:45 on Sunday (Becka carrying the rose plant the two had given Nancy), they'd found Bob home from the Arizona trip, and because a week had gone by in which Jeff hadn't seen his father, he had "popped in to the house," he explained, to say hello.

As was often the case, an argument started between his parents the moment his mother walked in. Jeff's younger brother, Greg, was graduating from Purdue University in a week (like his brother and his father, with a degree in automotive engineering). The graduation was a source of tension for Bob Seaman. For a year now, his younger son had not spoken with him, except to express his anger at his father for what he viewed as Bob's abandonment of their family, in favor of the Dumbletons. Greg had not invited his father to his Purdue graduation, though on his Arizona visit with his brother, Bob had expressed the hope that maybe, at the last minute, he might.

But on Mother's Day, when Nancy had returned home after her weekend with Jeff and Becka, she'd asked Bob to lend her his Ford Explorer to transport Greg's belongings home from school. Nancy owned a Ford Explorer of her own, but more significant for Bob was the fact that it now seemed clear that no invitation for the graduation ceremony was coming his way.

Bob told Nancy that she and Greg "would have to make other plans." Then the yelling began.

Becka, who had experienced the violent relationship of her own parents, told Jeff she wanted to leave, and walked out to the car. Jeff followed a few moments later.

Shortly after that, Jeff's cell phone rang. Because Jeff was driving and the rain was coming down particularly hard, Becka was the one to pick up the phone, but she didn't answer it. Observing the caller ID, she told Jeff it was his father.

Jeff didn't want to talk, in part because he was tired of all the arguments between his parents, but also because the rain was making the driving treacherous, he said, even for a skilled test-car driver like himself.

Later, he and Becka listened to the message and heard an apology from Bob about the argument with Nancy, but they erased the message without calling back. They spent the evening watching a baseball game on ESPN and turned in around eleven.

Meanwhile, Jeff didn't hear anything from his father and couldn't reach him. Later, he would recount the events of those days in his typical engineer's style, one of which he described as follows:

[Monday:] Stopped in the office to check e-mail . . . headed to Dearborn Proving Grounds to begin testing and get fuel for the Explorer that I had checked out over the weekend. Went through calibration data until about 10 A.M. . . . went to the test track to work on inferred barometric pressure calibration and speed control calibration. Ate salad for lunch. Went through the data from the test track . . . went back to the track for an hour to rerun bp data points because calibration took it that commands throttle angle does not actuate the VDT units or the IMRC's. . . . Came back and saw a message from Julie or Dick Dumbleton, asked if I had seen my dad. . . .

Jeff spent much of the rest of that afternoon trying to reach his father, though he also fit in a haircut at Fantastic Sam's and "a Braves or a Cubs game . . . possibly both" on WGN/TBS. He called his mother, who expressed irritation that Julie Dumbleton had interrupted Jeff at work to ask about his father. But he wasn't really worried about his father until he learned from Julie Dumbleton, when she called back later that evening, that Bob Seaman's Ford Explorer was still sitting in the driveway over at Briarwood Court. As Jeff knew, his dad never went anywhere without his car.

Tuesday morning, Jeff went to work, testing more Explorers at the Driveability Test Facility in Allen Park—"uploading changes into CFX in order to build a new calibration"—but he wasn't feeling well, skipped lunch, and left work early. He tried his father's cell phone twenty-five times, without a response, and after work stopped by his parents' house to look for his father. On the way, he passed his mother in her Ford Explorer on the highway, going the opposite direction. Then he went to the Upper Deck to look through the basement, where Bob Seaman kept his cars. He briefly took heart when it appeared that his father's 1954 Ford F series truck was missing, figuring his dad must have taken the truck down to the marina where he kept the boat, but when he called his dad's partner, Rick Cox, to report the news, Rick told him he was mistaken; the truck was still in the basement. That's when Jeff made the decision to call his uncle Dennis (though he had to track down the number first, from his cousin). Then he called the police.

He went to bed at midnight—late, he said, because the Tigers game went into extra innings. They lost (5 to 4, he said).

CHAPTER 3

"My Husband Is Trying to Find Himself"

T he first officer responding to Julie Dumbleton's missing person report concerning the disappearance of Robert Seaman was Lieutenant Saad. On Tuesday, May 11, just after 10 P.M., Saad knocked at the front door of the Seamans' home at 29812 Briarwood Court. The door was answered by Nancy Seaman, who said she'd been asleep.

"Did you call the police with a missing person report?" he asked.

"No, I did not call the police," she told him, so the officer returned to his vehicle to check the address on the report.

After verifying the address, Saad returned to the house and knocked at the door a second time. This time he asked if she was Nancy Seaman. She confirmed she was.

"Did you call the police for a missing person report?" he asked.

"No, it could have been his son that called," she said, evidently referring to Jeff, who was her son also, though a person hearing her response might have concluded otherwise.

She told the officer that her husband frequently disappeared for days at a time, stating that he had only recently returned from an absence of nine days during which time he had not informed her or his family of his whereabouts. "My husband is going through a midlife crisis," she said. "He's trying to find himself." The officer left.

Because of a shift change at the Farmington Hills police station that night, the report of Lieutenant Saad's visit that evening was overlooked by the dispatcher. Just an hour later, two other officers were dispatched to the Seaman home on Briarwood Court once again, this time to investigate a second missing person report on Robert Seaman, this one filed by his brother Dennis.

The lights were out at the house now, and the officers' knocks went unheeded. So—following the protocol of what is known as a "welfare check"—the two officers let themselves into the darkened Seaman home through the garage door, shining their flashlights through the rooms as they investigated. Upstairs, they heard snoring and saw a female figure in the bedroom, who appeared to be asleep. Like the first officer, they returned to the station with little to report.

The next day, Wednesday, Lieutenant Saad returned to the Seaman home on Briarwood Court. This time he observed that the older of the two Explorers parked in the driveway the day before had been moved and was now facing west, backed up near the grass. He also observed boxes near the bushes next to the driveway. Looking inside the older Explorer, he noted a pile of cardboard and some kind of large object in a tarp, but did not go to the door.

Detective Al Patterson—a senior detective on the Farmington Hills police force—was a friendly, downright affable-looking man in his late thirties with hair buzz-cut short enough to pass muster in an army boot camp and a soft-spoken manner that might lead a suspect to suppose, under interrogation, that Patterson could be, if not exactly a friend, at least moderately sympathetic to his or her side of the story. In fact, Detective Patterson was a graduate of the John Reid School of Interrogation, in Chicago, and, over the course of seventeen years of police work, had honed his seemingly nonthreatening manner of questioning to something close to an art, though he was not the type to tell you that. His small cubicle at the Farmington Hills police station—a far cry from the expansive, wood-paneled office of the chief, Bill Dwyer—was decorated with photographs of his wife and two young daughters, along with a computer printout of Patterson's dream car, a 1989 Mustang 350.

Now, after several days of unsuccessful attempts on the part of other officers to follow up on the increasingly troubling disappearance of Robert Seaman, it was Detective Patterson—along with Detective L. Fetherolf and Sergeant C. Hubbard—who had been dispatched to the scene. It was 4:25 P.M., May 12, 2004.

Pulling up in front of the house at Briarwood Court, the officers noted two vehicles in the driveway: a black 2002 Ford Explorer, Michigan plates VLM 991, parked closest to the street, facing east. The other vehicle was a black 1995 Ford Explorer, Michigan plates KNS 708, parked at the top of the driveway and backed in, facing west. They were greeted at the door by Nancy Seaman, wearing a T-shirt and capri pants. Mrs. Seaman said she was happy they'd come, because she had been about to call them.

She invited the officers in. Patterson sat with her at the kitchen table as Fetherolf and Hubbard perused the scene.

"Mrs. Seaman explained that the last time she had seen Robert was on Monday, May 10, at approximately 7 A.M., just before she left for work," Detective Patterson said. "She said that she and Bob were having financial difficulties and that the bank was about to foreclose on their home. Their car insurance had lapsed. She said she and Bob were in the process of a divorce but that their relationship was amicable."

Nancy Seaman told Patterson that on Monday, as she was fixing a submarine sandwich to take with her to school—her usual routine—her husband had informed her that he wanted "to start a new life without his current family."

She had informed him that this was OK with her, she now told Patterson, but that because she had to get to work, she didn't want to talk about it until after school was over.

She came home for lunch at 12:40, she went on. When she got to the house, Bob's Explorer was parked in the driveway, but there was no sign of Bob. She wasn't too concerned, she said, since he had just disappeared without notice the week before (though that time, he'd taken his car to the airport).

Now, two days later, the car remained in the driveway, and there was no sign of Bob. Nancy Seaman told Detective Patterson that the only thing she could think of was that maybe her husband had gone to St. Louis to see his parents, Ward and Helen, so Patterson suggested she call them to ask. She left the room, presumably to do that.

While she was gone, Sergeant Hubbard, who had gone outside to place a cell phone call, came back in and informed Detectives Fetherolf and Patterson that he had looked in the windows of the older Explorer—Nancy's—parked in the driveway. He said there was an object in the back, covered in cardboard, large enough to be a body.

Nancy Seaman returned to the kitchen to say she had been unable to reach Bob's parents, but gave Patterson their phone number.

"Continuing our conversation," said Detective Patterson, "Mrs. Seaman said that in the summer of 2003, Robert had discovered that an employee at the Upper Deck had been stealing large sums of money. Mrs. Seaman said that Robert had captured the theft on videotape, but told Patterson that instead of filing a police report, Robert had 'extorted' money back from the employee, and continued to let him work for him as long as he was paying back the money. She didn't know the employee's name, she said."

Then Nancy told Patterson that she suddenly remembered something else that might be relevant. When she'd gotten home from work on Monday afternoon, she'd found Bob's passport missing from his desk and approximately $500 in cash gone from the cookie jar. A bunch of hangers were lying on the closet floor, indicating that clothes were gone too. She suggested to Detective Patterson that the police should check the basement of the Upper Deck, as Bob spent a lot of time there.

Patterson asked if the officers could look through her home, and Nancy agreed. They started upstairs, looking in closets, under beds, in bathrooms. Then they checked the downstairs, the garage, and the basement.

"As we were completing the check of the basement, Mrs. Seaman began to get agitated," said Detective Patterson. "She said she needed to leave. She was supposed to meet her father in Woodhaven."

They walked outside together. As they approached her Explorer, Sergeant Hubbard asked Mrs. Seaman if she'd mind his looking in her vehicle.

She pointed to the 2002 Explorer—Bob's. She reminded the officers that they should look in the basement of the Upper Deck.

"We'd like to check your car," said Hubbard.

Together, the four of them made their way to the rear of Nancy Seaman's Explorer. Nancy took out her keys and opened the hatch.

At this point, Nancy Seaman had no choice but to open the car. Briarwood Court was not the sort of place a person takes off on the lam, even if she's not a fifty-one-year-old fourth-grade teacher, dressed in her capri pants and loafers. She put the key in the lock.

No doubt she had opened that hatch a thousand times in the past, loading in groceries and shopping bags from Marshall Field, materials for classroom projects at school, maybe the occasional plant or overnight bag. Never under circumstances like these.

Once the hatch was open, Detective Patterson reported, "we could see a large sheet of cardboard, approximately four feet long and two or three feet wide. The cardboard was covering a large object, partially visible. Mrs. Seaman stepped forward, pushing the cardboard down.

"She said, 'I'm moving. That's my condo stuff,' but Sgt. Hubbard and I took hold of the end of the cardboard and lifted it. Underneath, we saw a long object wrapped tightly in a blue plastic tarp, secured with a great deal of silver duct tape. There was dried blood all around the tarp and the tape."

The object was wider at the end closest to the rear of the vehicle, tapered down toward the front, and between five and six feet long. "A faint smell of decomposing body was also present," said Detective Patterson.

"I asked Mrs. Seaman what was in the tarp. She did not respond. Then I advised her she was under arrest and handcuffed her behind the back." The time was now approximately 4:57 P.M.

The Ramblewood subdivision, where the Seaman family made their home for seventeen years at 29812 Briarwood Court, was what's known as a gated community. A guard house stood at the entrance to the development, assuring residents that only individuals who had been given specific permission might pass through onto the well-maintained streets: Driftwood, Fox Chance, Turtle Creek, Greenspring. Driving through the development, a visitor was apt to pass several groups of women in pastel-colored jogging suits power-walking together, and a few younger ones pushing well-designed and expensive-looking strollers, but mostly those making their way along the flawlessly paved streets, past lawns green as golf links, do so in SUVs. Houses, too, were oversized, with expansive decks and gas-fired barbecues substantial enough to cook a dozen steaks. A half hour's drive from downtown Detroit, Ramblewood felt like another world from that bombed-out-looking city.

Life would have seemed to follow orderly patterns in Ramblewood. Every yard appeared to have been expensively landscaped. Every house was in good repair. This was the kind of place where a car with a dent on the side or a little rust, or a trash can tipped over, would stand out almost as glaringly as the sight of a homeless person or a scrawny and flea-bitten dog. A shrub that had died would more than likely be swiftly removed.

The sight of a resident in handcuffs would definitely have gotten the neighbors talking in Ramblewood, and perhaps for that reason—and also because he was an unmistakably decent sort of man—Detective Patterson suggested, after he placed Nancy Seaman under arrest, that perhaps she'd like to step up onto her front porch, a little less in the public view.

He took the handcuffs off—assessing, correctly, that Nancy Seaman would not be a flight risk—and suggested that she might prefer to go inside the house while they waited for other officers to arrive to secure the crime scene so that he could take her to the station. She agreed.

"It was an accident," she said. "He was beating me again. I have the bruises to prove it."

Part of Al Patterson's job in interrogating and interviewing a suspect was to build a rapport with the person. "Obviously I wanted to ask her about what had happened, but you can't talk to a person unless you read them their rights. I did that. She said she didn't want to talk without a lawyer present. Then, because she wasn't going to talk about the crime, we started chit-chatting about this and that, how warm it was out, that kind of thing. I asked her if she wanted a glass of water. She asked if she could call the automated system at school, to request a substitute teacher for the next day. I let her do that."

They went through the typical booking questions. Born May 13, 1952. The next day would be her fifty-second birthday.

A few minutes later, another officer arrived to transport Nancy Seaman to the Farmington Hills police station. The handcuffs were put on again for the ride. Just after 5 P.M., she was booked on the charge of first-degree murder.

PART TWO

Family History

CHAPTER 4

To Marry a Ford Man

N ancy D'Onofrio was born in the town of Lincoln Park, Michigan—Ford country. Measured strictly in terms of driving time, the trip from Farmington Hills to Lincoln Park takes about forty-five minutes, but the differences between the two places—in terms of class, culture, and standard of living—were as vast as those separating Milwaukee and Miami, or Nome and Mombassa. Both towns might have sprung up in the second half of the twentieth century, during the great heyday of the American automobile industry, but one place had formed its identity as the home of laborers who made the cars, the other, as the kingdom of management.

For Nancy D'Onofrio, getting from one place to the other—though the distance spanned little more than thirty miles—probably represented the grand journey of her lifetime, her arrival in the gated community of the Ramblewood subdivision as momentous an event, in her universe, as Lily Bart's arrival in the New York society of Edith Wharton, or the Clampett family's ascent to Beverly Hills.

Like most of those who grew up in Lincoln Park, Nancy was a child of the automotive industry. Her father, Eugene D'Onofrio (son of Italian immigrants, but born in the United States) had worked, as a

younger man, in a small nonunion shop supplying parts to the Ford
plant in nearby Dearborn. When the shop closed and he was laid off
in the sixties, the family struggled for a while before Eugene found
employment as a school custodian in Lincoln Park—a job he maintained until his retirement. His wife, Lenore, originally a homemaker,
had also gone to work during this period, as a secretary.

The couple had two children—Nancy and her younger brother,
John. They lived in a tiny brick bungalow on Merrill Street, identical to
every other house on the block; and like every other house on this
block and every other block on every other street in town, the mortgage contained a racial covenant, prohibiting the sale of the home to
Jews or Negroes.

These were the years of the Detroit race riots (beginning with the
terrible summer of 1967, when you could smell smoke and see flames
nearly every night). Back in 1967, if someone said the word "nigger"
in Lincoln Park, it wasn't likely that anybody would take offense at the
term. Detroit might be the home of Motown—a place where the
Supremes, Temptations, Four Tops, Smokey Robinson, and Gladys
Knight were turning out hits for Berry Gordy, just a few miles away—
but to white working-class people in a town like Lincoln Park, Detroit
meant the riots and a place to stay away from. Beginning in 1967, anyone living in the city of Detroit who could get away from there, did—
to the point where, within a span of five years, the population had
declined by seven hundred thousand.

But of the many places where people fled from Detroit, Lincoln
Park was not one. Not if you were black, anyway. No way would a
black family have been welcomed there.

Neighbors who remember them describe the D'Onofrios as good
parents, a little stricter than most, perhaps—with Nancy's mother taking the role as the more outspoken of her parents, her father the less
forceful of the two. The family went to the nearby Catholic church and
made sure their children learned the catechism. With little money in
the family, Nancy took baby-sitting jobs. She liked to go to the hardware store with her father, picking up materials for his handyman
projects, and it was from him that Nancy first learned to use tools. She
was always a hard worker and the type to take care of whatever needed
doing. She was always a good girl, Eugene said. She never gave him
any trouble.

At school, too, to hear her classmates from Lincoln Park High tell it, she was a quiet girl and a good student—top of the class. These were the years (from the late sixties, to her high school graduation in 1970) when the chief activity for teenagers in Lincoln Park was cruising up and down Woodward Avenue in the cars of the few kids fortunate enough to own them or to get the keys for the night. They listened to Bob Seger and MC5, McCoy Tyner and (for the stoners in the group) Jimi Hendrix and Janis Joplin. They drove around with no particular destination, arriving at one parking lot only to pull out for the next.

In those days, it was all about the cars, not where they took you. The boys in the cars greased back their hair and grew sideburns, and the girls smoked and wore tight sweaters and miniskirts and Cuban heels, but Nancy D'Onofrio was never one of that group. She belonged to the Future Secretaries of America. A petite girl, she wore her long hair straight down her back and her white blouses buttoned at the neck, and on the back page of her senior yearbook, her picture could be found—with a small, tight smile—alongside her fellow valedictorian. That year—1970—there had been two.

Despite her academic standing, Nancy did not go to college. Back in the late sixties and early seventies, the options for a girl in Lincoln Park were limited: you became a nurse or a secretary if you were smart. One way or another, you got married. Smart, pretty Lincoln Park graduates, if they were female, bet on men the way men bet on horses, and the greatest achievement for a girl in those days, according to more than one member of the class of '70, was to marry a man with a good job at Ford, a man with career potential.

If that was success for a Lincoln Park girl, there could be little better way of achieving it than to get a job as a secretary at Ford, where she'd be likely to meet up-and-coming young male Ford employees. This was precisely the job Nancy Seaman took after graduation. The man she met, not long after she started working there, was Bob Seaman.

CHAPTER 5

Smart, Single, and Short

Bob came to Dearborn from St. Louis, the second of four children born to Ward and Helen Seaman. Like Nancy's parents, Bob's had worked their way up to the low end of the middle class, without benefit of education or advantages. Like Nancy's, they were churchgoing people (but Protestant). They had known hard times, and took nothing for granted. The word "divorce" would not have featured in their vocabulary any more than it would have in that of Eugene and Lenore.

Ward and Helen had met back in Mattoon, Illinois, when they were kids, and married on the Fourth of July, 1936—when Ward was nineteen and Helen not quite seventeen. As their children had been told many times, they chose to get married that day because getting married on the holiday meant they'd have a whole afternoon and night off for the honeymoon, before getting back to haying the next morning.

They were farm kids, accustomed from childhood to long days of hard work. Nowadays, what his parents had him doing would be called child abuse, Ward liked to say. Back then it was just doing what was needed to keep food on the table: riding the tractor in the predawn hours before school; breaking up the clods for planting season; keeping on the lookout for chinch bugs that could wipe out a whole crop, and a whole family with it; tending the livestock. This being the Depression, Ward had to leave school at age ten to run the 180 acres of the family's farm—a little corn and beets, some oats, some clover, and two head of livestock per acre—while his father took a job in town. Although after that Ward never got to return to school for more than a few months now and then, he was a sharp boy and a natural with any kind of machinery. School or no school, he had a love of learning. He studied books where he could find them, and listened to stories of people who'd been to places outside of Mattoon.

Ward and Helen left the farm for St. Louis during the war years, when tool-and-die men were needed to turn out bullets and weapons parts, and even though he didn't have a degree, he showed such an aptitude that he'd done well for himself in the big city. By the time Bob had come along, Ward and Helen had moved from the first little tar paper shack they'd started out in, where they used to wake up to find their blanket sprinkled with snow that had blown in during the night. Nobody would ever have called Ward and Helen Seaman well off, but the house where Bob grew up was warm and tidy, and a day didn't go by that Ward wasn't tinkering with some project or other, to make things nicer. Helen too. By all accounts, the life they lived there was a happy one.

Ward was a hard worker and then some—taking a job with Buster Brown Shoe Company, running machines there and in a series of machine shops after that, two jobs a day, sometimes. In his mid-thirties, trying to save time on a tool-and-die job by not using the safety catch on a piece of machinery, he'd cut off both pointer fingers of his hands, simultaneously. He trained himself to do his work with his remaining fingers.

Never having had much time to play around as a kid himself, Ward loved taking his children to Cardinals games and coaching their teams. (Not that he knew all that much about the game, but, just as he had been all his life, he was ready to learn.) He was a member of the Loyal Order of the Masons, and a bowler; and Saturday nights, when he could swing it, he took Helen dancing. But the number one priority in Ward and Helen Seaman's house was their kids, and Ward's favorite thing to do with his boys, when he came home from work, was slot car racing. For most people, that meant bringing your little store-bought slot car in to a slot car racing joint and leaving it to chance to see whose car was fastest. But Ward, with his natural gift for engineering, wasn't about to leave the race to chance. Though the slot cars were not much bigger than a Matchbox, he and his boys would redesign their vehicles to make them go faster. He taught his sons how to file down the parts to cut down on friction, shopped for rubber to fabricate better tires, oiled the gears. Ward encouraged his sons to study the physics of the way those cars raced, in such a way that when one of the Seaman boys set his car out on the track, he was a sure bet to win.

Ward and his sons worked on real cars together, too—favoring big old used American cars you could pick up cheap and turn into something special. When Bob was fifteen, he got himself an old Nash and rebuilt the engine to where it could go a hundred miles an hour—not a piece of news he delivered to his mother, though Ward himself may have turned a blind eye and taken a certain pride in the thing.

Of the three Seaman boys, the one who had inherited his father's gift for working on anything with an engine in it was Bob, who took after his father so closely that even though he had all five fingers on both hands, he held his tools and worked with them in the same manner Ward did. In all the years he worked on engines with tools, Bob Seaman never used his pointer fingers either.

With his stocky build and short legs, Bob was never a natural athlete, but he always loved baseball. His own sport in high school was trampoline, and he'd won a medal for his gymnastics abilities. Famous as a joker at his school, he once left his footprints on the ceiling of the gymnasium—an accomplishment he'd managed to pull off by bouncing particularly high on the trampoline one day, with his sneakers on.

After graduation, he'd gotten into the highly regarded engineering program at University of Missouri-Rolla—a program known for being so tough that many who enter don't last beyond the first couple of semesters. At Rolla, Bob was known as something of a partyer—an outgoing guy who liked visiting bars and playing practical jokes. But though he wasn't top of his class, he had a kind of dogged ambition—enough that, after graduation, he won himself one of the more coveted positions a young engineer could ask for, working for Ford.

Although he wasn't particularly handsome or romantic looking (five foot seven at most, with a round face and a barrel chest), women always liked him. He had a few girlfriends over the years, and—shortly after getting hired at Ford—at least one serious love affair with a woman named Alice, a few years older than himself and divorced, with a young child. When he found out she'd been seeing someone else (an older guy, with money) he was evidently heartbroken. It wasn't long after this that his former Rolla classmate, Rick Cox, who also worked at Ford, told him about a cute secretary he should meet, a real dynamo. Her name was Nancy D'Onofrio.

Bob and Nancy dated only a short time before he asked her to marry him. They were married in the summer of 1973. He was twenty-seven; she had just turned twenty-one. Their wedding pictures show Nancy in a long white gown and veil—smiling for the cameras, alongside Bob in a wide-lapel jacket, with wavy hair and sideburns—no hint that either of these two people expected life to be less than perfect from that day on. Each of them the child of parents for whom marriage was till death do us part, there seemed no question that they would follow the same path.

Much later, when it was clear that things weren't good between Bob and Nancy, and hadn't been for a long time, Bob explained why he'd married her:

"She was smart, single, and short," he said.

CHAPTER 6

Home for the Holidays

It probably said something about Bob Seaman's priorities that he cared about being taller than his wife. He was a traditional guy. If Nancy Seaman was looking for a prince, he was probably looking for a princess, and for a brief while, anyway, he treated her like one.

This was the period in which Billie Jean King challenged (and defeated) Bobby Riggs in a tennis match that opened worldwide debate about women's equality and led to the creation of Title IX, the bill requiring equal scholarship funding for female athletes. This was the period in which previously all-male academic institutions like Yale and Princeton, one after another, were suddenly admitting women, and people were talking about a woman astronaut, and even a woman president. In 1973, the Equal Rights Amendment had not been ratified by all states, but *Roe* v. *Wade* had been decided. Young women on college campuses were reading *Ms.* magazine and Germaine Greer and Kate Millett. They were no longer taking their husbands' names when they got married, or simply not getting married in the first place.

But in suburban Michigan, in the world of Nancy and Bob Seaman, little evidence existed that any of this revolution was going on. The news that a woman might create her identity through her own accomplishments and not by snagging some potentially successful man did not appear to have reached Dearborn in a big way yet back in 1973.

"He was my knight in shining armor," Nancy said of Bob, as she viewed him back in those days.

Bob's responsibility, as knight, seemed pretty clearly laid out: to rise in the world of Ford Motor Company and provide a perfect and beautiful home for Nancy and the perfect, beautiful children she would surely present him with. If what a husband offered, for a daughter of Lincoln Park, was a ticket out, to a life of bigger and more exciting prospects, Bob Seaman must have looked like a good one to bet on.

Time proved Nancy right, at least in certain ways. After working for a time at Ford, Bob won a better job in the engineering division of Borg Warner, a company that supplied the automotive industry with engines. Bob and Nancy relocated to Muncie, Indiana, where their sons were born—first Jeff and then Greg two years later.

Bob was moving up through the ranks at Borg Warner. Nancy stayed home with the boys, cooking and cleaning and maintaining the house and being, by all accounts, the most devoted kind of mother, whose only failing, if she had one, was a certain tendency toward overprotectiveness, particularly where Greg was concerned.

Bob was more easygoing, but he wasn't around all that much. He was bringing in good money by this point—enough that he and Nancy bought a house, then a second car, and more vehicles after that—but he was a self-confessed workaholic, and when he wasn't working at Borg Warner, he could often be found under the hood of a car, working on an engine.

Always a lover of Mustangs since the first one came out in 1964, Bob found an old Shelby Mustang for sale, cheap, and bought it with the plan of rebuilding the car at some point—with one of his sons, maybe, in the same way his own father had worked with him on cars when he was young.

Then he found another great old Mustang—this one a Boss, orange, the same color that Parnelli Jones drove to victory at Laguna Seca in 1970. Bob garaged this car, like the Shelby, for some future day, to work on with his boys.

In the family where Bob Seaman grew up, one old used car was all they could dream of owning, but Bob was earning more now than his father, or Nancy's, ever dreamed of. He bought more vehicles, a rare Pantera among them. He got a pilot's license and purchased a small private plane. He bought a boat. For a boy whose mother had once worked for months, at $4 a week, to buy her wedding dress, it was a great thing to have an office at Borg Warner and buy a new car every two years, and one for his wife too.

Bob worked long hours back then, trying to get ahead in the corporation, with Nancy holding down the fort at home, but on the weekends, he tried to be a good dad for his sons. There was one time when Jeff and Greg were still very small, when their father told them they were having a special day together.

"We need to do something, just us boys," he told them.

So he threw them into the Boss and drove them to the airport where his plane was parked. He strapped the two of them in their seats and flew to Michigan. When he landed the plane, the Shelby was parked there, waiting for them, so they took off in that, drove to his boat, and went sailing. From there, they drove to the house of their D'Onofrio grandparents, and from there back to the airport, to fly home on the plane, with a stop at McDonald's on the way back to their house in Muncie. Looking back on that Saturday later, Jeff would refer to it as the Perfect Day.

Not all of them were perfect, however. According to Nancy, the first big fight of her marriage—and the first evidence of the violence she alleged to have taken place, with mounting frequency, throughout the marriage—occurred just weeks after their wedding. She and Bob had attended the wedding of Bob's younger brother, Dennis, and his wife, Lynn, in Georgia, and something she said had ignited an argument. Bob struck her, she said.

Over the years, she said, there were occasional incidents of physical violence—once or twice a year, she claimed—and a lot of verbal abuse.

One incident, at least, had been embarrassingly well known to everyone in the Seaman family. Back when Jeff and Greg were small, Bob and Nancy had gotten into some kind of argument in the car while driving to see Bob's parents in Missouri over the Christmas holidays.

Bob had thrown a Styrofoam coffee cup at Nancy in the car. When they had arrived at Ward and Helen Seaman's home, Nancy had immediately gotten on the phone to the police, who had shown up at the door soon afterwards to take a report, though in the end, no charges had been filed. For Nancy, the event served as early proof of her husband's violent nature. For Bob, it was a humiliating overreaction, and the fact that Nancy had chosen to make their dispute so public in front of his parents marked a moment, he told his brother Dennis, when the love he had felt for her up to then began to be replaced by bitterness and resentment.

Meanwhile, Bob was rising in the ranks at Borg Warner. He invented a five-speed manual transmission that earned him a patent. By now he was making a six-figure income and had a reputation as a man on the rise.

He had also had at least one affair. When Nancy learned about that, she'd gone to her competitor's house to confront her, bringing her two sons along for the purpose of driving home the point that the woman was a homewrecker. The affair ended. Either that, or Bob Seaman got better at keeping things secret.

In 1989, Bob was named vice president in charge of engineering at Borg Warner, and transferred back to the Detroit area. Bob and Nancy bought the house on Briarwood Court in the Ramblewood subdivision—a Tudor, on an oversized lot in a prime spot at the end of a cul de sac. Among the features the Seamans particularly liked about the house was its spacious three-car garage.

They'd come a long way from Lincoln Park and St. Louis, and made it known. For Christmas one year, Bob bought Nancy a fur coat, with a second surprise in the pocket: the keys to a brand new red Le Baron convertible. But on the home front, the couple fought a lot. According to Greg, his father was increasingly abusive (verbally, in particular) not only to his mother but also to him. Later he would describe an altercation he claimed to have occurred when he was eleven that ended with his father hitting him with sufficient force that it split his lip. He took a photograph of the injury with his Polaroid camera, he said, though at some point the picture had been thrown out.

Jeff viewed the situation between his parents differently. They fought, all right, but in his eyes, there was no one aggressor or one victim. He compared the situation around their house to the family on the show *Married, with Children* or the couple in the movie that was his mother's favorite, *The War of the Roses.*

"He called her names; she called him names," said Jeff. "My brother and I just took it for granted and tuned it out."

In one place, at least, the arguments between Bob and Nancy Seaman were noted, and a subject of considerable concern. At holiday times, the couple typically drove to Ballwin, Missouri, outside St. Louis, to visit with Bob's family—Ward and Helen, Dennis and his family, Margie (divorced from her husband) and her daughter, Bob's brother Dave and his children.

"The first time they came to visit after Jeff was born, Nancy wouldn't let any of us hold the baby. She just went off to the upstairs bedroom to be alone," said Margie. "But back then, we all just thought she was still adjusting to motherhood."

Over the years of family visits, however, the family observed that Nancy's behavior toward them remained distant and chilly. Although there were several cousins close to the ages of Jeff and Greg, Nancy continued to remove her sons from the family group, spending a significant portion of the visit in the bedroom, playing card games with her boys.

"The presents they brought always looked like something they'd picked up in ten minutes at K-Mart on the way to Missouri," said Dennis, noting another characteristic trait of Nancy's holiday visits: that although she was a woman who appeared to care a good deal about her appearance in certain circumstances, she always wore the same outfit—a sweatsuit—when she came to Missouri.

"It was like she was having to put up with this low-rent bunch of relatives when she came to see the family," he said. "Like she didn't belong with us."

The family got used to Nancy's habit of absenting herself from the rest of them during holiday visits. Eventually, Margie and Dennis maintained, Jeff resisted being isolated from his relatives, but Greg remained at his mother's side every visit, keeping his distance from the rest of the family, even the cousins.

"He was like her shadow," said Lynn. "There were all these cousins around, and what did Greg do? Play cards with his mother."

"You could tell Bob felt bad about that, but he never talked about it," said Dennis. "The way I figure it, he was just trying not to rock the boat."

Then Dennis and his wife split up. He'd been having an affair, and he left her—an event that inspired Bob to express concern over the assets his brother was going to lose in the process.

"I can earn it back," Dennis told him. But to Bob, the idea of splitting up, fifty-fifty, all the cars and savings you'd accumulated through your own hard work was reason enough to stick out a bad marriage.

"He kept adding up what it was costing me," Dennis said. "I kept telling him it was more important to be happy."

For Nancy, Dennis and Lynn's divorce brought about at least one surprising shift. Where in the past she had remained unfriendly to Lynn (resenting her, Lynn believed, for having upstaged Nancy's own bride status years earlier by getting married herself, just a few weeks after Bob and Nancy's wedding), now Nancy sought out Lynn as the injured party, snubbing Dennis even more visibly than before and virtually ignoring his new wife, Robin.

"She started sending me Christmas cards," said Lynn. "Like we were friends all of a sudden. But we weren't."

The truth was, Nancy Seaman didn't have close friends, though she did sometimes socialize with Paulette Schleuter, the wife of Bob Seaman's old classmate Dennis. When she did, she'd report later to Bob about all the things Dennis Schleuter, who worked for American Axle Corporation, did for Paulette—the gifts he bought her for her anniversary, the trips they took—that Bob had failed to provide.

The visits to Ballwin grew less and less frequent over the years, but the elder Seamans and the extended Seaman family grew closer to Jeff when he made the choice to attend the same engineering program his father had at University of Missouri-Rolla.

"That's when we finally got to know him," said Dennis. "And he told us, 'All these years, I've been hearing you guys are some kind of ax murderers.'" That was his mother's story, he said.

So Jeff became close with his grandparents, his uncles and aunt, and his cousins. "I think this made Nancy crazy," said Dennis. "She got this idea—she'd lost Jeff, but she'd hold on to Greg." No way was he coming to Rolla like his brother.

Although he too chose to study engineering, Greg went to Purdue, in Indianapolis (after a year of college in Michigan first). By this time, Bob's brothers, sister, and parents had grown accustomed to hardly seeing Bob and Greg, except for one fondly remembered Christmas when Greg and Jeff were both out of high school; Bob and the boys came to visit without Nancy, and they had all laughed and talked—even Greg.

"The boys had actually joked about how their mom was going to give them a hard time for having so much fun with us," Dennis said about that visit. By now everyone understood that for the two sons of

Bob and Nancy, any allegiance to their father and his family would be viewed as a betrayal of their mother. The way some people lay claim to possessions when a marriage breaks down, she was holding on to the one son whose loyalty she believed she could still guard: Greg.

But though Greg didn't go to college to Missouri, he was gone from home, and as a woman who didn't have many hobbies or outside interests or close friends besides her family, Nancy found that hard enough. There was, however, one other source of fulfillment in her life. After years at home as a full-time mother, Nancy Seaman had embarked on a career, and she was loving it.

As Jeff and Greg had grown older, Nancy had made the decision to return to school and fulfill her longtime ambition of becoming a teacher. It had taken a number of years of commuting to Eastern Michigan University, in Ypsilanti, but she earned her degree and her teaching certificate. Eventually she had earned her master's degree at Eastern Michigan as well, writing a dissertation on the subject of fostering nonviolent conflict resolution.

CHAPTER 7

The Best Batting Cage in the State of Michigan

Right around the time Nancy earned her degree, several unexpected events rocked her world. Not yet fifty years old, Bob Seaman suffered a heart attack. Around the same time—in an event whose details vary depending on the source—Bob lost his high-paying job at Borg Warner, an event Nancy's allies later alleged to have come about, directly or indirectly, due to his hotheaded behavior.

"Bob had a temper," said Rick Cox. "Everyone who knew him knew that."

His friends suggest a somewhat different scenario, in which his refusal to demote an employee (coincidentally, an African American man) whom he regarded as valuable and loyal had brought about his own professional ruin. He had taken a strong stand, all right, but one that demonstrated courage and loyalty, not explosiveness.

Likewise, the stories vary considerably as to how Bob Seaman dealt with the news of having been let go from his position at Borg Warner. To Nancy, the event marked the beginning of a dramatic downward spiral characterized by increasingly irrational and violent behavior. To Jeff, Dennis, and others, Bob Seaman was a happier man after his release from the stress of corporate life.

He received a substantial buyout package. After he left, he invested the money—some of it in stock deals that lost money, which Greg Seaman cited as an example of his father's imprudent behavior during this period. The stock fared poorly and lost a lot of its value—a source of considerable bitterness on Nancy Seaman's part.

The other investment Bob Seaman made during this period might have seemed even less well thought out. A few years earlier, his Rolla classmate Rick Cox had bought an old Ford plant, the Waterwheel Building, named for an actual waterwheel out front, no longer functioning. The place was in need of both capital and major repairs and remodeling (not to mention a handyperson) to fix it up. Rick—who ran a marine supply business there called R and D Enterprises—offered to let Bob buy into the building to become a 49 percent stockholder for an investment of several hundred thousand dollars. Bob agreed, with the additional plan of using part of the space in the building to start a business that was a kind of fantasy for him (particularly, no doubt, as the father of two ball-playing sons): a batting-cage operation. But this would be no ordinary batting cage: it would be the best batting cage in the state of Michigan, the best batting cage in which any ball player had ever swung a bat, probably. He'd call it Put One in the Upper Deck.

Initially, Nancy appeared to take a positive attitude about the batting-cage business, though it was unlikely she could have felt happy at her husband's leaving the high-profile life of an automotive executive. Later she claimed that she had pitched in to help Bob set up the Upper Deck facility, along with their sons. But she had also begun to work at the first job she'd held since leaving her secretarial position fifteen years earlier, having been hired to teach fourth grade at Longacre Elementary School.

Once again, the stories vary here. In Nancy's telling, her husband felt jealous of her career—castrated, even, by the knowledge that she was now bringing home a bigger paycheck than he was. Old acquaintances like Rick Cox and others from his days in the automotive industry—Dennis Schleuter, Ron Schoenbach—described Bob as a man fallen from grace, depressed, humiliated, and bitter.

But to many others, who came to know Bob only during his years of running the Upper Deck, Bob Seaman was a happy man who loved his new work, helping kids learn how to hit and throw a ball.

"This was his dream," said Scott Gardner, a former Triple A ball player Bob hired to work with kids at the Upper Deck, echoing the observation of many others. "The guy loved what he was doing. The only thing that wasn't good in his life was his marriage. So he stayed away from home as much as possible."

Around this same period—the nineties—Bob Seaman embarked on another project that allowed him to live out a longtime fantasy. As his son Jeff neared driving age, the two of them set out to rebuild one of Bob's two classic Mustangs. The Shelby being the more valuable in the marketplace, Bob chose to start his son in with the Boss. For the next three years, the two of them worked on that car to the point, Jeff said, where he knew every centimeter of the engine. All through high school, Jeff drove the Boss, with its sleek fastback and racing stripe and souped-up muscle engine, though the car remained in his father's name. When he turned eighteen, he left home to attend Rolla, his father's alma mater, and returned the car keys to Bob.

"That was OK," he said. "I got everything I needed out of working with my dad on the Boss. I knew I could buy my own Mustang and fix it up after that. I like being independent. I like taking care of things myself."

With Jeff off to college, it might have seemed time for Bob and Greg to get to work on a car project, but that didn't happen. According to Jeff, Greg had a short attention span for projects that didn't produce an immediate and gratifying reward. Greg was accustomed to having things handed to him, Jeff said. He might be Ward Seaman's grandson, but his mother had raised him as a child of privilege, and Farmington Hills, Michigan, was a long way from Mattoon, Illinois.

There may have been more to the story. Where Jeff had always idolized his father (whom he resembled closely), Greg (who resembled Nancy, and bore seemingly no resemblance to Bob) remained much more closely identified with his mother. Perhaps Nancy felt threatened by the closeness that developed between Jeff and his father, over the hundreds of hours they spent working on the Boss, knowing there was no equivalent activity she could engage in with him. And in the same way that Bob Seaman appeared to emulate at least some of the ways his father had raised him (working on cars with his sons, for instance), Nancy seemed equally invested in providing, for Greg, the kind of high school life—of carefree privilege—she herself had never known.

Not many seventeen-year-olds get to drive a $130,000 car to their high school prom, but Greg Seaman did. Bob let him use the Ferrari for the evening. But the two had never put in the time, as Bob had with Jeff, rebuilding a Mustang engine together.

"My brother wasn't that interested," Jeff said, though in Greg's telling, the problem lay not in his own lack of interest but in his father's growing absence from the family and his overinvolvement with the Upper Deck.

Where Jeff had played baseball and ultimately saved up college money working as an umpire, Greg had never held the same enthusiasm for the sport his father loved, preferring cross-country running. Despite a physique strikingly ill suited to distance running, Bob had made efforts to run with Greg over the years, though Greg's main running partner had not been his father, but rather his father's old classmate Dennis Schleuter. Sometimes, now, when they argued—as they so often did—Nancy would tell Bob that Dennis would have been a much more satisfactory father to her son than Bob had proved to be.

"Maybe Dennis Schleuter would like to pay for Greg's college," Bob had suggested.

But it wasn't just a lack of passion for the sport of baseball that caused Greg's gradual alienation from his father. It was Greg's growing belief that Bob's attachment to baseball and the Upper Deck had become dangerously connected to an insidious attachment with another family, whose place in his father's life now threatened that of himself and, most of all, his mother.

They were called the Dumbletons.

CHAPTER 8

A Man Who Could Make
a Pork Chop Interesting

T hey might have seemed unlikely friends: the stocky, scrappy, outgoing, big-talking, life-of-the party lover of big V-8 engines and baseball, who drove fast and told off-color jokes and loved the Dave Matthews Band and Rush Limbaugh, and the much quieter homebody couple, Dick and Julie—who tried to eat every meal with the family, never used bad language, subscribed to Christian magazines and attended Bible Study classes, and never raised their voices in front of the children. Dick too was an engineer, but not—as Bob had been—a particularly brash or high-profile one. He put his money into family vacations and the college fund, not cars, and was more inclined to listen than to talk a lot.

Where Bob had made a name for himself in the industry some years earlier with his invention of a five-speed manual transmission for big American cars, Dick worked (in Detroit, the mecca of the American automobile) for a Japanese company, Nissan. Dick was a trim, soft-spoken man who never missed a softball game but never took center stage with his advice to players. He sported a neat, brushy moustache and wire-rimmed glasses and thinning hair generally topped with a baseball cap. A person might describe him as possessing a faintly receding chin, but he had a sweet face, and appeared unembarrassed by how easily tears came to his eyes, by how often he choked up when he talked about his wife and kids.

Julie, a highly attractive woman of Korean American origin—raised in Maryland, the daughter of a surgeon—had the trimmest figure of any mother on the bench, but never flaunted it. She favored a shirt that said Fastpitch Mom, kept a bag full of healthy treats—nuts, dried fruit, and low-fat Twizzlers—to pass out during games, and always wore a simple gold cross around her neck. She liked to be there waiting for her kids when they got home from school, and took the family's big dog, Bailey, wherever she went. Except for the hours she spent helping out at the Upper Deck and in her part-time job as a crossing guard at school, she had been a stay-at-home mother ever since Jake was born.

The Dumbletons were one of those couples who reminded you of a sixties family situation comedy, with their tidy front yard (displaying a plywood baseball cut out with a jigsaw and painted with Jenna's number, 16) and big, friendly dog; pictures of the family on the mantel; calligraphy of happy and inspirational sayings ("Friends are the family you get to choose") hung in frames on the walls. When you called their house, the voice on the answering machine featured a sweet-voiced Jenna, around age six, saying "We aren't home right now, but please leave a message." When you dropped in to see them, it was a good bet that there would be cookies coming out of the oven if they weren't set out on the plate already.

Julie and Dick met back in Pennsylvania, when she was working as an ultrasound technician, and Dick—son of a highway shovel operator—had a job in the lab. He lived on rice and beans for a month, he said, after he bought a pair of skis so he could accompany Julie to the slopes. He went back to school to get an engineering degree, he said, "so I'd be someone she could be proud of."

After they married, they'd waited a few years to have children—wanting to make sure things were secure for them first and that they could provide for their children as they wanted to. They were loving but strict parents who kept a close eye out on their kids, making sure they didn't get exposed to violent movies or bad language, and neither Jake nor Jenna had let them down in that department. They called adults "Mr." and "Mrs.," shook hands, and sent thank-you notes.

Twenty-five years after his wedding day, Dick Dumbleton still brought his wife flowers, though she said it was a waste of money. If he didn't call out, "Honey, I'm home," when he walked in the door at five o'clock, it was probably because Julie would have been there to greet him already.

They had met Bob when Dick brought Jake—then around age ten—to the newly opened batting-cage facility to work on his hitting. Pretty soon both Jake and Jenna had hitting cards of their own, with Jenna—then only six years old—showing as much promise as her brother. Sometimes, after batting and hitting practice, Dick invited Bob to join him and his family for pizza, and they got to be friends.

Bob volunteered to coach Jenna's softball team. All his life, he'd been accustomed to the highly competitive world of male athletics—but he discovered, to his surprise, that he loved working with the girls. Not that the competitive side of his personality had disappeared, however. Recognizing Jenna's talent, he began working with her one-on-one to improve her pitching, and started encouraging Dick and Julie to sign her up for a higher level team, the Northville Girls' fastpitch twelve and under team. Jenna was just nine at the time—and Dick worried that she might not be able to keep up with the older girls and would feel discouraged, but Bob wasn't buying it, and it turned out he was right. Three years younger than her teammates, she was a star.

"Bob told us she could handle the pressure, and he was right," Julie said. "That was Bob for you. He got us to think bigger."

The friendship went beyond softball, though. Although neither of Julie nor Dick said it outright, it was a safe bet that Bob Seaman must have represented a certain kind of excitement and drama seldom present in the wholesome stability of the Dumbleton household.

"Bob could take anything—a pork chop he had for dinner the night before—and make it interesting," said Julie, who—sweet as she was—would not be described as a raconteur. "He had this way of telling stories. We never heard anything like it before."

Sometime in 1999, Julie volunteered to work part-time for Bob, first as a paid secretary in the office, assisting with the payroll, billing, and scheduling of customers, then, a year later, becoming an unpaid helper. She did so, she said, because the business wasn't making much money, and she felt uncomfortable taking any from a man who was, by this point, like a member of the family.

At first, Julie said, she and Dick liked Nancy Seaman. The families socialized together several times and attended a Tigers game together. It was at Jeff's wedding in Illinois, where Jake had been asked to be one of the ushers (a job not given to Greg), that the Dumbletons first experienced Nancy's obvious resentment.

"At the wedding, she barely spoke to us," said Julie. "All she said was, 'Oh, you're here from Michigan.'"

According to Julie, in fall 2001—shortly after Jeff Seaman's wedding—Nancy Seaman burst into the office at the Upper Deck and stole a bunch of picture frames displaying photographs of Julie's children. At home, Nancy had begun accusing her husband of neglecting her in favor of the Dumbletons, whom she referred to as "the Dumbies." They were taking him away from his family, she said. They were usurping her place in his life and causing him to neglect his own children.

But the big problem between Nancy Seaman and the Dumbletons started—at least on the surface of things—with a car. Not surprisingly, it was a Mustang.

In the summer of 2001, Bob bought a beat-up Mustang—a 1989, priced at $500—with the plan of rebuilding the car with Greg over the course of the months he'd be home from his first year of college. Bob hoped that the Mustang would serve as a father-and-son bonding project like the ones he'd engaged in with his own father and with Jeff, when the two of them had worked together on the Boss.

At first Bob and Greg were full of energy and ambition for the project, though Bob had been a little surprised at Greg's decision—once he got the car home and parked it out in front of their house on Briarwood Court—to completely disassemble the entire engine all at once.

They spent a few nights working together on the car. Then, according to Bob, Greg lost interest. Alternatively, it may be that Bob found fault with how Greg was approaching the job, and lost his temper—an event that occurred frequently when Jeff worked on cars with his father, though when it had happened with Jeff, he said he never took his father's flare-ups very seriously or registered deep concern about them.

Whatever the reason, the Mustang sat in the driveway, parts all around, for the rest of the summer and into the fall. Instead of bringing Bob and Greg closer, the car became an endless source of contention between the two, with Bob telling Greg he had to get the car out of the driveway or the neighbors would complain, and Greg doing nothing about it.

Then, without consulting Bob, Nancy presented Greg with a surprise: a newer Mustang, in much better shape, in no need of work. To Bob, his wife's decision to purchase a different car for their son without consulting him felt like a deep betrayal.

Greg drove off to school in the fall, at the wheel of the newer Mustang. Months passed in which he had taken no interest in the older vehicle. With neighbors in the subdivision complaining—and a $400 fine ultimately levied against him for keeping an unsightly mess in his driveway—Bob had the car hauled down to the Upper Deck. He began working on it in the basement there, with Jake Dumbleton, who was nearing his fourteenth birthday and already looking forward with great anticipation to getting his learner's permit the following year.

To Bob, learning to drive and getting out on the road was one of the major rites of passage in a young person's life. Even before Jake got the permit, Bob had been taking Jake out in the car with him, same as he had his own sons. (Later, once he was legal, Jake practiced driving with his father too, but it was Bob who taught him how to use a manual transmission and instructed him in the shifting techniques of a pro, including some his mother would probably have preferred he not know about.)

One day, while the two of them were in the basement of the Waterwheel Building working on the Mustang, Bob told Jake the car was his.

Jake was thrilled, but even then he was concerned—and so were Dick and Julie—as to whether Greg might object to Jake's receiving the gift of a car that had originally been purchased for him. Jake spoke directly to Greg about the Mustang to ask if it was OK that Bob had given it to him. According to Jake, Greg told him that was fine; he had his own, newer Mustang now. So Jake began using his savings from his job cleaning the bathrooms at the Upper Deck to purchase parts for the car.

But even if Greg didn't want the 1989 Mustang, from all appearances Nancy did. In February of 2002 she called Julie Dumbleton.

According to Julie, Nancy told her, "You better make sure you keep Jake away from that car. If you don't, I'll make sure I do."

"She also said 'If you're thinking about calling Bob to whine, I'll . . . be at your front door so fast and kick your fucking . . . Got that, girl?'"

This was the point at which Julie Dumbleton decided to keep notes on her dealings with Nancy Seaman.

"I just had the feeling I might need them some day," said Julie.

After the phone call, Dick and Julie were set to return the gift of the Mustang, but Bob wouldn't hear of it. He didn't intend to be bullied, he told them. Greg clearly didn't want the car. End of story. At least, they all wanted to believe that.

After the Mustang incident, the Dumbletons kept their distance from Nancy. Bob and Greg seemed to be close for a while—working out together at the gym that next summer when Greg came home from Purdue again, and spending long hours bent over the engine of Greg's newer Mustang. Greg took Bob out to lunch that winter, Julie recalled, presenting him with a card that read "Thank you for all the tools you gave me"—referring to tools for living, she said.

From the looks of things, Bob Seaman was eager to do whatever it took to reinforce and deepen the bond with his younger son in the aftermath of some difficult times between them. He spent hours driving around searching for parts so that he'd have what they needed when Greg came over to work on his car. Greg and Bob took a road trip together to Tennessee to buy an old Ford F100 truck Bob had found online, stopping in Cincinnati to show Nancy's brother the truck. Greg and his girlfriend had shown up at a tournament in Kalamazoo where the Compuware girls were playing.

As Julie reconstructed it, the break between Bob and Greg had been touched off just before Greg's birthday over the summer of 2003. Nancy showed up at the Upper Deck that day, and a huge fight took place between her and Bob. Bob told Nancy to leave and to stop embarrassing him at his place of business. From that point on, Greg became increasingly hostile to his father.

But the final break occurred, most agreed, on August 16 of that summer, the date of an event in which the Seaman family always participated, the Woodward Avenue Dream Cruise, where Bob traditionally put his beloved Shelby Mustang out on display. In years past, it would have been Nancy or Greg or Jeff in the Shelby with Bob, but that year, Nancy expressed no interest in attending the Dream Cruise with him. Bob offered a ride to the Dumbletons. When Greg saw that, he exploded. "You have to choose between your friends and me," he told his father.

Nancy had made the lines clear as a penmanship lesson. There was no way Bob could be friends with the Dumbletons and still have his son in his life. There was no way Greg could truly love his mother without rejecting his father. No way for the son to have both his parents in his life. Back home on Briarwood Court later that day, in the aftermath of a Dream Cruise that had felt more like a ten-car pileup, Greg Seaman swung a pool cue at his father and told him, "You're not my father anymore."

CHAPTER 9

A Broken Fingernail, Caught on Film

From that August day, Greg Seaman's communication with his father was confined to similar expressions of contempt, the word "asshole" featuring with increasing frequency in the vocabulary of a young man most people would have described as mature, upstanding, and precisely the kind of person a parent would be proud to have raised. One of his parents certainly was: Nancy.

Over the course of the fall, according to Julie Dumbleton, Bob made a series of overtures to Greg, attempting to mend the growing acrimony between them, without success. Meanwhile, Jeff and Bob continued to spend time together—going out for lunch, working side by side on their cars, and coaching kids on Saturday mornings down at the Upper Deck.

One person who didn't share Bob Seaman's enthusiasm for girls' softball, however, was Nancy. If to some people it might have appeared that Bob sought refuge at the Upper Deck and occupied himself coaching girls' softball and hanging out with the Dumbleton family out of a growing sense of frustration in his marriage, his wife appeared to interpret the evidence differently. To Nancy Seaman, her husband's involvement in softball activities, and the time he spent with Julie and her family, was not a symptom of trouble in the Seamans' marriage, but its cause. (Conversely, then, she must have reasoned that if Bob stopped coaching girls' softball and discontinued his relationship with the Dumbletons, things between them might be good again.)

And from all anyone could tell, Nancy Seaman desperately wanted the marriage to endure. Bob might be sleeping in the basement, and she might be sleeping alone in the master bedroom. She might complain of his inattentiveness, his failure to appreciate her, the lack of interest he displayed in her school activities, his failure to provide her with the kinds of romantic gifts or trips that couples like the Schleuters seemed to share. They might barely speak to one another, in fact, and (though she wasn't sharing this with anyone in her family at this point) he might be hitting her (as she would later say) with increasing frequency. Still, from what she said to her sons and others, it appeared that she believed the two of them should stay together.

Anyone paying close attention to Nancy Seaman's demeanor in fall 2003 would have spotted indications of trouble, though. One fellow teacher, Jill Fleming, was not a friend, precisely, but a colleague who had gotten to know Nancy while they were both on the same committee having to do with writing issues for elementary school students. Jill had noted, when school resumed that September, that the large diamond ring Nancy used to wear was missing from her finger and that her characteristic good humor and easy laughter, too, seemed to have disappeared.

"I almost said something to her," said Jill. "But it didn't seem my place. I didn't want to intrude."

And there were other signs. In earlier years, the house on Briarwood Court was always maintained in pristine condition, but now nobody seemed to be making the effort. More significant, Bob and Nancy appeared to be in a kind of standoff.

"My parents had a disagreement about whose responsibility it was to keep the house up, because . . . neither one of them had been maintaining the house for the last three or four years," said Jeff.

The grass was long, uncut for weeks. The shrubs and bushes had gone untrimmed. The sprinklers no longer functioned, and neither did most of the Malibu lights out front. The basement carpeting had water damage. The furnace needed routine maintenance. The larger of the two garage doors didn't open anymore. Most bizarre, neither

Bob nor Nancy appeared willing to carry the trash out, so it had piled up in the garage, emitting, Jeff said, a powerful odor—all the more baffling in the context of a family for whom the garage had been a crucial part of the property, and, in the past, the place that housed whatever vehicle (probably a Mustang) Bob was working on at the time.

Bob wasn't working on cars in his own garage anymore, however. He had shifted his tools over to the basement of the Upper Deck. More and more now, he spent his days there, and sometimes his evenings too. More and more, Julie Dumbleton observed, the Waterwheel building had become a refuge from his increasingly stressful home and his life with Nancy. Now and then, though, Nancy would enter into that territory too, and when she did, things nearly always went badly.

On Friday, November 7, 2003 (a date Julie recorded in her growing list of notes documenting unpleasant encounters with Nancy Seaman), Julie was at the Upper Deck, waiting for Jenna, who was having a pitching lesson with Bob. Because she had the family's dog, Bailey, with her, she was watching from a spot near the entrance, while one man, a regular customer, worked out in the batting cage, and an employee, Jenny Metz, took care of the desk.

Sometime after four-thirty, Julie said, Nancy entered the Upper Deck and approached Bob. She was making a drive to Woodhaven to see her father, evidently. She told him she was concerned that she might have car trouble in her Explorer. Some of her irritation may have come from the fact that Bob had recently taken back the expensive Lincoln LS she had been driving and sold it—leaving her with the far less impressive-looking 1995 Explorer.

Now she was stopping by to say she wanted to trade cars with Bob and take his newer Explorer (a 2002 model) to Woodhaven. Bob stopped Jenna's lesson and approached the counter to talk with Nancy. As they started moving toward the door, Julie said, she stepped back with her dog to clear the path.

"What happened after that was laughable and embarrassing," said Julie. "As Nancy walked past me, she made a face and stuck out her tongue." Julie said that what happened next was a little less clear, because she was trying to get Bailey out of the way, but it appeared that Nancy gave her the finger.

Julie Dumbleton was not a large or physically threatening person, but she was not the type to shrug off Nancy's behavior, as her husband had often advised her to do.

"I followed them to the door and said, 'Bob, did you see what she did? She just stuck her fat tongue out at me.'"

According to Julie, Nancy then turned around and called her a name. Julie Dumbleton was not used to repeating this word out loud, she said, but it began with *F.*

"Then she started flailing her arms and screaming, 'Stay away. Don't touch me. I'm going to call the police and tell them you pushed me and hit me.'"

Bob tried to get between her and Nancy, Julie said. He tried to move Nancy away from the door. Finally he got her away. A moment later he returned, and a moment after that, Nancy followed him. Still screaming profanities, according to Julie, she demanded a telephone to call the police, accusing Julie of having assaulted her.

Bob told Nancy to leave. According to Julie, Nancy continued screaming, demanding the phone.

Finally, as Julie later reported to the police, "Bob pulled Nancy out of the counter area, and she appeared to trip on the pitching tunnel netting. She stumbled into the scaffolding that was near that area. Bob grabbed the back collar of Nancy's coat and her arm and dragged her out. Nancy resisted and tried to grab on to the nylon netting of the pitching tunnel."

Eventually, Bob succeeded in getting Nancy out the door. For a few moments, the yelling continued outside. Then Bob came back in. He resumed his pitching lesson with Jenna.

A few minutes later, Nancy returned with Officer Evans of the Northville Police Department. She repeated her allegation that she had been assaulted, accusing Julie Dumbleton of slapping her on the right side of her face with an open hand. She told Evans that Julie then pushed her against the wall of the building, using both of her hands, against Seaman's chest, causing an injury to the knuckle of her right hand and breaking a fingernail.

According to Nancy Seaman, her husband had witnessed this alleged assault, but had done nothing to intervene. When she attempted to reenter the building for the purpose of locating a phone to call the police, Bob Seaman had grabbed her by the sleeve of her jacket and escorted her out to her car. He told her not to call the police and said that if she did, the two of them were "through."

Nancy then made her way to the health club in the Waterwheel Building to use their telephone to summon the police.

Officer Evans interviewed both Bob Seaman and Julie Dumbleton, as well as Nancy Seaman. As he wrote in his report later that day, "Both denied any physical altercation. Their story was very similar to what Mrs. Seaman told me except they said Seaman and Dumbleton were only yelling at each other while outside and that no pushing or slapping occurred." When Officer Evans asked Bob Seaman if his wife was lying, Seaman answered that she was.

Neither Jenny Metz nor Jenna Dumbleton, who'd been at the Upper Deck that afternoon, had witnessed any assault, though both attested, in the police report, that they had heard yelling. The man who had been practicing in the batting cage said he'd heard nothing.

Following the conclusion of his investigation, Officer Evans suggested that Nancy Seaman follow him back to the police station for the purpose of having her injuries photographed. A picture was then taken of her broken fingernail.

Upon receipt of Officer Evans's report, the police dropped the assault charges against Julie Dumbleton, and the case was closed.

CHAPTER 10

"Your Dad Grabbed My Arm"

N ancy's mother, Lenore, had been hospitalized in November of 2003 for diabetes. The following month, after her release from the hospital, she died unexpectedly.

Colleagues of Nancy Seaman, who observed her over the days that followed, described—not surprisingly—the intense grief and devastation she displayed at the loss of her mother. Although Jeff said that Lenore D'Onofrio and Bob Seaman had always enjoyed a good relationship—and that his father had been deeply saddened by her death—in Nancy's opinion, Bob had once again failed to offer the kind of support she believed a better and more loving mate might have provided at such a difficult time. Specifically, she expressed to Bob the view that with her mother dead, he should be making more of an effort to repair their marriage. As Julie Dumbleton reported it, Bob had responded by telling his wife that whatever sorrow he felt about her mother had no effect, for him, on what he saw as the breakdown of their relationship.

This was the end of December 2003—not, by all accounts, a happy Christmas. Then came the new year, and whereas in the past, Nancy Seaman had apparently chosen to conceal the truth of what was going on between herself and her husband, she seemed ready now to reveal to her family—her son Jeff, at least—the abuse she claimed to have been taking place between herself and his father and the hell, she told him now, that she'd silently endured.

For years, it had been something of a joke in the Seaman family, Jeff said, that Nancy Seaman was a klutz. There was a particular step leading out from the front door of their house on Briarwood Court where she had tripped once injuring her wrist—so that now, every time one of them approached it, she'd remind them to be careful. (She also commented on her husband's continued failure to repair the step.) Nancy had a history of injuries, her son said—bruises she'd gotten on the family boat or from bumping into chairs, she had told them.

In January of 2004, Jeff said, his mother changed her story.

It was on one of their Saturday lunches at his parents' house—with his father absent as usual, and Becka at his side—that Nancy had announced she had a confession to make. Bob had been beating her, she told them. Up until now, she said, she'd wanted to protect them—and to protect Bob. She had wanted so badly for her sons to love their father, she said, that she'd concealed the truth from them, but now things had gotten so much worse that she'd decided the time had come to be honest. She rolled up the sleeve of her blouse then, holding out her arm for her son and his wife.

"She had a bruise on one of her arms," said Jeff.

"See this?" she had said. "This bruise is from where your dad grabbed my arm."

And there was more. "Remember that wrist I said I hurt, falling on the sidewalk five or six or seven years ago?" she told them. "That was when he threw me into a wall."

The news came as a terrible shock.

"My wife immediately jumped in," Jeff said, "because her parents had gone through a very painful divorce where there was domestic abuse."

"And she immediately said, 'You have to leave now. You have to call the police. You have to do something. I mean, you can't sit back. You have to get out. This is a problem.'"

The thing was, Jeff recalled, that when Becka said that, his mother seemed to back off of her allegations.

"I mean, all of a sudden she did not want to follow through on the course of action my wife was talking about. Like, when we said, 'You have to get out of here,' that wasn't really what she wanted to hear. And my perception at the time, and what I still believe, was that she was testing out her story for the upcoming divorce. It seemed like . . . she was figuring out what she was going to say at the divorce. But she hadn't bargained on our reaction.

"The other thing was," he went on, "she had a scratch on her hand. She said, 'Your dad grabbed a bunch of what he thought were Post-it notes out of my hands.' He had scratched her. Those were the three instances she gave us of this so-called abuse," Jeff said. More and more, as he listened, and watched his mother, he wasn't buying it. She had a scratch, all right, but it was barely visible. "It was like somebody scratched you with their fingernail," he said. "It was like nothing."

Still, he and Becka had offered to let his mother come and stay with them at their apartment. Becka had been even more insistent, initially, that if in fact Bob was beating Nancy, as she said, something had to be done. She urged Nancy to find a place to live, away from Briarwood Court and her husband. This was when they made the plan to go look at condos together.

In January (having sworn her sons and their partners to secrecy), Nancy put a down payment on the condo unit at King's Crossing with money provided by her father. She returned to the unit several times after that, accompanied by Jeff and Becka and by Greg and Kristin, for the purpose of choosing colors and fabrics and appliances for the unit, which would be ready the following August. For someone who appeared to be fearing for her safety, the date seemed curiously far into the future; in fact, there had been a unit at King's Crossing available for immediate occupancy, but Nancy didn't like the floor plan of that one as well.

In February came the anonymous letter to Compuware, suggesting that Bob Seaman had been behaving inappropriately with the girls on his team.

The letter was typewritten on a computer. The heading, in all capital letters, read "ATTENTION: DIRECTOR OF COMPUWARE GIRLS' SOFTBALL PROGRAM." Beneath those words, the note was short and swift as a punch to the gut:

> *Your coach for the girls 12 and under fast pitch softball program, Bob Seaman, shouldn't be coaching "little girls." Didn't you ever wonder why a man with no daughters is so obsessed with little girls. You should have done your homework. Compuware is responsible for the safety of these girls. You've been warned and if you don't take action then you are liable for damages. Find yourself another coach or find yourself in the news.*

There had not been a signature, only the words, at the bottom of the note, once again in all caps, "SOMEONE WHO KNOWS."

The letter had been mailed to the Compuware team office, where the board of men who oversaw the workings of all Compuware-sponsored teams had read and swiftly dismissed it.

When Bob confronted Nancy with the letter, she said that maybe Julie Dumbleton had written it, just to try to get her in trouble.

On February 29, 2004, Bob wrote Nancy a letter to say he was no longer paying the mortgage on their home. Nancy and Bob were communicating almost exclusively through angry written notes by this point (with Nancy's ending up, eventually, in the Nancy Crap File). In response to her charges that he never did anything around the house, Bob began leaving Post-it notes on various items he'd fixed or installed, in the kitchen and elsewhere. With a bitter eye toward the future division of property, he posted one such note on a roll of toilet paper in the house, with the words "Bob's toilet paper." In other notes, he called her a bitch.

In March, Greg came home for a visit without informing his father—a source of new anger for Bob, who still held out hope that he might salvage their relationship. Greg had won an award at Purdue, but did not invite Bob to the awards ceremony.

Later that month, Bob learned of the condo purchase. When he asked Jeff if he knew about the purchase, Jeff lied to him, saying the condo was for Greg. Bob didn't believe him, but didn't press the issue further, though he reported to Julie his sadness that now his older son appeared to be moving apart from him, as his younger one had. It wasn't true, in fact: Jeff Seaman hated lying to his father, but didn't know what else to do at the time, he said.

Also that spring, Nancy learned that she'd been turned down for a mortgage due to a bad credit rating brought on by Bob's recent decision to discontinue paying the mortgage. In the end, she succeeded in getting a mortgage for the condo, but due to the credit problem, she had forfeited the original rate she'd hoped to qualify for. "I could kill your father," she told Jeff when she got the news.

In March, Bob Seaman traveled to St. Louis to see his parents. Although his father had undergone minor surgery, Bob reflected on Ward's amazingly good overall health and sharpness of mind at age eighty-eight. This reminded Bob that he could have another thirty years of life ahead of him too, his brother Dennis reported. Still, he couldn't get past the idea that a divorce from Nancy would mean losing many of the things he'd worked so hard to earn.

Then came the strange-tasting bowl of ice cream and Bob's remark to his fellow coach, Dave Brubaker "I sleep with one eye open now." Then came the trip to Arizona and the news, from his brother, that in a divorce, he would be entitled to half of Nancy's share of the condo.

The value of half-equity in the condo might have added up to only five thousand dollars, but to Bob, it seemed, that discovery changed everything. That—and a week of observing what it felt like to live in a house (Dennis and Robin's) where people carried out the trash at regular intervals and talked with each other and displayed affection, instead of leaving angry notes, not to mention going to bed at night in the same room, not two floors apart—seemed to have brought Bob Seaman to a new point in the decades-long standoff with his wife. That, and his easy, relaxed evenings eating pizza and watching ball games with the Dumbletons, and hearing Jake Dumbleton call him "Mr. Seaman" and ask for his advice, while his son Greg called him "asshole" and hung up the phone on him. That, and waiting all spring to be invited to Greg's college graduation (from a college whose tuition he'd paid for four years now) and finally realizing, a week before the event, that he wasn't going to be asked to attend. He had thought, once, that he owed it to his sons to stay with their mother. Now he was asking, where had that gotten him?

After thirty-two years of marriage to Nancy, Bob Seaman was flying home to deliver the news to her that he knew about the condo and he was happy she had bought it. He was going to tell her what Dennis told him: half of that purchase belonged to him. He was ready to accept that he wouldn't have as much retirement savings as he used to, but he felt confident now that he could earn it back again. He'd been talking to some engineers over at Hyundai about doing some consulting work. He could have another thirty years of life ahead of him; it was time he started living.

There were other women out there who might not think of him as "fucked up," the way his wife did. He didn't have to spend his nights in a basement forever, eating takeout food and waiting for the sound on the floorboards overhead of the little cart Nancy used to wheel her school supplies out to the car every morning, his signal that it was OK to come upstairs and take a shower.

He was leaving for good. He would tell her the next day, once he got home. Mother's Day.

PART THREE

Building the Case

CHAPTER 11

The Body on Briarwood Court

—〰〰— Within half an hour of Nancy Seaman's arrest for the murder of her husband, a team of police officers and evidence technicians, overseen by Detective Al Patterson, arrived on the scene. One, Officer Parsons, took photographs of the Explorer with the wrapped body in the back. Only then could firefighter Larry Gauthier step forward "to confirm that the person was dead." Gauthier made a twelve-inch incision in the tarp. A box of Febreze deodorizer had been placed in the back of the SUV next to the wrapped body, but once the tarp was cut open, the Febreze was no longer enough to mask the odor of what lay inside. As the plastic was cut away from the body, the smell hit them, thick and terrible.

The Farmington Hills police began the task of notifying the family, but not before the media had gotten word that a body had been found in the Ramblewood subdivision. Although the name of the victim had not yet been released, at least one of Bob's friends—Jack Thomas, an employee of Rick Cox at the Waterwheel Building—was watching the news as the first word came from the helicopters.

"Just from looking at the house they were flying over, I knew what that meant," he said. That's when he told Scott Gardner, a former Triple A ballplayer and batting coach at the Upper Deck, to turn on his radio.

The first person the police reached was Dennis Seaman in Arizona, who was informed by Assistant Chief Nebus that his brother was dead. Nebus then turned the phone over to Lieutenant Swanderski for further questioning.

Although in a state of grief and shock, Dennis Seaman managed to make a statement to the police that day.

For many years, Dennis told Swanderski, he himself had been the object of Nancy Seaman's greatest ire, ostensibly because of a business partnership he and his brother had entered into early in their respective marriages that had not gone well. Nancy never got over blaming Dennis for that, and remained unfriendly on the rare occasions when the two saw each other, but in recent years his sister-in-law's greatest resentment had been reserved, he said, for his brother's good friends, the Dumbletons.

"I always thought I should have sent Julie Dumbleton a thank-you note," he said, "for putting me a little lower on Nancy's hate list."

He told the investigating officer about his brother's visit to Arizona the week before—his decision to tell his wife he was leaving her, his hopefulness about the future. The picture of the Seamans' finances portrayed by Dennis differed markedly from that suggested by Nancy, earlier, to Detective Patterson. Bob had not paid the mortgage or the car insurance for several months, Dennis said, but not for a lack of money. He was just fed up with supporting a household in which he'd been relegated to the basement.

While visiting, Bob had told Dennis that Nancy had racked up a credit card debt of about $30,000—a figure that included payments to Purdue for Greg's tuition—and then transferred the balances to Bob's cards. The part about the condo purchase that had troubled his brother was not the news that she intended to leave the marriage, Dennis said. The part that upset him was the realization that from the looks of things, not only Greg but Jeff too had been party to the condo deception.

"He felt like he'd already lost Greg," said Dennis. "He didn't want to lose Jeff too."

As the interview concluded, Dennis Seaman explained that he'd be flying to St. Louis first, to tell his parents in person what had happened to their son. Ward and Helen Seaman were both in their late eighties. It would be hard news to deliver. After that, he'd head to Michigan.

Jeff Seaman had spent all that Wednesday morning in Dearborn again, "working on DTF testing, speed control and torque validation." Although he had continued to place calls to his father's cell phone, he had carried on with his routine. He had made dinner for Becka: "chicken nuggets with mac and cheese." They were just eating when the call came from Scott Gardner.

"Turn on the radio," he said. "They found a body in an Explorer on Briarwood Court."

A minute later, Robin called from Arizona to say the body was Bob's. "You don't sound very surprised," she said to Jeff.

Jeff called his uncle John—his mother's brother—and, despite the fact that they weren't close, he called his own brother, Greg, but neither John nor Greg answered. He left a message on Greg's cell phone, saying that something had happened at home. Only that much.

Then Jeff went into engineer mode. "I told Becka I was going to work to drop off my laptop and keys to the Explorer," he said, "because I wasn't going to work tomorrow, or maybe Friday, because something terrible happened. Drove to Dearborn [twenty minutes in the opposite direction]. . . . Got a cell call on my way from the Farmington Hills Police. Forgot my employee badge so I dropped off the keys in the fuel tank door of the Explorer and drove to the police station."

At the Dumbleton house, the news had a devastating impact.

"It was around six-thirty in the evening, and I was just returning home from my game," said Jake Dumbleton. He'd been in the last weeks of his senior year of high school at the time, and heading into his favorite months of the year, baseball season.

"The sun was shining. I can remember these specks of white that covered the blue sky as I walked in my garage. I was worried about Mr. Seaman, but I was feeling good about the game. Then as I entered the house, I heard a sound that seemed at first like some kind of hysterical laughter, coming from the family room. Then I saw my sister crying, and my dad holding her. He was solid as a stone, with this look on his face I had never seen before.

"Behind them, I could see the TV set on. The news. I saw a helicopter view of Mr. Seaman's house, with the two Explorers in the driveway and police tape wrapped around the perimeter. I didn't even have to read the caption, *Man found dead in back of SUV.* I already knew."

CHAPTER 12

News Travels Fast

In the first moments after her arrest, Nancy Seaman told the police her husband's death was an accident. She told them he'd been beating her. As soon as she reached the Farmington Hills police station, she asked that photographs be taken to document what she asserted to be injuries incurred by her husband, both on the day of the killing and over the days, weeks, and months leading up to it.

Just before 11 P.M., two nurses, Margaret Lane and Sherry Berg, arrived to perform a physical examination. On preprinted sheets, with a template of a naked female figure drawn on the front and back, the women indicated places on Nancy Seaman's body where bruises or signs of injury were visible: one 2 cm abrasion on her right upper arm, a 5 cm bruise on her lower right leg, a couple of 3 cm bruises on her right and left knee, a .5 cm laceration on the nailbed of her third left-hand finger.

All told, the body map filled in by the nurses denoted approximately a dozen minor bruises to Nancy Seaman's body, though none of a particularly dramatic nature. As Berg continued to photograph the suspect's body, Nancy sat down on the chair and extended both legs. "The bruises are easier to see if I sit," she said.

Sometime a little before eleven that evening, not far from the room where his mother was being examined, Jeff Seaman sat down at the police station for an interview with Sergeant David Stasch. He reviewed for the officer the series of efforts he had made to reach his father over recent days, and the surprising fact that so many calls to his parents' home had also gone unanswered. When his mother finally picked up the phone late on Monday, he reported to Stasch, she had explained to him that she didn't answer earlier because she was cleaning.

He also told Stasch about how, while heading over to his parents' house the day before (Tuesday, May 11) to look for his father, he had passed his mother's Explorer on the road, heading west. She appeared sufficiently distracted, he said, that she did not recognize him.

Wednesday night, following the interviews with Jeff and Dennis Seaman, an officer was sent to the home of Julie and Dick Dumbleton, and two other officers, Lieutenant Kohls and Sergeant Stasch, were dispatched to West Lafayette, Indiana—a four-hour drive from Farmington Hills—for the purpose of locating Greg Seaman at his apartment near the Purdue campus. It was three o'clock in the morning when the two officers reached the apartment building where Greg Seaman lived with Brandon Kolosiwsky, his roommate, who came to the door.

Brandon had not seen Greg since the previous Saturday, he told the officers. He understood that Greg was driving home to Michigan with his girlfriend, Kristin Sears, to get a truck for transporting his belongings. Having been away himself for several days, Brandon had been surprised to return to the apartment, a few hours earlier, to find that Greg's things were still there. He had no idea of Greg's whereabouts, but gave the officers the description of Kristin's car, a black Saturn with Indiana plates.

It was a day later when Bill Dwyer, the Farmington Hills chief of police, placed the call to Greg Seaman's cell phone.

"Making a notification of death call is one of the most difficult parts of my job," he said. "Of course, we prefer not to notify the family over the telephone, but in this case we had no choice."

In the case of Chief Dwyer's call to Greg Seaman, however, it was apparent that by the time he was reached, Greg already knew at least part of what had taken place.

"I didn't go into the specifics of the nature of his father's injuries or the means of death," Dwyer said. "Just the basics."

Greg Seaman responded, he said, "in an unemotional manner." But Dwyer also understood, from past experience, that not everyone expressed grief in the same fashion.

Greg was not in fact driving home to Michigan with Kristin. When he got the call, he was in his Mustang, in the company of two friends, driving back to Indiana from St. Petersburg, Florida, where they had gone on a short fishing trip.

They had left St. Pete the night before, probably at right about the time his mother was being brought into the police station and booked. He knew by the time of Chief Dwyer's call that something must have happened, because there were six messages on his cell phone telling him to call the police. (His first thought, on hearing that the police were trying to reach him, he said, was that "My father must have killed my mother.")

He had also received a call from his roommate, Brandon, to say that the police had come to the door in the middle of the night. Now, in the morning, he returned the police officer's call. After telling Greg the news, Chief Dwyer turned the phone over to Detective Patterson, who continued the interview. Greg asked Patterson what the cause of death had been. Patterson said it was unknown at the time.

Greg explained that he had last been home on the first weekend of May—the first through the third, to sign a lease on an apartment in Troy—before returning to school for finals. While he was home, his mother had helped him load up some of his personal possessions. She had wanted him to stay at their house before driving home, but though his mother had assured him his father wasn't around, he didn't stay, out of concern that he might see his father. He said his dad would work till close to midnight, then come home drunk. It was "weird," he said.

According to Greg, things had been bad between his parents for the past six years. Sometimes he'd see bruises on his mother's arms, but when he asked her about them, she said they were from banging into the swivel chair.

His own relationship with his father was "on and off." Greg told Detective Patterson the story of the '89 Mustang his father had originally bought for him, and later took back to give to Jake Dumbleton.

"We'd gotten past the problem," Greg said. But he added that his father's relationship with the Dumbletons was "almost creepy."

Just before taking off on his trip, he said, he'd ordered flowers from FTD to be delivered for his mother. He'd called her that Thursday to make sure she'd received the flowers. Roses.

The interview continued, Greg Seaman remaining surprisingly composed throughout. Detective Patterson asked Greg if he thought anyone else might have helped his mother in what had taken place. Patterson asked Greg if he believed his mother could have moved the body by herself. Greg told him that no, she could not have done such a thing, but he didn't know who could have helped her.

"I don't know much about her personal life," he added. "I've been away at school."

By the time the interview ended, Greg and his friends were approaching Lexington, Kentucky, a four-hour drive from school, he thought. He told Patterson he'd load up his belongings as soon as he reached Indiana, and then proceed to Michigan.

Meanwhile, back in Oakland County, the media swarm had begun. The six o'clock news featured an interview with Chief Bill Dwyer, offering his initial impression that the murder had been committed in the Seaman family's kitchen, not the garage—a mistake his critics would later cite as an example of his attempt to sensationalize the crime.

One way or another, however, what attracted attention was simply that the crime had taken place in the kind of family, some might have said, where this type of thing didn't happen.

Oakland County had known its share of notorious and bizarre crimes in recent years: a crazed husband who murdered his family following his gambling loss of all their assets; a young wife and new mother of an infant daughter, newly emigrated from Japan to follow her husband, suffering from postpartum depression so extreme that she had drowned her daughter in a lake near their home in an upscale suburb, and left her there.

Chief Dwyer could tell you (and did, with a certain grim relish) about the sex-slave operation in Farmington Hills. But there was no question that people held a particular fascination for situations—like the one involving the Seamans—in which the victims and perpetrators were not part of the so-called criminal element, but, rather, belonged to the white, upper-middle-class living in gated communities like Ramblewood, with good jobs and expensive cars and children enrolled at places like Purdue or employed at corporations like Ford. And when they did become involved in crimes—when someone like Nancy Seaman was arrested for murder, let alone the additional stir created, when the weapon turned out to be a hatchet—the public couldn't get enough of the story.

CHAPTER 13

"Let's Try to Focus on Our Schoolwork"

Longacre Elementary was the kind of school you might have pictured Beaver Cleaver attending—a school where many of the students still arrived from their neat suburban neighborhoods on foot or bicycle, or were dropped off by their mothers (driving SUVs more than likely, with a car seat or two in the back) on the way to pick up groceries or put in a few hours at the gym. There were a sizeable number of Asian, Indian, and Pakistani students at Longacre, but virtually no African Americans.

Children here mostly came from comfortable middle-class families—with dads who worked in the auto industry, more than likely, but not, by and large, in the portion of the industry affected by downsizing. To say that because these children live in Farmington Hills, their parents had succeeded in shielding them from trouble or pain would have been an oversimplification, but it wouldn't have been stretching things to surmise that the children of Longacre were probably more protected and sheltered than children growing up in many other parts of the country or, certainly, just a few miles down Woodward Avenue, in Detroit.

Of all the teachers at Longacre Elementary, Nancy Seaman—though she had been teaching for only seven years—was known as one of the most dedicated, as well as the most outstanding. Often the first to arrive at the building in the morning (in fact, she was often waiting when the custodian, Ray Wyss, arrived around six), she had a reputation for thoroughness and standards so high, some said, she made other teachers feel a little guilty. Not long before, Nancy had been recognized for excellence in the classroom, with the presentation of the Rainbow Award for promoting an understanding of diversity in the classroom. At the awards ceremony, she had been presented with a plaque by the Governor of Michigan herself.

Now, two years later, principal William Smith and his staff were faced with a problem, as students filed into their classrooms Thursday morning, May 13, 2004. The news of Nancy Seaman's arrest had made it to the television screens the night before, and certainly within a few hours, the entire community would know what had happened. A substitute teacher, Kristen Siskowsky, had been assigned to take over Nancy Seaman's classroom, but the news was going to be upsetting to everyone, and especially to the twenty-five children who had spent the last eight months with Mrs. Seaman as their teacher—children at an age when the teacher represented, at least for many, the most important adult figure in their lives after their parents. Many of her former students were in the upper grades. Some of them were in high school now, too. Even there, the reverberations of what had happened were sure to be felt.

Then there were the teachers to think about—Nancy's two fellow fourth-grade teachers, Jeff Rehbine and Christine Brueck, in particular, but the entire community of Longacre faculty and staff as well, all of whom, as they learned the first fragments of the story, had entered into a state of disbelief, grief, and shock.

The night before, Chief Dwyer had placed a call to Estralee Michaelson, a former teacher who, for a number of years now, had held the position of "director of safe schools and student services." Michaelson's job description called for her to step in at precisely this kind of moment—not that anything like this had ever occurred before, but in a school system of thirty schools and twelve thousand students, some form of crisis was a regular event—and coordinate the effort to maintain order, calm, and stability.

Michaelson did the best she could. By ten in the morning, she had distributed an alert to all administrators and secretaries in the district:

> We regret to inform you of the tragic death of a Longacre staff member's husband. As was reported by the *Detroit Free Press* this morning, Robert Seaman was found murdered last evening. Robert was the husband of Nancy Seaman. The entire incident is under investigation and nothing more has been confirmed. It is important that false information or rumors not begin. We will keep you updated as we confirm more information. This incident may command media attention directed at Longacre, therefore police presence may ultimately be necessary.

In Estralee Michaelson's first bulletin, no mention was made of Nancy Seaman's arrest, but by noon that day, a follow-up was sent out to say that "unfortunately, Nancy is the named suspect, however NO further information has been confirmed."

By the end of the school day, a letter for parents had been prepared to send home with the children. "In the wake of recent events and media coverage," the letter began, "you and your children may experience reactions that are new and confusing. These may include sadness, anxiety, fear, aggression, withdrawal, numbness, guilt, powerlessness, hopelessness. Reactions may include: decreased academic functioning, decreased concentration, difficulty making decisions, and increased aggression."

The letter went on to offer suggestions to parents that they limit their child's exposure to the media and remind him or her that stories on television are not always completely factual.

"We suggest that you ask your child what they have seen and heard and then truly listen to their stories," the letter continued. "Drawing pictures is also helpful. The goal is to help have them externalize, or just get out of their system, what they are feeling. They may not be easily able to find the right words."

To help parents deal with specific questions that might come up, a sample script was provided, in which a hypothetical child asks, "Did you hear about a murder with a man named Mr. Seaman? Do you think that this man is related to Mrs. Seaman?"

And the response: "Yes, we are hearing about the tragic death of Mr. Seaman. We know the police are investigating. . . . It is important that rumors not get started. . . . Let's try to focus on our schoolwork today."

Finally, parents were reminded, "Mrs. Seaman has been truly devoted to her teaching career and her students. Due to the current circumstance Miss Siskowsky will be replacing Mrs. Seaman for the remainder of the school year."

Over in Woodhaven—downriver, as it is known to those in the Detroit area—Nancy's father, Eugene D'Onofrio, was confused. He had understood that his daughter would be picking him up the evening before. But she never showed up, and nobody had called.

At seventy-nine years of age, Eugene remained physically spry— lean to the point of wiriness, with the appearance of a man who had spent his life working hard, which he had. He bore a striking resemblance to Frank Perdue, but unlike the chicken-selling mogul, Eugene D'Onofrio was a man of extremely modest means.

A dozen or so years back, he and his wife, Lenore, had sold the little house in Lincoln Park where they'd raised their kids, and moved a few miles away to Woodhaven. They had been enjoying their retirement until that terrible day, just before the previous Christmas, when Lenore had died suddenly, and for the first time in almost sixty years, Eugene was on his own. Life had been hard for him, in the days since, and he thanked God for his daughter, Nancy, who had recently purchased a condominium just down the road from him, where she would be moving soon, she'd told him.

The one thing about this condo was that Nancy's husband didn't know about it, and they had to keep the whole thing secret. That's why Eugene had given Nancy $10,000 out of his retirement savings for the down payment. He didn't have much, but Nancy had explained that her husband had burned through all their money and left her near to penniless. What kind of father would he be if he didn't help out his daughter in her time of need?

Particularly since Lenore's death, Nancy had been the best daughter a father could ask for, coming over to fix meals and take him places—as she had said she would be doing the previous evening. All that night, Eugene D'Onofrio had wondered what was going on. Finally, the next morning, came a call from his sister, who read the paper every day, to say that something had happened, some kind of mix-up no doubt.

"According to the paper, she says, Nancy's in some kind of trouble down at the police station. So we headed to Farmington Hills. And what do you know, they tell us she's been arrested for murder."

CHAPTER 14

Changing the Locks

round noon on Thursday, informed by the front desk personnel at the police station that Nancy Seaman seemed depressed, Detective Al Patterson, along with female Detective Stacey Swanderski, made their way to the cell block to check on her.

"I opened the door and asked Mrs. Seaman if she was OK, if she needed anything," he said. "She asked me what was going to happen from here.

"Since this was obviously a new and traumatic experience for her, I asked Mrs. Seaman to come with me to the cell block interview room so that we could sit down and I could explain things to her. As Mrs. Seaman walked out of her cell she said, 'When am I gonna get my clothes back? I didn't wear those on Monday. I put those on yesterday.'" Because her clothes had been taken as evidence, Mrs. Seaman was wearing a department-issued paper gown.

Patterson advised Nancy Seaman that he would get some clothes for her. Once they were seated in the interview room, he explained the process of requesting a warrant, arraignment, preexam, and exam. After her arraignment, he told her, he would assist her in the completion of a request for a court-appointed attorney if she wished. He asked if there was anyone she wanted him to contact. The only thing she wanted, she said, was to write a note to her son Greg.

"Greg," she wrote, in the clear, even hand of a teacher accustomed to instructing children in the formation of cursive letters for the first time. The rest of the letter read, in its entirety, as follows:

> The title to your car is in the black file box, I think, in Grandpa's basement. The car is paid in full.
>
> Also—you are the beneficiary on my credit union savings and checking accounts. They are:
>
> Dearborn Federal Credit Union #2123776
>
> I think there is a statement in the dining room on the credenza. Account #40105.
>
> This money is yours.
>
> Also: In the vase on my dresser close to the bed—look inside. There should be an envelope with about $200 inside. Also: In my purse is about 300+ in my wallet.
>
> I'm sorry. Dad wouldn't stop beating me.

By Thursday afternoon, Dennis Seaman had reached his parents' home in Ballwin, Missouri, just outside St. Louis. Ward Seaman was eighty-seven years old, but still sharp as a tack.

Even now, with his wife Helen's having been diagnosed with Alzheimer's, Ward wasn't complaining. The two of them had more than sixty good years together (going on sixty-eight of them now, truth to tell).

It was Bob's older sister, Margie, and one of their grandsons, Scott Seaman, who got to Ward first and told him what had happened. (No need to tell Helen. It was just as well she wouldn't understand.)

"My father took the news like he took everything," said Dennis.

"That man is as tough as Kroger's meat," he added, referring to a popular supermarket chain in the area. "Not that he doesn't cry. He just said, 'Bob's in a better place now.' That's how he saw it."

Over at the Waterwheel Building, Rob Berlin, who owned a design business there, ran into Bob Seaman's partner, Rick Cox, a tall, lean figure with the ramrod bearing of a man in possession of a devout

Christian faith (as anyone would learn, who talked with Rick for more than a minute).

"We've got to get to the bottom of this and find out who killed Bob," Rick told Rob. The statement baffled Rob. It had seemed pretty clear, based on what the police were saying, that there could be little doubt who was responsible for the murder.

That day, Julie Dumbleton had also returned to the Waterwheel Building to retrieve some of Bob's belongings. She met up with Jeff Seaman, who was gathering up some papers—financial records, she thought—when a group of police officers arrived, evidently summoned by Rick Cox's wife, Diane. To Jeff's indignation, he was informed that he was to vacate the premises.

"We're changing the locks," Rick said.

Julie never returned after that. She was glad that she'd had the good sense to remove Bob's "Nancy Crap File" some days earlier. If she had waited until after the discovery of the body, she strongly suspected, the file might have been gone.

CHAPTER 15

One Good Thing About Store Surveillance Cameras

T he chief medical examiner for Oakland County, Dr. Ljubisa Dragovic, would have seemed like some television executive's idea of a medical examiner to build a series around, to be portrayed by a particularly dashing, though unconventional, older actor. Jeremy Irons, maybe, with his hair dyed silver.

A man of compact build—trim as a tap dancer—Dr. Dragovic was famous for his bow ties. Handsome in a princely sort of way, with a perfectly groomed moustache, he was well known in Oakland County—a locale whose high crime rate ensures that he would remain busy—for his staunch advocacy of the prosecution in all matters relating to the murders whose victims he examined, often in the aftermath of brutal injury. He was also known for his highly outspoken and controversial position on the issue of Sudden Infant Death Syndrome.

Dr. Dragovic took the position that no such syndrome existed and that the term was manufactured exclusively to alleviate the guilt of negligent parents who allowed their children to die of asphyxiation because they slept in the same bed with them or laid them on their stomachs when they put them down to sleep or—less benignly—smothered them.

His views on this, and all else that he expounded on (which was to say, a lot), he conveyed in an accent richly evocative of his native country, formerly known as Transylvania. Now, however, he made his home in Grosse Pointe, perhaps the priciest suburb of Detroit, with his physician wife and their six children.

On the morning of May 13, 2004, the body of Robert Seaman was rolled into the examining room of Dr. Dragovic for the purpose of undergoing forensic examination and autopsy.

Because Bob Seaman's body had been left wrapped tightly in a tarp in a hot car for a number of days, the process of decomposition was well under way by the time Dr. Dragovic was able to examine it, though for a person in his line of work, this was by no means an unusual or abnormally distasteful situation. It was part of the curious quality of elegance Dragovic conveyed that a person could never forget, while in his company, how recently those well-manicured fingers had been engaged in the act of dissecting the bodies (horribly mutilated, sometimes) of dead people.

Dr. Dragovic's report on the autopsy of Bob Seaman began with a listing of personal effects found on the body: one black T-shirt, one pair of white shorts, two white socks, two black tennis shoes, one watch, one brown belt, one pen, one comb, two key rings with six keys, one key ring with eight keys, one white handkerchief, $1.00 in Canadian coins, $14.64 in U.S. currency.

"The body is received tightly wrapped up in green and pink blankets and a dark blue tarp sealed with gray duct tape," the report of external examination began.

A small, all metal, gray colored pocket knife is found in the blankets. The partially decomposed body is that of a five foot nine inch, hundred and seventy six pound, medium developed, well nourished white male, reported to be 57 years of age, clad in a blood soaked, black polo style, short sleeved shirt ("BONDURANT" brand, [named for race car driver Bob Bondurant], blood soaked, stone colored cargo shorts ("Sonoma" brand) with a light brown leather belt, blood soaked white underwear briefs, black athletic shoes and white sweat socks.

Rigor mortis is absent (passed) in the cool body, except in the hands, where residual rigor is still detectable. Rigor mortis is dorsally distributed and fixed. The scalp hair is brown gray, measuring up to 3" in length. The scalp is further described under "evidence of injury."

There is marbling and slippage of the facial skin due to early decomposition. The eyelids are altered by decomposition as are the corneae, sclerae and conjunctivae, so that the color of irises is not discernible.

Because so much time had elapsed before the discovery of the body, Dr. Dragovic explained, it had not possible to pinpoint the exact time of death. Nevertheless, a great deal could be learned from the body itself.

The report went on to list a series of sharp force injuries, most of which were described as "chop injuries," one so deep it penetrated clear to the cheek bone. These included injuries to the back of the neck, the top of the head, the left ear, and the face. In addition to the series of ragged and deep chop injuries, Dr. Dragovic went on to list a series of stab wounds, these inflicted by a different instrument: a knife (from all appearances, the small pocket knife found wrapped up with the body). The majority of the wounds were located around the victim's neck and shoulder, but the blade had also perforated his voicebox, thyroid, esophagus, trachea, and lower cervical spine. Examination of the victim's heart revealed the presence of "arterioschlerotic cardiovascular disease"—not surprising perhaps for a man who had undergone a heart attack nine years earlier. This disease, however, was not the cause of death.

The cause of death, Dr. Dragovic's report concluded, was multiple sharp force injuries: "multiple chop injuries (16) to the head and neck, multiple stab wounds (21) of the neck, chest and back, slashing of the left side of the neck, superficial cuts of the right and left hand, and blunt force trauma of the head."

"In consideration of the circumstances surrounding this death and the findings at this postmortem examination," wrote Dr. Dragovic, "the manner of death is homicide."

Over on Briarwood Court, meanwhile, a team of evidence technicians from the Farmington Hills Police Department had taped off the area and begun its crime scene investigation, with a focus on the Seamans' garage, where it appeared that the fatal injuries had been inflicted.

The first thing a person would have noticed, stepping into Bob and Nancy Seamans' garage, would have been the black-and-white floor tile Nancy and Greg had laid down a few years earlier, with track lighting installed over the three car bays where, in better days, Bob Seaman liked to work on his cars.

Had they visited the Seaman garage a week earlier, the police investigators would have encountered the mountain of trash that had been accumulating over the many months of Bob and Nancy's standoff, but during the week of Bob's disappearance, when Jeff had returned to Briarwood Court to look for his father, he had found, to his surprise, that the trash had finally been disposed of. Now, as the evidence technicians got to work in the garage, they found the place not just clean but spotless.

Closer examination revealed why. Not only had the floor been bleached and hosed down, but a portion of drywall between the two garage doors had been replaced and painted. Investigators located a paint roller, still damp, and a container of white paint.

The black-and-white tiles had been mopped, but a few brown stains between them suggested the presence of dried blood, and removal of those tiles revealed blood stains on the cement underneath. Remnants of blood spatters were also found on the exterior wood trim next to the garage door. A black garbage bag containing bloody wash clothes and paper towels was found. Another bag held a pair of used yellow rubber gloves.

The two bays that normally held the Explorers were empty, but a third car remained in its place at the far end of the garage: the Mustang belonging to Greg, which Bob had towed home from Indiana the year before in the hopes, once again, that he and his son might work on rebuilding it together. Closer inspection of that Mustang revealed the presence of human blood and hair on the rear bumper as well as a very small amount of human tissue.

The police search of the Seamans' home yielded another discovery. In a plastic bag in the kitchen, the investigating team located a bunch of store receipts. Among them was one dated May 9, 2004—Mother's Day. At 7:37, less than an hour after Jeff and Becka had left her house to avoid witnessing more of her argument with Bob, Nancy Seaman had evidently taken off, in the driving rainstorm, for the nearest Home Depot. She had visited another branch of the store earlier that morning with Jeff and Becka—a trip about which she later expressed her frustration over having forgotten to pick up trash bags. This time, once again, she failed to purchase trash bags. She made only a single purchase: a hatchet. Cost: $19.93.

The Home Depot trip was not Nancy Seaman's only shopping expedition that week, however. The next day, Monday, as her bag of receipts indicated, she had paid a visit to the Meijers store on Haggerty, after work. This time, her purchases included two pairs of Playtex rubber gloves, four bottles of bleach, a roll of duct tape, a bottle of Lysol, and a tarp, for a total cost of $22.28. A little way down the road, she made a second stop at Target, also on Haggerty, where, for $12.84, she purchased an item called a Rough Tote.

The next day, Tuesday, she evidently returned to Target, this time to return the Rough Tote. On Wednesday, May 12, just before filling up her gas tank and returning home, and probably at about the time Detective Patterson and his team were preparing to head over to Briarwood Court themselves, Nancy Seaman returned to Meijers, this time to purchase another pair of rubber gloves, a set of napkins, three sets of picture hangers, and a container of Febreze air freshener.

One other transaction was documented in the receipts found by the officers. This one puzzled them at first. Like the first receipt, from Mother's Day night, this one came from Home Depot, but it was dated two days later, May 11. The receipt indicated the return of a hatchet whose price suggested it was identical to the one Nancy Seaman had purchased on May 9.

The officers were baffled. If, as they believed, Nancy Seaman's purchase of the hatchet on Mother's Day night had been the act of an angry and vengeful woman in search of a weapon with which to strike her husband, what did it mean that this same hatchet had evidently been returned (presumably unused) two days later?

Now, on Thursday afternoon, Sergeant Haupt paid a series of visits to the stores where Nancy Seaman had made her recent purchases. At Meijers and Target, nothing of note was learned, though he studied surveillance tapes of the parking lot during the period in which Nancy Seaman made her visits, and examined still photographs of transactions at the store. The only aspect of note was that a woman with a dead body in the back of her car would take the time and effort necessary to return a Rough Tote valued at $12.84. And purchase picture hangers.

At Home Depot, Sergeant Haupt, joined now by Sergeant Hubbard, met with the store manager, Ben Kroll, and the loss prevention manager, Chris Cockfield, to review surveillance videos of the sale on May 9 as well as the return on May 11. In the first, Nancy Seaman was observed entering the store in her capri pants, carrying her purse. In the tape, she could be seen making her way, purposefully and without deliberation, directly to the aisle where the hatchets were sold, known as the "tool corral." The officers studied the images of Seaman palming a couple of hatchets before settling on one manufactured by Vaughn, weighing twenty-two ounces, then proceeding to the checkout.

The officers then reviewed the video of the hatchet return, showing Nancy Seaman presenting her original receipt. While watching the video of the return transaction, Haupt and Cockfield noted that Seaman's entry to the returns counter—the direction from which she made her approach—seemed odd. Although a person making a return would be expected to approach the returns counter from the bottom of the screen, where the door was, Seaman appeared to approach it from the side.

Haupt then asked Cockfield to check the video surveillance of the tool corral. When they did that, they made a surprising discovery: Nancy Seaman could be observed selecting a hatchet, then concealing it under her purse. She moved directly from the tool corral to the returns counter, where she returned the hatchet she had evidently shoplifted moments before.

What Nancy Seaman had accomplished, with the second Home Depot transaction, was now clear: by returning the hatchet, she had created a record suggesting that the hatchet she'd purchased on Sunday night had been returned, unused, to the store of its origin.

The police officers found the original hatchet—the one purchased in the middle of the Mother's Day downpour—on the floor of Nancy Seaman's Explorer, under the seat. The handle had been cleaned with bleach, but on the blade remained a single human hair, believed to be that of Robert Seaman.

CHAPTER 16

The Chief Takes Charge

Chief William Dwyer was no stranger to the television cameras. A thirty-five-year veteran of the force, Bill Dwyer was a handsome, charismatic man in his mid-sixties, whose silver hair was always perfectly combed and held into a dashing wave with the help of styling products. His shirts bore his initials on the cuff.

Where Detective Patterson seemed comfortable staying just out of view in high-profile cases like this one, Bill Dwyer welcomed the opportunity to speak with the media. Now, with Dr. Dragovic's autopsy complete and the details emerging concerning the way in which Bob Seaman had met his death, it seemed clear to him that the time had come to call a press conference about the Seaman case.

So the six o'clock news on May 14, 2004, featured heavy coverage of the Seaman murder, including an account from Chief Dwyer of what he believed to have happened in the altercation between Nancy Seaman and her now deceased husband, in the minutes leading up to his brutal murder.

No doubt some people in Farmington Hills viewed Chief Dwyer as a grandstander, possibly even an egomaniac. There was another way to look at the man, though: he loved his police force. He was hugely proud of the work they performed. There was no denying his affection for appearing on camera, but he also possessed an unmistakable zeal for putting criminals behind bars and letting the public know they could sleep safer once he'd done it.

But in this particular case, at least, Chief Dwyer had little opportunity for reticence. Within minutes of the news that a body had been found there, the media had swarmed the cul de sac on Briarwood Court, where Chief Dwyer was already on the scene. Now they were hounding him for a statement.

In his original take on the crime, Chief Dwyer stated that the murder had actually been committed in the couple's kitchen, with Nancy later dragging her husband's body out to the garage and hacking it up more out there. The fact that later investigation would reveal that Chief Dwyer and his team had briefly misconstrued the course of events became one of the many aspects of the case that the defense claimed to have prejudiced the residents of Oakland County against Nancy Seaman from the beginning. Not that a hatchet murder in the garage was necessarily so much less troubling. But there was something about the kitchen—maybe that food had been prepared there?

Most upsetting, though, to supporters of Nancy Seaman (and no doubt, to Nancy herself) was the TV interview with Jeff Seaman. On-screen, Jeff came across as strangely calm and blunt, almost flippant, as he weighed in, but it was what he said that would reveal the beginnings of a fissure soon to utterly divide the family. Far from supporting his mother's allegation that her husband had been a violent and abusive man, Jeff spoke of Bob Seaman as a wonderful father and his best friend. It wasn't a picture that would help a woman whose only hope for freedom lay in convincing a jury that she killed in self-defense.

It was plain now that two very different stories were forming—one, of a desperate woman fighting for her life against an angry and violent husband. The other, of a premeditated murder. One way or another, what had happened to Bob Seaman presented a disturbing picture, and to a lot of people who saw the photograph of a reasonably attractive, neatly groomed 130-pound middle-aged woman flashed on the screen alongside the burly figure of her 180-pound husband, the idea of a woman doing something like that was simply unimaginable. Particularly for those who knew Nancy Seaman as a teacher ("an award-winning teacher," as she was now being identified in the media), there had to be some justification for her actions—the only justification being that she was an abused wife acting in desperation, fighting for her own survival.

Up until this point, not a single act of violence naming her husband as an abuser appeared to have been reported by Nancy Seaman or anyone who knew her. The absence of any substantial wounds or injuries on her body, of the sort that would be expected when a person was fighting for her life against a significantly more powerful adversary, was a mystery to all who were learning about and discussing the case after Dwyer's press conference.

Over the course of the next five days, police officers interviewed Christine Brueck, Jeff Rehbine, and others, who now recalled a black eye Nancy Seaman had a year or so earlier, and a time she'd shown up at school with her arm in a sling. She had explained the black eye as the result of an unfortunate collision with her own car door, the arm injury as the result of a fall. Abuse victims are often known to be fearful and ashamed to acknowledge what is going on in their lives, of course—and inclined to protect the very person who has been injuring them. A teacher, in particular, might well worry about her reputation, if word got out that her husband was beating her.

To many, there was ample reason to believe that as Nancy Seaman now asserted, years of horrific abuse and fear for her life had led up to the final terrible confrontation that left Bob Seaman dead, and to imagine that if Nancy hadn't killed Bob, he surely would have killed her.

To some in the community, this was the only thing that would make comprehensible and forgivable what Chief Dwyer was now presenting to the community as the most unspeakable kind of murder: a hatchet attack, followed (in what is known in the world of law enforcement as "overkill") by a series of stab wounds. If Chief Dwyer was portraying Nancy Seaman as a brutal ax murderer—the Lizzie Borden of Farmington Hills—Nancy's colleagues and defenders would find another explanation, one that would not rattle the gates of their gated communities or shake their sense of how life was supposed to work for a person like Nancy Seaman in a world like theirs: Nancy Seaman had to be an abused wife. Which meant that Bob Seaman had to be an abusive husband. The only way to prove Nancy Seaman not guilty of murdering her husband was to prove Bob Seaman capable of murdering his wife.

CHAPTER 17

"Just a Girl Who Loves to Put Criminals Behind Bars"

O ne thing about the prosecutors and assistant district attorneys in the office of Oakland County prosecutor David Gorcyca: they moved fast. With an average of approximately two hundred homicides a year to move through the court system (many of them vehicular, the majority committed by one family member against another), it was important to keep those cases moving through the courts.

In a matter of days after Nancy Seaman's arrest—and with the investigation of the case, led by Detective Al Patterson and the Farmington Hills Police Department, only just getting under way—Gorcyca's assistant in charge of handling high-profile cases, Deborah Carley, had handed this one over to a young prosecutor by the name of Lisa Ortlieb.

Thirty-seven years old, Lisa was known around the courthouse as one of the hardest working and most likeable prosecutors on Gorcyca's team. Although she was unmistakably a rising star, with a close to perfect conviction record, she had also earned the reputation as one of the most down-to-earth attorneys at the courthouse, someone with whom you could imagine hanging out at a sorority pajama party or going shopping or sharing a big bag of peanuts at a Tigers game. There remained a quality of something like innocence about her, despite her high-powered profession.

"It's pretty simple," she said. "I'm an open book. I'm just a girl who loves to put criminals behind bars."

Lisa Ortlieb preferred talking about perpetrators and their victims to engaging in discussion about herself, but when pressed, she explained further:

"To be a good prosecutor, you have to have a passion for what you do," and she definitely possessed the passion. Back in law school (where she knew right off the bat that civil law "bored me to tears"), she had recognized that she could make a lot more money as a criminal defense attorney than she would working for the state. But she also knew that "it would be tough to put my passion into defending anyone who killed a person.

"I love being on the side of justice," she said. "I feel like the luckiest person, doing this job.

"I'm all about the truth."

Lisa was also—at five foot eleven, with a great figure and a mane of dark hair she did not typically pull back into a lawyerly bun—a dazzlingly attractive woman, whose legs were shown off to best advantage when she opted, as she tended to, for high heels and a skirt that just missed being daringly short. Asked if she often heard that she resembled the actress Kirstie Alley in her slimmer days on *Cheers*, Ortlieb said the name that came up more frequently in such comparisons was that of Brooke Shields, which also made sense.

Lisa Ortlieb grew up north of Detroit, Rochester Hills, where her father worked for General Motors. "A small-town girl," she described herself as quiet and a little shy, a lover of reading, reluctant to put herself in the limelight outside of court. She'd been married briefly, in her twenties, and later divorced, with no children. At the time she got the high-profile assignment of prosecuting Nancy Seaman, she was recently married to Oakland County prosecutor David Gorcyca.

A few years older than Lisa, Gorcyca had made his name, and his career, during the highly publicized Jack Kevorkian case some years back. Tall, handsome, square-jawed, with a full head of well-styled hair, Dave Gorcyca resembled a B movie actor. To many at the courthouse, Gorcyca's ascent to the top prosecutor's position was a prime example of being at the right place at the right time. He had won his last election to office with assistance from the Christian Right.

Gorcyca had twins, a boy and girl, just a couple of years old when he and Lisa Ortlieb, recently divorced from her first husband, had gotten together. He also had a wife at the time.

But Lisa Ortlieb loved David Gorcyca, and after a longer engagement than she might have chosen, they were married in spring 2003, but Lisa had been so busy prosecuting crime she had no time for a honeymoon. Devoted to her husband's twins, whose photographs were prominently displayed around her office, among the pictures of murder victims and murderers she kept around for inspiration, Lisa remained relentless in her crusade against the criminal forces of Oakland County and was in possession of an almost missionary fervor at seeing criminals put behind bars. Now the person she'd be gunning for was Nancy Seaman.

For some, there might have seemed to be a contradiction in the fact that even as she prepared to build a case against Nancy Seaman—an alleged battered wife—Ortlieb headed up the Oakland County Domestic Violence Fatality Review Team and served as cochair of another domestic violence prevention organization. For Ortlieb, no conflict whatsoever existed.

"If I see a battered woman and she commits a murder, that's not a crime I want to prosecute," she said. "I've seen some horrible cases. A woman who murdered her husband in his sleep, when he was passed out on the couch, and she still had tuna casserole in her hair from where he threw it at her. I'm very attuned to that kind of tragedy. A guy like that is a rat bastard, and a woman who kills him may be just as much of a victim or more so as him. Nancy Seaman, though . . . that was a different story. A woman like that, who commits a brutal murder and then calls it self-defense, makes a mockery of all the truly abused women out there who really were fighting for their lives."

From the moment Nancy Seaman was arrested, she had made it plain that she considered herself a battered woman. The fact that she had not previously mentioned this to most of those people closest to her, including her father and brother, or her colleagues, was not out of keeping with the patterns of denial common among abused women— the urge to conceal and protect the abuser and to deny what had been going on, possibly even to herself.

Although Nancy Seaman did not fit the typical profile of the weak, unassertive, powerless woman—someone who feels trapped by her circumstances, a passive individual with few options, low self-esteem, and no financial or professional independence—the simple fact of her affluent lifestyle hardly ruled out the possibility of domestic violence. Anyone who studied the literature of abuse could tell you that the problem cut across all socioeconomic lines. Just because a woman lived in a gated community and wore nice clothes didn't rule out the possibility that her husband might be beating her or that she might be keeping quiet about it.

What was typically harder to conceal, for most abused women, was the physical evidence of what had been going on in their lives, visible on their own bodies. With her husband's corpse in the morgue, and dressed in a jail-issue jumpsuit, Nancy had requested that photographs be taken, not only to document the injuries she said had occurred during her husband's final attack but also to support her contention that she'd been suffering this kind of thing for years.

There were definitely bruises on her body when she was brought into the Farmington Hills police station—not particularly dramatic ones, perhaps, but bruises nonetheless, as well as a small laceration on her hand. She had suggested to the nurse who examined her, and to others over the days that followed, that a look at her file at Henry Ford Medical Center in Detroit would reveal multiple visits (though as it turned out, there had been only one, for a sprained wrist). To prove her claim of abuse, it became clear, she would need the corroboration of those closest to her—most particularly her sons Greg and Jeff.

It was obvious, from the moment of her arrest, that Greg Seaman would support his mother's account of what had been going on between her and her husband. So would Nancy's father, Eugene, and her brother, John D'Onofrio (though he and Bob had appeared close in the past, working together on home improvement projects at John's home in Ohio), who had made the trip to Farmington Hills shortly after Nancy's arrest.

"She doesn't belong in jail," John said angrily. "We've got to get her out of this place."

But there remained one crucial member of the family who saw things differently: Jeff.

"She's my mom. Of course I love her," he said, shortly after her arrest. "But she committed a murder. There has to be a consequence to something like that."

It might have seemed like a simple enough statement, but with those words, the lines were drawn, with Greg and Nancy on one side, Jeff on the other. And Bob in the morgue.

CHAPTER 18

Personal Protection Order

T he day after Nancy Seaman's arrest, Julie Dumbleton came home to find a message on the family's answering machine.

It was from Marcia Low, a reporter with the *Detroit Free Press,* to say that she had learned about something called a PPO that Nancy Seaman had taken out against Julie, in February of 2002. The *Free Press* would be running its story about this in the next day's paper.

Julie didn't know what a PPO was until she called her brother in-law, a policeman in Chicago. When she learned that the letters stood for *personal protection order,* she was confused. Julie Dumbleton was a soft-spoken woman who weighed 115 pounds and stood five foot five. It would be hard to imagine anyone viewing Julie as a threat to his or her physical safety.

In her message, Marcia Low had named February 22, 2002, as the date Nancy Seaman had taken out a PPO against Julie Dumbleton. This was a help. Because of her practice of keeping a record of her interactions with Nancy Seaman, begun when the relationship first began to break down, Julie now consulted her notes. When she did, she was reminded of the fact that February 15 of that year—a week before the filing of the PPO—was the date on which Nancy Seaman had called her up, warning her to stay away from Greg's Mustang. When Bob had heard about the call, he'd had a fight with Nancy about it, but things had been quiet after that. Julie had wanted to believe the incident was finished.

Now, more than two years later—the day after Julie's discovery of Bob's murder, and Nancy Seaman's arrest—came the call from Marcia Low.

"She said in her message that she'd be writing about this whether or not I talked to her," Julie explained. "So I called her back." And after talking with the *Free Press* reporter, the facts of what had happened became clear to her.

After Bob had spoken angrily to Nancy about her threat to Julie, evidently Nancy had paid a visit to Oakland County Courthouse. In the petition she filed with the court that day, Nancy Seaman accused Julie Dumbleton of the crime of "stalking."

On February 22, the same day it was filed before the court, Judge Rae Lee Chabot denied the request without a hearing, on the grounds of "insufficient factual allegations to establish reasonable belief that irreparable and immediate injury will occur." For this reason, Julie and Dick Dumbleton had never heard about Nancy Seaman's complaint until Marcia Low discovered it the day after Nancy's arrest.

"I told her 'Please, just don't mention my name in the paper,'" said Julie. "But she did. And it came out that we lived in Northville. So then all of a sudden, we had TV news trucks parked in front of our house and people calling all the time, coming to the door. I stopped answering the phone.

"I thought we were going to be grieving over Bob's murder, quietly," said Julie. "All of a sudden it turned out we were part of the story. In my whole life, I don't think anybody hated me before. Now I realized how much they did."

And not just Nancy Seaman, now, but Greg. There had actually been a time when Greg and Jake were friends, when the family used to spend time with him. Jake had looked up to Greg. But if Bob's younger son was willing to embrace his mother's view of what had happened, as it appeared he did, then he too must have come to view the Dumbletons as representing everything that had brought about the destruction of his own family.

CHAPTER 19

This Call Is
Being Recorded

N ancy Seaman was arraigned for the murder of her husband, Bob Seaman, on May 14, 2004. Only after ten o'clock on the night of the arraignment, was Nancy finally able to speak by telephone with her father and her younger son, from Oakland County Jail, where she was being held. This represented the first communication between Nancy and Greg since the murder of his father.

There was a standard procedure concerning telephone calls between inmates in Oakland County Jail and those with whom they communicate: a voice coming on the line before the beginning of the conversation announced to the parties on either to be aware that the state maintained the right to tape-record the communication about to take place. These tapes could be turned over to the Oakland County prosecutor.

A second crucial procedural policy at the jail concerned prisoner visits. These were limited to two per week, and could take place only within designated hours on visiting days. In virtually all aspects of life, those in the jail possessed no control over their lives, but one choice (and it may have been the only one) remained within the rights of the prisoner herself: nobody was allowed to visit an individual incarcerated at Oakland County Jail unless the prisoner chose to see her. For a visit to take place, a person's name had to appear on the prisoner's visitor list.

Greg Seaman's name was on Nancy's list, of course. So were those of Eugene and John D'Onofrio. Nancy's attorney, Don Ferris, was allowed to see her (though he would shortly be replaced). But no one scanning the names on the list could have failed to notice a curious omission. The name of Jeff Seaman was not among them. By now it was clear from Jeff's remarks after his mother's arrest that he wasn't buying her allegations of his father's abuse. Not surprisingly, Greg Seaman and his mother spoke of this in their first phone call.

"Jeff, you know, he said he wanted to come visit you," said Greg. "You know he said, 'let me know about visitation.'"

"I don't want to see him," Nancy said.

"I know," said Greg.

"He saw bruises," said Nancy.

Because the Purdue University class of 2004 was so large—4,386 students were receiving undergraduate degrees—graduation exercises were held in four groups over the course of the weekend of May 15 and 16. Just after noon on Saturday, May 15, the day after Nancy Seaman's arraignment, the president of the university, Martin Jischke, delivered his remarks to the first group of graduates on the school's campus in West Lafayette, Indiana.

In his remarks, Jischke alluded to the four years of work that had led up to this day for the students: "a journey that would ultimately be filled with triumphs and struggles, laughter and late-night study, strong coffee and cold pizza." Finally, he said, "it has all paid off."

Greg Seaman, though he was a member of the class, did not make it to West Lafayette that weekend. Right around the time President Jischke was delivering his remarks, Greg was once again speaking by telephone with his mother, Nancy Seaman, in Oakland County Jail. Reportedly, Nancy had had her outfit for the Purdue event picked out and laid on the bed of the family's home on Briarwood Court at least a full week in advance of the graduation exercises, but now she wore a jail-issued jumpsuit and paper slippers. Once again, her conversation with her younger son was recorded on tape.

They talked about the hiring of an attorney and how to pay for it. As she had done in the previous conversation, Nancy reiterated to her son that the murder weapon had been an old hatchet she'd found lying around the garage and not the one she'd purchased on Mother's Day night, which she said she'd returned. This was good news, Greg said, since the use of the new hatchet would have reinforced the impression of premeditation.

No doubt Nancy Seaman was unaware, as she discussed this with her younger son, that the police had learned about the shoplifting incident at Home Depot and of Nancy's return of the shoplifted hatchet, and that the whole event had been recorded.

"You hanging in there?" Greg asked her.

"I'm worried about you," she told him. "I want you to get your apartment set up," she said.

CHAPTER 20

His Mother's Son

T he preliminary examination charging Nancy Seaman with the murder of Robert Seaman took place at the Farmington Hills District Court. This was the first time Lisa Ortlieb would lay eyes on Nancy Seaman and the rest of the principals in the case.

Outside the courtroom, Lisa introduced herself for the first time to Dennis and Robin Seaman, Jeff and Becka.

Lisa understood that as the one prosecuting Eugene D'Onofrio's daughter and John's sister, she would be viewed as a hostile party, but her position in relation to Greg Seaman, the son of the murdered man, was more ambiguous. She knew that Greg Seaman took a position of extreme sympathy for his mother and that he was supporting Nancy's contention of self-defense in the face of alleged abuse.

Still, she said, "I figured he'd lost his father, and as the person responsible for seeing that justice was done, for his dad, I thought it seemed like the right thing to do to go up to Greg and give him my card.

"I told Greg how sorry I was for his loss," she said. "He made it plain he wanted nothing to do with me."

Inside the courtroom, it was clear, from the side of the room where people chose to take their seats, where their sympathies lay. Dennis and Robin Seaman sat on the right side, behind the prosecution. So did Jeff Seaman and Becka. Eugene D'Onofrio, John and Barb D'Onofrio, and Dennis and Paulette Schleuter (old friends of Bob and Nancy's from school days and the early years at Ford Motor Company) had positioned themselves on the left, closest to the defense. In the front row, seated behind the rail, directly in back of his mother, was Greg Seaman.

Just as anyone would know, on meeting Jeff Seaman, that he was Bob's son, it was evident from one look at Greg that he was Nancy's. Jeff and Greg were brothers, born two years apart, but except for one feature—their large and penetrating eyes, and lashes a woman would envy—they seemed to bear no resemblance to each other physically. (And in fact, they differed in the eyes too: Jeff's were blue, like his father's. Greg's, like Nancy's, were brown.) Maybe it was easy to imagine this now, given what had taken place in their family, but even photographs of the brothers from years before seemed to suggest a haunted, almost yearning quality in their gaze.

Everyone who knew them also agreed: the two brothers possessed totally different personalities and styles. From early youth, Jeff had been the bolder, more outgoing one, loud and brash. Depending on who you were asking, he was either admirably self-confident—or an insufferable know-it-all. Like his father, he had a mind for machines and an engineer's way of looking at the world, founded in numbers, parts, statistics. He was not one for a lot of emotional expression. Jeff was a joker.

He was also dazzlingly smart. He'd gotten top grades in high school without apparent effort, earning his engineering degree (at a top school, Rolla, in St. Louis) in just three years. His sport—and for him it reached the level of obsession—was baseball. Even now, at twenty-five, he continued playing on a local team and coached a group of kids known as the Hitters' Club every Saturday morning at the Upper Deck.

He was married (had been, for three years) to a former engineering classmate, Becka. They had no children yet, though they wanted them someday. Jeff had a few good friends, but his favorite thing, apart from playing or watching baseball, was doing home improvement projects around the house and working on his cars.

Greg had always been the quiet one. Where Jeff tended to carry a few extra pounds, Greg had a lean build, slight as a girl. There had even been a time, Bob used to tell Julie Dumbleton, when the son with whom he felt the most connection and tenderness was Greg, who, unlike his brother, possessed a visible softness, a sensitive side.

"Even as a baby," Bob had told Julie, "you couldn't cuddle with Jeff. Greg was like this little koala bear." And Nancy and Jeff's tendency to monopolize the conversation around their house left Bob (who was outgoing elsewhere, but had little to say at home) feeling a sense of kinship with his younger son as the two of them sat back, mostly listening to Jeff and Nancy.

Greg had played on a Little League team, as had Jeff, but though he possessed more natural grace than his brother, and certainly more speed, baseball was never his sport. He was twelve when he discovered running—tagging along with his dad and Dennis Schleuter during the period following Bob's heart attack scare, when Bob (the unlikeliest of runners) had taken up jogging. He took the sport up for his heart, Julie said, but got deeper into it when he saw how Greg loved running, though by senior year in high school, Greg's knee trouble had pretty well benched him from cross-country.

In the courtroom now, Greg Seaman sat impassive, waiting for the proceedings to get under way, dressed neatly in a shirt and tie, in slacks not jeans.

"If he was upset, you wouldn't have known to look at him," said Dennis Seaman. "Cool as a cucumber, that one."

Dennis Seaman was a tall man, built on a whole other scale from Bob, and, as he would be the first to admit, a much more emotional type than his engineer older brother. He was well aware of the alienation that existed between Bob and Greg. Still, this was also his brother's son, and he knew Bob loved Greg and that he'd hoped for a reconciliation.

"Greg was also a mama's boy," Dennis said, "so naturally he was going to be upset about seeing his mom in jail. It was understandable that he'd be pretty traumatized right about then. You had to make an accommodation for that.

"My main purpose for going to Michigan that day was to come to the aid of my nephews, my brother's children," said Dennis. "I knew they were both going through hell, and it seemed like my responsibility to offer any support I could. My wife was saying it too: 'He's still your nephew.' So I went over to Greg and gave him a hug. I told him, 'We just want to let you know, anything you need, we're there for you.'"

Greg did not return his uncle's embrace. "I think he said something like, 'Well, thank you,' and smiled," said Dennis. "But after I got back to my seat, it was like a chill went through me."

Nancy Seaman entered the room then, in a prison tunic made of a thick, paperlike material. She took her place at a table in the front next to the attorney, Don Ferris, from Ann Arbor, Michigan, whom Greg had hired, hastily, in the first hours after his mother's arrest.

In some photographs from happier days, Nancy Seaman comes across as a woman of above-average looks, though perhaps not a beautiful one. Those who knew her from school spoke of how well groomed she always was. As a girl, she'd been petite, with thick dark hair worn halfway down her back, in the style of many female members of the class of 1970, though for some years now, Nancy had been coloring her hair blonde. Now it hung lank, pulled into a ponytail.

Her best feature, most agreed, was her large dark eyes, which she usually outlined in dark liner, though on this particular occasion, makeup had not been an option. A heavy chain was wrapped around her waist, with her shackled wrists attached, but she wore the handcuffs as much as a person could as an unusually heavy piece of jewelry. She stood very straight as she entered the courtroom, as if in charge of a fire drill or lining up students for the lunchroom, except for the moment when her eyes met Greg's and she smiled. The only emotion she seemed to display, according to one reporter who observed the scene, was a certain stunned surprise at finding herself in a place like this, at just around the time she should have been taking attendance or leading the Pledge of Allegiance.

At the hearing, Ferris laid out Nancy Seaman's contention that the injuries she had inflicted on her husband, which brought about his death, had been an act of self-defense, undertaken in response to Bob's threat that he would kill her. According to Nancy, the murder had not taken place, as the state purported, on the night of May 9, but rather on the morning of May 10, as she was preparing to go to her job at Longacre Elementary. She had been fixing a sandwich in the kitchen, she said, when Bob began to threaten her, first verbally, then with a knife. He had chased her into the garage, she said, where—with no avenue of escape—she had reached for the first thing she could find to defend herself, a hatchet. As for the knife wounds on her husband's body, she had no memory of inflicting those. She had blacked out, her attorney explained. She had been in a state of shock, fearing for her life.

Then it was Lisa Ortlieb's turn to present the basic allegations of the state: that Nancy Seaman had set out to Home Depot with the express purpose of purchasing a hatchet to kill her husband. That she had committed this murder not, as the defense asserted, on the morning of May 10, but shortly after her return from Home Depot the night before. Seaman then spent the next two-and-a-half days attempting to clean up the scene and, at the moment of her arrest, was on the brink of disposing of the body.

After hearing the two opposing positions, Judge Chabot ruled that Nancy Seaman should be held without bond at Oakland County Jail on a charge of first-degree murder, with a probable cause hearing to be held shortly and a trial sometime later that year.

Greg Seaman, Eugene and John D'Onofrio, and other supporters of Nancy Seaman had evidently anticipated that she'd be released on bond. Now that she was not, they expressed outrage and shock as she was led out of the courtroom, headed for Oakland County Jail.

Among those in the family, only Jeff expressed the view that when a person kills someone, there must be consequences. Even if the person is your mother.

CHAPTER 21

"A Totally Reasonable . . . Individual"

A woman of small though sturdy stature, with an interesting geometrically cut hairstyle, unusually daring for a subur-ban wife and soon-to-be grandmother approaching retirement age, and the energy output of a bumblebee, Rose Christoph had known Nancy Seaman for a number of years through her work as a reading specialist at Longacre Elementary School. A teacher for almost four decades, Rose was married to Carl Christoph, a magistrate for the City of Farmington Hills—an appointed position carrying a certain level of political clout in the city.

Now, with Nancy in trouble, Rose flew into action, incensed that the arraignment had not resulted in the swift release of her friend from jail. To Rose, this called into question the skills of the attorney who had represented Nancy at those proceedings, Don Ferris.

"He wasn't prepared. He looked like a college professor. He had patches on the elbows of his jacket . . . that type.

"He should have got her out on bond," said Rose. "It was immoral, keeping a woman of Nancy's stature in jail. It's not like she was some common criminal who was going to strike again or what have you."

Part of the problem, as Rose saw it, was Chief Dwyer and his press conference. "Bill Dwyer left the impression that Nancy had committed this grisly crime, chopped up the body, and dragged it around the garage or some such," she said. "The man just wanted to get attention, same as he always does."

To Rose, there was no question that her friend was innocent and that jail was no place for her, but she had to concede that this business of keeping the body in the car wasn't going to make things any easier. Nancy needed the best attorney in Oakland County, and in Rose's opinion (hers and Karl's; he was an attorney himself, after all, and knew more about these things), the best in the business was Larry Kaluzny.

They let Greg know their recommendation, and after discussions with Rick Cox and Nancy, the decision was made. Kaluzny wouldn't be cheap, but what was money at a time like this?

Larry Kaluzny had taken an unconventional route to becoming a highly paid defense attorney in Oakland County. After getting his undergraduate degree in physical education, he began his career as an elementary school gym teacher, before going back to school and earning his law degree in his late thirties. Since then, he had made a name for himself defending a long and impressive list of clients—often white-collar types. Among his most notorious cases was that of Steve Szeman, known as the Ski Mask Rapist, a twenty-year-old from an affluent Oakland County suburb, who had terrorized his community for a period of over a year before he was finally apprehended. Szeman got life without parole.

Interestingly, considering Kaluzny's high-profile reputation, his record for winning acquittals remained less than impressive, although as he reminded you, "The attorneys who say they never lost a case don't try the cases I do."

Although Oakland County legal observers remained hard pressed to come up with memorable or particularly dazzling courtroom performances by Kaluzny, most spoke of his decency as well as his humility.

No question: Larry Kaluzny didn't possess anything close to the showmanship of Oakland County's star defense attorney, Elbert Hatchett, who was a self-made man, raised in poverty in Detroit, and schooled on the poetic eloquence and passion of black Baptist preachers. But Kaluzny had an earnest, unintimidating way about him. An avid golfer with a 12 handicap, he maintained a reputation as an enormously likeable guy around the courthouse, the kind of person who might remind you of, say, your old school gym teacher. "I carry out the garbage just like everybody else," he said.

Recently, Larry had been joined at his firm by his older son, Todd. With the challenging Seaman case in front of him, now seemed like the ideal moment to fulfill his longtime dream of running a defense with his son. Kaluzny and Kaluzny versus the prosecution.

Larry met first with Greg Seaman. "A nice, clean-cut young man," he said. "When I talked with him it was never about the money, just what was best for his mom." Jeff, on the other hand—"well, I reached out to him. He had lost his dad, and I appreciated his loss. But he wasn't responsive. The way I see it, he was the one who told his dad about Nancy buying the condo, which is what brought on this whole thing. He had to have a lot of guilt feelings about that."

Larry met with Nancy Seaman at Oakland County Jail, where she laid out her story—years of abuse by Bob Seaman, she said, leading up to that deadly night when he had let her know she'd never live to set foot in that condo she'd bought.

"It's bizarre," said Larry Kaluzny, reflecting on the story. "You just don't get a middle-class woman killing her husband with a hatchet. A woman like that gets divorced. For such a person to take that kind of action, I truly believe she had to have been battered."

The question would have to be addressed as to why—once she'd acted, as she maintained (in self-defense)—Nancy Seaman hadn't picked up the phone to call 911. Then there were the two-and-a-half days she'd spent cleaning the garage, making trips to the store, teaching school (some of that time with her husband's dead body in the back of her vehicle). Perhaps an insanity defense might be appropriate, or short of that, an examination of the mental health of the accused?

"We had Nancy examined by a psychologist," said Larry. "But she never would have stood for an insanity plea. We never even discussed it. This was a proud woman. She wasn't about to say she was sick, and if you talked with her you would know she was a totally reasonable, intelligent, normal individual. Like anybody you might associate with socially."

Nancy Seaman had told Larry Kaluzny she'd bought the hatchet to get rid of a stump in her yard that had been bothering her. The fact that the piles of trash hadn't been taken care of, and the grass hadn't been mowed, didn't change this about her: she was a woman who liked doing yard work. And buying tools.

"As for the cover-up," he said. "I truly believe she was going to turn herself in. She knew she was going to jail. She was just trying to take care of a few last-minute things first, before she had to go away."

Picture hangers. Three sets of them.

CHAPTER 22

Two Sons, Two Mustangs

Bob Seaman died without a will, and though reports concerning the extent and value of his assets varied dramatically, one thing was clear: the man owned a number of highly collectible cars. If you considered the kind of bitterness that had come about in a conflict over a vehicle as relatively insignificant as the '89 Mustang, it was not hard to imagine that when the time came for dividing the more valuable cars in Bob Seaman's collection—as well as his other assets—strong differences were likely to arise.

In this family, it would appear, questions regarding the acquisition and disposition of material objects occupied a significant amount of attention, even in those first few days following the violent death of the man described by his wife as "the patriarch." Nobody disagreed with the assessment of Bob Seaman as a man who had subscribed to the belief that "the one who dies with the most toys, wins," and although when Bob was alive he and his son Greg saw many things differently, in this one area, perhaps, the apple did not fall far from the tree.

It was not news to Jeff Seaman that the relationship he enjoyed with his mother was different from the one between her and his brother. Now he learned that long before the murder of his father—before any appearance of bad feeling between him and his mother over his unwillingness to support her allegations of abuse—she had made Greg the sole beneficiary of her credit union account. More significant, she had given Greg power of attorney over her financial affairs.

About the credit union account, Jeff claimed to feel no consternation, asserting that his mother's choice to make his brother sole beneficiary was consistent with her long-established pattern of coddling Greg in ways he himself had never been—and the truth was, he liked it that way.

Jeff had held jobs all through high school. When it came time for college, he had over $3,000 saved from umpiring kids' baseball games to contribute to his tuition at Rolla. He took an obvious pride in covering his expenses, buying his clothes and incidentals, and being largely self-sufficient from age eighteen on. (No doubt it helped that unlike Greg, Jeff was content to wear not particularly fashionable or up-to-date clothing, while Greg favored a preppier look: Abercrombie and Fitch to Jeff's Men's Wearhouse style).

In contrast to his brother, it appeared, Greg had not contributed to the cost of his college tuition. Far from it, according to Jeff. Throughout his college years, he had appeared happy to avail himself of financial assistance from his parents (not only tuition, but also money for rent, and a charge card). To Jeff it was not surprising that after his brother had, in his view, lost interest in the project of rebuilding the '89 Mustang their father had bought him, their mother had bought him the newer, road-ready red Mustang.

"That was just Greg," said Jeff. "It was like my mother knew my brother couldn't manage on his own, so she got into the habit of taking care of everything."

At the point of his father's death, Jeff, at age twenty-five, was pulling down what was probably a high-five-figure income as a Ford engineer, paying a mortgage, supporting a wife, and investing in his own growing fleet of vehicles.

"I knew my parents were well off," he said. "But it wasn't of concern to me. I can take care of myself."

Still, the financial mess surrounding the death of his father could hardly have left Jeff Seaman totally sanguine. Particularly not the disposition of his father's retirement account.

Three days after the arrest of Nancy Seaman, her first attorney, Don Ferris, had arranged for the removal from the family home on Briarwood Court of several boxes of financial documents, including papers relating to Bob Seaman's 401K plan, valued at somewhere around $100,000. Although she was charged with the murder of her husband, Nancy had managed to claim the funds as his widow, which she immediately transferred in their entirety to Greg. As coexecutor of Bob Seaman's estate (with his brother), Greg would have been legally prohibited from liquidating these funds, but as he had not yet been named coexecutor, there appeared to be nothing stopping Greg from liquidating the 401K account.

Whatever it was Greg ultimately chose to do with the money, one thing was certain: Jeff Seaman was going to be kept out of it. And although Jeff may not have felt an overwhelming need for the money himself, there was a certain grim irony in seeing the money his father had set aside for retirement now being used (it appeared) to pay Larry Kaluzny to defend Nancy against the charge of having murdered Bob.

And it didn't end with money. Roughly a week after Bob Seaman's murder, his sons met up with each other at the Upper Deck, where they argued over what should be done about the contents of their father's office. A pushing match got started, and the police were called. (Perhaps there was a certain sense of déjà vu here for the Northville police officers.)

As had been the case in the past, nothing came of the police visit. Afterwards, though, Kristin Sears was reported to have commented to Jeff Seaman, "I'm sorry Greg was such an asshole."

A second encounter between the brothers occurred not at the Upper Deck but back on Briarwood Court, where Jeff and Greg met up again, this time for the purpose of dividing up the contents of their father's home office.

"I was actually worried that my brother might want to take some of the things that mattered so much to me," said Jeff, who had wanted, as a keepsake of his dad, an autographed ball from a Tigers game he and his father had attended some years before. Most important of all, to Jeff, was the metal plaque acknowledging Robert Seaman as the holder of a registered U.S. patent for a particular style of five-speed manual transmission he'd invented, during his Borg Warner days.

"To me," said Jeff, "those were the only things I cared about. I didn't want another fight with my brother."

Jeff needn't have worried. It turned out that Greg had no particular interest in the game ball or the patent. What he wanted were the fax machine, computer, printer, and scanner.

Among the cars in his father's fleet of vehicles, however, he chose the two that were, by far, the most valuable: the Shelby Mustang (worth well over $100,000) and the Ferrari. Jeff got the boat, but most important, as far as he was concerned, was that he got the car that meant the most to him emotionally. On eBay, and in the world of collectible Mustangs, it might have gone for around $30,000, but to Jeff this was the irreplaceable vehicle, because it was the one he'd rebuilt with his dad: the Boss.

CHAPTER 23

Choosing Sides

A s a parent in the Longacre School District, Michelle Siskowski had known Nancy Seaman for a few years at the time of the murder and arrest. The year before, her daughter Emily had been a student in Mrs. Seaman's fourth grade classroom. Michelle had requested Nancy Seaman as Emily's teacher, in fact, based on her outstanding reputation for teaching. Even before she won the Rainbow Award, it was well known at Longacre that Mrs. Seaman was among the most highly regarded teachers in the school.

And the decision to place Emily in Nancy's classroom had been a wonderful one, Michelle felt—a decision she credited for Emily's transformation from lackluster student to a real achiever who loved to read and brought home report cards with no grade lower than a B. More even than bringing up her daughter's grades, Michelle said, her year with Nancy Seaman had changed Emily's whole outlook about school and learning.

"My daughter was a different person, once she had Mrs. Seaman for a teacher," Michelle said.

Because she liked to stay closely involved in her daughter's educational life, Michelle Siskowski had also volunteered as a classroom mother that year.

"My feeling has always been that if I could take a burden off the teacher, that would give her more time to spend with students," she said. "So another mom and I used to come in on a regular basis to do copying for her and help out preparing materials for projects."

Not only that, but Michelle's older daughter, Kristen, was a student teacher, who substituted for Nancy Seaman on occasion. After the arrest, in fact, it was Kristen—young as she was—who'd been chosen to step into the difficult situation and finish the year with Nancy Seaman's fourth grade students.

Michelle had gotten the first news about what happened—part of it anyway—the very night of Nancy's arrest.

"Emily's softball team had a game, and we happened to be playing against a team where one of the dads was a policeman," she said. "I remember it was a beautiful day. Kites were flying. Younger kids on the sidelines were kicking around a soccer ball. This guy mentioned something about a murder. He made a joke, something like 'this lady must have been really mad at her husband' but he didn't say any names.

"Then the next day, I was over at school as usual, helping out at my daughter's classroom, and someone pulled me in the office. She told me, 'I just wanted to let you know about the dead body they found last night. It was Bob Seaman.'

"That afternoon, when I picked Emily up from school," Michelle went on, "I had to tell her the news that Mrs. Seaman's husband was dead. 'That's so terrible,' Emily said. 'She lost her mother and her husband all in just a few months.'"

Then she asked her mother, was it a car accident?

He was killed, Michelle told her daughter, keeping her eyes on the road.

"Did they find the killer?" Emily asked her.

"I hate to say this," Michelle said. "But it looks like Mrs. Seaman was the one that did it."

It was not the kind of conversation a parent expects to have with her child, she said. It wasn't exactly like having the class hamster die, or having the field trip cancelled. You just hoped these kids wouldn't carry long-term scars, but only time would tell.

Elsewhere in Farmington Hills, meanwhile, the Seaman family was finally getting around to holding a service for Bob. Because Nancy Seaman's first defense attorney, Don Ferris, had ordered a second, independent autopsy following the autopsy of Dr. Dragovic (hard to imagine why; there seemed little question as to the cause of death), days had passed before Bob's body was released to the family. By the time they got the body, the family decided to forgo a funeral. They opted instead for a memorial service held at the Upper Deck. Eventually there would be a second memorial in St. Louis.

Dennis Seaman returned to Michigan for the service, with his wife, his children, his brother Dave, and his sister, Margie Palmer. Bob's parents, Ward and Helen, also traveled to Michigan for the service. Hardly regular visitors to Farmington Hills, they had paid a visit a few years earlier to Bob and Nancy's home, memorable—at least to Margie—for Nancy's insistence that Ward take his shoes off before entering their home.

On that last visit, Ward an old Cardinals fan—had admired Bob's beloved Upper Deck. Now, with the ball machines silent and trays of antipasto from Bob's old hangout, Ginnopolis, laid out on tables, this would have been the last way anyone would have wanted Ward to make his return visit. As for Helen, she seemed dimly aware that Bob was gone, but did not dwell on the particulars.

A good-sized crowd assembled for the service—an unlikely mix of friends from Bob's two different worlds: ball playing and automotive engineering. From the engineering group were men who had worked with him, mostly under him, in his years at Borg Warner, and one or two from back in the Ford days. There was Don Shim, a Korean American independent contractor, who had traveled with Bob on trips to India and Korea in recent years—part of a plan of his and Bob's to build business relationships with what both recognized as the increasingly powerful force of Asian business, Chinese in particular. There was an African American junior executive with Borg Warner who said it was Bob's unwillingness to see him unfairly passed over for a job eight years earlier that had brought about Bob's departure from the corporation. He stayed only briefly, paid his respects, and disappeared.

One striking aspect of the transition Bob Seaman had made from high-level automotive engineer to girls' softball coach was what virtually all his friends agreed was Bob's absence of regret about having left behind the high-profile, high-paying lifestyle of the auto executive.

To Nancy, Bob's departure from Borg Warner had represented the beginning of the end, "the worst mistake Bob ever made in his life." But the consensus of those with whom he spent most of his time during those last seven years suggested otherwise.

"Bob loved his life at that batting cage," said Rob Berlin, a commercial interior designer who ran a business in the same building that housed the Upper Deck. "Bob had some projects in mind. My guess is, he was going to cook up some kind of engineering work again down the line. But I never heard him talk about missing the old days when he was a big-deal engineer."

Friends of Nancy Seaman evidently saw it differently. In their eyes, Bob had become an increasingly embittered and angry man who had felt threatened, overshadowed, and emasculated when his wife started bringing in an income of her own as a teacher, right around the time his own career seemed, in their eyes at least, to have taken a dramatic downturn.

Rick Cox—though he was present for the memorial service with his wife, Diane—appeared to share this view of Bob. So did Dennis Schleuter. Like Cox, Schleuter had been an engineering classmate of Bob's, and in their younger days, he and his wife, Paulette, had socialized with Nancy and Bob, gone out on Bob's boat together and sometimes to dinner. Some years earlier, Dennis and Bob had gotten into the routine of running together—an activity that had ultimately inspired Greg to take up the sport.

The two men had grown apart, however. The two couples had seen little or nothing of each other in recent years, though Nancy still had lunch occasionally with Paulette. Now, at the memorial, Schleuter made his way to the front of the area set aside for guests, where a sort of altar had been set up with photographs and memorabilia of Bob: model cars, a baseball, pictures of Bob as a young man and on his boat and coaching softball. After studying the other pictures on display, Dennis Schleuter propped up a framed photograph of his own to add to the group, setting it in a prominent position.

Julie approached the photographs and studied them. "I felt sick when I saw what Dennis Schleuter had put there," she said. It was a picture of a group of old classmates from Rolla at a recent reunion. Bob was there, of course, and so were Dennis and Rick. But in the front, clearly and, to Julie, painfully visible, was the smiling face of Nancy Seaman.

Jake Dumbleton saw it too. When he did, he turned the photograph over and set it face down on the table.

No formal speeches or eulogies were delivered at the memorial for Bob Seaman held at the Upper Deck. Most people milled around, exchanging stories and eating, but the mood was hardly jocular. It was clear by now that a division existed among the people in Bob Seaman's life: a split between those like Rick Cox who chose to believe that Bob had abused his wife, and those like Julie, for whom it seemed unfathomable that anyone would fail to recognize that the abused party in the marriage had been Bob himself. Few in one group communicated more than a stiff greeting to those in the other. A division had developed, in which there now seemed to be no way a person acquainted with the Seaman family could simply inhabit a place of sadness and compassion over what had happened, and not align himself or herself with either Nancy or Bob. It was probably not so surprising that those who loved and thought highly of Bob Seaman would feel outrage at Nancy Seaman, who had indisputably wielded a hatchet to his skull. But at the service it was plain that the bitterness went both ways and that those whose sympathies lay with Nancy chose to view the murder victim as if he were a criminal.

To some, like Nancy's father, brother, and son, Bob Seaman evidently got what he deserved. Even Rick Cox, Bob's longtime business partner and, according to Rick, his closest friend, now portrayed Bob as a rageful bully, and Nancy herself as the victim. Stranger still, perhaps, was the way in which all of those aligned with Nancy Seaman—Greg, Rick Cox, Nancy's friends Dennis and Paulette Schleuter—seemed to extend their animosity to anyone who had been associated closely with Bob. This included not only Jeff but also Bob's brother Dennis, as well as the Dumbletons. Ever since Marcia Low's story had run in the *Free Press*, Julie had been viewed by some people with a kind of chilly suspicion she'd never before encountered.

"Some people actually think I was having an affair with Mr. Seaman," she explained to Jenna, knowing that Jenna would hear talk at school soon enough, if she hadn't already.

"*Big duh,*" Jenna said. "I knew that would happen."

One person who was absent from Bob Seaman's memorial service was Greg Seaman. He did show up a few weeks later for the service in St. Louis, and briefly paid his respects to his grandparents Ward and Helen Seaman on his way to the church.

"We thought he was going to stop by after for more of a visit," said Ward. "But I guess he just took off. We didn't see him anymore after that."

Later Greg would complain that his brother did not inform him of when or how he'd chosen to dispose of their father's ashes, but apart from that expression of discontent about the arrangements, nothing in Greg Seaman's behavior in the days following his father's death gave evidence of grief. If he had loved and admired his father once, as all evidence suggested he had, there was room in his universe now for only a single truth: his father (or, as he referred to him now, his mother's husband) had been a brutal, violent man, whose death left him with a single regret: it was messing things up for his mother.

CHAPTER 24

How to Poison
Your Husband

‌I‌n the offices of the Longacre School District, crisis intervention director Estralee Michaelson called a special meeting for parents and students at the school, to give the school community a chance "to process their feelings about the Nancy Seaman situation."

"Some children were having nightmares," said former classroom mother Michelle Siskowski. "Even up at the high school, kids who'd been her students in the past were crying about what happened. But I think the ones who took it hardest were the other teachers."

As the weeks passed since the murder, the teachers were pulled in two directions. On the one hand, they were loyal to their colleague and incredulous that the woman with whom they'd worked side by side for so long—the exemplary, award-winning teacher who sometimes made the others look like underachievers—could have attacked her husband with a hatchet. At least as far as the press—and the police— was concerned, they formed rank around Nancy, saying as little as possible about what had happened.

On the other hand, these were people who had dedicated their careers and lives to the needs of children. Many of them were also angry that Nancy Seaman, a role model for her students, could have done something that would have traumatized so many children at such an impressionable age. Some teachers began to remember things about her that seemed ambiguous at the time but now perhaps alluded to a dark side of Nancy that people had never spoken of before.

Jeff Rehbine now remembered a time, just a couple of weeks before the murder, when he and Christine Brueck and Nancy Seaman had been discussing an upcoming fourth-grade sex education presentation. During the meeting, Nancy had pulled a file folder of curriculum materials out of her filing cabinet and told the two of them, "I just want you to know where this stuff is in case I end up dead."

One teacher spoke—off the record—about a time when a parent had just slightly bumped Mrs. Seaman's car out in the parking lot and she'd "totally lost it."

Then there was Tim Prince, another teacher at Longacre. With a certain reluctance, he admitted to police, speaking of Nancy Seaman, that "it always had to be her way." He told them about a time when he didn't get something done that Nancy felt he should have accomplished, and she had "hounded" him about it. He was sufficiently troubled at the time to speak with the principal about the matter, but Principal Smith had told him that Nancy had domestic issues and left it at that.

One other thing Tim Prince couldn't get out of his mind: several weeks before the murder, in the student lounge, he had overheard a conversation between Nancy Seaman and "an unknown person"—almost certainly a faculty member, but one whose identity Prince had either forgotten or chosen not to reveal. The other individual had evidently been discussing some kind of poison, at which point Nancy had responded, "I need to know how to make that poison for my husband."

At the time, Prince said, he figured it was just a joke (the two were "giggling as they were talking"), but in consideration of recent events, the comment took on a new and ominous significance.

CHAPTER 25

A Fixer-Upper Goes on the Market

I t was July now. School was out. Baseball season and softball season were well under way, though over in Northville, at the Waterwheel Building now presided over by Rick Cox alone, the facility known as Put One in the Upper Deck had now been gutted, leaving no trace of Bob Seaman's state-of-the-art batting cage operation.

Greg Seaman had moved into his apartment in Troy, a few miles from Farmington Hills, and though the work he was doing did not approach the level of his brother's over at Ford, he had begun his job at a manufacturing company called American Axle—"a world leader in the manufacture, engineering, validation and design of driveline systems, chassis systems, and forged products for trucks, buses, sport utility vehicles, and passenger cars."

Dennis Schleuter—Bob Seaman's former friend—had pulled a few strings to get Greg the position, though initially it had been Bob who'd arranged for Greg's internship with the company, back when he was at Purdue.

Sometime in the summer, Greg had proposed to Kristin Sears, his longtime Purdue girlfriend, who was now sporting an impressive-looking diamond. Under other circumstances, this was a purchase his mother might have assisted Greg in making, but with Nancy Seaman locked up in Oakland County Jail, her friend Paulette Schleuter had accompanied him on the shopping trip to pick out the ring. He continued to visit his mother when he could and communicated with her by phone between visits, and as he told her regularly, he remained optimistic that, as he put it, "we've got a winner here."

All in all, viewed strictly on the basis of appearances, the life of Greg Seaman in summer 2004 wasn't all bad. His father was dead, but to hear him tell it, he no longer thought of Bob Seaman as his father anyway. He no longer had a relationship with his brother, but it hadn't ever been much of a relationship anyway. His mother was awaiting trial for murder, but he expressed confidence that, given the evidence, the jury was bound to see things her way.

Meanwhile, not many twenty-two-year-olds could boast as secure a situation in life, materially speaking. He had a well-paying job with great benefits, a nice apartment, a pretty fiancée, and money in the bank. Greg's fleet of vehicles included a 1975 Mercury Montego, his father's Ferrari and Shelby Mustang, and the hatchback Mustang that had been in the garage at the time of his father's murder—the car on whose front grill had been found portions of Bob Seaman's brain tissue.

And there was one other car in the fleet: the 1995 Ford Explorer that had held his father's body not long before. Since the murder, Greg had had the vehicle detailed.

You could clean up a car, but the facts were on the record, and they would have presented a challenge for any attorney representing Nancy Seaman. But at the offices of Kaluzny and Kaluzny, in Bloomfield Hills, Larry Kaluzny was hard at work preparing Nancy Seaman's defense—with the strategy of portraying her as a battered woman who had killed in self-defense.

On this case, Larry was working for the first time with the older of his two sons alongside him. In his early thirties, Todd Kaluzny bore a striking resemblance to his father. There was a bland, midwestern congeniality about the two of them, absent of silver-tongued rhetoric or the capacity for memorable courtroom theatrics. But juries tended to like Larry. The hope was that some of that goodwill would inspire them to feel sympathy for his client.

Working side by side with one of his sons on a case was a longtime dream of Larry's. (It was an aspiration that might, oddly enough, call to mind the image of Bob Seaman down at the basement of the Upper

Deck, bending over the engine of a Mustang, rebuilding a car with one of his boys.) What could be a better feeling, he said, than passing the baton to the next generation? And there was one side benefit: they could confer about the case on the golf course together.

In a visit with Larry at the jail, Nancy had explained to him how—on one of her last visits to Henry Ford Medical Center with an injury inflicted by Bob—she had planned to finally admit she'd been abused. Then, in the waiting room, she'd spotted the parent of a student from Longacre Elementary, and it was too much for her to think of word getting out at school about what was going on. So she had left without receiving treatment.

In Larry Kaluzny's telling of his client's story concerning the events of the previous spring, Bob had found out from Jeff about Nancy's secret purchase of the condo. The fact that she was leaving him had so enraged Bob, Larry would suggest, that he'd escalated his violent behavior toward her. As the defense would portray it, Bob Seaman was a man embittered by his failure to remain at the top of the corporate world, losing money rapidly, drinking heavily (and combining alcohol with prescription medication), and jealous of his wife's career success.

"Nancy finally gave up on the marriage. She was going to leave Bob. That's what made him go crazy," said Larry.

It wouldn't be easy to come up with a comprehensible story to explain Nancy Seaman's choice to hide her husband's body in the back of the Explorer for several days and to clean up the garage as she did. To do so, Larry would remind the jury that his client had been in a state of shock and denial. She didn't fully comprehend that her husband was dead. She was trying to save her son Jeff the trauma of seeing his father's body. But above all, Larry Kaluzny would call on his "fixer" theme: Nancy was going to turn herself in; she just wanted to fix things up first.

Preparing for trial, Larry understood he would have the assistance of several associates of Nancy's to mount his battered woman defense. Rick Cox was on his list. So were Dennis and Paulette Schleuter and several of the teachers who remembered seeing Nancy with bruises and, in one instance, a black eye. Eugene D'Onofrio would testify, as would his son—Nancy's brother—John. Larry had also hired Dr. Lenore Walker, a nationally renowned expert on Battered Woman Syndrome—the woman who invented the phrase, in fact. And of course there would be Greg, a crucial part of the defense, unwavering not only in his support for his mother but in his utter contempt and, it might be said, apparent hatred for his father. As for the other of the Seaman brothers: To counteract Jeff's assertions that their father was not an abuser, Larry would portray him as a liar.

If Jeff tried denying he'd seen the Post-it notes and the bruises Nancy had rolled up her sleeves to show him, Greg pointed out, Larry could nail him for perjury.

"No matter how much he hates to do it," said Greg, "he's gonna have to come clean."

It was a sad situation. Not only was Bob Seaman dead and Nancy in jail, but the two remaining members of the family, Jeff and Greg, no longer spoke to each other. Here were two brothers, only two years apart in age, the only two people on earth who shared the loss of this particular father, the incarceration of this mother. But instead of finding any comfort from each other, the two—never close in the first place—had positioned themselves as the bitterest enemies.

Of course, if their mother were found guilty of murder, they would also be the joint beneficiaries of Bob Seaman's sizable estate, whenever it finally got out of probate. Meanwhile, they had to deal with each other, at least enough to figure out what to do with the cars, the boat, the house. And to come up with money for Nancy's swiftly mounting legal bills. The $100,000 in Bob Seaman's retirement account had been a start, but not enough to pay the bills from a Bloomfield Hills defense attorney.

Bob Seaman had no insurance policy. As joint executors of the estate, Jeff and Greg together now held control over disposition of the house on Briarwood Court, and they put the place on the market. Under normal circumstances, a home of that scale (four bedrooms and large landscaped lot in the Ramblewood subdivision) might have been priced upwards of half a million dollars, but because of the longtime standoff between Bob and Nancy over yard work and home maintenance, the place had fallen into disrepair. So much time had passed in which nobody mowed the lawn that a substantial part of the lawn had died. Pieces of fence were falling down. The sprinklers no longer worked. Of the Malibu lights Bob had installed in the front yard—to cast a nighttime glow on the impressive Tudor façade—only one remained functional.

More troublesome, from the point of view of a prospective sale, however, was that anyone showing up for an open house would be aware they were visiting the site of a gruesome murder. It would be difficult for a realtor to proudly display the roomy three-car garage, with its track lighting and unique Indy 500–inspired black-and-white floor tiles, knowing that several of these tiles had been removed in the course of the Seaman investigation for the purpose of testing the residue of blood that had evidently seeped through the cracks onto the cement beneath. The walls were newly painted—by Nancy Seaman, in the hours following the murder, also to disguise evidence of blood.

And then of course, out in the yard, there was the stump that Nancy Seaman never got around to removing, despite her well-publicized trip to Home Depot, back on Mother's Day, to purchase a tool for the job.

CHAPTER 26

"I Love You So Much, Darling"

A s the days passed, Nancy settled into her new routine at Oakland County Jail, and the telephone conversations with Greg (and, now and then, her father or brother) came to take on a familiar pattern. There would be a businesslike exchange of information about car titles, mortgage payments, taxes, a new cell phone number, Greg's birthday. Then they'd settle into the real issue at hand: the upcoming trial, at which—as they continued to remind themselves—the jury was sure to recognize the groundlessness of the charges against Nancy and come back with a speedy verdict of not guilty. The focus now was to get her home in time for the holidays.

It was August now. Julie and Dick Dumbleton drove with Jake to the campus of Albion College, a little over an hour from home, to help their son move into his dorm room for the beginning of his freshman year. They hoped the change of scene and the excitement of college would take Jake's mind off Bob's death. Not that they'd managed to get their own minds off of it. Jenna, in eighth grade now, was faring a little better. On the outside at least.

Back at Longacre Elementary, a new school year had also begun.

The students from Nancy Seaman's fourth grade class, who'd finished out the year with a substitute, had moved on to new classrooms now, and the hope was that with a new teacher to focus on, the memory of what had taken place the previous spring would fade.

Over at the Ford Test Facility, in Dearborn Heights, Jeff Seaman was hard at work on the 2007 Explorer—and not just in Dearborn Heights, either. He flew to Las Vegas and to Arizona to the proving grounds there, for the purpose of test driving the new car. Many times over the course of that fall, situations had come up in the engine design that had left his team at least temporarily in a state of turmoil and uncertainty about the future of the new model, but he liked to say, "I thrive on chaos."

On the rare moments when he wasn't in overdrive, calibrating the Explorer, he was coaching a baseball team for twelve-year-old boys or playing, himself, in a baseball league over in Ann Arbor—using wooden bats, because that was more challenging than the metal kind. (Harder on his rotator cuff, but his was shot anyway.) His father was gone from his life, his mother was gone, his brother had never been there much in the first place. But he had Becka. Weekends, they went out on the boat or worked on home improvement projects. Never an effusive man, he made it plain nevertheless that the sun rose and set with her.

Maybe it was the new job, but as the weeks passed, Greg's conversations and visits with his mother became a little more infrequent. In discussions with her father and aunt, Nancy could be heard observing, now and then, that "Greg must be traveling for his job" or that "Greg must be busy." He had a lot going on, that was for sure. No doubt he'd be visiting again soon.

Meanwhile, Eugene D'Onofrio continued to make his regular Sunday afternoon visits to the jail to see his daughter and to speak with her by telephone. Her brother called, along with her Aunt Minnie, who reminded her, "You did everything right, Nancy. You were an exemplary mother.

"If we'd ever have known, Nancy," Aunt Minnie observed late that October, speaking of her failure to understand, until the murder, what a terrible, abusive man Bob Seaman had been, "I would have come and dragged you out of that house myself and kicked him in the shins on the way out."

In early November, the house on Briarwood Court was sold to a couple with three children—stay-at-home mom, husband working for the automotive industry. The S's were aware of what had taken place at the house, of course. Had the murder not occurred there, they would not have gotten such a great deal, and they knew it. Just because one family hadn't been happy on Briarwood Court didn't mean another one had to be miserable.

The price was $380,000. After deducting the real estate commission and the $60,000 remaining on the mortgage, this left roughly $150,000 for each of the two Seaman sons, before taxes.

Most of that money, if not all—or at least, Greg's portion of it—would go to attorneys' fees for the upcoming trial, of course. The irony was that even as one brother was turning over his share of the estate to help in his mother's defense, the other appeared ready to sell her up the river by cooperating with the prosecution and refusing to support her allegations of abuse.

Jeff's unwillingness to testify in Nancy's defense remained a central theme of her telephone conversations with Greg and her father, taped during the period before the trial.

"You have to remind him," Eugene D'Onofrio told his daughter, speaking of Jeff, "you gave him life."

"Every time he needed something I was there," Nancy agreed.

"I can never repay you for everything you've done for me," Nancy told Greg.

"I'm just making up for everything you've ever done for me," Greg said.

"I love you so much, darling," she told him. "Whatever happens, you know I love you so much."

CHAPTER 27

Guilty of Telling Blonde Jokes

O ver at 1200 Telegraph Road, on the fourth floor of the impressively scaled building that houses Oakland County Courthouse and, next to it, the office of prosecutor David Gorcyca and his team, Lisa Ortlicb was working even harder than usual in the preparation of her case against Nancy Seaman, with the trial now set to begin November 29.

Lisa and her husband, Gorcyca, had been married close to a year by now, but because of their busy schedules, they hadn't found time to take a honeymoon. Now, finally, they were taking off for two weeks in early November, but doing that meant getting everything ready for trial before Lisa left for Hawaii. She had only just received copies of the tapes of Nancy and Greg's telephone conversations from jail.

The tapes were a breakthrough for the prosecution, revealing a side of Nancy Seaman's personality her fellow teachers and friends like Rick Cox might have found alarming: a combination of eerie detachment and businesslike coolness, and occasional vulgarity on the part of Greg Seaman, as well as his mother. Recognizing that the tapes would form a crucial part of her case, Lisa played them over and over, even in her car, until she could recite parts of the conversations from memory.

And there was plenty more to work with, she believed: the absence of defensive injuries on Nancy Seaman's body at the time of her arrest and, similarly, the absence of the kind of injuries on Bob Seaman that would seem to indicate a struggle.

Then there was the return of the shoplifted hatchet, an event the jury would actually be able to witness on tape, thanks to Home Depot's store surveillance cameras.

The Post-it notes that Larry Kaluzny would be describing to the jury—as evidence of Bob Seaman's irrational anger and hostility toward his wife—would actually become a part of the prosecution's case as well, though the notes that Lisa Ortlieb planned to introduce revealed a different side of the story. She had gotten them from Julie Dumbleton, who had retrieved them (along with a selection of Nancy's letters to Bob) from the files Bob had left in his office at the Upper Deck.

In preparing her case, Lisa had also studied the extensive records of the police investigation headed up by Detective Al Patterson. But now, with the trial approaching, she brought in another investigator, Don O'Chadleus, who worked not for Farmington Hills but for the prosecutor's office. It was O'Chadleus's job to contact defense witnesses and attempt to conduct interviews with them, in an effort to give Lisa Ortlieb an idea of what they were likely to say on the stand.

A retired Madison Heights policeman who bore a strong resemblance to Kirk Douglas (a characteristic that could not have hurt, when interviewing female witnesses face-to-face), O'Chadleus always began by making telephone contact with those on the defense witness list. He understood that sometimes a witness close to the accused was likely to be hostile to the prosecution. Still, it had been surprising how many of those on Larry Kaluzny's list—individuals who would have seemed like the type less concerned with protecting the accused than with establishing the truth of the events in question—had simply refused to speak with him or even to return his calls.

"They don't have a legal obligation to talk with me, but if they don't, they'll have to explain in court why they didn't cooperate," he said. Among those who chose not to return O'Chadleus's calls were a group of school colleagues (Nancy McCoy, Barb Mikel, Sue Duncan, Gerry Pugh, Ray Wyss, and Elaine Gilbert), as well as Nancy's friends Ron and Ginger Schoenbach and Dennis and Paulette Schleuter. Jeff Rehbine, also a teacher at Longacre, did agree to speak with O'Chadleus—cautiously describing to him Nancy Seaman's occasional display of temper and her desire "to be in control."

John D'Onofrio, Nancy's brother, told O'Chadleus of seeing bruises on his sister's body. His wife, Barb, offered that she never liked Bob, though when asked why was only able to say that he "told blonde jokes." (Barb D'Onofrio was a blonde.)

Greg Seaman chose not to speak with O'Chadleus. Principal William Smith, from Longacre Elementary, returned O'Chadleus's call only to say, "Please note for the record that I returned your call."

Rick Cox told O'Chadleus that Bob was a "very explosive" person and needed to be in control. Cox had been a witness, he said, to "verbal and mental abuse" on the part of Bob Seaman toward his wife. He conveyed his belief that Bob Seaman had an affair a few years back with a secretary of his. Cox was, O'Chadleus said, "unusually supportive" of Nancy, to the point where O'Chadleus asked Cox if he had a relationship with the accused. With some consternation, Rick Cox had told him definitely not.

One defense witness who had been willing to speak with Don O'Chadleus was Eugene D'Onofrio.

"Mr. D'Onofrio doesn't like victim Robert Seaman because of an incident involving a cake when victim yelled at him," O'Chadleus wrote in his report.

"He found out that victim was having an affair," O'Chadleus wrote. "He doesn't remember who told him that.

"I got the feeling," O'Chadleus offered, "that this was a man who was trying to be honest with me. But it was his daughter, too. He wanted to believe his daughter."

CHAPTER 28

"She Swung for Her Life"

It was November now. As the months had passed since the discovery of Bob Seaman's body in the Explorer, one question had haunted Don O'Chadleus, as it had Detective Patterson and Chief Dwyer: How did Nancy Seaman get her husband's body in the back of the Explorer? Greg Seaman himself, in his first interview with the police shortly after his mother's arrest, had expressed the view that it would not have been possible for his mother to lift the body without assistance. This was a 130-pound woman—and not one who visited a gym, either; her own lawyer described her as "a couch potato." The body she had lifted represented 180 pounds of dead weight.

The seeming impossibility of Nancy's lifting the body unassisted had caused Patterson to look hard, once again, at the movements of Greg Seaman during the period surrounding the murder, but it was clear from phone records and the testimony of his friends that Greg had been out of state, on his road trip to Florida, during the days in question. Jeff certainly didn't help his mother, and, judging from Eugene's age and circumstances, Patterson had also ruled him out.

Larry Kaluzny had wondered about this question, too. But his client had offered an explanation that satisfied him, at least: just the week before the murder, she told him, she had been teaching her students about levers and angles, in connection with a unit about physics. Faced with the dead weight of her husband's body on the floor of her garage, she had thought back on that unit she'd just taught, and constructed a ramp and lever of her own, to ease Bob's body into the car.

This probably wasn't the use for physics most teachers had in mind when they instructed students about levers. But it had worked. One way or another, nobody chose to pursue the issue, and whatever lingering questions anyone had about how on earth Nancy Seaman had lifted that body into the vehicle, they kept them to themselves during the trial. The last thing Lisa Ortlieb would want was an open question in her case. So she let this one go. She took off on her honeymoon.

Her intention was to put the whole thing out of her mind for those two weeks in Hawaii. But she couldn't. Even on the beach, she thought about Nancy Seaman. Even when she and Dave Gorcyca were supposed to be enjoying their romantic dinners by the ocean, she found herself thinking about Bob.

Over at the county jail, meanwhile, Nancy Seaman—with the help of Larry Kaluzny—had managed to win what was, for her, an important pretrial victory. The judge ruled that Nancy could wear her own clothing at the trial.

A selection of her suits from home was brought over for her. If they hadn't actually come from a Talbot's store, it was safe to say that these suits would have appealed to any Talbot's customer. Well cut, conservative. Certainly not cheaply made. They spoke of quality, class, and a certain quiet dignity. Murderers didn't wear suits like this.

Because Nancy had been coloring her hair up until the murder and was no longer able to keep up with the maintenance of hair coloring in jail, her roots had come in gray, but there was nothing to be done about that. The question had remained unclear for a while, however, whether or not she'd be allowed to wear makeup at the trial. Larry was working on that one.

It was her father who informed her that the judge had approved her petition requesting permission to wear makeup at the trial.

"Thank God," she said.

Makeup or makeup, though, Nancy knew what was coming. "It's gonna be ugly," she told her father. "It'll be really ugly. It'll be ugly, but it will be over in a couple of weeks."

"It will work out," Greg told his mother on the telephone on November 25, four days before the start of the trial. "You just stay strong, because we're staying strong out here."

"Well, I will, but if it doesn't work out—" she began. He interrupted before she completed the thought.

"We're hoping for the best," he said. Then (perhaps surprisingly for a young man inclined toward a predictably upbeat outlook) he qualified his optimism slightly: "Like anybody, we're bracing for the worst," Greg added.

"You know, whatever happens, you know I love you so much," Nancy told him

Then Greg again: "I know. Whatever happens you're always gonna be there and you're always—"

"Yeah," said Nancy, her voice flat. "I'll be there somewhere."

Back in May, when the Seaman story first broke, a huge amount of press attention had focused on the murder, as was inevitably the case in Oakland County when a victim or perpetrator was white and affluent.

In the months since Chief Dwyer's initial press conference, however, and those that had followed soon after, the Metro Detroit press had found other stories to fill its pages. Other murders occurred. There was the Detroit Lions professional football team to occupy people's minds, and the war in Iraq, and the presidential election. And always, in the Motor City, there was the automotive industry to think about, the ever increasing loss of market share to foreign carmakers, the sorry state of the economy, the ever dwindling job market.

Now, however—with Nancy's trial just days from getting under way—the reporters were back on the Seaman murder. It wasn't just the *Detroit Free Press* and the *Detroit News*, either, or the local television stations. *Inside Edition* was preparing a segment on the case. So was *Good Morning America*. Jeff Seaman was talking to the press, and Chief Dwyer was back on television.

That, in particular, offended Greg Seaman. He and his mother were convinced that Jeff's big mouth, combined with Dwyer's grandstanding for the media, as they saw it, would leave them with a hopelessly prejudiced jury pool—one convinced before the trial even got under way that Nancy Seaman was a cold-blooded killer.

Greg decided to do something about it. He called up the *Detroit Free Press* and offered to give an exclusive interview. Clean-cut and well dressed, as usual, he made his way to the *Free Press* offices in downtown Detroit and met with reporter Marcia Low.

"For months he had remained silent as his older brother, Jeff Seaman . . . touted their father as a man of honor," wrote the *Free Press* reporter. "Now, Greg Seaman is telling what he says is the truth. And it begins with a fist to the face."

According to Greg, he was eleven years old when his father had first hit him—for reasons not explained—bloodying his lip so badly that he had taken a Polaroid photograph of his face, just in case he needed it at some point down the line. (Unfortunately, he'd thrown out the photograph a while back.) At the time, Greg said, he had threatened to go to the police with his evidence, but he had not done so, though he went on to say there had been other incidents of physical abuse from his father over the years that followed.

He also recalled an incident in which, as a very young child, he'd witnessed his parents arguing on a stranger's lawn after his mother learned that her husband was having an affair.

"He was a closet wife beater," Greg explained to Marcia Low. "She always had bruises, and she was not a klutzy person. He did not like women, he had little patience for children, he drank and he cheated."

Greg went on to describe how his mother, fearing for her life, had "squirreled away" her savings to buy the condo in Woodhaven that January. He told how she had come home from work one day to find "hundreds of sticky notes inside drawers and on the refrigerator, walls, kitchen cabinets and bathroom mirrors," with Bob Seaman's handwriting scrawled over every one, and the words "I'm going to divorce you, bitch" or just "bitch."

Even in the context of a sympathetic interview, there was no getting around the facts of the murder itself, but Greg filled the reporter in on how it was that a woman like Nancy Seaman had reached the point of hitting his father with the hatchet.

Bob Seaman had chased his mother with a knife and cut her, pushed her down, and punched her, Greg explained. He had kicked her. She was curled on the floor of the garage when she'd caught sight of the hatchet.

"She grabbed it," wrote Marcia Low, recounting Greg's words but adding her own journalistic flourish. "And she swung for her life."

In the months since the murder, Greg told Low, he and his brother had broken off all communication. The story went on to say that "his brother scattered their father's ashes without telling him, taking away his final chance to say goodbye."

"Now he says he's moving on," she concluded, "comforted by the fact that his mom no longer lives in fear. Now he, too, looks forward to a new life, after the trial."

It sounded good, if not altogether convincing.

PART FOUR

The People Versus Nancy Seaman

CHAPTER 29

The Fixer

*T*he *People of the State of Michigan* v. *Nancy Ann Seaman* got under way on Tuesday, November 30, 2004. Almost seven months had passed since the sunny May afternoon of Nancy Seaman's arrest. No snow covered the ground yet, but a chill hung in the air, signalling colder days ahead. On Mother's Day, the sidewalks in front of Home Depot had been filled with plants and gardening tools, but now spring merchandise had given way to snowblowers and shovels, storm window kits and driveway salt.

The clothes Nancy Seaman had relinquished the day she was brought into the police station had been a T-shirt and capri pants. Now she was dressed—by special dispensation of the court—in a dark suit, with a turtleneck. She wore a bun, which partially concealed the fact that her hair was growing in all gray.

A petite woman when she was younger, Nancy had gained weight over the years, having gotten up to a 130 pounds on her five-foot-one-inch frame at the time of her arrest, but since then she had lost at least 20 pounds. Her face—even after Larry Kaluzny had succeeded in winning her the right to wear makeup—looked gaunt and worn, but she appeared to have gotten her hands on a manicure kit.

Nancy was brought into the courtroom before the arrival of the jury—with good reason. She was wearing shackles—not only a chain around her waist and attached to her wrists but also a second set of shackles on her ankles, which required her to walk slowly, with a shuffling step. Seeing this, a group of teachers on the bench a few rows back, who'd taken off from work to support her, let out a collective gasp. They whispered disapproval among themselves at this latest offense to their friend and at the absurdity seeing her treated like some kind of dangerous criminal when anyone who knew her could tell you she was the farthest thing from it. Now, catching the eye of their former colleague, they mouthed words of encouragement and waved. She nodded and offered a tight smile, shrugging her shoulders as if to say, "What's a person to do?"

Once Nancy reached the table where Larry and Todd Kaluzny were seated, the shackles were removed. Taking her place at the table now, she looked surprisingly composed, though Lori Brasier, a *Free Press* reporter, characterized her as having "a rabbitlike countenance"— mouth pursed, eyes darting around the room as if in search of a safe place to burrow down.

At the table across the aisle from that of the defense sat Lisa Ortlieb, and the contrast was dramatic. Only recently returned from her honeymoon, Lisa was looking particularly striking in a dark blue suit, with her hair down. Some women as attractive as Lisa would come across as vain or full of themselves, but she maintained the appearance of obliviousness to the impression she left as she strode purposefully into the courtroom in a short skirt and high heels, as if she were truly nothing more than a "small-town girl who likes to see justice done." Next to her sat Detective Al Patterson, his hair in a military-short buzz cut, his suit not nearly so well tailored as that of his chief of police, Dwyer.

Behind the two tables, a larger than average group of onlookers had assembled. Like guests at a wedding choosing the bride's side or that of the groom, they seemed to understand, without being informed, where to sit on the bench. Because any individual who would be testifying in the case was prohibited from observing any portion of the trial prior to giving his or her own testimony, many of those who would ultimately take their places in the courtroom—like Dennis Seaman, Greg and Jeff Seaman, Julie and Dick Dumbleton, and Rick Cox—had yet to appear, but as they did, one by one, they would position themselves (as the group of teachers had already) in direct alignment with the side they supported.

There was also an unusual preponderance of press in evidence. Not only Lori Brasier, the *Detroit Free Press* reporter, and Mike Martindale, her counterpart from the *Detroit News,* but others as well. Producers of the CBS program *48 Hours* were evidently planning a segment on the case. Rumor had it that a producer from *Oprah* might be attending. And in the back of the courtroom, as powerful a presence in its own way as that of the judge or jury, a television camera with boom mic stood on its oversized tripod, aimed directly at the witness box. Court TV had come to town, and now the cameraman zoomed in on the players: Nancy Seaman, Larry Kaluzny, Lisa Ortlieb. The cameraman expressed regret that Lisa's hair was hiding her face. She would look so good on camera.

At nine o'clock the bailiff announced the arrival of Judge John McDonald—a tall, gray-haired figure, patrician, with a deeply lined face. Then the jurors were brought in.

First to address the court was Lisa Ortlieb for the prosecution. She turned to the jury now, her voice indignant.

"Bob Seaman spent the last week of his life in Arizona with his brother, Dennis," she began. "When Dennis said goodbye to him at the airport, Bob was contemplating his future. He was looking forward to returning to Michigan and filing for a divorce.

"Bob Seaman never got that chance. Within twenty-four hours, Bob Seaman laid *[sic]* bloodied and butchered on his garage floor.

"Within twenty-four hours, someone bought a hatchet, drove to Bob's house, came at him in the garage, aimed that hatchet—with such force and such destruction—at his head and started attacking him in the head over and over again.

"That person wasn't a stranger. The person that bought that hatchet wasn't a stranger who attacked a defenseless, unarmed man in his own garage. It was Bob's very own wife, the person he intended on divorcing, the Defendant, Nancy Seaman."

Studying the face of the accused as Lisa Ortlieb spoke the words, a juror would have had a hard time determining much in the way of her emotional state in the courtroom. Nancy Seaman, seated beside her attorney, might have been attending a school district meeting, for all

the emotion revealed in her expression as Ortlieb went on to sum-
marize the case she would be presenting in the days ahead: the upcoming testimony of Jeff Seaman, the purchase of the hatchet, the
Dumbletons' increasingly desperate search for their friend, and finally,
the discovery of the body in the Explorer.

"When this case is over," Lisa concluded, "you will know several
things. First, you will know that Bob Seaman died a gruesome death.
Gruesome.

"Most importantly, you will know that the Defendant had time to
make decisions and choices. She chose to be a killer.

"You will know that she is a cold-blooded murderer.

"You will know when this trial is over the Defendant is guilty of
first degree murder."

It was Larry Kaluzny's turn next, offering a very different picture
of how the story had played out.

"Imagine growing up in a loving household where marriage is sacred, important, forever, through good times and bad times," he began.
"Then imagine being married, yourself, and two weeks after you're
married, as you're driving the car with your newlywed husband you
get beat up, you're sworn at, there's a threat to throw you out of the
car, two weeks after you're married.

"Thirty years ago, Nancy didn't have to imagine that. She was living it. She went through that.

"Imagine spending the next thirty years, sometimes good times,
but maybe once, twice a year, being beaten up physically, emotionally.
And imagine during that time your husband says, 'I wish you were
dead. Die, bitch, die. That's all you can do.'"

For Larry Kaluzny, building a successful defense for a client was
about telling a story. You needed to help those jurors look beyond the
shock and horror of a violent murder—get to know the person who'd
committed the crime and understand what might have happened in
her life to bring her to the point of doing something they might otherwise view as indefensible.

The story should be simple enough that anyone could follow it. You
didn't want to throw in too many complicated elements. For Kaluzny,
at least, the way to go in Nancy's case was to establish a simple theme,
clear enough that even a child might understand, and pound it home
as forcefully as possible.

As Kaluzny saw it—and as he framed the story now, in his opening remarks—Nancy Seaman was a woman who had always fixed things. (She did yard work. She did little projects around the house all the time. She bought tools.) But there had been one thing in Nancy's life that defied all her best efforts at fixing: her marriage to Bob Seaman.

Kaluzny went on to lay out a portrait of escalating abuse spanning thirty years. He described his client's deep-seated Catholic faith, her belief in the sanctity of marriage and her commitment to her marriage vows. "She would write him notes to avoid verbal arguments," Kaluzny explained. He talked about a couple of times, over the years, when Nancy had gone so far as to go to the police with her reports of abuse, but—unwilling to see her husband put in jail, and given no alternative by the police—she had chosen not to press charges against him.

"She was a religious person. A Catholic. She truly believed in her marital vows."

For thirty years, she confided in no one about the abuse that was going on, he reminded the jury now. "She tried to . . . fix things and avoid confrontation."

She had begged Bob to spend more time with her and the boys. But he wouldn't listen. He just kept spending time with the Dumbletons. And abusing her.

"She wanted to wait until the kids were grown . . . to leave," said Kaluzny. "She was trying to squirrel away some of her own money so that she could get out of this relationship finally."

Having at last given up on her marriage, Nancy had bought the condo in secret that January, out of fear that if her husband learned she was leaving him, he might kill her.

She was right to be afraid, Kaluzny told the jury. Because, he continued, when Bob Seaman discovered Nancy's secret, he'd attacked her with so much violence that he left her no choice but to reach for the one thing she could find to defend herself: the hatchet.

Kaluzny didn't dwell on the next part of the story—the murder itself, or the elaborate cleanup. He focused on the psychology behind it.

"It didn't happen, if you fixed it," Kaluzny said, gravely.

Maybe it was not such a big jump, then, from repairing drywall and touching up paint to wrapping a dead body in a tarp and stashing it in the back of the SUV.

"Now the fixer comes out in her," Kaluzny suggested, of the three-day cleanup effort in the garage. "She told herself, 'I can fix this like I've fixed everything for thirty years.'"

"She never intended to get rid of the body," Kaluzny said. "Her only intent was not to let Jeff see his father like that.

"If you're going to plan a murder," he pointed out, touching on the planner theme, "do you do it before you go teach? The weekend before your son's going to graduate that you're looking forward to?"

In closing, Kaluzny told the jury that he would bring in a couple of experts on Battered Woman Syndrome to enlighten them about the mental state of a woman experiencing abuse of the sort he alleged his client to have suffered. They would be hearing from none other than Dr. Lenore Walker, the woman who coined the term *Battered Woman Syndrome,* he told the jury. He added that Dr. Walker had "been on every major television program you can think of: *Nightline, 48 Hours,* you name it.

"We believe that you will decide that on May 10, 2004," Kaluzny concluded (suggesting the morning after the evening on which the prosecution alleged the murder to have taken place), "Nancy was acting in legal self-defense. And we're confident at the end of this case that you will find her not guilty."

CHAPTER 30

"A Dynamic Happening"

ith the opening statements concluded, the prosecution called Dr. Ljubisa Dragovic, the chief medical examiner for Oakland County, who had conducted the autopsy on Bob Seaman.

In the meticulous manner required of a medical examiner, Dr. Dragovic walked the jury through the process of his examination of the body, beginning with how he'd peeled back the blood-encrusted duct tape, the tarp, the blood-soaked blankets. The jury was sent from the courtroom while photographs were displayed, showing images of Bob Seaman's swollen and partially decomposing face and the shaved image of his skull, with deep gashes where the hatchet had struck.

Larry Kaluzny objected to the introduction, into evidence, of a number of these photographs, suggesting that the medical examiner's words might be sufficient. He further suggested that black-and-white photographs be substituted for the more gruesome color images. Judge McDonald took several moments to study the photographs himself, selecting several (particularly those of Bob's face) that he felt the jury should see only in black and white, and the jury was brought back into the room to hear Dr. Dragovic's testimony.

For a person unfamiliar with the world of forensic medical examination, the language of Dr. Dragovic's testimony might have come as something of a jolt. He spoke of "chops, blows, slashes, stabs, multiple chop injuries, blunt force injuries . . . gaping skin, skin that is basically falling apart, sloughing off, decomposition."

To explain the angle and force with which the hatchet wielded by the defendant must have made contact with the victim's skull—and penetrated it—he then reached for People's Exhibit 32, a Styrofoam model of a head, of the sort more typically used in places like Wal-Mart to display hats for sale. He held up a hatchet (not the actual murder weapon, it was explained) and re-created the angle of swing.

"This is a dynamic happening," he explained. "The head may be bent forward or to the side. And it certainly doesn't stay straight all the time."

The question was raised, by Lisa Ortlieb, as to whether Bob Seaman could have remained conscious during an attack of the kind he experienced. Studying the photographs, a person could only pray the answer was no.

"The multiple blows to the head suggest, at least, that the decedent was rendered unconscious," he concluded. "And then under a relatively controlled, physical circumstance, those multiple stab wounds to the left upper back were inflicted where the decedent was not moving."

The question was asked, Could Bob Seaman have survived the hatchet attack, had he received treatment afterwards, rather than being left in the garage?

"None of these injuries are instantaneously fatal," Dr. Dragovic offered. "It takes many minutes to die from injuries of this kind."

"Were you able to determine or estimate the timeframe when all these injuries were supposed to be inflicted on him?" asked Ortlieb.

"I would consider this to have taken minutes," said Dr. Dragovic.

Finally, Ortlieb asked Dr. Dragovic about the presence of defensive injuries on Bob Seaman's body—wounds that would indicate the presence of a struggle with his wife, the attempt to fend off injury, or actions that might support the defense allegation that it had been Bob, not Nancy, who acted as the aggressor.

"Not what I would consider overt defense-type injuries," said Dr. Dragovic, adding that the relatively insignificant wounds on Bob Seaman's hand "would likely represent passive types of cuts simply coming from the hand being somewhere in the way when the knife was coming into the body."

The implication was plain enough. When Nancy Seaman started stabbing her husband, on the floor of the garage, he wasn't in any position to fight back. And still, she had kept on stabbing him.

"This Is Robert's Toilet Paper"

T he next witness called by Lisa Ortlieb was Dennis Seaman. He recalled his early and cordial meeting with Nancy shortly before her marriage to his brother, when she had evidently described him, after watching him play tennis, as "poetry in motion." The good feeling did not last long, however, at least to Dennis Seaman's way of thinking.

"I was married three weeks after she was married," he explained. "I think there might have been a little animosity, from the fact that her marriage . . . was . . . overshadowed a little by my marriage. . . ."

But what sealed Nancy's dislike of him, Dennis testified, was a business deal he and Bob had entered into a year or two later, around 1975, in which Bob had funded a company the two started. "And after it didn't work out, it seemed like there was no relationship," he said. "I was her number one most hated person."

On cross-examination, Larry Kaluzny asked about Dennis's idea that Bob should have transferred his valuable cars to Dennis's name, to protect them in a future divorce from Nancy. "You were trying to cheat her out of whatever you could, right?" he asked Dennis.

"It couldn't be done," said Dennis.

"Were you aware that Bob was putting notes on all the property in the house: 'mine,' 'mine,' 'Robert's toilet paper,' 'Robert's property'?"

"The notes I heard he wrote were 'bitch' and 'I fixed this,' 'I did this,' because he was accused of never doing anything around the house."

It was not a pretty picture, all right, but nobody was pretending here that there had been love lost between Bob Seaman and his wife by the time she murdered him. It was stunning, in fact, to grasp how much bitterness and contempt two people might possess for each other and still continue to live under the same roof.

So far, the allegations Kaluzny was attempting to support were familiar to most of those involved with the case: the idea that Bob had behaved angrily and abusively to Nancy, that he had a reputation for bullying and physical violence. Now Larry laid a new card on the table during his cross-examination of Dennis Seaman.

"Did he confide in you at all that he may have had an affair with Julie Dumbleton?" Larry asked.

If the idea of an affair might have shocked some people—the Dumbletons, top of the list—it wasn't a particularly shocking notion to Dennis Seaman, any more than it shocked him that his brother might have called his wife "bitch" on a Post-it note when, in his opinion, she most definitely was one.

"I asked him flat out, had he had an affair with Julie Dumbleton, and he said no," said Dennis. "I asked him flat out if Jenna Dumbleton was his daughter, and he said no."

On redirect examination, Lisa Ortlieb chose to revisit only a couple of questions.

"Why did you ask him if Jenna Dumbleton was his daughter?" Lisa asked Dennis.

"Just because at this point we were talking about what was going on, and he [Bob] had mentioned that Nancy was obsessed with this relationship."

Next on the stand for the prosecution was Marjorie Palmer, Bob Seaman's older sister, now age sixty-seven and living near her married daughter, Dawn, in Kansas. Ortlieb asked her about a conversation she had had with Bob on the afternoon of Sunday, May 9, 2004, when he called to wish her a happy Mother's Day.

"He was happy," she said. "Said he was feeling real good. He'd just spent a week in Arizona with our younger brother."

"Did he tell you anything about what his intentions were?"

"He said he was tired of all the fighting and that he was going to get a divorce. The marriage had been over for a long time. He'd told me that before."

And when he spoke of the divorce, how did he sound?

"He sounded relieved."

CHAPTER 32

"A Great Mother-Son Relationship"

—⟁— fter a break, the prosecution continued its case, calling Jeffrey Robert Seaman. He took the stand briskly. He did not look in the direction of his mother as he settled into his seat in the witness box. He gave his age as twenty-five, but despite his round, baby-faced countenance, something in the way he carried himself suggested a man significantly older. It was easy to see, within the first few moments of his testimony, how Jeff Seaman could rub some people the wrong way, without caring that he did. If there was a soft place in him, he wasn't about to go around displaying it.

"What was your relationship with your father like?" Lisa Ortlieb asked Jeff.

"My dad was my best friend in the whole world.

"He went to University of Missouri-Rolla. I went to University of Missouri-Rolla. He was an engineer. I became an engineer. . . .

"I would call him and talk about work, or talk about cars. He had classic Mustangs. I had classic Mustangs. We both loved working on cars. We both—we're really like home improvement nuts. Like, I'm finishing my basement now. He finished his whole basement."

His relationship with his mom had always been great too, he went on to say. He and his wife went to see her every Saturday. "I would always encourage them to go out and go shopping and do some damage to the credit card," he explained. "Anytime my mom needed anything, I always tried to help her out. . . . We had a great mother-son relationship."

Given the weight Larry Kaluzny had placed on Nancy Seaman's role as the fixer and the tool buyer (possessor of a Sears Craftsman Tool Club card) in the family, Lisa Ortlieb now asked Jeff, "Do you remember your mom ever buying the tools?"

"She would go with my dad to buy like Christmas gift tools for the kids maybe, but my dad would kind of pick it out.

"My dad was like Mr. Tool. I mean, he was the tool man. We used to joke about him being sort of like Tim Taylor from the show *Home Improvement* . . ."

Lisa asked Jeff if he had seen his mother with bruises. Yes, he had, he said.

"She had a bruise on one of her arms. . . . and she claimed that my dad had grabbed her by the arm. This was . . . the only time that we ever talked about any sort of domestic violence or abuse. My perception at the time, and what I still believe, was she was testing out her story for the upcoming divorce. I mean, it seemed like . . . she was figuring out what she was going to say at the divorce and trying to let us know basically this was going to be the route that she was going to go."

This had been the spring of 2004, Jeff told Ortlieb.

Lisa moved on then to the topic of stump removal. Had Jeff ever known his mother to do any stump removal in the yard?

No.

Anything with a hatchet?

No again.

Would it surprise him to learn that his mom had a Sears Craftsman Tool Card?

No. (Laughter here.) He had a tool card, his dad had a tool card. Becka had a tool card. His mom bought tools for Christmas presents. No big surprise she'd have the card. But as for being a major tool user: "She had a yellow and black tool box that she kept in the pantry that had, like, a hammer, tape measure, Phillips screwdriver, a flathead screwdriver, some picture hangers.

"I mean, she could hang a picture and pound a nail into a wall. But you know, she wasn't actively taking on construction projects or anything."

He described his trip to the house on Briarwood Court Tuesday after work, and how he'd passed his mother on the road, but she hadn't seen him. He described how, to his surprise, he'd found that the mountain of trash that had been accumulating over the last year had finally been removed, though it had been there so long that "the whole garage did stink like garbage."

Inside the house, only one thing had seemed odd to him. "The window was broken in the downstairs basement, and it was broken from the outside in, because there was glass on the floor. And there was a vacuum cleaner next to where the glass was. . . . It hadn't been broken the last time I was over. And there was a rock on the floor. There was a box on the table, filled with broken glass.

"It looked," said Jeff, "like somebody had been cleaning up the window that had been broken."

In a voice startlingly absent of emotion, he told about getting the call from Scott Gardner the next day, to say that a body had been found in the back of an Explorer on Briarwood Court, and of how, rather than tell his wife what happened, he'd instructed her to turn the radio on.

Lisa Ortlieb asked Jeff to reconstruct a conversation he had with his father the previous fall, about how his mother never paid any of the bills for their home, and another conversation with his mother, held more recently, when she'd complained about his father not taking care of the mortgage for two months in a row, ruining her credit. Now, as a result, she would have to pay a higher interest rate on the mortgage for the condominium.

"I was so mad at your father I could have killed him if he was there," she told him. She was angry, that was for sure.

"Your mom would call your dad names, your dad would call your mom names?" Lisa asked Jeff.

"It went both ways," he said.

Larry Kaluzny—getting his shot now—wanted to know Bob Seaman's state of mind, back in 1995, after his firing from Borg Warner. Did Jeff notice any change in him after that?

"Not immediately. He bought an acoustic guitar and hung around the house a lot more." But not long after, Jeff explained, Bob bought into the Waterwheel Building previously purchased by Rick and Diane Cox.

Jeff went on to add, however, that Rick Cox was never a close friend of his father. When his parents left Michigan in the early eighties and moved to Indiana, he said, they never saw the Coxes. Later, when Bob and Nancy returned to Michigan, the two couples both owned boats at the Ford Yacht Club, and knew each other "somewhat" from there.

Did Jeff ever tell his mother that she could have a place at his home if she wanted?

"I told both my parents they were welcome to stay with me."

"Was it ever told to her in the context, 'If you need a place to go to immediately, you come to us'?"

"No, it was told as in, 'If you two ever have arguments and don't want to be around each other . . .' "

Larry Kaluzny pounded away at him: What about his father's drinking? What about his dad abusing medications? ("He took vitamin E. He had a pretty big vitamin drawer.") What about that nickname they had for Bob Seaman in their family—"Psycho dad"? (It was a joke, Jeff said, taken from an episode of *Married with Children,* when the father on the show was called by that name.) What about fistfights with Greg? . . . Bob kicking in a door . . . stealing Nancy's teaching certificate . . . having an affair with Julie Dumbleton? . . . Had Jeff written to his mother or attempted to see her in the months since her arrest? (No, he had not.) How about any concerns that his father might have been abusing children? (No again, with something resembling a chuckle thrown in. The judge, seeing this, did not appear amused.)

On the surface, as Nancy Seaman had evidently liked to remind herself and others, this had been an enviable family living out a form of the American Dream, with a big house and an expensive gas-fired barbecue, big SUVs in the driveway, season tickets to the Tigers, a 401K plan socked away. But for all the family get-togethers at Applebee's, the father-and-son times working on cars, the jokes about mall shopping trips where the women "did damage to the credit card," a sense of the Seaman family was already taking shape on day one of the trial as one in which lines were forever being drawn, sides taken, points scored, accusations and counteraccusations leveled, wounds (not, up until now, the deadly kind) incurred. As Jeff described the goings-on at Briarwood Court, a sense came across of something rotten infecting the life of this family, with a scent putrid as the garbage that had piled up in an ever growing mountain on those neatly laid black-and-white floor tiles. It was the stink of a decaying marriage, a desperately unhappy couple, no doubt creating considerable injury to their children in the cross fire.

"Did you see the Post-it notes?" Kaluzny asked Jeff.

"Yes."

"And there were notes, like, on the toilet paper?"

"I didn't see any notes on the toilet paper."

"Did the notes say, 'This is mine, bitch'?"

"I didn't read any notes that said 'This is mine, bitch.'"

"How many notes did you see?"

"I probably saw forty Post-it notes."

"Didn't that strike you as being a little strange?"

"It looked like somebody had a lot of free time."

Larry Kaluzny—still married to his original wife, who sat in the front row now, observing her husband at work (a woman who, it was safe to bet, was not accustomed to being called "bitch" by her husband)—was unlikely to have experienced anything like *Life with the Seamans* in his own tidy Bloomfield Hills homestead. To look at his son Todd—the spitting image of his father, on whose shoulder his hand now rested as the two conferred at the defense table—it was hard to imagine he ever called his dad "asshole," either.

"Do you feel that your mom was closer with Greg than with you?"

"No. I felt I was closer with my dad than Greg, but we were equally in good standing with my mom."

Jeff Seaman, saying these words, seemed to have positioned himself in the witness box in such a way as to ensure that his mother's face would be outside the range of his gaze. He almost reclined in the seat, as if relaxing with a beer—though there could have been nothing remotely relaxing about this moment for him.

If it had ever been the case that, as he suggested, he and his mother enjoyed a great relationship, those days were definitely over. Nancy Seaman had been shaking her head and rolling her eyes throughout her older son's testimony—passing hastily scrawled notes to Larry when something she heard in the testimony particularly incensed her, as it apparently often did. During Jeff's testimony, her face suggested that of a woman listening to the words of a political candidate who will not merely fail to earn her vote, but one she has been actively campaigning to defeat.

"You've said you've lost your best friend in this whole thing."

"Yes." Still, as he spoke, Jeff Seaman kept his blue eyes steady. And never looked toward the defendant.

"The person that you were closest to in the whole world," Larry added, by way of clarification.

"Except for Becka," said Jeff.

"You want to see your mother convicted in this case, don't you?" Larry asked Jeff.

"No," said Jeff, the flippant tone absent for once. "That doesn't fix anything, does it, Larry?"

On redirect examination—the opportunity for an attorney to attempt to clean up whatever damage might have been done to her case during cross-examination from the other side—Lisa Ortlieb returned to the question of Jeff's apparent failure to make contact with his mother since her arrest. Was it possible to call Nancy in jail, she asked? (No.) Had Nancy called him collect? (No.) How many letters had he received from her? (None.)

But there was a more potentially damaging fire to put out, and Lisa went for it. "Mr. Kaluzny also asked you something—'Did your mom tell you your dad was abusing kids?' And you laughed. Why?"

"Because he ran a kids' business. He ran a batting cage and coached a girls' softball team. Obviously he loved being around kids, otherwise he wouldn't have done those things."

"Did your dad accuse your mom of sending an anonymous letter typed on a computer to Compuware that he was abusing kids?"

"Yes. He showed me the note. It was a typed letter that said—"

"Objection," Larry Kaluzny interrupted. This was the first word the jury had heard that accusations had been made suggesting pedophilic behavior on the part of Bob Seaman, and as damaging to the prosecution as it might have been for the jury to hear it, the idea that his client had been the source of an anonymous letter was probably not the best way to introduce the concept, either.

Judge McDonald sustained the objection. The contents of the note would not be divulged, though it appeared that the defense had planted in the jury's minds the idea, at least, that maybe there had been more than a love of coaching softball on Bob Seaman's mind when he agreed to coach Jenna's team. They had heard now—obliquely at least—suggestions of two different varieties of sexual impropriety on Bob Seaman's part: the possibility that he'd been having an affair with Julie Dumbleton (age fifty) and the possibility that he'd had a thing for Jenna (age twelve).

As damaging as either of those allegations would have been to the jury's image of Bob Seaman were they to be proven true, there was something confusing in the way the defense appeared to be suggesting both scenarios at the same time. Men with a predilection for very young girls seldom took an interest in their mothers as well. It might be hard for Larry Kaluzny to sell both the Julie and Jenna Dumbleton stories to the jury simultaneously. It was not yet possible to see from their faces how they viewed Larry's suggestions. But the trial was just getting under way.

CHAPTER 33

Enter the Dumbies

Out in the hall during the break, those on the opposing sides of the case (Bob supporters, Nancy defenders) kept their distance from each other, though they shot each other wary or visibly hostile glances. Bystanders huddled and kept their voices low, as if fearful that someone on the other side might pick up some piece of valuable intelligence. The group of teachers was probably the most vocal—expressing again their indignation at what their friend was forced to endure.

"Anybody would do what she did, faced with a nightmare like that," said one of the teachers to her friend.

"Her husband was an animal," said another woman.

Lisa Ortlieb called a woman named Nichole Coughlin to the stand—the cashier at Home Depot who had sold Nancy Seaman the first hatchet. Her testimony was followed by that of Cheryl Krokos, who had been on duty at the Home Depot returns counter the night Nancy Seaman received the credit for the shoplifted hatchet.

The implication, from the testimony, was clear: by creating the appearance of having returned the hatchet she'd purchased on Mother's

Day, Nancy Seaman had attempted to remove the impression that she had premeditated the murder when she set out to purchase it that night. It was much better for the defense if Nancy could claim that the murder weapon had been an old hatchet that was simply lying around the garage.

Dick Dumbleton took the stand. After going through the story of how the Dumbletons had gotten to know Bob Seaman, Lisa asked Dick to describe his wife's relationship with Bob.

"She had a good relationship with him," said Dick, speaking, as always, in the quiet, level tone of a man whose definition of drama, up until recently, would have been "Bottom of the seventh, score tied, full count, runner on base, with Jenna on the pitcher's mound."

"Mr. Dumbleton," Lisa began gently. "Did even for a second throughout all the time you knew Bob Seaman, did you ever suspect something was going on with him and your wife, ever once?"

His voice was steady and firm, answering the question. "Absolutely not," said Dick.

"Did you know what [Nancy's] nickname was for you?"

"I think it was Dumbies."

It was striking to watch how two such radically different portraits could be painted of the same relationship. In one version—that of the prosecution—Bob Seaman was a treasured member of the Dumbletons' extended family: attending softball games with them, working with Dick on home improvement projects (here, too, there had been a basement renovation), helping Jake fix up an old car, taking Jenna Christmas shopping so she could pick out presents for her parents. In the defense version—as portrayed by Larry Kaluzny—the relationship was twisted, sick, filled with troubling sexual undertones. What was Jenna Dumbleton doing, sitting on Bob Seaman's lap? ("She sat on my lap, too," said Dick.) What did it mean, that Bob took Jenna shopping? Why didn't Julie get paid for her work at the Upper Deck? Why wasn't Bob paid for his help with the basement renovation?

In recent years, Nancy Seaman had evidently enjoyed making jokes about the Dumbies—about what she viewed as the pathetic cluelessness of Dick, the cuckolded husband, and the diabolical machinations of Julie as she attempted to take the place of Nancy in Bob Seaman's world. Here was a Brothers Grimm quality to this story, as Nancy spun it: with Jenna, the young temptress, and Jake, the pretender to the throne, weaseling his way into the basement of the Upper Deck in a shameless effort to usurp the position of Bob's true son, Greg, the rightful heir to the '89 Mustang and all the wonders of the Seaman kingdom. What could a man like Bob Seaman—worldly, brilliant, and a little flamboyant—want with a family as unsophisticated, and—let's face it—boringly wholesome as the Dumbletons?

The only explanation in the Nancy Seaman view of the universe was sex. (The part that didn't quite fit was where to put Dick Dumbleton in the scenario, given that he seemed to have had a close relationship himself with Bob Seaman. Not to mention the ever present Dumbleton children and even the Dumbleton dog.)

But if the notion were impossible for Nancy Seaman to fathom, that the Dumbleton family, and her husband, might simply enjoy each other, it might not have been all that hard for a jury to understand. Given the picture that was emerging in the courtroom of the Seamans' own home life, a person might have recognized easily enough the appeal for Bob Seaman of just hanging out at the Dumbletons' kitchen table and spending time with a couple of teenagers who were as likely to call him "asshole" as they were to start dealing marijuana at softball games or to open fire in their school cafeteria.

Five years into the friendship, in fact, Jenna and Jake still called Bob "Mr. Seaman." That's how their parents had raised them. It was a sign of respect.

CHAPTER 34

"Even My Dog Liked Him"

The next session of the trial, held December 2, began with the showing of a videotape: Nancy Seaman's shopping trips to Home Depot. She could be seen proceeding to the checkout, paying for her purchase (evidently the automated payment aisle confused her, so she found herself a live cashier), and from there, making her way out the door again. Her entire transaction, from the moment she entered the store to when she left, took less than ten minutes.

The tape of the purchase on May 9 was followed by a screening of the second tape, documenting the shoplifting episode and the return of the shoplifted hatchet. As in the first tape, Nancy Seaman would have come across as the most ordinary Home Depot shopper to anyone who encountered her that evening. Even now, in the courtroom, though her eyes were turned to the screen, Nancy Seaman appeared strangely unfazed by the sight of herself on tape, purchasing the murder weapon. She might have been watching the news.

When Julie Dumbleton's name came up in the newspaper reports on the Seaman case—as it had often—it was her western name that was printed, but now, as the bailiff called her to the stand, she was called Ye-ok, her Korean name, followed by Julie, her American middle name. She was dressed in a conservative suit, with a gold cross around her neck, and her shoulder-length hair turned under. She was a strikingly attractive woman, without appearing to have cultivated it, though events of the last year had taken a toll on her youthful appearance. (Nancy Seaman, in filing her affidavit seeking the PPO, had evidently guessed her age at almost a full decade younger than her real age, which was fifty.)

Approaching the stand, Julie Dumbleton did not look in Nancy Seaman's direction and seemed almost pained as she came within range of the table where the defendant sat. For her part, Nancy retained the cool, dispassionate gaze of one with no particularly strong feeling about the witness.

Once Julie was on the stand, Lisa Ortlieb led her through questions and answers about the early history of the friendship and the decision she'd made to help out with office work at the Upper Deck.

"On Saturday, December 15, 2001," said Julie, "[Nancy] went into the office [at the Upper Deck] . . . and knocked over all of my daughter's photographs."

Then had come the call to her home the following February, in which, Julie said, Nancy had threatened her and her son Jake with conspiring to take away Greg's Mustang.

"She said 'You better make sure you keep Jake away from that car. If you don't, I'll make sure that I will,'" said Julie.

"She . . . called us 'the God-damned Dumbleton family.' She also said 'If you're thinking about calling Bob to whine, I'll' . . . something about 'fucking ass . . . got that girl?'" Julie had all of this documented, she explained. From this point on, she had kept extensive notes.

"Anything happen after that?" Lisa asked Julie.

"The following Thursday, February 21, 2002, . . . she went into the office and stole one of my daughter's photographs."

"Why do you say that?"

"Because Jake called me from there." One of the stolen photographs had shown up later in the dumpster, Julie said.

After that, Julie said, she tried to stay away from Nancy. Then came the incident the previous November, when Nancy had accused Julie of hitting her and breaking her fingernail, and filed the assault charges.

The last time Julie and her family saw Bob was on Mother's Day. He had just come back from his week in Arizona with his brother. Jenna was umpiring a softball game, and Bob had stopped by the ball field to watch her ump.

"Do you remember what he was wearing?" asked Lisa.

"Either a navy blue or a dark polo shirt and khaki shorts, white socks, and a brand new pair of black shoes, and a gold chain around his neck." Apart from the chain, these had been the clothes on Bob Seaman's body when it was found in the back of the Explorer several days later.

"He was very happy," Julie said of Bob's mood that day.

"Did he indicate whether he was going to be filing for divorce?"

"Yes, he did. Right after Greg's graduation."

Lisa asked Julie if she had noticed anything when she had gone to the Upper Deck the next day, Monday.

"His Franklin planner was on the desk," she said. "It was left open. And the automatic coffeemaker was on, with hot water for his tea."

"Is it unusual for his planner to be there?"

"He took it with him wherever he went," said Julie.

She ran through the next few days—her concern for Bob's well-being, and her efforts, with her husband and son, to look for him. More strongly than anyone else, perhaps, Julie had understood from the first that something was terribly wrong. It was her belief that something might have happened to Bob that had inspired her to re-move from Bob's office at the Upper Deck the "Nancy Crap File," which Lisa Ortlieb now placed into the record as People's Exhibit 44, containing Nancy's letters to Bob, Bob's letter to Nancy, and a selection of Post-it notes he'd written to her.

Lisa's final question to Julie might have seemed like an odd one. She asked, first, when the last time had been that Julie had seen Nancy Seaman, before that day in court. November 7 of the previous year, said Julie. The day of the alleged assault.

"And does she appear to weigh the same now as she did back in November?" said Lisa.

"No," said Julie. "She's lost a lot of weight."

It was not entirely clear what the relevance of this information might be, but perhaps the prosecution was suggesting to the jury that the small woman on trial before them that day had not been quite as small when she swung the hatchet at her husband's head back on Mother's Day.

"Mrs. Dumbleton," Larry Kaluzny began. "How would you describe Bob's relationship with the family?"

"He was like another parent to my children," said Julie.

"He was closer to Jenna than Jake. Is that a fair statement or not?"

"He was close to them both."

"And apparently [Jenna] liked him from what you observed."

"Very much. Even my dog liked him."

"Now, isn't it true that you encouraged Bob to leave Nancy?"

"Absolutely not."

"He used to stay overnight at your house, correct?"

"Absolutely not."

"He stayed overnight at the Upper Deck?"

"Yes."

"And you were aware of that?"

"Yes."

"Did he do that often?"

"Yes he did."

"He used to go with the baseball team that your daughter played on."

"Softball team. Yes."

"Out of town?"

"Yes."

"And where would you go out of town?"

"Different places. Toledo. Cleveland. Marian, Wisconsin. The nationals one year was in Virginia. The next year it was in Atlanta."

"Some of these trips would be more than one day?"

"Yes."

"Were you aware that there was a rumor that maybe you were having some kind of affair with Robert?"

"Yes, I was aware of that." Julie looked Larry Kaluzny square in the eye.

"On these trips, would your husband go at times or not?"

"When Jake had a tournament, he didn't go. When Jake didn't, he went."

"So obviously you had spent a lot of time out of town with Robert and the family?"

"With Robert and all the team members and all the other coaches and their parents."

It wasn't difficult to see where Larry Kaluzny was trying to go with his questions, but a motel filled with softball players and their parents wouldn't have seemed a likely site for a torrid extramarital affair between the mom who subscribed to *Christian Woman* magazine and kept score at games and the coach whose favorite pastime was rehashing plays in girls' softball games over pizza with the team parents.

Maybe Larry Kaluzny himself sensed that. He moved on to the question of Bob Seaman's prescription medications—Zocor, for his heart—and whether or not he was "drinking pretty heavily."

"He liked to drink," said Julie. "I wouldn't say heavily."

Then came the issue of Bob's relationship with his son Greg, the fight over the Mustang leading up to an argument with Greg that had marked the beginning of the alienation between father and son.

"You didn't tell [Bob] 'You were right to throw him out of the house?'"

"I sent Greg an e-mail telling him his father loved him and there are always two sides to every story and to think about it."

"Isn't it true that Nancy begged you to stay out of the family's problems?"

"She never said that. When she called me, she threatened me."

"Threatening you because you were interfering with the family's problems, right?"

"She threatened me because she thought we were conspiring to get—to take Greg's car, which we did not."

"When you talked about the pictures that you put in the Upper Deck, you used the frames that Nancy had her family pictures in, and you took the pictures out of the frames that she had there and put your family in those frames, correct?" he asked.

No, Julie answered. She had not substituted her family's photographs for those in Nancy Seaman's picture frames.

"What did you do with the frames where the pictures were?" asked Larry.

"She stole my picture frames thinking that they were hers. She had a picture frame that had a "Number One Dad" card in it. She thought I was using that frame. But that frame was on the top shelf. Bob even took it home and . . . showed it to her. I did not use her frame." The episode, examined in so much depth, had begun to take on an almost comical overtone. It sounded like the kind of feud a couple of junior high school girls might get into over something like a bottle of nail polish or a pair of shoes.

"What did you do with the frames of the pictures that were there that you changed?"

"I didn't change anything."

Had Julie attended the Dream Cruise with Bob? (Yes. With her family.) Had she and Bob driven downriver, to Brownstown, to take a look at the condo development where Nancy's secret condo was located?

(Yes.) And would Jenna "sit on his lap all the time"? (Yes.) And Bob would not only coach Jenna's team but watch her when she served as an umpire? And go to her school for events sometimes? (Yes on all counts.) That certainly sounded like an unusual amount of togetherness.

Lisa Ortlieb, when it was time for redirect examination of the witness, went right to it. "Did you have a relationship with Bob that was ever intimate?" Lisa asked Julie.

"Never," said Julie.

"You knew that the defendant called you the Dumbies?" Larry Kaluzny wanted to know, when it was his turn once again.

Yes, said Julie, she did.

"Did you know that your husband had a nickname too?"

"I think she called him 'Pathetically Weak.'"

"How about 'whipped,' 'whoosed,' or 'pussy'?" asked Larry.

Lisa Ortlieb had one final question for Julie Dumbleton too.

"Right before we broke for lunch," she asked Julie, "Mr. Kaluzny asked you if the defendant had a nickname for your husband. Did the defendant have a nickname for her own husband, Bob Seaman?"

"Yes. She called him Mole Man," said Julie. "Because he lived in the basement."

CHAPTER 35

"It's a Scent I'm Familiar With"

W ith the completion of Julie Dumbleton's testimony, the prosecution moved on to the law enforcement officers responsible for the Seaman investigation.

First up was Lieutenant Saad, one of the two policemen who'd paid a visit to the Seaman home in response to the initial missing person report, who recalled telling his partner "This is like the cleanest garage I've ever seen."

Next came Detective Al Patterson, describing his visit to Briarwood Court on the afternoon of May 12—the visit that had led to the discovery of Bob Seaman's body in the back of the Explorer. For a man who dealt, on a regular basis, with the darker side of human behavior, Detective Patterson maintained a surprisingly mild demeanor. Now he walked the jury through his inspection of the Seaman home that day, almost as if it had been a visit to Mr. Rogers' Neighborhood—describing his search like a hide-and-seek game in which someone is calling out "You're getting warmer."

"I was finishing looking around in the basement," he said. "Nancy had gotten more and more agitated and said she had to get going.

"At one point, while I was still looking in the basement, she turned the lights off on me. Then she quickly turned them back on and said she was sorry, but then turned them right back off again."

"What did you do when the lights were off?" Lisa asked Detective Patterson.

"I was pretty much done anyway at that point," he said. "We walked upstairs and out the front door. . . . At that point, we asked if we could look in her vehicle, the 1995 Ford Explorer.

"I started to notice a slight odor of a decomposing body," he continued, of his examination of the vehicle.

"Unfortunately," said Detective Patterson, "it's a scent I'm familiar with."

The prosecution called Officer John Piggot, an evidence technician with the Farmington Hills Police Department, who had worked with Officer John Markey and the evidence tech team on the laborious but crucial process of examining the crime scene.

Officer Piggot's responsibility had been taking the precise measurements necessary to ascertain the position of the victim and his assailant at the time the injuries were incurred, the angle from which the hatchet had entered the skull, the force with which it had been wielded—all of which were determined largely on the basis of the blood spatters still visible, though only faintly, despite Nancy Seaman's aggressive cleaning efforts. In addition to examining the walls and ceiling, Officer Piggot and his crew had also gone over every centimeter of Greg Seaman's 1998 Mustang fastback, which had been parked lengthwise in the garage on the day of the murder.

"It appeared as if the vehicle had been wiped down with a wet rag," said Officer Piggot. "You could see the faint red tint, which we believed was blood which had been wiped from the vehicle . . . smeared across the hood."

There was more. A series of photographs submitted as People's Exhibits 111 through 129 detailed the traces of blood and tissue the officers had detected on the car—on the taillights, rear left wheel, the rear driver's-side tail lamp, across the hood. Four hair samples were found stuck to the back of the Mustang in the vicinity of the rear tail lamp, and a tissue sample was taken from the back of the vehicle and the grille. The final photograph—Exhibit 129—showed a single blood spatter in the center below the trunk lid along the back of the vehicle, directly above the label of the car—the spot displaying the word "Mustang."

In addition to the spatters on the car and walls, there was evidence of blood spatters on the ceiling of the garage, and not only on the floor tiles but on the cement beneath them. The quantity of blood from Bob Seaman's body that had spilled out into parts of the Seaman garage and under the tiles had evidently been considerable.

Now it was cross-examination time. "If I said to you that a hose was used and there may have been some splashing, are you able to say, yes, that could have happened; or no, I can't tell; or no, it didn't happen?" Larry Kaluzny asked Piggot.

The answer came swiftly, and it was not what the defense would have wished to hear.

"I would . . . have to say that the concentration of the blood, to me, would not suggest that it had been watered down and then carried by another fluid."

In other words, any blood that had landed high on the walls or ceiling of the Seaman garage did so by the sheer force of the impact from the wound, and the gushing of the blood from the wound itself. It did not seem possible that this could have occurred if the person inflicting the wound had done so from a position on the floor of the garage, where—as the defense wanted the jury to believe—she had crouched, cowering, in fear for her life.

CHAPTER 36

Just a Man Who
Loved His Daughter

———

On the afternoon of December 2, following the testimony of Officer Piggot, the prosecution rested its case. It was now time for Larry Kaluzny to call his first witness, Eugene D'Onofrio, father of the accused.

With a quick glance in the direction of his daughter, D'Onofrio made his way to the witness box. He adjusted his suit jacket and stared out at those assembled in the courtroom with the look of a man who had somehow gotten on the wrong bus and now, a couple of hundred miles down the highway, has awakened to realize he's lost.

Kaluzny asked if he had ever worked for Bob Seaman. Yes, for approximately three weeks, sometime after his retirement from his job as a school custodian.

"Can you tell me whether or not Bob Seaman had a reputation for any violence or temperament?" Kaluzny asked.

"Yes, he was violent."

"Are you talking about his reputation for violence?"

"His reputation. Yes."

"Did you ever see him physically abuse Nancy?"

"I never seen him abuse her, no."

"Did you ever see any marks on Nancy?"

"Yes I did. Back in November of '03."

"And what . . . did you observe?"

"I observed she had a black eye. She had marks on her arms and legs."

"Where was she when you observed these things?"

"She came over to my house."

"Now, were there any other times where you saw any injuries on her?"

"Well . . . let me think for a minute. I would say yes. . . . It was . . . just before my wife passed away."

"And what year would that have been?"

"December of '03."

They moved on then to the purchase of the condo, and Eugene's decision to give Nancy $10,000 for the down payment, and Nancy's request that he and her sons say nothing about the condo to Bob.

"It took place in—let's see—January, February—I believe it was February '04," said D'Onofrio.

"Was a reason given why Bob shouldn't be told?" Kaluzny asked D'Onofrio.

"Because he would probably explode if he found out."

"Was she afraid of what he would do?"

Oh yes.

Lisa Ortlieb had a difficult task as she approached Eugene D'Onofrio to begin her cross-examination. No question, her goal was to discredit his testimony and challenge the credibility of the witness. But he was also an old man who had lost his wife less than a year before, and now here he was, watching his only daughter on trial for murder. The jury was not likely to look kindly on a prosecutor who chose to hammer a senior citizen when he was down.

She started gently. "You love your daughter very much, right?"

"You better believe it." His answer came back almost defiant.

"You have not been very happy with the situation she's in, correct?"

"Right."

"Now, knowing that, when's the first time you told anyone in law enforcement about the fact you saw your daughter with—I believe you testified—a black eye?"

"I didn't tell law enforcement. I saw it when she came over to my house."

"OK. Do you remember coming to the police department on Thursday, May 13, at 1:45 in the afternoon?"

"Yes, I remember that."

"Do you remember Detective Al Patterson, the man sitting right in front of you?"

He remembered.

"And you were concerned and you wanted to know what was going on, right?"

"I wanted to know."

"He asked you, 'Have you ever seen any evidence of domestic violence?' Do you remember that question?"

No response from Eugene D'Onofrio.

"'Has your daughter ever told you of any domestic violence issues?' Do you remember that question Detective Patterson asked you?"

Yes.

"Do you remember what your answer was?"

"I—" He sat there. She wasn't interrupting him. He just didn't have an ending to that sentence.

Now Lisa Ortlieb supplied it. "That you had never seen any evidence of any domestic violence."

"Now, do you remember on November 24th, having a conversation with a Don O'Chandleus, an investigator for the prosecutor's office?"

"I may have, yes." Eugene was on to Lisa Ortlieb now, from the sound of things. From now on, he was going to give himself a little margin for error.

Now came the moment when Lisa Ortlieb would collect on all those hours she'd spent listening to the taped conversations from Oakland County Jail between Nancy Seaman and Greg, and with her father. Evidently Nancy had discussed the Don O'Chandleus interview with her father in advance, and while there was nothing illegal about that, some of what had been recorded in those conversations reflected on her case now.

"Your daughter . . . when this happened, she sent you a list of things to remember, correct?"

"She told me there's some things to remember."

"And she wrote you a letter, too, of things to remember, right?"

"She may have."

"Can I see that letter that she told you to—"

"I don't have it with me. No."

"So she did tell you that a private investigator was going to come meet with you and you should not show him that list?"

"I can't recall offhand."

"Do you remember your daughter saying, 'Do you remember that paper I sent you a long time ago with those things you needed to remember? I hope you still have it. You don't need to give it to him. Don't even show it to him. That's just for you'?"

"I may have heard that."

"Who did you share that paper with?"

"I didn't share it with nobody."

"Do you remember that your daughter said, 'You need to remember that in January I . . . told you I needed to get out and I might need to get out fast. That was January and that's when you gave me the money. And in February we all went to put the money down on the condo. Those are the important dates'?"

"Yes."

Lisa wasn't finished yet. She was reminding Eugene D'Onofrio now that Nancy Seaman had had more to say to him, more reminders about what to tell the investigator. She was quoting, again, from Nancy's telephone conversation with her father from jail.

"Do you remember your daughter talking to you about what you should say under oath if I asked you how come you didn't say you knew anything about domestic violence?"

"When was this?"

"It would have been November 10th, this year, at 7:34 in the evening. She called you collect quite often, right?"

"Yes, she did."

"Thirty-one times since she's been in?"

"She calls me on occasion."

"Thirty-one times."

"To see how I was doing." He wanted people to understand what a considerate person his daughter was. Anyone looking at his face could see him trying hard to get that across. And knowing it wasn't going as well as he wanted it to.

"Do you remember what she told you you should say if I asked you why you didn't tell Detective Patterson about domestic violence?"

"I don't recall."

"Would this tape refresh your memory?" Lisa Ortlieb tossed her long, wavy hair as she moved over to the tape recorder and inserted the cassette. Any impression Eugene D'Onofrio might have had before, that she was just a sweet and pretty Michigan girl having a heart-to-heart with him about all the hard times he'd been through this year, was long gone now. She might as well be sticking a knife between his ribs as playing that tape.

The jury heard Nancy's voice now, coming from the tape recorder: firm and sharp, less like a daughter talking with her elderly father than a schoolteacher, at the close of a particularly stressful day, perhaps, at the end of her rope with a difficult student.

"If the police ask you how come when they interviewed you when this happened you didn't say anything, cause they asked you if you knew anything about domestic abuse, all you have to say is you were in shock—"

The jury was listening hard to this. Several of them leaned forward in their seats, so as not to miss a word.

"—because you know, you thought I didn't do it? Remember how concerned I was it was that manager he was blackmailing was going to kill him? That man embezzled money from the Upper Deck. . . ."

Lisa Ortlieb shut the tape player off.

"Yes, I remember that," he said.

But there was more.

"Do you remember," she asked him, "having a conversation with Don O'Chadleus, the investigator from the Oakland County Prosecutor's Office, where he called you November 24th of this year? And do you remember telling—did your daughter tell you that . . . [Bob] threatened not only to kill her but he was going to go to your house and then kill you, too?"

"That's right," said Eugene. "He did."

"And [Bob would] take everything you owned."

"Right."

"And who told you that?"

"My daughter told me that her husband told her that."

"That he was going to kill her and then go to your house and kill you?"

"That was after this violence in—I believe it was the garage that they were in."

"And she told you that she wrapped him in what?"

"In a carpet or something like that."

"Did you tell Investigator O'Chadleus that you didn't understand how she could do it? How she got him in the Explorer?"

"She lifted him up and put him in there."

"Do you remember asking your daughter, 'Well, how could you pick him up, because he weighed twice as much as you?'"

Here was the question that had baffled everyone. From his silence, it appeared that Eugene D'Onofrio didn't have an answer to this one either.

"Do you remember her response was, she said she didn't know how she did it?"

"That's right."

"Is your daughter pretty strong?"

"I would say she is, for a small—you know she's a small girl."

Larry Kaluzny approached Eugene now.

"Sir, how old are you?" he asked.

"I'm eighty years old."

"Have you had any problem remembering things?"

"Once in a while, yeah. And of course many things have happened to me."

"Your wife died recently."

"That's right. That's when things started to happen."

"When the police talked to you about domestic violence, do you know what domestic violence is?" asked Kaluzny.

"Somebody kills somebody, I guess."

Did he ever lie intentionally, here in the courtroom or to the police? Larry Kaluzny asked.

"I don't lie," said Eugene. "I don't lie to anybody."

He was allowed to step down then. Court adjourned for the day, as D'Onofrio, in his good brown jacket, made his way back to his seat.

CHAPTER 37

A Loyal Brother

John D'Onofrio, younger brother of the accused, had come to testify, with his wife, Barb, and their two teenage sons, from their home just outside Cincinnati, Ohio. A compact person like his sister and father, John approached the witness box with an air of cautious defiance—shoulders thrust back, back stiff. In his younger days, he'd enlisted in the army and gone to Vietnam, though given his age—forty-seven—he must have been among the very last to have done so.

All these years later, there was still something of the Vietnam vet about him: a wariness, maybe—the air of a man on the alert for trouble.

"What kind of contact have you had with Nancy over the years, John?" Larry Kaluzny began.

Almost every month or two months, he said, they'd get together, either in Michigan or Cincinnati.

"Any response when you would hug her?"

"Most of the time she'd pull back or wince."

There had been more, too. "I seen a black eye, bruised-up face, marks on her hands." The first time had been two, maybe two-and-a-half years ago, he said. "The more I visited, the more and more things you would see."

More than one black eye?

"I seen the covering up of a black eye with makeup and stuff. I knew something was there."

"Did you see any other injuries?"

"Marks on the forearm." He'd seen those, he explained, when she was washing dishes at their parents' house and rolled up her sleeves to keep them from getting wet. She had told him, "Well, I bumped into the door," or she'd banged into a table. "She never looked me in the eye," John D'Onofrio added.

"And how would you describe the relationship [between Bob and Nancy] as you observed it?" Kaluzny asked him.

"Bob was extremely controlling," said John D'Onofrio. "He would just bust out in violent anger sometimes."

And what, Larry asked John, was Bob's reputation for anger and violence?"

"Arrogant. Controlling. Violent."

Lisa Ortlieb approached the witness box for the cross-examination.

"You've known Bob for . . . many years, right?" she asked John.

"Many years."

"In fact, he helped you with your house in Ohio, right?"

No response.

"Helped you remodel it?"

"Not exactly, but he was there."

"What year was that?"

Once again, no response.

"September of 2003?"

"Yes."

"Okay. This person that you said is extremely controlling, bursts out in violence, arrogance, do you remember, you've given him some pretty nice gifts throughout the years, haven't you?"

"It was usually after we had our little arguments, yes."

"What kind of gifts would you give Bob?"

"Mainly tools."

"Special tools that were hard to find?"

"Not particularly hard to find."

"What's the nicest tool you gave him?"

"I would say an air-cutter for restoring cars, cutting body panels off, that kind of stuff." John D'Onofrio—unlike his father, perhaps—seemed well aware, as he said this, that what he was telling the court wasn't helping his sister any.

"Did you ever give your sister any information about domestic violence shelters or domestic violence help information?"

"No."

"Never called the police and asked for help for her?"

"No."

"When was the first time you told anyone in law enforcement about this—the marks you've seen on her?"

"Law enforcement never contacted me."

"Did you know there's an officer in charge and a prosecutor on this case?"

Nobody ever contacted him, John D'Onofrio said.

So the first time anyone in law enforcement ever heard his account of black eyes, bruises, and pain so great that his sister winced when he hugged her would be now?

"Yes."

When it was Larry Kaluzny's turn for redirect examination of the witness, he had only a few more questions for him. Wouldn't John have told the police about the abuse he believed to have taken place if they had just asked him?

"Absolutely. I assumed they had my name."

Kaluzny returned to the topic of gifts, then. Had John D'Onofrio given presents to Nancy?

He had, of course. A cordless drill set. A decorative colored box. And for her anniversary, a pair of engraved champagne goblets.

Those who sat on the Bob Seaman side of the courtroom might have called this an odd gift for a brother to give a sister to share, presumably, with the brother-in-law he now said he saw as a violent, explosive abuser, who—in his family's view at least—suffered from a drinking problem.

CHAPTER 38

The Boy You Want
Your Daughter to Go
Out With, Maybe

Except for their beautiful eyes, there seemed to be not a single physical trait shared by Jeff Seaman and his brother Greg—a fact few could have failed to observe watching Greg take the witness stand now, with the memory still fresh of his older brother's testimony the day before.

Where Jeff—like his father—exuded an exaggerated macho toughness, Greg conveyed an almost feminine softness. Perhaps he had supposed that the dark suit he wore might give a certain heft to his appearance or make him appear older than his twenty-three years, but it had the opposite effect. His body seemed lost inside his clothing. Who he might remind a person of—though the image would probably not have come to the minds of this particular jury—was David Byrne in the Talking Heads movie, *Stop Making Sense,* when he wears the comically oversized suit and (looking for a moment like a businessman) launches into "Psycho Killer."

But this was no rock and roller taking the stand. This was a young man mothers all over Farmington Hills would want their daughters to go out with: clean-cut, well spoken, well mannered, polite, and above all, devoted to his mom. (It was too late for their daughters, though, as he explained at the beginning of his testimony. Greg Sea-man had recently become engaged to his longtime Purdue girlfriend, Kristin Sears.)

How did he and his brother Jeff get along? Kaluzny asked Greg. Not very well, Greg told him, until recently.

"Six months ago," he said (though he must have had his timetable off, because six months ago he had been conferring with his mother about taking Jeff's name off her visitor's list) "we started getting very close."

"We started bonding," he continued, "over the fact that my father was mentally deteriorating."

"How would you describe that change?"

"It was . . . a slow degradation. It all started when he got fired from his job."

That would be the Borg Warner job, seven or eight years back?

"He started making financial decisions that normally he wouldn't have made. He started losing a lot of money and kind of gambling on investments. . . . He would lose his temper a lot more quickly than be-fore. He was a lot more irritable. You could tell he was getting stressed out at the fact that he had been fired and he couldn't find work and that all of his business investments were going south."

There had been "heart complications," Greg said. His father went on medication.

"Did you observe any abuse . . . between your mom and your dad?"

"Almost constant verbal abuse, all the time. He would constantly belittle my mother, her profession, all the choices that she made. And there was also physical abuse that I personally observed. . . . I saw him hit her with his forearm, just kind of shove her out of the way."

"Did you ever talk to your mom about any abuse of any kind?" asked Larry Kaluzny.

"There was a time when her hand was smashed up pretty good, and it was wrapped up. And I asked her what happened. She told me, 'It was your father. He threw a chair.'"

Had this episode caused problems in Greg's relationship with his dad? Larry asked.

"Yes. I had called him on his cell phone and I asked him . . . why he did that."

Greg had threatened to call the police, he said. His father had stayed away for a while after that. But a few months later, Greg had spoken to his father again about his treatment of Nancy. This would have been a year before the murder, more or less.

"It was at a restaurant, and he started yelling at her, and mom went to the restroom and she was crying. And I said, 'I can't believe you treat your wife this way. This is despicable.' And ever since then . . . we were a bit more distant. I think he had a problem with me telling him how his marriage should be."

Kaluzny asked Greg what he had thought that day in May, when he had been returning from his trip to Florida with his college friends and got a message on his cell phone suggesting that something terrible had happened back in Michigan.

"My first thought was that my dad killed my mom and that he probably killed himself."

"Why did you think that?"

"The situation was just getting . . . scarier by the day. And we were all so excited that she was moving out."

His mom had a talk with him and his brother after she put the money down on the condo, he explained. "She said 'Listen boys, you cannot tell your father about this. He will kill me.'"

"Greg, what was your mom's reputation for truthfulness?" Kaluzny asked him.

"She's got a reputation for being very honest and very caring and very loving."

"Do you know of your dad's reputation for honesty and truthfulness?"

"He had a reputation for being kind of a wild, violent brawler."

How did Greg know this?

"A lot of friends that he had worked with would tell stories about my father, and he told me himself about his younger days and getting into bar fights."

"And how would you describe things that your mother did around the house?"

"She did everything. Everything to do with the maintenance of a typical yard and the house, including patching drywall, doing all the yard work. Pretty much everything that goes wrong with a house . . . or when the furnace went out she'd get the repair people there."

"Were you aware whether anybody in your family belonged to the Sears Craftsman Tool Club?"

His mom again. "We had made a joke about it several years back. That there were three mechanical engineers, and she was the one with the tool card. So we would also go to her to buy tools."

And who did the yard work in the family? Kaluzny asked.

"That was all my mom," Greg replied. "She would mow the grass. She would take care of the weeds. She would cut down branches. There was a lot of growth towards the back yard that she would take care of. There was gardening. She had flower beds all around the house."

He recalled for the jury now the Post-it notes around the house and his father's habit of kicking in doors when he got upset. Then it was time to consider the question of the Dumbletons.

"And what kind of relationship did you have with them, if any?" Larry Kaluzny asked Greg.

"They were kind of a cancer on our family."

"Why do you say that?"

"They wouldn't leave my dad alone. A number of times we had told them, 'Leave us alone.' And 'My dad's never around. We want to hang out with my dad. We want him to be around, and you guys are taking up all his time.'"

As Lori Brasier of the *Detroit Free Press* noted, watching his testimony, "It was as if his son believed Bob Seaman had no free will of his own." Greg apparently subscribed to a view of Bob Seaman's powerlessness similar to that of his mother, with regard to the Dumbletons. They had stolen him away from his rightful family, and to hear Greg tell it, Bob himself had been no more capable of escaping their grasp than a kidnap victim.

"Did you ever give your mom any advice about divorce?" Larry asked Greg.

"I was very adamant in telling her that she needed to leave my dad because the situation was growing horrible."

"Did she respond?"

"She would respond in her typical way by saying, 'You know, I'm just going to give it one more chance. I'll give him one more chance.'"

From the expressions on their faces, the jury appeared to look favorably on this young man sitting upright in his big suit, his Adam's apple protruding from a neck that did not fill out the collar of his shirt, ears sticking out more even prominently than they might have, had he not been sporting what looked like a fresh haircut, schoolboy neat. All in all, Greg Seaman could have been working one of those summer jobs young men sometimes take in college, selling knives or air purifiers or magazine subscriptions door to door to finance their education, earnestly explaining the advantages of his product, with his commission on the line. If he had been, he would have done well.

He looked a person in the eye. His tone was direct, not overly emotional, but totally lacking in the disconcerting flippancy his brother had seemed to display on the stand earlier.

Now Larry Kaluzny asked what happened between Bob and Greg when the two had a disagreement.

"He would always say, 'Get out.' "

"He threw you out of the house one time, didn't he?"

"Yes."

"Told you not to come back?"

"Yeah."

It was Lisa Ortlieb's turn. As she had with John and Eugene D'Onofrio, she asked Greg when he had first informed the police about his observations concerning his father's alleged abuse of his mother. As with his grandfather and uncle, the answer was, never before now.

She asked about the money from his father's 401K plan, that he'd liquidated. He was using it for his mom's expenses, he said.

"And who's the power of attorney for your mother?"

"I am."

"And who's the beneficiary of her will now, solely?"

"I don't know that. I would assume that I am." Greg shot a look in the direction of his mother here, as he had been doing regularly from the start of his testimony.

Now Lisa asked him why he didn't like the Dumbletons.

"They were removing my father. . . . He was gone coaching little girls' softball almost every weekend." Something in the way he said this last—not "girls" but "little girls"—lent an unseemly air to Bob Seaman's coaching.

"You've said 'I had nothing to do with Jeff not visiting my mother in jail,' " Lisa Ortlieb now stated.

"That's correct."

"You've had many conversations with your mother since she's been in jail, correct?"

"Yes."

"And?"

"I encouraged her to take Jeff off the list, but she wouldn't listen to me. . . . but after a certain conversation, in which Jeff's stance on this became known, I told Mom, 'I don't think it's a good idea that you talk to Jeff.' "

"So it's a little bit different than what you just testified when you said 'I had nothing to do with taking—'"

"I had no control over who she put on the list and who she took off."

"Do you remember telling your mom, 'Jeff is not your friend. Jeff is evil'?"

"I probably mentioned it."

"OK. 'He's a greedy bastard'?"

"Certainly after working with a civil attorney with Jeff, I said that."

Next, Lisa asked Greg about a conversation he'd had with his mother, recorded on tape, in which the two of them had discussed the murder weapon.

"Your mom told you that the hatchet that she used . . . was not the hatchet she bought at Home Depot that day. She told you [it] was an old hatchet that she had in the drawer?"

"I think that's what she said."

"She said the hatchet that she bought on Mother's Day . . . she didn't use that hatchet to kill your dad."

"Could you say that again?"

"Did she tell you which hatchet she used to kill your dad?"

No response from the witness. Greg sat there.

"What did she tell you?"

"I honestly don't remember."

"Perhaps playing the tapes would refresh your memory," she told Greg.

Larry Kaluzny apparently understood the damaging effect of the tone of these conversations between Nancy and her son.

"Objection," he said.

After an argument from Lisa Ortlieb, Judge McDonald made the decision that certain portions of the tapes might be played for the purpose of refreshing the memory of the witness, but only after the jury had left the room.

Then came the voices of Nancy and Greg Seaman, discussing, with that same curiously dispassionate tone, the ongoing issue of which hatchet had been used to kill Greg's father.

When Lisa Ortlieb finished playing the excerpts of the jailhouse tapes, the jury was allowed to reenter the courtroom. She continued with her questioning of the witness, whose memory, presumably, was now refreshed.

"Do you remember which hatchet your mom told you . . . that she used to kill your dad?"

"At the time she said it was an old one that we've had."

"Do you remember her telling you that, 'There's another one in the drawer. We had two'?"

"Yeah."

"Did you say to her, 'Please tell me it was the old ax that we had in the garage for—like—ever'?"

"Yes."

"She told you the hatchet that she bought on Mother's Day, she returned that one, right?"

"Correct."

Now Larry Kaluzny was back, on redirect.

"In spite of all the problems you had," he asked Greg, "how did you feel towards [your father]?"

"I loved him," said Greg. "I mean, he was my father. We had an on again/off again relationship. But at no point do you ever feel that you're going to be off again."

Lisa Ortlieb, back in front of the witness box, had one more line from the jailhouse tapes to run by the witness now.

"Do you remember, when you talked about the fact that [Bob] didn't have a will, you said 'Your husband didn't have a will'?" No one needed to point out to the jurors that Greg Seaman had chosen the word "husband" as his way of referring to his father—chosen that word, on the very same day he'd first learned of the murder.

"I don't remember that phrase," he said. "But if you have it tape recorded—"

She did, of course. No further questions.

Greg Seaman made his way back to the bench behind his mother. Her eyes, so much like his, followed him.

CHAPTER 39

"It Looked Like a Regular Marriage"

W̲ith the completion of the crucially important testimony of Greg Seaman, Larry Kaluzny handed the baton over to his son Todd, for now anyway. Todd began with a brief, workmanlike debriefing of William Smith, the former principal of Longacre Elementary School, who had retired shortly after the arrest of Nancy Seaman. Smith recalled an occasion when he'd seen Nancy Seaman with a black eye and asked about how she had gotten it. Car door, she had told him, which made sense to Mr. Smith, he said, because the exact same thing had happened to him once.

Officer Craig Dersa, the Farmington Hills police officer who had transported Nancy Seaman from her home on Briarwood Court to the station following her arrest, reported that she had told him, "I need to take picture of my injuries." This had been taken care of. When asked by Lisa Ortlieb to describe the scratch on Nancy's hand that had been of particular concern to the defendant, Officer Dersa described it as "red in color . . . an inch or less in length. . . . It looked . . . just like a scratch you'd get on a daily basis from anything," he said.

The defense called Christine Brueck, one of the two other fourth-grade teachers at Longacre Elementary, who described herself as having worked closely with Nancy Seaman. She too remembered seeing the black eye and bruises over the years, as well as "some kind of arm brace." She recalled a discussion she had with Nancy and another teacher in late April of 2004, regarding a sex education presentation they were going to be giving to their students.

"[Nancy] opened the cabinet where the materials were because they were housed in her classroom. And she said, 'In case anything happens to me, here's where I keep all the materials.'"

Next up was Dennis Schleuter. After meeting in the engineering program at University of Missouri-Rolla, he and Bob Seaman had worked together at Ford Motor Company and saw each other every day, socializing once a month or so with their wives. Dennis and Bob had competed together in a race called the Howell Melon Run with Greg Seaman.

Todd Kaluzny asked Schleuter about Bob Seaman's reputation for aggression or violence. On occasion, Dennis recalled (when the two would "sit down and have a beverage together"), Bob would "brag about his younger days, getting in fights."

They had had a falling out a few years back, he said. This would have been after Bob was fired from Borg Warner, when Dennis was running a small engineering company. Bob had taken on some free-lance consulting work and needed a laboratory and some facilities to work in. He had called Dennis.

Dennis had agreed to make some kind of arrangement, evidently. But shortly after this, his business had folded. When Bob got back in touch to arrange for coming in to do the work, he had been upset to learn that Dennis had neglected to tell him about what happened. "He was mad and he hung up," said Dennis.

"I think Bob changed a lot when he was released from Borg Warner," Dennis observed.

". . . I was working and busy—and I didn't have the time that he did. He withdrew from our entire . . . circle of college friends."

Paulette Schleuter, Dennis's wife, described going out to lunch with Nancy Seaman in March of 2004. "She said she would leave [Bob] after Greg graduated from college," she said. "She did mention that Bob would have to divorce her, that she would not divorce him. . . . Her marriage and family were very important to her."

Todd Kaluzny asked Paulette to tell the court Nancy's last words, when the two women had parted after lunch that day. "Pray for me," she said.

Still on day two of the case, the defense continued (Todd at the helm again now) with yet another Seaman acquaintance from the old days, Rick Cox, Bob Seaman's partner in the Waterwheel Building and former Rolla classmate. Depending on who you asked, Rick was either Bob's closest friend over the years (as he represented himself to be) or someone Bob had simply known a long time, with whom he had financial dealings.

Now Cox offered his assessment of Bob Seaman's emotional state following his firing from Borg Warner.

"It's a very difficult time in anybody's life when you think you've done a great job and you've been fired. And I talked to Bob many times about trying to put that behind him. But it was tough for him. I suggested that he get counseling because he was not dealing well with having lost his job." But Bob had not taken Rick up on his suggestion, he said.

"Bob was a very bright engineer and had an awful lot to offer," Rick continued. "And he was not pursuing those avenues. He had many many contacts in the engineering field.

"I was observing a man basically lost in what he was trying to accomplish and not pursuing what he really knew how to do." He didn't say it, but the implication was plain enough: in Rick Cox's eyes, the batting cage and a life filled with girls' softball were a sad comedown.

In the early days, Rick said, Bob and Nancy had "what I would have considered . . . a regular marriage."

Later, though, after Bob lost his job, "there was less and less time spent at home. I didn't understand why. . . . I would observe him at midnight in my building when I would go home."

Bob "was explosive," Rick reported. "He had a reputation in school for not taking any guff off of anybody.

"If things did not go the way he wanted them to go . . . I many times stood before him with him yelling in my face with clenched fists," said Rick. He spoke in a tone that suggested he himself was not inclined to raise his voice. "Then I would wait until he was done and tell him that we would have to solve this in another fashion."

Did he know the Dumbletons? Larry Kaluzny asked Cox.

"Yes I did."

"Mostly I knew Julie," Rick added. "In fact, I did not know Julie had a husband for a number of years, because I never saw him."

"Were you aware of divorce plans between [Bob and Nancy]?" asked Kaluzny.

"I was. . . . About six weeks before this incident, he called me into his office and said, 'I'm divorcing Nancy.'

"And I said, 'Don't throw thirty some-odd years of marriage away. I can get you counseling.'"

"Did he respond to that?"

"He said, 'I will not go to counseling, and she will never get a part of my estate.'"

Lisa Ortlieb, when it came time for the cross-examination, had many questions for Rick Cox.

He had spoken of the Waterwheel Building as "my building." "That was actually part Bob's building, too, right?"

No response.

"He gave you a substantial amount of money for it?"

"I bought the building a year before he became involved. He came in and purchased 49 percent of the building."

Lisa asked what that 49 percent would be worth now, but Larry Kaluzny objected.

"You're working now with the defendant's power of attorney—correct?—with that building."

". . . At either my death or his, there was an automatic guaranteed buyout by the other party. It was all spelled out . . ."

Next up was Sherie Berg, the nurse who had conducted the physical examination of Nancy Seaman's body following her arrest. Under questioning by Larry Kaluzny, she described a number of bruises on the arms and legs of Nancy Seaman. Some discussion ensued regarding the severity of the bruises, which were not particularly impressive looking, at least as they came across in the photographs projected on the screen in the courtroom. Nurse Berg explained that different people bruised more easily than others, so it was impossible to determine from the appearance of a bruise how serious the event might have been that had brought it about in the first place.

A series of photographs (requested by the defendant) was submitted as evidence, showing the bruises on Nancy Seaman's body on the day of her arrest. When a photograph was submitted that showed

Nancy dressed only in her underpants with a piece of paper partially covering her breasts, Larry Kaluzny made the motion that the image not be projected on the screen in the courtroom as the others had been. The motion was granted.

When it was Lisa Ortlieb's turn to cross-examine the witness, Ortlieb brought up Nurse Berg's comment that at least a few of the bruises on Nancy Seaman's body had been "consistent with defensive injuries."

"You can't say for sure, is that correct?" she asked.

"Correct."

"Could it have been . . . from being on her hands and knees scrubbing a floor for hours?"

"It could be."

"Using soap and bleach?"

"Could be."

"Was it possible, by taking a long time taping and taping a body, rolling it over and over, and over and over again?"

"Um-hmm."

"Lifting?"

"Could be."

Several jurors scribbled notes at this point. If Larry Kaluzny had been hoping that Sherie Berg's testimony might bolster Nancy Seaman's claim of having been abused, it was just as likely, perhaps, that her remarks left the impression her injuries may have been incurred while covering up a murder.

CHAPTER 40

Ten Ways to Spot
a Battered Woman

From November 30, when the trial began, the jury had been hearing about Nancy Seaman. Now, finally, on December 5, the defendant would speak for herself, and there was no one in the room who didn't understand that how she came across was likely to affect substantially the jury's ultimate decision for a verdict of guilty or not guilty.

The jurors seemed, noticeably, to intensify their concentration as Nancy Seaman took the stand and was sworn in—wearing, as always, one of her neat suits. She wore a different one each day; the styles nearly identical, the colors varying. This time her suit was green, with a gold-colored turtleneck underneath. Her gray hair was pulled back in a bun, but her eyebrows remained black, and due in part to the application of makeup and the pronounced, almost theatrically exaggerated arch they had been given, they stood out even more prominently than they might have otherwise. With her large round eyes and small face, paler than ever after seven months in jail, her brows seemed to serve like exclamation points, rising dramatically when she spoke, as she began to now, in a voice that sounded firmer and more confident than anticipated.

Larry Kaluzny began his questioning gently, seeking the kind of answers a person doesn't have to think hard about to provide. How old was Nancy? When was her birthday? What kind of family did she come from?

Her parents had been married over fifty years, she said. She described her home as "very peaceful." "I never saw my parents fight," she said. "My father never raised his voice to me or my mother."

She had been valedictorian of her high school class in Lincoln Park, Michigan, and her dream had always been to become a schoolteacher, though she had not entered college until many years later. After high school graduation, she'd gone to work as a secretary at Ford Motor Company. That was where she met Bob Seaman. She had been twenty-one years old.

All through the relatively brief courtship, Bob treated her "like a queen," but two weeks after the wedding, she said, on a trip to Georgia for the wedding of his brother Dennis, he had abused her for the first time. He'd called her by his previous girlfriend's name, called her a whore and a slut, and ripped her gown. He'd had too much to drink, Nancy went on. She decided to leave him that night.

"I went to his mother and sister's motel room to get my wedding proofs," she said, "because my parents would have to pay the $250 if I didn't get them returned. . . . They calmed me down."

In the early years of her marriage, she continued, the abuse had been "sporadic"—once or twice a year, usually triggered by alcohol consumption.

But leaving was not an option. For one thing, she was a devoted Catholic. "My religion is very important to me," she said. "Family is everything for me because of my culture."

"Imagine the sacrament," she said. "You take a vow and it's for better or worse. That's how my parents raised me."

Then came the verbal abuse. "I was always the 'no good fucking bitch,'" she said. "That was my name, 'you no good fucking bitch.'"

Once or twice a year, however, there would be an incident of physical abuse as well—Bob would shove her or kick her, or throw something.

There was, as reporter Lori Brasier noted, a curious discrepancy here between the demeanor of Nancy Seaman, as she testified, and the story she told. Seaman sat up as tall in the witness chair as her five-foot-one-inch stature allowed. She spoke with self-assurance and an attitude bordering on impatience—an air that might, to some, have come across as self-righteousness.

"In the eighties I finally told myself I've got to take a stand," she said. "I told him if he ever put his hands on me again I'd call the police."

It was shortly after this that the incident with the coffee cup occurred in the car, as they were driving to St. Louis to visit Bob's family. When they got to her in-laws' house, she had made good on her promise and called the police. But when they came, she said, "Bob was very charming. He was a Vice President of Engineering for a major corporation. He had cousins on the St. Louis Police Force. He was a St. Louis homeboy, and here I was, this little homemaker, and Bob just . . . explained his way out of it. And I just stood there and felt more battered than I had when he battered me."

Things got noticeably worse, according to Nancy, around 1995 when, at the age of forty-one, she completed her degree and got her teaching certificate. Bob didn't think much of the idea of her becoming a teacher, she said.

"He would belittle me. He said . . . 'this is meaningless.' He was making six figures. He said a teacher is not going to ever make anything."

Very shortly after, Bob lost his job. "Suddenly his six figure income was gone, and I was the only income, the only health insurance. And throughout our whole marriage Bob's goal was to be CEO of this corporation. When he was fired that disappeared and suddenly my career was taking off. . . ."

The abuse intensified, she said. She "tried to run interference for my sons." She wanted the boys to love their father, no matter what. But eventually, Greg had figured out what was going on.

"He always looked for me when he came home from work," Nancy explained. "And he found me in the bedroom. I had just come back from the emergency room. My hand was wrapped. It was black, blue and swollen. I was crying. My arm was packed in ice. He saw me laying [sic] there all crumpled and crying and he said, 'Did Dad do this to you?' "

Recounting the conversation with her son and her son's support of her that day, Nancy made crying noises and dabbed at her eyes.

"I know this is hard for you," said Larry.

Nancy went on with the next chapter—Bob's curious decision to start the batting-cage facility. At first Nancy had helped him set up the business, she said. "I was always welcome at Bob's office. And then . . . after Julie started working there I wasn't welcome anymore.

"I was told by people that they were having an affair," Nancy said. She told the story then—her version—of coming to Bob's office and finding that picture frames that had originally held photographs of her sons playing baseball now displayed images of Jenna Dumbleton.

Once Julie Dumbleton and her family entered her husband's life, she said, he was never available to help Greg with his car or provide the kind of close father-and-son times she said Greg longed for. On Greg's birthday, she went on, Bob had called their younger son "an asshole" and threw him out of the house. Then "he took the car away and gave it to the woman he was . . . having an affair with, her son."

"Did you ever confront Julie about interfering with your family?" Larry Kaluzny asked Nancy.

"I called her. I begged her. I said, 'Julie, please, please don't create a wedge between my son and my husband.' I said, 'I don't want my family hurt like this. Not over a car, please. Just don't do this to my family. That's Greg's car. Just leave it alone. Surely you can buy your own car.'"

Here was a version of events that contrasted starkly with the account Julie Dumbleton had given. There was a contrast, too, between the words spoken by Nancy Seaman and her demeanor as she uttered them, the striking stiffness with which she recounted her story. The woman she portrayed in her telling—a plaintive supplicant, humbly begging her rival to take pity on her son and herself—bore little resemblance to the one Julie Dumbleton had described in the parking lot of the Upper Deck that day, sticking out her tongue.

With a strangely clinical detachment, Nancy went on to describe a series of physical confrontations with her husband: "If I asked questions, it was always bruising. Usually Bob would shove. That's what he liked to do, shove and push against walls. Most of my bruising is where either he would grab me by an article of my clothing or by an arm, he'd squeeze my arm, push me against the wall. Sometimes I'd get knocked down. That's why most of my bruises are arms and legs.

"Sometimes he'd use household objects, like he'd throw a chair," she said. "Or he'd throw objects."

One time at the emergency room, she told the court, she had planned to report an act of abuse, but a parent from her school had been there, so she'd remained silent. "I worked so hard for my career," she said. "I couldn't have something like this come out because parents would say 'My child might not be safe in Mrs. Seaman's room. What if her husband shows up at school?'

"I am a fifty-two-year-old woman. He beats me and he kicks me to the ground and spits on me. I can't let people know that."

One other time, however, in the summer of 2001, she had driven to the Farmington Hills Police Department to report an act of abuse after a fight, and talked to the officer at the front desk, but he had presented her with only two options: she could file a complaint and have her husband put in jail, or she could apply for a PPO.

"I said, 'There's got to be something in between, I can't put him in jail. I can't do that to my sons. I can't do that to my career.'"

According to Nancy, the officer had told her there were no other options. So she'd gone home.

Now came the moment for Larry Kaluzny to unveil the twin themes around which, it was increasingly apparent, he meant to build his case. Theme one: Nancy Seaman was a planner. Under questioning, she explained to him that in May of that year, she'd had all her project materials assembled for the 2005 school year, "labeled and ready to go."

"I pride myself on having everything ready," she said. "I always . . . had my outfits from head to toe laid out the night before." In fact, she'd had the clothes she planned to wear to Greg's graduation already out, on their hangers, the day of the murder. She had also made hotel reservations and dinner reservations two months in advance, still hoping, she said, that Bob would attend the graduation, though in her telling of the story, it had been he who refused to attend, not Greg who refused to invite him.

Theme two: Nancy Seaman was a "fixer." She dealt with the problems in her marriage, Kaluzny explained, by "fixing" things. Wherever Bob's violent outbursts resulted in damage to their home, the defense maintained, there was Nancy, following behind, with her tool kit and her Sears tool card, making everything look good again.

In case there was any confusion about the psychological implications here, Nancy Seaman provided the explanation. "It made me feel that I could deal with what I was living with because it was like it didn't happen. And all the ugliness would go away. Because I didn't see the damage. It was like it didn't happen."

There was the time, for instance, when Bob had thrown a mail organizer, and it shattered. "I went to half a dozen different Meijers stores to find the exact organizer so that when Greg came home he wouldn't ask questions," she explained. (It was an odd picture, Lori Brasier observed: that a twenty-year-old college student, observing a desktop mail organizer to have been broken while he was away at school, would have felt the need to investigate. But maybe this one would have.)

In the same spirit of "fixing," she said, she used makeup to cover up her bruises. She patched drywall when her husband threw things at the wall, and rushed out to buy replacement chandelier globes when Bob threw something at the chandelier and broke them. Another time, when a chair Bob had thrown at their Thanksgiving table had broken a bunch of crystal glasses and china, she had headed out to the store again (on Thanksgiving) and bought new ones, and set the table all over again. Then she glued the chair back together.

"Then it was like it never happened?" Kaluzny inquired.

"Exactly," said Nancy.

In response to more questions from her attorney, she went on to recite a litany of conditions and events that sounded strangely like a checklist of "Ten Ways to Spot a Battered Woman."

"I was not allowed to participate in the financial decisions," she said, in her flat, midwestern schoolteacher tone. "There were times when Bob's short fuse and his anger and rage would erupt, but I could usually identify the triggers.

"Bob had a real problem with strong, independent women.

"I was always there for my children.

"He was like a Doctor Jekyll and Mr. Hyde.

"It was a real roller coaster."

Bob had taken away the files containing her teaching certificate and her diploma, she said. He almost burned down the house, twice. Asked to elaborate, Nancy explained that these incidents occurred when Bob had left a pot on the stove and forgot about it, so the pot had melted. Maybe the house hadn't burned down, exactly, but the place smelled like burned plastic for a long time after that.

CHAPTER 41

A Sex Game and
a Pesky Possum

A s the afternoon of Nancy Seaman's testimony wore on, a change became visible in the jury. When she had first taken the stand, the jurors had leaned forward in their seats and looked at her with compassion or, at least, eagerness and openness to hear her story. Now several jurors were leaning back in their chairs, arms folded on their chests.

"There were numerous incidents that were just tormenting," she said.

"Such as . . . ," Larry Kaluzny asked her.

"Endlessly tormenting," she said.

"I loved him," she said, explaining why she put up with Bob's treatment of her. In the months leading up to the murder, she said, the "torture" escalated sharply. Her mother's death was a contributing factor, she thought.

"Bob was afraid of my mother. I didn't have the courage to tell, but my mother would have put him in jail if she had known."

By her calculation, there had been twenty-four episodes of abuse in the first twenty-one years of her marriage, she said. Ninety-four, in total. The tally was strikingly precise.

In case the relentless abuse wasn't enough, there had been more humiliation and pain for Nancy Seaman to endure, and now Larry Kaluzny asked her to revisit that part of the story. Could Nancy share with the court her observations of the relationship between her husband and Jenna Dumbleton?

"I thought it was creepy," she said.

There was the way Bob took Jenna Christmas shopping, she said. "A twelve-year-old girl. . . . And it's just the two [of them] going shopping."

"And there were other times," Nancy continued, "when we would go to the Woodward Avenue Dream Cruise and she was sitting on his lap."

Kaluzny asked Nancy to describe her sleeping arrangements with her husband. Bob slept on the sofa in the basement, she said. She slept two flights up, in the master bedroom.

How did that come about, Larry asked?

Brisk and teacherlike as ever, Nancy Seaman continued. "Summer of 2003, everything changed as far as our sex life," she said. "We'd always had a good sexual relationship. It was always mutually satisfying for all the time that we were married."

"What changed?"

"Bob liked to role play when we had sex, and I don't have a problem with that. I enjoyed it as well. Except that there was one particular role playing game that he liked to do, starting in that summer, that made me very uncomfortable."

"And what was that?"

"I had to be a twelve-year-old girl and he was the softball coach. And depending on how I pleased him I could earn a spot on his team. Depending on how I sexually performed."

For a woman more accustomed to addressing fourth graders than a jury in a capital murder case, Nancy Seaman recounted the story with surprisingly little sign of discomfort, but the discomfort on the faces of the jurors was palpable. Whatever they thought of the story, it was more than they wanted to know about a person, though there was no denying a certain element of fascination at hearing "an award-winning schoolteacher" describe her foray into sexual role playing. The courtroom was dead silent as the words took hold.

"For the first two times we engaged in this role playing it was okay with me," Nancy Seaman continued, "but it became the only way that we could have sex. That was all he ever wanted to do. And I told him I couldn't do it anymore. I was uncomfortable with it. He got mad."

That's when Bob moved to the basement, she said.

It was getting late—no time to begin questioning Nancy Seaman about the murder. Larry Kaluzny asked her, instead, about the pest problem on Briarwood Court that, according to his client, had inspired her quest for information about poison.

"We had a problem with moles eating my plants," Nancy explained. "We have a problem with a lot of critters. . . . We eventually bought a cage. We were going to try to trap them.

"And we put the cages in the backyard. . . . And [Bob] trapped a possum by mistake. When he found it he filled a trash can, a 32-gallon trash can, with water and stuck the trap with the possum in it, and put the lid on. He was going to drown it.

"Except when he took the lid off several hours later the little possum was just hanging there for air. And I said 'oh my god, you can't do that.' I mean, he's not drowning.

"So Bob got a hammer and he tried to hit the possum so that it would fall into the water to drown [but it didn't]. . . . Eventually he pulled it out of the trash can and we took it and drove it to a field and let the possum go."

It was hard not to picture that opossum, then: slinking out of the cage and high tailing it off (or retreating, dazed and limping) into somebody else's subdivision, to eat up someone else's garden or simply die a slow, brain-damaged death. And Nancy and Bob, driving back home with that empty cage in the back, the car smelling faintly of possum, perhaps.

But something was unsettling about this story, though it had nothing much to do with the murder of Bob Seaman, and perhaps Nancy Seaman herself, as she told it, had failed to recognize this part.

The day had ended with a haunting image, of the possum. The animal had survived incarceration in a squirrel cage, near death by drowning, followed by an unsuccessful bludgeoning with a hammer. But here was the strange part: Nancy and Bob Seaman had disposed of the possum together. Whatever else they felt about each other, they had chosen to share this singularly unappealing chore, and the fact they had done so spoke of a curious connection that had evidently endured, long after affection, tenderness, or goodwill had departed, from the sound of it. They had driven, together, to get rid of the animal. For a brief moment, they had been co-conspirators, with a common enemy, instead of facing off against each other.

CHAPTER 42

"Crab Trees Are the Worst Offenders"

Nancy Seaman was back on the stand the next morning, Tuesday, December 7, in a different but equally well-tailored suit, with an explanation of the ins and outs of membership in the Ramblewood Property Owners' Association. The association was very strict about certain rules concerning home maintenance, as evidenced by the $400 fine that had been levied against the Seamans a few years earlier, when the '89 Mustang with its dismantled engine had sat in the driveway for too long, becoming an eyesore.

Moral of the story: you couldn't let your yard get out of control if you lived in the Ramblewood subdivision. The association was very strict about that.

The issue of property maintenance had come up that Mother's Day night, in fact, Nancy now explained under questioning by Larry Kaluzny. As if the argument concerning Nancy's desire to borrow the Explorer hadn't been enough for one night, they'd moved on after that to the issue of yard work.

"I had told [Bob] we had clean-up to do," Nancy explained, "and I said I could use some help this year, because he usually didn't help.

But it's a big job and I didn't have a lot of time . . . because, as you know, other things were going on.

"He said 'do it yourself,'" she said. They launched into an argument. Though it was seven in the evening by this point, she said, and raining hard, Nancy decided to get started on cleaning up the yard, or at least assembling the tools to do so.

"I went into the garage like I always did and gathered all my stuff together," she said. "I gathered a spade shovel. . . . Gathered my hedge trimmer, my extension cord. I went and got the gas can for the lawn mower. Made sure we had enough gas in the can. I gathered everything and put it out at the far end of the garage. I . . . opened up the drawer to the workbench and got out my hand trimmers."

There had been an old hatchet in the drawer that she'd used the spring before, she said, but it was twenty-five years old, and dull. It didn't make nice, clean cuts. And the bench grinder she would have used to sharpen the blade was unavailable because Bob had taken it down to the Upper Deck.

The hatchet was necessary, she said, to cut shoots off from a large stump in the yard. To illustrate this point, Larry Kaluzny placed a transparency of the backyard at Briarwood Court on the overhead projector, giving Nancy a laser pointer so that she could indicate areas in the yard requiring her work. "Locust trees . . . ," she said. "They are very messy, locust trees. . . ."

And crab trees. "Crab trees are the worst offenders," she said. "They have all of these little tiny trees that are always growing at the base of the tree." Then she showed more bushes. "They are not wanted," she explained, her voice uncharacteristically full of feeling. "They have to be chopped out."

Normally she would have attended to all this in the fall, but that last fall her mother had been in the hospital. "Then there was the assault by Julie Dumbleton," she added. "It wasn't a good fall."

She had looked at the clock then, because she wanted to go to Sears to buy a new hatchet. (Sears, because she owned a tool card.) But Sears would be closed by this time. So she went to Home Depot instead, her second trip that day.

Once at Home Depot, she went directly to the display of hatchets, because, as she explained, "I went for a specific purchase." Then she drove home. She went into the garage and set the hatchet on top of the generator she and her husband had purchased to provide emergency power during an outage. Then, according to Nancy, she went up to her room, turned on the television, and went to bed. (This was a different scenario from the one Lisa Ortlieb hypothesized, in which the murder had taken place shortly after Nancy's return that night.) She went to sleep not long after that. "I had a very busy week ahead of me," she said.

Next morning she got up early, as usual—her strategy, she explained, for avoiding morning confrontations with Bob. But where typically she would manage to get her breakfast and make her exit to school without laying eyes on her husband, that particular morning when she came down to the kitchen, she had found him waiting for her, sitting on one of the two bar stools at the kitchen counter. No coffee, no tea. He was just sitting there, waiting.

"When I saw him, I just took a deep breath," said Nancy. "It's like, oh God, I can't do fifteen rounds this morning."

"I walked into the kitchen and I didn't say a thing. I pretended he wasn't there. . . . I'm making a lunch."

She had shifted to the present tense now. "I have a dish and a sub bun and I get the knife," she said.

"There's no eye contact. I slice open the sub bun . . . start assembling the sandwich. Still no words are spoken.

"I walk over to the opposite side of the room where the refrigerator is because I keep the Saran Wrap in the drawer over there. I take out the Saran Wrap.

"He said, 'I think it's time we talk about going our separate ways.'

"I said 'Bob I can't have this discussion in the morning.' I said, 'What time are you coming home tonight?'

"He said, 'I want to settle it now.'

"Always in the past," Nancy continued, "I would say, 'Oh let's get counseling. Let's try to work it out . . . every marriage has bumps in the road. . . .' This time I didn't. I said fine. I said, 'I am so ready for this.'"

Had she ever said this before, Larry asked her?

"Never. . . . He loved begging and I wasn't going to beg this morning.

"I said, 'I am so ready for this. Let's just do it.' . . . I said, 'I'm moving on.' . . . That's when things got heated."

What happened next?

"He said, 'You no-good bitch, you think I don't know that condo is for you?'. . . I was stunned. I had no idea that he put the pieces together. . . . I'm more than stunned. I'm scared. . . . Because the whole purpose about keeping a secret about the condo was that I knew he'd kill me."

Back in April, she explained, Bob had found the folder that held her condo papers—a folder she kept under her pillow so that he wouldn't find it, marked "moving on." Initially Jeff had told his father that Nancy had purchased the condo for Greg, but once Bob knew the real story, Nancy said, his rage was terrifying.

"I wasn't allowed to make any large purchases or be part of any large financial decisions," she said.

"I'm standing there," she said. "My eyes, from so many confrontations before . . . look around the room for my things because I know I've got to run. I've got to get out."

Now, she said, he had picked up the knife she'd been using to cut the sandwich bread.

"Bob used to play with silverware when he was talking," said Nancy. "Sometimes he would bend forks and spoons and throw them at me. I had to buy all new silverware the year before last. I was getting kind of short on forks and spoons."

What did she do at this point? Kaluzny wanted to know.

"I'm looking for my keys. I'm looking for my purse. I'm getting out of the kitchen.

"He had the knife in his hand and he just pointed it at me. He just dragged it across my hand as I am reaching for him. . . . It filled with blood right away. . . . I wiped it on my pants. I had black slacks on. . . . And I just stood there . . . in disbelief . . . because nothing like that has ever happened before. There's never been a knife.

"I start running down the hallway toward the front door," she continued. "When I got about two feet from the front door I noticed the dead bolt key, the chunky key fob that we have was missing, and it's never missing. . . . We never removed it because if you remove that key you are locked in the house. . . . I'm locked in now."

So she headed to the garage, she said. She had one foot in the house, one foot in the garage. "The next thing I know I get shoved from behind . . . and I go flying.

"There's stuff all over the floor where Greg had left some things from working on his car," Nancy continued.

"I'm crashing into things . . . trying to catch my balance. . . .

"I'm crawling to get to something to lean against. . . . To cover up. To cower like I usually do. . . . I'm covering my face because I don't want to be bruised for graduation.

"He's coming towards me. I hear his footsteps coming for me. . . . I'm on the ground but he's got my arm and he's squeezing it and he said, 'What is it you don't understand, bitch? I don't love you any-more.'" She paused.

"I'm crying. I'm on the floor. . . .

"He's angry because he said he's wasted his life with me. He says 'Why can't you just die? I don't love you anymore.'

"He kicked me. . . . I'm between the wheel well of the Mustang and the generator.

"And he starts pacing like he always started pacing and he's still yelling at me. About the boys, his relationship with Greg is fractured. It was all my fault. . . . He said 'I told you, I'll never let you take Jeff away from me.' And he was angry that Jeff had helped conceal the condo.

"He says . . . , 'What do you need a three bedroom condo for, you no-good bitch?'

"I told him, 'I'll give it back.' I said, 'I'll cancel the contract.' And he says, 'You know you can't do that you lying bitch.'

"Begging didn't work . . . ," she went on.

"He says, 'You are never going to live . . . to move into that condo.' Begging isn't working. . . . He was pacing back and forth. . . . and he came back the last time. . . . I can hear him coming because things are rolling around in the garage. There's rattled cans of paint that Greg has left; at least a half a dozen cans of paint. . . . I'm hearing pinging . . . the cans rolling . . . things are getting kicked. So I know . . . he was pretty close . . . he comes closer . . . he starts to bend over. . . ."

Until this moment, Larry Kaluzny had been taking an almost in-visible role in eliciting Nancy Seaman's testimony, his questions largely limited to "What happened then?" and "How long did that go on?" Now, though, he asked Nancy to demonstrate her position on the garage floor.

She stepped down from the witness box to the front of the court-room. Glancing first to the judge for a sign of approval, she lowered herself to the floor, crouching low.

"All right. This is the Mustang. . . . This is the generator," she began.

"He's coming toward me. . . . I'm just laying [sic] there. I'm scared and I'm thinking to myself 'I've got to get off the floor. I've got to run somehow because he's coming towards me and he's mad. He's mad.' . . . He bends over like he might be getting something off the floor but I don't know what he's picking up. . . . I can see his shoes, just like your shoes. . . . He grabbed my leg. . . . I feel him grabbing my leg and I think I'm going to get pulled back down toward him.

"As I'm getting up there's a . . . railing around the generator and I'm using it for leverage. . . . And as I get up I can feel the handle of the hatchet. I pick it up and I swing it at him."

Something happened in the courtroom when she said this. Nancy herself appeared unchanged, but something seemed to have shifted for the listeners in the room, once the defendant reached the part in her story where she raised the hatchet.

They already knew the outcome of this battle, of course. Nobody had any question that Bob Seaman would end up a dead man in this showdown. But the moment when Nancy swung the hatchet was the moment the line had been crossed, the moment the two players had moved beyond the point of no return, and it seemed clear (if not at the moment, certainly now, listening) that if two people had entered that garage on their own two feet, only one would walk out of it.

"Did you make contact?" Larry Kaluzny asked Nancy.

"Yes I did."

"How were you swinging it?"

"I just swung it at him and sliced him across the face."

"Were you looking at him or just swinging?"

"I just swung it. . . ."

"Did he go down at that point?"

"No . . .

". . . He didn't let go of my leg. It just stunned him and all I could say was, 'Oh my god, oh my god.'"

"Was he saying anything at that point?"

"No, but he didn't let go of my leg."

"Are you constantly swinging the hatchet?"

"I'm swinging."

"You can take a seat now."

"I'm swinging it."

Nancy returned to the witness box. She patted her hair. Larry Kaluzny resumed his questioning.

"You know you hit him more than once. You've heard the testimony?"

"I kept swinging it and I kept swinging it and I kept swinging it."

"Were you thinking about what you were doing?"

"I was terrified. . . . All I knew was I had to stop him because so many times before we would be face to face like that, when he got his hands on me his grip was like a vice. When he got his hands on me he would drag me around like a rag doll. . . . Before I hit him, the last words he said to me, as he was bending over, was 'Before I let a no-good fucking bitch like you have half of everything I'll see you dead.' . . . I had to stop him."

Was there any intent to kill him? Kaluzny asked her.

"I never thought about death. I never thought about killing. . . . I just wanted him to stop hurting me."

He asked her about the angle of her swings.

"I'm swinging it in all directions. I'm swinging it at different angles. I'm swinging it and swinging it and swinging it, and it's like a blur. It is not like individual swings. It melds together in a blur."

"At some point you stopped swinging the hatchet, is that correct?"

"Yes, I did."

Her husband had lost consciousness. He had slumped against her. "You remember," she said, in an almost conversational tone, "I was not laying [sic] all the way on the ground. I was halfway up and halfway down. . . . He slumps towards me."

"Was he touching you at all?"

"Touching me. Yes."

"What's going through your head at this point?"

"We hadn't had any good touching like in six months," Nancy offered. "The only touch we had had was pain for me. It was some kind of battering, and when I felt his body I just kind of freaked out."

Here it was then. The all-important explanation for why—after inflicting enough hatchet blows to render her husband unconscious—Nancy Seaman would have proceeded to do what came next. "It was like a panic because the only touch I associated with Bob for a long time was pain. And when I felt him I started screaming, 'Get off me, get off me,' . . .

". . . I felt the knife on the floor," she said. "I picked it up. . . . The knife from the kitchen. . . ."

"What happened then?"

"I don't physically remember stabbing him, but . . . obviously I did. I was screaming at him to get off of me, get off of me, get off of me, just get off of me."

"He's not responding?"

"No."

She got up then, she said. She ran into the house. She ran up to her room and slammed the door.

"I'm shaking," she said. "I'm just waiting to hear him come up the stairs."

Given the injuries sustained by Bob Seaman by this point, the idea of his reentering the house and mounting the stairs to wreak revenge on his wife might have seemed like a grim joke, which was pretty much how Nancy Seaman described the next scene.

"I'm shaking like a leaf, cause I know he's coming upstairs because he always came upstairs after me. I could hear his footsteps on the stairs. I know he was coming. . . ."

"Did you think at all to get help or anything like that?"

"All I'm thinking about at this point is my safety."

"You don't know he's dead at that point?"

"No."

She was sitting there—"for it seems like an eternity," she said. Blood on her hands. Blood on her clothes. She stood in front of the mirror. Blood on her face. In her imagination, at least, the figure of Bob Seaman might still be stalking her, like a character out of a horror movie—bloody, mangled, and vengeful.

Still, she stayed in the house. She stripped off her clothes and got in the shower, she said. She threw her bloody clothes in the bathtub. She went to the phone to call the substitute teacher request line, but the automated system informed her it was too late to get a sub, and the sub coordinator's line—when she called it—was busy.

"I remember looking at the clock and thinking my students will be in the room and I've got to get to school," she said. She grabbed some clothes—not her teacher clothes, she said (that would have been her suit jacket), but slacks and a top. She didn't put on makeup. Didn't do her hair. Didn't return to the garage. She drove to Longacre Elementary School. She was late for work.

CHAPTER 43

No Running
in the Hallway

I kept telling myself, 'This isn't happening. . . . I'll be okay . . . ,'" Nancy continued from the stand. "I was always okay when I got to school. School was a place that . . . when I got there I was always safe."

The hallways were empty and quiet, she said. "I'm thinking I'm not supposed to run in the hall. . . . It's against the rules."

She looked at her shoe. Blood there.

She was late enough by now that her students had been taken from her classroom and brought to Christine Brueck's room, where she retrieved them. One boy asked her about the cut on her hand, she said.

"I'm in the room in the morning and I'm telling myself over and over again, I've got all these children in there and they are all working," she said. "They are doing what they normally do in their routine. But it was not a normal day. . . . I'm thinking I've got to go home. . . . I can't be here."

She drove home for lunch. Bob's car was in the driveway, of course. Did she realize he could be dead? Kaluzny asked her.

"I couldn't think death. Do you hear me? I couldn't think death."

She opened the door to the garage, but she didn't go in. "I see his shoes, his legs. . . . There is blood everywhere." She slammed the door and went back out. Back to school.

"I can't believe what I saw," she said. "You don't understand. Nothing ever stopped Bob. It was always me on the floor not him. And he's not moving, he's not moving." The pitch of her voice, as she said this, rose noticeably.

"Then this terror . . . creeps over me," she said. "I realize that Jeff and I hadn't worked out the car plans yet for the graduation and he was going to come to the house. I can't let Jeff see his dad like that.

"He's all broken," she said of Bob—echoing Larry Kaluzny's carefully developed theme. "He's all broken on the floor. He's not moving and there's blood everywhere. . . . I had to fix it. I had to make it okay."

"So you are still thinking of fixing things," Larry offered helpfully.

"I had to."

She described going to Meijers then, to buy the cleaning supplies and the bleach. She couldn't let her son Jeff see his father like that. "He'd lose his mind," she said, at the prospect of Jeff seeing Bob in the garage, dead and mutilated.

Meanwhile, she was struggling with injuries of her own, she reminded the court. Her hand was bleeding, and her knuckles were scraped.

"Do you know how you got those injuries?" Kaluzny asked her.

"I don't," she said, though earlier she had mentioned the cut produced by the kitchen knife.

"Things were not calm in the garage that morning," she added. If this was an attempt at irony, it would have been the first evidence of such in Nancy Seaman's testimony.

Back home again from the store, Nancy said, she laid out the tarp she'd bought.

"I can't look at Bob," she explained. "I drag him to a clean place in the garage. . . . I put him in the tarp. . . . I drag him and I roll him on the tarp with my eyes closed."

Then she opened a gallon of bleach. "I just pour it all over everything. I'm pouring bleach on everything because . . . there's blood everywhere. It's everywhere . . . it's everywhere. . . . Blood on the car . . . blood on the walls . . . blood on the cans of paint . . . blood on the generator . . . blood on the lawn mower . . . blood on everything."

She threw bath towels on the puddles of blood, but there was more than the towels could soak up, so she took out the hose.

"When I turned on the hose," she said, "it's like when you turn on a hose the first time, when there's air and water in . . . the line, and it sputtered and spurted. Blood just . . . I just made things worse."

"Did the blood splash?" Larry asked.

Right, said Nancy. Particularly in the area where "the conflict" took place, she said.

Even after hosing down the garage, though, Nancy's work was not done. There was painting to do. Drywall to fix. Who knew what time it was, but finally she was done.

"It was perfect," said Nancy, with an air of satisfaction still apparent, recalling her hard work that day. "I had fixed it all."

"So what's going through your mind?" asked Kaluzny.

"I fixed it. I'm fixing it . . ."

"Like you did—" he reminded her.

"I can do this. I can fix it," she interrupted.

"Like you did for thirty years?"

"Like I did for thirty years. . . . Like I always had."

She went to bed then. She hadn't even heard the police officers when they entered her house later, responding to the missing persons report of Dennis Seaman, or when they stood in the doorway to her bedroom and saw her sleeping there. Who wouldn't be tired, after a day like that?

Nancy Seaman was up to the events of that next morning in her testimony now—the day after the murder, by her account. She came downstairs. She looked in the garage.

"And it's perfect. . . . It didn't happen. . . . Every time those thoughts of that horrible morning came, when I looked, I fixed it, just like I fixed everything."

The jurors, initially riveted, were looking a little weary, but Nancy Seaman seemed not to notice.

"I got dressed and ready to go to work, just like always," she said. "I always went on with my life after the ugliness."

She didn't remember anything about the school day, she said. But after school, she knew she had to return the hatchet. Not the hatchet, actually. *A* hatchet. The one she'd used to defend herself, she said, was "with his body."

"If I could put everything back the way it was Sunday, this didn't happen. It wouldn't happen," said Nancy. "I had to get out of this nightmare. I had to wake up from this nightmare."

After shoplifting and returning the hatchet, Nancy was—not surprisingly—exhausted once again. Imagine her surprise when the doorbell rang and she opened it to find (talk about your worst nightmare) the Dumbletons. Dick and Jake Dumbleton were standing there on the porch, with those concerned, eager-beaver faces of theirs, looking for Bob.

"I couldn't have been myself," Nancy said, "because I would have told them to leave . . . and yet I stood there and just looked at them and I just looked at them and talked to them. And I never would have done that, I would have always said, 'Leave. What are you doing here?' Because they weren't welcome."

At some point, did she realize she couldn't fix the situation? Larry asked her now, gently.

Yes.

And when was that?

"Wednesday morning."

She woke up early, as usual. She went out to the garage, and for the first time since "the conflict," she stepped inside.

"I sat down and cried next to his body," she said. "I just sat down and cried.

"I cried because I couldn't fix him," she said. "I could fix everything else. I had fixed everything else but I couldn't fix him. I couldn't fix him no matter what I did. I couldn't fix him. . . ."

"Is that the first time you really confronted the fact that he was dead?" asked Larry, in his most gentle voice yet.

"Yes," said Nancy. "I just sat there and the hatchet was on top of him, and he was all wrapped up, and I laid across him and I just said, 'Why did you do this to me? Why?'"

Then she called the substitute teacher line, she explained. This time, however, she had called early enough to get a sub.

CHAPTER 44

What to Do with a Body in an Explorer

N ext came the business of getting Bob's body in the car—a superhuman-seeming task, but maybe not so incredible for a woman who had, in the last seventy-two hours or so hosed down, bleached, painted, and drywalled her entire garage; disposed of several trash bags full of bloody towels; pulled off a hatchet heist at Home Depot; tarped and taped a corpse; purchased picture hangers; and taught twenty-five fourth graders for the last two days. Not to mention killing her husband.

Larry Kaluzny did not linger on the particulars of how Nancy Seaman managed to get the body into the car, appearing satisfied with Nancy's explanation that "I know how to use ramps because I've used them before." She had a little cart with wheels on it, too, she said—a cart her husband presumably had used to scoot around underneath the vehicles he worked on, back in the days before she murdered him.

Once the body was safely in the back of her Explorer, the question came up: What was she planning to do with it?

"At any time during this whole thing did you ever consider . . . dumping the body?" asked Kaluzny.

Hearing the suggestion, Nancy Seaman's face—somewhat forbidding at the best of moments these past few days—took on a particularly stern appearance, as if the suggestion barely deserved a response.

"He was my husband," she said. "He stayed with me for two and a half days in the house. I couldn't get rid of him."

She was not going to contact the Farmington Hills Police Department, she said, almost equally indignant at this latest suggestion. "The last time I went to the Farmington Hills Police and asked them to come to the home and help me to please scare Bob, . . . they said they couldn't do it unless I had him arrested. . . . I would never have called the Farmington Hills Police."

She needed to get to her dad's house, she said. "I wanted to turn myself in on my own terms, not theirs." Except that before she had a chance to do that, who should show up on her doorstep but Detective Al Patterson and his buddies, nosing around again.

"They asked about my life," she said. "And the whole time they are asking I'm telling them my life story about how bad things had been, all I am thinking is, 'Why do you care now? You didn't care the last time I saw you. You didn't care the last time I went to the police station. Now you care? It's too late to care now.'"

Her voice, as she said this, was filled with righteous indignation. For a moment there, you might have thought the ones on trial were Detective Patterson and the entire Farmington Hills police force.

When her turn came to cross-examine the witness, once again Lisa Ortlieb wanted to play the tape of Nancy Seaman's first telephone conversation with Greg from jail, the day after her arrest—the one in which the two had focused the majority of their concern on the question of the difference between an ax and a hatchet, and the additional question of just which hatchet it had been that Nancy Seaman had used to kill the man Greg referred to as "your husband." Interestingly, Larry Kaluzny offered no objection.

After the tape was played, Ortlieb asked Nancy about her statements to her son to the effect that the hatchet used to kill Bob Seaman had not been the one she purchased at Home Depot.

"When you talked to Greg on that tape, you were lying about the hatchet?" Ortlieb asked Nancy.

"I said I returned a hatchet," Nancy said.

"You lied to him again about the hatchet that you used on Bob?"

"No, I did not. It said that the hatchet that I used on Bob was with the body. It says that on the tape."

It was a fine point—the kind of technicality a kid might use to argue his way out of a dented fender in the family car (by saying he hadn't dented the fender; it had been the grille). But Nancy Seaman, making her distinction, seemed satisfied with her response, whether or not the jury appeared to be.

"The first words out of your mouth [after her arrest] were, 'It was an accident'?"

"It *was* an accident that he was dead. Yes." Once again, an expression of something close to triumph passed across Nancy Seaman's face.

"You saw the pictures of your husband?" Ortlieb asked. Nobody who had been in the courtroom the day the images of Bob Seaman's chopped, swollen, and decomposing face had been shown was likely to forget those images.

"Yes I did."

"That's the first time you saw them?"

From the look on Nancy's face, hearing the question, Ortlieb might have been asking Nancy Seaman to engage in some indecent sexual act or take an illegal tax deduction. "I never looked at my husband," Nancy said, indignant. "I wouldn't do that."

"At what point did you turn the hatchet around and bash him in the forehead?" Lisa asked.

Never, said Nancy. Not intentionally. "This was not a calm situation," she said.

"You were able to swing fifteen times, and he still had your leg?"

"I didn't say that. I said he . . . had my leg. . . . I said he still had my leg after the glancing blow."

"Let's stop for lunch," suggested Judge McDonald.

"You said you went home and you saw what had happened," Ortlieb continued, when court resumed. She was speaking of Monday, the day Nancy Seaman claimed the murder had taken place.

That was correct, Nancy told her.

"No 911? No Farmington Hills Police? No Oakland County Sheriff? No Michigan State Police?"

"None of that ever entered my mind," said Nancy, without apology. "I was in a state of shock."

"And then after school you were in such a state of shock you went and bought cleaning supplies?"

"I explained why. Yes."

"OK. Cleaning supplies. Rough Tote, tarp, tape, Lysol—"

"I did not buy Lysol," said Nancy.

"And before you shoplifted the hatchet you went shopping and you returned that Rough Tote, to a different store?" Ortlieb asked her.

"It was too big."

"Now, the next day . . . Officer Saad comes over, and you tell him that Bob is having a midlife crisis and is trying to find himself?"

"Yes I did."

"That's a lie."

"No," said Nancy. "He actually *had* been having a midlife crisis. And he was trying to find himself a lot."

"He wasn't trying to find himself. You knew where he was."

"That's not what that means. He was trying to find himself. He was having a lot of ——" Nancy Seaman wasn't backing down on this one.

"So that wasn't a lie? He was trying to find himself?"

"That's how——"

"Even though he was dead? Butchered? In your car?"

No comment.

"OK. So when Officer Saad came to you, when you said, 'He's having a midlife crisis and is trying to find himself,' you used the present tense?"

"I wasn't aware I was using the present tense."

"Well he *is* having a midlife crisis, and *is* trying to find himself? In the back of your car?"

"He was not in the back of my car at this time."

"Now when the officers come to you that day, you told them you were in the process of a divorce and it was amicable?" said Ortlieb.

"It was, to me. I was leaving."

"Amicable?"

"For me it was. I was leaving peacefully."

"And you repeated that the detectives should look in the basement of the Upper Deck?"

"Yes."

"Because he spent a great deal of time there?"

"And [when the detectives opened the back of the Explorer], you touched the cardboard it went down on the body concealing it even more."

"That didn't conceal much of anything. Because it looked like a body in the car."

"So you actually didn't do a good job concealing it?"

"It was not my intent to conceal it. I was going down to my father's. . . . If I wanted to conceal it, it would have been concealed."

"You had days to call all types of law enforcement agencies?"

"That is correct."

"Days to call lawyers?"

"I explained that. Yes."

"You had days to talk to anybody? Friends? Family?"

"Yes."

"And you certainly do have friends, right?" Lisa asked.

"I do not have close friends, actually," Nancy told her. "I have wonderful acquaintances, but I do not have people that are close to me."

"Do you remember your husband accused you of sending an anonymous letter to Compuware [the managers of the softball team Bob coached]?"

"Yes, he did. It was a terrible fight."

"In fact, he included that letter in the 'Nancy Crap File,' a letter he thought you wrote, and he confronted you with this letter."

"Yes."

"Accusing him—a horrible letter—"

"I did not send that letter."

"Do you remember asking [Bob] on February 17, which would be after he accused you [of sending the letter to Compuware], 'Why don't you talk to me anymore?' Do you remember what his response was?"

"I don't recall it."

"Was it, quote, 'After you sent that letter there is nothing more to talk about.'"

"One of the names you called him was 'bastard?'"

"I have called him bastard, that's correct."

"Did you tell him 'your automobile colleagues are laughing behind your back'?"

"They were."

"Do you remember calling him an 'asshole'?"

"It's very likely I did."

" 'Son of a bitch?' 'I hope he's burning?' "

"Yes."

Lisa Ortlieb moved on to the tape-recorded conversations from jail—specifically, Nancy's conversations with Greg about Jeff. Once again, it was startling to see how easily the defendant confirmed what, in the eyes of some, might have been painful admissions concerning her feelings about her older son. From the looks on the faces of the jurors, it appeared that they had been growing weary of the defendant's tendency toward nitpicking semantics. "Do you remember saying 'I'm sorry [Jeff] turned out to be such a weak person'?" asked Ortlieb.

"He *is* a weak person," Nancy told her.

"OK."

"He was always weak."

"Greg said 'But we knew that, Mom. We knew that.' "

"We knew that."

"And you said yes."

"Yes we did." (There it was again, that "we," unmistakably referring to the core unit of Nancy and Greg.)

"Do you remember saying, 'He never wanted to share a damn thing with anybody, now he's not going to end up with anything'?"

"I don't recall saying that."

"Remember telling your father, 'I just want Jeff to leave Greg alone'?"

"Yes."

" 'Greg's got enough on his shoulders. He's doing everything himself and you don't need that Greedy Bastard Number Two trying to give him trouble'?" Once again, Lisa was quoting from Nancy on the taped conversation with her father.

"That's right."

"That Jeff 'would screw you out of your last dime'?"

"That's true. He would."

"Do you remember August 7th saying 'The lawyer asked me if I wanted to see Jeff, and I told him I don't ever want to see him'?"

"That's true."

It was a striking moment: a mother acknowledging, in open court, her lack of interest in ever again laying eyes on her firstborn child. She might have been expressing a dislike for seafood or rap music or hockey, for all the emotion with which she delivered the news.

The afternoon was winding down. On the witness stand, Nancy Seaman was looking visibly tired. Lisa Ortlieb's ponytail remained perky, however, and if her feet in their three-inch heels were sore, she wasn't letting on.

"You were aware that [Bob] had talked to an attorney, J. Robert Rock?" she asked Nancy.

"Yes."

"In fact, when he told you, you laughed and said 'You'll never get the Shelby'?"

"I never said that."

"You didn't laugh?"

"Cars mean nothing to me," said Nancy.

Larry Kaluzny got up again, for the final round of questioning. With the bearing of a baseball team manager heading out to the mound to talk to a pitcher who's just given up four walks in a row, he got to work, cleaning up as best he could.

He revisited her seemingly coldhearted decision to take her older son's name off her visiting list at the jail. Wasn't it true that just the other day, after Jeff had testified (for the prosecution!), she had gone so far as to put his name back on the list? If that wasn't a sign of forgiveness, what was?

He asked her about that seemingly superhuman feat of getting Bob's body into the Explorer. The trick was using an incline plane, she told him. "I could do a piano the same way if I tried to."

"Did you roll him feet first or head first?" Larry inquired.

"I don't know feet from head," Nancy said. Whatever words might have been interjected here, concerning the differences between one end of a dead body and the other, nobody pursued this topic, and the witness stepped down.

CHAPTER 45

As Seen on *Bill O'Reilly*

T he defense concluded its case with the testimony of its two expert witnesses, speaking on Battered Woman Syndrome. One was Dr. Michael Abramsky, a Michigan-based forensic and clinical psychologist, who had interviewed Nancy Seaman on two separate occasions, conducting a battery of psychological tests meant to evaluate her psychological state and identify the possible presence of mental illness. The other was Dr. Lenore Walker, a nationally known expert in the field and the woman who had invented the term Battered Woman Syndrome.

In addition to his interviews with the defendant, augmented by the test results, Dr. Abramsky had evidently interviewed Greg Seaman, as well as teachers from Nancy's school and Paulette Schleuter. He had also reviewed police reports on the case.

On the basis of the testing and interviews, Dr. Abramsky testified, he concluded that the defendant suffered from what he referred to as Battered Spouse syndrome. Her symptoms included anxiety, hypervigilance, nervousness, and denial. All classic symptoms of the syndrome, he added.

He had provided the results of his inquiries into the defendant's mental status and the background of the case to Dr. Lenore Walker, who would be testifying directly after him, having flown in from Florida the day before for this express purpose. She would serve as the number one expert witness for the defense—the big gun.

Dr. Walker's testimony began with a lengthy examination of her training, awards, honors, and publications. In 1979, she told the court, she had published *The Battered Woman*—now a classic in the field. In 1984 she'd followed that one up with *The Battered Woman Syndrome.* She had taught seminars around the country, testified before Congress and in Europe, and had worked for the United Nations and the World Health Organization. Asked by Larry Kaluzny what TV shows she'd been on, she named *Donahue, Oprah, 48 Hours, 60 Minutes,* and *Bill O'Reilly.* (This last name may not have carried the impact it would have once, given that at the very moment of the trial, Bill O'Reilly was somewhat visibly in the news for charges of alleged sexual harassment of an employee, a case that was later settled out of court.)

Dr. Walker—a formidable-looking individual, wearing a large-print dress, big jewelry, and, surprisingly, long hair in the style of the eighties—told the court that she had served as a witness in many trials of this sort. Always for the defense.

A major obstacle for the expert witnesses in Nancy Seaman's case lay in the fact that Michigan law prohibits a psychologist from making a direct assessment of whether or not a particular defendant suffers from Battered Woman Syndrome. As a result, and despite Dr. Abramsky's testing and interviews of the defendant, all Dr. Walker was able to offer on the stand was a general discussion of the traits of a battered woman, the misconceptions about battered women, and the behavior patterns one might expect to see in an individual who had suffered abuse of the kind Bob Seaman was alleged to have perpetrated against his wife. The fact that she had not actually ever met the defendant did not stop Dr. Walker from expressing, with fervor, her conviction that Nancy Seaman had been a battered woman.

Unlike every other witness in the trial to this point, Dr. Walker offered her testimony in the form of a lecture from the witness stand, virtually uninterrupted by questioning from the defense.

She listed the traits of a battering spouse: "They blame everybody else for their problems. . . . It's their way or get out. . . . They use abuse as a way of getting control. . . . Aside from battering," she said, "they may look like normal, everyday people."

Alcohol might contribute to the battering, she explained, but it was not the cause. Stress or health problems, too, could exacerbate a battering situation. A batterer might be charming and loving on occasion—the Jekyll-and-Hyde situation, she said, using the very phrase the defendant herself had employed to describe her husband. A batterer "puts wedges between [the victim] and her family." As for the battered spouse (not necessarily a woman, though the vast majority of battered spouses were female), you might find such a person in any socioeconomic category, rich or poor. Like abusers, abuse victims, too, "look like everybody else."

"Batterers do not share well," she said, once again echoing the words of Nancy Seaman about Bob, "and they don't share their children well."

Battered women "have an uncanny ability to keep it hidden and not tell people," she said. "They're willing to accept the responsibility and the blame that the batterer gives out if that will keep peace in the family.

"It's like walking on eggshells," she said. "They blame themselves for not keeping [their partner] calm."

"Does the spouse who's been battered have any kind of a break with reality at times?" Larry Kaluzny asked Dr. Walker.

"The most common is what we call dissociation," she said. "That is the kind of separation of your mind from your body. It helps you not feel what's happening.

"People in the middle class and professional classes who are being battered are often so ashamed that they don't see the police as a resource," she added. "They feel they'd die of shame if a police car pulled up in front of their house in their neighborhood."

Larry Kaluzny asked her why it was that so many battered women didn't leave their spouse.

First of all, she told him, they did. Battered women actually leave their marriages in roughly the same percentages as the general population.

"If a woman starts to gain some independence, either through a job . . . or starts to seek out some ways to have independence, how does that affect the relationship with the man?" Kaluzny asked.

"It threatens the relationship. It threatens the batterer's control over her. And the more independence she may have, the more he's going to try to control her."

It was also true, Dr. Walker explained, that "the highest risk period for somebody to get severely hurt" occurs "when the woman was preparing to leave."

Lisa Ortlieb began her cross-examination of Dr. Walker by introducing herself. "As the head of the Domestic Violence Section of the Oakland County Prosecutor's Office," she said, "I've heard a lot about you." The fact that even as she challenged this particular defendant's claim to Battered Woman Syndrome she was identifying herself as an advocate for abused women within this very jurisdiction was hardly lost on anyone in the courtroom.

"Now, your whole testimony today is about the characteristics of a battered woman," she said. "So you're assuming there's been a battering."

"That's right."

"In this case, you have not reviewed anything other than what Dr. Abramsky supplied to you?"

"That's right."

"You didn't meet the defendant?"

"No."

"Didn't listen to any of the phone calls that she made from the Oakland County Jail?"

"No."

"Or [read] the personal protection order that she tried to get against a female?"

"No."

"Were you able to read any of her letters, written to Bob, her husband, in this case?"

"No I have not."

How much was Dr. Walker paid for providing her testimony today? Ortlieb inquired.

$3500, plus expenses.

Did she ever testify for the prosecution in cases of this kind?

That situation tended not to arise.

"Now, there's obviously women who kill that haven't been battered, correct?"

"That's correct."

"I believe you've written many books," said Ortlieb. "Thirteen or fourteen? And you talk a lot about how the batterer tries to control his victim."

"That's correct."

"And one of the things is jealousy, he's over-possessive, is that correct?"

"Yes."

"He's very intrusive of the woman?"

"That's correct."

"He isolates her?"

"That's correct."

"Usually the woman is not permitted to do anything without his approval."

"That's correct."

"He expects her to remain unassertive?"

"Well . . . unassertive to him."

"Do you remember writing in your book that, 'He cuts her off from others. She is paralyzed with loneliness'?"

"Some are. Some are not."

" 'His domineering and jealous nature often prevents her from seeking friendship of others.' "

"That's correct."

"And . . . in one of your books you talk about a study where you said all the battered women mention the fact that their batterers were extremely jealous of every person in their life, including family, friends, people at work, and especially children?"

"Yes."

Lisa Ortlieb didn't come out and say it, but the implication was clear enough: an unassertive woman did not generally call her husband an asshole to his face or accuse him of being a terrible husband and father. Given the tendency of abusive men to express their anger in a physical manner, behavior of this kind would seem likely to bring about a fairly major beating.

Ortlieb didn't point it out, but any listener in the courtroom, hearing Dr. Lenore Walker's recitation of the traits of a battered spouse, could probably have drawn the conclusion by himself or herself: if there were a person in the Seaman marriage who had manifested extreme jealousy and possessiveness, the desire to cut off outside friendships of the other partner, and fear of abandonment, that person would not be Bob Seaman. It would Nancy.

Nancy Seaman may have purchased a condo in the apparent act of leaving her marriage. But Bob had also gone to see a lawyer and announced his decision to get out, and from everything the jury had heard in the courtroom in recent days, he was about to take action, finally.

In fact, a bystander listening to Dr. Walker's testimony might have noted that virtually every trait the defense might have hoped the jury would associate with Nancy to identify her as a battered wife, and those pinned on Bob to mark him as her abuser, could be flipped around. Dr. Lenore Walker had said it herself: a battered spouse might cover up abuse pretty well, to the point where it might be hard to determine who was the abuser and who was the abused.

CHAPTER 46

A Woman Like That Wouldn't Ruin Her Son's Graduation

T he weather had been warm and sunny where I live in Northern California, the week the Seaman trial got under way. In Detroit the temperature was well below freezing. I had left a cold-weather climate almost a decade before, out of a particular dread of winter and winter driving. There had been more to the leaving than that, of course—a divorce and its bitter aftermath—but it was true, I hated cold.

When I'd made my decision to come to Detroit to explore the Seamans' story, my friend Rebecca (whose husband, Bill, wrote about the automotive industry for the *Detroit News*) offered me her guest room. Rebecca lived in the comfortable suburb of Birmingham, Michigan, just a few miles from the courthouse—and less than a mile, oddly enough, from the street where my children's father had grown up.

It was from my ex-husband, over twenty years ago, that I had first heard stories of the Woodward Avenue Dream Cruise, the parade of lovingly restored and gleaming vintage cars that sailed by every August, just blocks from his house. And it was from him that I got my first small glimmer of understanding of what it meant to have grown up in the Detroit suburbs. His father was an executive with Goodyear—a tire man. All around in his neighborhood and those surrounding it, like the one where Bob and Nancy Seaman made their home, were people whose lives centered in one way or another on the American automobile.

I had never spent time in this place before (his parents having retired to Hilton Head around the time of our marriage), so the trip I now prepared to make was taking me to largely unfamiliar territory.

I reserved a rental car and, having given away my serious winter gear when I left New Hampshire, borrowed a coat and gloves, boots and a hat. Leaving my ten-year-old Honda Civic at the airport in San Francisco, I hopped a red eye—landing in the early hours of dawn, in the middle of a snowstorm, crawling along the icy and unfamiliar Southfield Freeway to 1200 Telegraph Road, the address of Oakland County Courthouse.

It was December 13, 2004, a chilly Monday morning, when the court reconvened for the final portion of *People of the State of Michigan* v. *Nancy A. Seaman,* for the purpose of hearing the closing arguments of Lisa Ortlieb and Larry Kaluzny.

When I walked into Judge McDonald's courtroom that morning, all I knew of the case was what I'd seen on *Good Morning America* a couple of days earlier and a few short newspaper reports I'd read online. I had not heard the testimony of Greg or Jeff Seaman or of Julie Dumbleton or of Nancy herself—only gathered the headlines and the sensational aspects of the case, as the media tended to present them. I had not heard the tapes of Nancy's conversations with Greg from jail or spoken with the attorneys representing either side. I had read the allegations of abuse and infidelity and Nancy Seaman's much-publicized story about her husband asking her to engage in sexual role playing as a twelve-year-old girl wanting to get on his team. I knew about the divided positions of the Seaman sons. But I had no sense yet of whom I might believe and whose testimony I might ultimately question.

I took a seat on a bench beside an attractive blonde woman a few years younger than I, with her hair almost as unkempt as my own that morning, whom I guessed to be a reporter on the basis of the notebook in which she was scribbling. She turned out to be Lori Brasier from the *Detroit Free Press*. Because she looked friendly, I leaned over and introduced myself as a freelance writer from out of town. Somewhat uncharacteristically for a local journalist in whose territory an outsider like myself might be viewed as a carpetbagger, she introduced herself and greeted me warmly.

"I can't talk now," she said. "But we can grab a cup of coffee later."

Today the benches in the courtroom were nearly filled, though the proceedings had not yet gotten under way. Rick Cox was back. So were Julie and Dick Dumbleton, along with their son, Jake, seated with Michelle Cernits, the victims' advocate from the prosecutor's office, and Eugene D'Onofrio, John D'Onofrio, and an angry-looking teenager who appeared to be his son, Nancy Seaman's nephew. And there was a cluster of teachers, along with a row of press (the row in which I'd taken my place) and the ever present Court TV camera.

Lisa Ortlieb wore her hair down loose, to the consternation of the Court TV cameraman, to whom I also introduced myself, with the thought that down the line, I'd be wanting to get hold of his tapes.

It wasn't anything close to a party atmosphere in the courtroom, of course, and yet a certain amount of socializing went on that morning. Larry Kaluzny, affable as ever, greeted Greg Seaman as if he were one of his golf foursome stepping into the clubhouse to play eighteen holes, though Greg's demeanor was considerably less expansive. He made an attempt at a smile before slipping silently into his seat, wearing the same suit he'd had on when he testified, Lori told me. It looked to me like something from a high school drama department costume room.

Jeff Seaman had not put in an appearance in the courtroom since finishing his testimony, and remained among the missing.

Nancy, in the latest of her well-tailored suits, with her hair pulled into a tidy bun, was brought in by the bailiff. Familiar now with the procedure of unshackling, she extended her wrists for him to release the chains that bound them and lifted her arms slightly so that the heavy chain around her waist could also be removed. As she often did, she shot a look in the direction of her younger son and took her seat next to Larry and Todd Kaluzny.

I felt a strange, almost sick feeling, watching her. I pictured myself in her shoes, imagined one of my sons witnessing a moment like the one now playing out in this courtroom. There was a hardness to Nancy Seaman's face that I hadn't anticipated, but then, she had lived through terrible experiences, witnessed things I couldn't conceive of. How should I know what the face of a woman should look like, who has felt the blade of a hatchet she herself wielded, making contact with a human skull?

I felt afraid—not for any risk of physical injury, only the sense that to know this woman would require me to go to a dark place I didn't want to visit. For a fleeting moment I registered the thought, "I shouldn't be here." To witness a woman being shackled like this, in front of her own child, seemed like an intrusion into an intensely personal family tragedy. On the other hand, I told myself, the fact of my presence here would make possible, for Nancy Seaman, the opportunity to tell her story and be heard. It was my job to visit those dark places, and if I could, to shed light on them.

The jurors entered the room—five men and eight women, including the alternate. All but one of them were white, most in their forties and fifties. They looked like middle-class people of the sort, I supposed, who might have a hard time picturing an award-winning schoolteacher from Farmington Hills committing a hatchet murder for any reason but self-defense.

Now came the judge—tall and stern-looking in his robes. It was not unlikely, I thought, that he lived in a gated community himself.

"You may be seated," he intoned.

First up for closing statements was Lisa Ortlieb. Taking her position in front of the jury box, she recapped what were for her some of the most telling moments of the previous days' testimony, including that of Nancy Seaman herself. There was Nancy Seaman's "injury," ostensibly incurred during that final confrontation with Bob. She reminded the jurors of what one of the police officers had said about it: "I'm familiar with knife wounds, and this was not a knife wound," and of Detective Patterson's observation, "I thought nothing of that little tiny scratch."

This was my first glimpse of Lisa in action, and it was impressive. There was an aura surrounding her, of sincerity and fervent love of the law. She was like a Girl Scout making a badge presentation, who's done her homework and knows it, but more than that: one who truly believes in the subject she's made it her business to study.

"Think about her story," Lisa told the jury. "Think, any of you, about one 'glancing blow' to your face with a hatchet. What do you do? The first thing you do, you certainly wouldn't continue holding on." And yet—as everyone in the room remembered from her testimony (everyone but myself, at that point)—Nancy Seaman had claimed her husband hung on to her leg.

She went on to ask the jurors to consider the stab wounds that had come after the hatchet wounds. The depth of the incisions suggested, she said, that they had not been inflicted—as the defendant wanted the jury to believe—by the kitchen knife Bob Seaman had supposedly been wielding, but by his own pocket knife, removed from his pocket once he'd lost consciousness, and inserted, far from lovingly, into his back, throat, and chest.

Ortlieb revisited the question of whether the murder had occurred on the morning of May 10, as the defendant alleged, or on night of May 9, which would be much more damaging to the defense, because this would more closely link the murder to the purchase of the hatchet, suggesting premeditation.

"Look at Bob Seaman's clothes, as described in the autopsy report," she said. Same dark shirt and khaki shorts he'd been wearing at the game Jenna Dumbleton had been umpiring Sunday afternoon. Same white socks and dark sneakers his sister-in-law had teased him about at the airport, as improper attire for a newly single man who might be in the market for a date at some point in the not-so-distant future.

"You know why [Nancy's] clothes were frumpy [when she showed up at school Monday morning]?" Lisa speculated. "Because after she killed [Bob] and cleaned herself up, she starts cleaning right away, covering her tracks. She didn't sleep a wink on Sunday, *not a wink.*

"She wants you to believe that she was out of control, wildly swinging," Ortlieb continued. "Really? How come Bob had not one wound on any part of his body that's not a vital area?

"She said 'I had to get out. I had to get out. I had to get a condo.' But she just happens to buy one that's not available until mid-August.

"The defendant testified she tried to be fair to her sons? Remember she said 'I give one something, I give the other something'? That's not what we observed once she was arrested. She wrote only to Greg. He's the beneficiary of everything.

"She said 'it was ice packs and it was x-rays.' . . . Thirty one years of abuse and she came up with, maybe, maybe one hospital record, maybe. . . . It's the one from 2001 where she said she had the collision with a chair and hit her palm and an x-ray was given to her and there was nothing wrong. They wrapped her up with an ace bandage.

"She didn't like the fact that her husband was spending less and less time at home. He was spending time doing what he enjoyed, what made him happy. Working on cars and being involved with softball, helping other people. Does it sound like he was a jealous man, or does it sound like she was a jealous woman?

"He writes at the end a self-fulfilling prophecy. He writes, 'I have lived with you for the last twenty years without love for the sake of my sons. Now you want to bludgeon me with the threat of turning Jeff against me as you have with Greg.' . . . That's what he writes. And she did bludgeon him to death not too long after he wrote this.

"Look how she attempted to fool the detective, this scary detective. She said 'He wanted to start a new life without his current family.' No, just without her."

As Ortlieb ran down the list, her voice rising, she paced the front of the courtroom, long hair moving like the tail of a race horse. As much distaste as was conveyed on the faces of Greg and Nancy Seaman as she spoke, the thirteen jurors followed Ortlieb's every movement with intense concentration. It was hard to take your eyes off Lisa.

Her beauty accounted for this in part, but more was going on. There was an incongruous quality to Lisa Ortlieb that had taken me by surprise when she got up to speak: the curious combination of unminced words concerning the very grittiest of details—her easy, almost offhand references to hacking, throat slitting, puddles of blood, pieces of human tissue—all the while uttered in her wholesome, idealistic sorority-girl tones. She could have been a teenager describing the plot of *Halloween III* at a sleepover with her girlfriends, but it was real life, real death, real hacking she was talking about, and what made the scene I now watched more arresting was that someone like Lisa Ortlieb—a woman you might expect to find getting her nails done and reading *Cosmo*, or trying on cute outfits at Marshall Fields—was here in this room instead, discussing things like getting a dead body up an incline plane or the depth of knife incisions to the voice box.

The sense of outrage Lisa conveyed at the violation of justice she believed to have occurred was unmistakably authentic, as was her allegiance to the victim—a man she knew only after death, from the testimony of others, a handful of snapshots provided by the Dumbletons, and a bunch of autopsy photographs that would become the stuff of nightmares for most people. I could tell this was the kind of woman who might actually get a tear in her eye when the national anthem was sung at a Tigers game, the kind of woman for whom the Constitution was a sacred document, a woman who would not rest until she'd seen every criminal in Oakland County safely locked behind bars. There was no doubt in my mind that she believed, with every fiber of her being, in the American justice system.

"Think about how much time she had when she had the first swing," Ortlieb was saying now. "*Aim, swing. Aim, swing.* Over and over again; plenty of time. She chose not to stop. She chose to be a killer.

"Take the hatchet back with you [to the deliberation room]," she said, "Try swinging it once, let alone sixteen times. It takes a concerted effort.

"'Bastard,' 'heartless bastard,' 'screwed up,' . . . calling his best friends names. Does that sound like a woman who wants to avoid a beating?

"What we forget, and please don't forget," she said, standing squarely before the jurors as she spoke, "is that prior to Mother's Day, Bob Seaman was a living human being. He was a cherished family member. He was a cherished friend. He was loved by many. . . . The facts in this case lead to one verdict, and it's the verdict of first-degree murder. Miss I-Plan-Everything deserves a first degree murder conviction."

Lisa Ortlieb sat down. There was silence in the courtroom. Then Larry Kaluzny began to speak.

"'I got flowers today,'" he said. "'It wasn't my birthday, or any other special day. We had an argument last night. He said a lot of cruel things that really hurt me. I know you're sorry and didn't mean the things you said, because you sent me flowers today.'"

For a moment, the jurors appeared baffled. So was I, actually, but at this point I attributed my confusion to having so recently gotten off the plane.

"'I got flowers today,'" he continued soberly. "'It was the day of my funeral. Last night he finally killed me. He beat me to death. If only I had gathered enough courage and strength to leave him. I would not have gotten flowers today.'"

He had been reading from a poem sent to Ann Landers, he explained, written by a woman who had witnessed her mother's death at the hands of her husband.

"Our case is a little bit different, because Bob never said he was sorry," he said, taking a meaningful pause. "If the defendant had not defended herself, this poem would have applied to her."

It might have occurred to some, hearing Larry Kaluzny's words (not to me, once again, because I was not yet acquainted with the testimony to date), that Nancy Seaman had not said she was sorry for murdering her husband. But Nancy Seaman, at least, appeared moved by her attorney's words and the undeniably poignant circumstance they described. He didn't stop there.

"In order to convict Nancy, you have to believe a peaceful, well-respected school teacher decided to kill her husband with a hatchet," said Kaluzny.

"You have to believe that a person who would never ruin her son's graduation would do this the week before. That a person who finally decided that she was going to leave [her husband] by setting up the condo months before would do this . . . a person who struggled to get her degrees, and finally at the age of forty-two gets her degree would throw everything away. In order to convict her you're going to have to believe that a person who had her own accounts, had a retirement, had credit cards, had the condo set up, and a career, would do this."

"Bob had every reason to get rid of Nancy," said Larry Kaluzny. "Because he was losing control, he was going to lose some of his toys. . . . After thirty years, he couldn't handle her finally standing up to him and saying, 'Go ahead and do it.'

"Remember," said Kaluzny, "he put forty bizarre notes, sticky notes, between the front door and the kitchen. Those were bizarre. His behavior was becoming more bizarre. Putting your name on toilet paper?"

Now he was on to the matter of the Dumbletons, who sat there stiffly on a bench, a few rows behind the prosecutor. I had tried not to be obvious about it, but I had to turn around periodically to study their faces—attempting, as I did so, to assess the likelihood that the attractive Asian American woman sitting beside Dick Dumbleton had been Bob Seaman's lover. It didn't seem likely, but I was still just getting my feet wet, I knew. And as unfamiliar as I was with the particulars of the case at this point, I knew well, of course, that every marriage has its secrets. Maybe that was theirs.

Now, though, Dick and Julie Dumbleton were holding each other's hands, and Dick had a protective arm, too, around the shoulders of the young man I thought must be the couple's son, Jake. At the mention of his name by Larry Kaluzny, Dick Dumbleton managed to maintain an outward appearance of calm or at least numbness, but Julie looked as though one strong gust of wind could knock her over.

Beside her, Jake sat rigid and glowering. This may not have been a young man much acquainted with rage or bitterness but they were evident on his face now. There might be no way for him to shoot looks of hatred at Nancy Seaman, but the *Free Press* reporter, Lori Brasier, remained within his range of vision, and though she was not Marcia Low—the one responsible for the highly sympathetic Greg Seaman interview—he regarded her with a look of contempt which suggested that he supposed she was—a look which said that if laser beams were to emanate from his irises, she'd be a dead woman.

"Every single one of us would be upset about the Dumbletons' intrusion into her ability to try to save the marriage," said Larry Kaluzny, earnest and reasonable sounding. "That was going on for years. An intrusion in trying to keep a good relationship between the sons and their father. Is it any wonder why she was so upset with them?

"And the relationship that he had with them was bizarre," Kaluzny continued, replacing "creepy," the adjective the defense had favored in its earlier portrayals. While the woman Lori Brazier pointed out to me as Larry Kaluzny's wife looked on approvingly, he reminded the jury of Nancy's words concerning Bob's alleged desire for sexual role playing, with an emphasis on twelve-year-old girls.

In no particular order, then, he tossed out a number of reasons why the jury should find Nancy Seaman not guilty. "A person who plans like that doesn't commit a murder like this with no plan," he reminded them.

"Remember . . . the nickname the boys had for their dad? 'Psycho dad.' *Psycho dad.*"

As opposed to Nancy: "A planner. . . . A fixer. . . . A handywoman. . . . A peaceful person. Everybody knew that except Julie or that family."

For a man known around the courthouse as the quintessential nice guy—a man who, even as he championed the cause of the defendant, went out of his way to speak well of the prosecutor and the police, a man who spoke well of just about everybody, come to think of it—Larry Kaluzny launched into an uncharacteristically aggressive attack.

Above all, he took aim at Jeff. He asked the jury to consider the Seaman brothers. *Compare and contrast.*

"How can we explain two brothers having such different opposing views in the same family?" he asked. "I think part of it is that Jeff was so close to his dad, his best friend, and he idolized him. . . .

"Look at his demeanor. When he testified, it was so inappropriate. I don't know, am I making this up? If I am, you disregard it. He was jovial. He was telling jokes. He was throwing things in. That's not a kid whose father, your best friend, has died, and your mom's on trial for murder. . . . It was so inappropriate."

But there was a good son in the Seaman family too, Kaluzny reminded the jury now. Greg. "Greg . . . saw through this façade," the attorney said. "He saw what was going on in the home. He was serious when he testified. He was responsive to the questions, and he was trying to be truthful. . . . He took the different path than Jeff did. He took the path of the truth, and that's a much tougher path when you're dealing with what was going on. He knew what his dad was capable of."

The question Larry Kaluzny raised here concerned the psychological phenomenon of denial, of course. In Kaluzny's view, Jeff Seaman could not look honestly at the actions of his father and see the man for who he truly was. Lisa Ortlieb, though she had not stated it quite so baldly, no doubt believed about Greg the very things Larry expressed about Jeff. One thing was certain: one of the sons in this family was living in a state of denial concerning one of the parents. The jury would ultimately have to decide which was which.

There was one more thing about Nancy Seaman they needed to remember, Kaluzny reminded the jury. She still loved her husband. "Even Greg said," Larry reminded the court, " 'in spite of what he was like, there was love.' "

"I must have missed the part where she said how much she loved him," Lori Brasier whispered to me now, scribbling on her notepad. It would have been hard, she added, to find a single moment, throughout the trial, in which either Nancy or Greg Seaman had recalled a single affectionate memory of Bob or described a single endearing characteristic of the man who had been Nancy's husband and Greg's father. The best either of them had been able to do in that regard (and it was the line Larry now urged the jurors to remember) had been Nancy's observation that Bob had possessed "charm," that "he could light up a room." One look at the ravaged face of Jake Dumbleton, seated in the courtroom, near tears, suggested that Bob Seaman had inspired a deeper kind of feeling in some people, whether or not his younger son had been one of them.

"Ralph Waldo Emerson, over a hundred years ago, said that one man's justice is another man's injustice," Kaluzny went on.

The lines that followed, however, belonged to the attorney himself, and he delivered them with the closest thing he had yet demonstrated to passion:

"If ever there was a case that should not be guilty, this is it. If there ever was a case that depicts Battered Wife Syndrome, this is it. If there was ever a case that cries out for justice for the defendant, this is it.

"She's been through enough," he concluded. "She deserves not guilty."

With a certain air of anticlimax, then, the defense rested its case. Larry Kaluzny took his seat beside his son. Julie Dumbleton and Jake exchanged uneasy glances. Nancy Seaman shot a look in the direction of Greg. Eugene D'Onofrio sat resolute on the bench, staring straight ahead, looking like a sleepwalker.

The last word belonged to Lisa Ortlieb. I felt an immediate eleva-
tion in my interest level as she got up to address the court again. As
great looking as she was, she wasn't the type to coast on that. She was
working hard here.

First she reminded the jury of Nancy Seaman's words to Greg, "The
Dumbletons ruined our life."

"The Dumbletons?" she said. "This case is about *the Dumbletons?*

"Look over at the defense table," she told the jury, pointing in the
direction of the stony visage of Nancy Seaman. "Put the face of a man
on her. Would any of you let her walk out of this courtroom if she
were a man?"

She asked the jury to consider the likelihood that Nancy had been
on the verge of turning herself in that Wednesday afternoon, when
Detective Patterson beat her to it and interrupted her in the final stages
of her preparations over on Briarwood Court.

"There's not an actual place where you can drop off a murdered
body," Ortlieb said. No attempt at levity here, though a certain dark
humor could be found if you conjured an image of a location somewhere in Oakland County, in which someone like Dr. Dragovic,
maybe, could be found standing at the drive-through, ready to receive
corpses.

Lisa Ortlieb was skipping around quite a bit here, but the jurors
appeared to be with her. She reminded them how Greg had said, "I
was jealous of the Dumbletons. They took my dad away."

"But in the next minute he's saying, 'Dad's a bad guy. Dad was beating Mom.' So why would he care?"

"You think a woman who's battered is going to refuse sex?" she
pointed out (on to a new idea again, with lightning speed), referring
to the sleeping arrangements at Bob and Nancy's house, following the
alleged role-playing incident involving twelve-year-olds and the softball team.

"Don't you think you'd get a beating for refusing sex since December? Don't you think sending a letter accusing your husband of being
a pedophile, hurting someone he loved, . . . don't you think that would
get a big beating?

"The most dangerous time is when someone is leaving, absolutely,
for Battered Woman Syndrome," Lisa Ortlieb asserted, echoing the
words of Dr. Lenore Walker.

"Only the person leaving here was Bob. He just didn't know he'd
be leaving in the back of Nancy's car."

She was almost done, but Lisa had one final point to make. She reached now for a brown paper bag and held it out, in clear view of the jury box. She reached her hand into the bag, to reveal People's Exhibit 31, a hatchet. She held it out over her head—in a manner not unlike that of Nancy Seaman, perhaps, as she had faced her husband on the black-and-white, Indy 500–inspired tile floor of the garage on Briarwood Court that day, just before taking that first swing and all the others that followed it. This hatchet was not the murder weapon, however. This was the hatchet Nancy Seaman had shoplifted and then returned a moment later at Home Depot, on the night of Tuesday, May 11. Although the hatchet had been submitted into evidence earlier, this was the first time it had actually been taken out of the bag.

"Notice something?" Lisa Ortlieb asked the jurors. "A blade cover. *A blade cover.*

"You have to take the blade cover off to cause the injury that she did."

I could almost hear a gasp in the courtroom then. "Oh, my gosh," said Lori Brasier. "We weren't expecting *that.*"

Lisa Ortlieb took her seat with the air of a woman who knows she's knocked it out of the park with that last at-bat. The trial was over.

Only, as it turned out, there was one more person to be heard from. Nancy Seaman had been silent all this time, except during her testimony. But Lisa Ortlieb's final, dramatic moment of unveiling the hatchet with the blade cover had touched off in her a cry as piercing as if the blade itself had struck directly at her heart.

Now Nancy Seaman covered her face in her hands and let out a high wail. "It's not fair," she cried out.

From the bench behind her, where her father and brother and the rest of her supporters sat, a rumble of dismay arose. Even the unflappable and forever easygoing Larry Kaluzny—a man who looked as though he wouldn't lose his temper even if he shanked his golf ball—appeared at least momentarily agitated. At the very moment they were about to head off to weigh the evidence and come up with their verdict, the jurors had been left with the indelible image of that blade cover. Only a day earlier, they had witnessed Nancy Seaman's dramatic reenactment of her final confrontation with her husband in the garage and heard her testify that she had reached up to the generator in a moment of terror and fear for her life, grabbed the hatchet, and swung.

Now suddenly they would have to revise that picture to incorporate a whole new step, one that considerably altered the picture of wild, uncontrollable panic. It appeared that before striking, Nancy Seaman would first have had to remove that blade cover, and though the defense might have argued that this particular hatchet had not come with a cover or that Nancy had removed the blade cover as soon as she got home from Home Depot, there would be no opportunity for any of that now. Lisa Ortlieb had gotten the last word. She, and Nancy—whose near-scream of outrage had left a powerful impression as well.

For the first time, perhaps, those who'd been in the courtroom to hear her might have felt they'd caught a glimpse of the side of the defendant's character that had sufficient rage and pain to commit a murder. The sound of Nancy Seaman, wailing, was disconcerting, revealing in the defendant a capacity, perhaps, for the very kind of outburst that might have taken place in the garage on Briarwood Court.

The jury was escorted from the courtroom. There would be no further rebuttal allowed, but in the eyes of the defense, the damage done as a result of the dramatic way in which Lisa Ortlieb had chosen to conclude her remarks was inestimable. Now, over the sound of his client's weeping, Larry Kaluzny approached the bench to offer his objection and move for a mistrial. For the first time in the trial, my new friend from the *Free Press* observed, Larry actually appeared angry.

Lisa Ortlieb stood firm. What she had done was totally within the bounds of law, she pointed out. The shoplifted hatchet had been submitted into evidence days before, along with a written description clearly identifying the hatchet in question as being encased in a blade cover. Judge McDonald ruled Lisa Ortlieb's action admissible. The defendant was once again shackled and led from the courtroom.

The reporters raced to file their stories—Lori Brasier, hair flying, among them.

"You're welcome to come down to my office in the basement tomorrow morning, while we're waiting for the verdict," she said. I scribbled down her number. Then, with no pressing deadline, I decided to introduce myself to a few of the main characters in the case.

I pushed my way through the crowd of bystanders now toward Larry Kaluzny, standing with his son near the front of the courtroom. Larry was upset over what he viewed as Lisa Ortlieb's shenanigans with the blade cover. But even in his state of what for him constituted anger, he remained affable and open to meeting with me later. Hearing that I was a writer, he reached into his briefcase, where he evidently had been carrying around a copy of a self-published novel written by his other son, Ryan (he too had two sons), called *And Guest*. (It was a title that referred to the invitations single people get when invited to their friends' weddings. He described the book as "sort of *Sex and the City* for guys" and mentioned that it would be great if I knew the name of a good agent.) I slipped the book into my purse.

"Of course I'm anxious to speak with Nancy," I said. "But I'm sure that until the jury comes in with its verdict, she'll be in no mood to think about anything else."

"We'll work it out," Kaluzny said, warmly. "It's important that Nancy's story gets out. If she can save just one battered woman from the hell she went through—"

"Give me a call after the verdict," he told me. "We've got *Oprah* interested, and *48 Hours*." This was life in the media, I thought. For now, Nancy Seaman was big news.

Over on the other side of the room, Lisa Ortlieb, even in the first flush of euphoria from finishing her case, was equally welcoming and friendly, talking a mile a minute. Her husband, David Gorcyca, had come down from his office to see her deliver her closing remarks. She gazed up into the strong-jawed countenance of Gorcyca with the look of a woman in love, and though—as she reminded the many who now circled round to congratulate her—the jury had yet to come in with its verdict, she looked not only beautiful but happy and confident, a woman on top of the world.

Not so, the bystanders. The Dumbleton family—who had heard themselves described during the proceedings as having a "creepy" and "bizarre" relationship with Bob Seaman—had staggered numbly out the swinging doors the minute closing statements were over, looking as if they might need to throw up. Eighteen-year-old Jake, in particular, was a portrait in grief.

Out in the hall as I left the courtroom, I saw that members of Nancy Seaman's family and a small cluster of teachers had lingered to commiserate about the latest offense on the part of that young prosecutor. Eugene D'Onofrio shook his fist. John D'Onofrio looked ready to spit. Nobody wanted to talk to anybody he or she wasn't related to (as I learned when I tried to speak with first John D'Onofrio, then his wife), though in the case of certain Seaman family members, blood connection alone hardly ensured trust and good will.

Greg Seaman stood a little way apart from the group, not talking. I approached him cautiously—in the manner, I hoped, less of a hard-driving journalist dogging her story than of a mother of a son just about his age and someone who felt, as I truly did at that particular moment, an abundance of sympathy and compassion.

Having missed all of the trial until today, and having yet to speak with any of those most centrally involved in the case, I had formed no opinions about the guilt or innocence of Nancy Seaman, the likelihood that Bob Seaman had been an abusive husband, or the veracity of one brother's testimony over that of the other.

But as a woman with her own long history at that point, I approached the case with a certain natural, almost automatic loyalty to another woman, a mother like myself, just about my age, and to each of the two young men who were her sons. I was not a victim of domestic abuse, but I had known plenty of women who were. So finding sympathy and compassion for Nancy Seaman required little effort, as I watched her led off in shackles that day. As I approached Greg Seaman, I found myself imagining how it would be for one of my sons (like Nancy, I speak of them still as "my boys") to sit in a courtroom and see me led in wearing shackles, on trial for murder. I pictured my son Willy in his suit—sleeves a little short, pants a little long—stepping into the witness box, knowing that his words might save my life or doom me.

That image was still in my mind as I introduced myself to Greg Seaman in the hallway of the courthouse that afternoon.

"I know this is a hard time," I said. "I wouldn't expect you to feel like talking now. But I'll be writing a book about what happened in your family, and I'll need to talk to you."

Need to, I told him. I could not imagine telling this story, the story of the decimation of the Seaman family, without the insights of this heartbroken-looking young man, the same age as my son Charlie, who, like Greg Seaman, had graduated from college the previous May.

I did not press my telephone number into Greg Seaman's hand and didn't have a business card. I told him I'd be around for a while and would wait till he was ready. Our eyes met briefly, and I saw that haunted gaze of his.

He stood there a moment, saying nothing. Then he turned and disappeared down the hall.

Out in the parking lot, I spotted him again. He was standing alone in the snow, getting into his car. It was a Ford Explorer.

CHAPTER 47

The Jury Decides

The proceedings finished for the day, I drove back to my friend Rebecca's house a few miles down Telegraph Road and spent a night of uncharacteristically troubled sleep. The next morning I brushed the snow off the windshield of my rental car and made my way back down Telegraph to Oakland County Courthouse, to await the verdict.

My first stop was the basement of the courthouse, to take advantage of Lori Brasier's invitation to visit her office, so we could talk while the two of us waited for the jury to come in with the verdict. This could take days, of course, but Lori's guess, based on years of covering Oakland County criminal proceedings, was that we'd hear from them soon.

We sat now in the tiny and hopelessly messy basement room, drinking bad coffee, while she filled me in on some of the players in the case—Ortlieb, Kaluzny, Chief Dwyer, Gorcyca.

I might have expected a local reporter on a story like this one to possess a territorial attitude and to view an outsider like me with chilly suspicion, but this time I was lucky. A voluptuous woman with a big laugh and a blunt, noir-ish way of talking that would have made her a natural as a character in an updated Raymond Chandler novel, Lori gave me a chair and a stale cookie, and complimented me on my shoes. She was the type—like me, and nothing like Nancy Seaman, in this regard—who, if she put on a suit, would probably discover that it was missing a button or that there was a coffee stain on the lapel. I liked her right away.

Lori had somehow managed to combine spending her days with an unlikely mix of activities: reporting on unspeakably violent and horrifying crimes (a full decade's worth of stories about mothers scalding their babies, a man who kidnapped his wife and drove around with her in the trunk for three days until she died of thirst, a man who'd injected bleach into a woman's veins for reneging on a drug debt), and overseeing the mundane details of kids, husband, and family life: phone calls home to arrange figure skating lessons for her thirteen-year-old stepdaughter and doctor's appointments for her ten-year-old son. More than once, over the course of the morning, she engaged in brief, playful conversations with her husband, Mike, a former reporter himself, who now worked in construction—and was the love of her life. She was writing a mystery novel on the side, she told me, between calls and courthouse gossip, and I had a feeling—based on our conversation that day—that her fiction would probably be considerably spicier than Ryan Kaluzny's.

At three-thirty that afternoon—after less than five hours of deliberation—word came down to the little basement bunker where Lori and I had camped out that the jury had reached a decision. Trials tended to move swiftly through the system in Oakland County, Lori told me—but this jury had made its decision even more quickly than average. Within fifteen minutes, everyone who had scattered to wait for the verdict reconvened in Judge McDonald's courtroom: Lisa Ortlieb, Larry Kaluzny, the Dumbletons. I took my seat again, notebook in hand, on the bench with the other reporters. I had seldom been in a room in which more was about to happen, or more at stake. Only when giving birth, probably. And at my mother's bedside, when she lay dying. Then, too, you had the feeling that life as you knew it was about to be changed forever.

To nobody's particular surprise, Jeff Seaman was absent. At Nancy Seaman's specific request, Greg and the rest of Nancy's family had also stayed away this time. It would have been too difficult for her, she'd told her attorneys, to see her younger son's face when she got the word from the jury. But if things went her way today, she could be home by midafternoon.

Nancy herself was brought in, her shackles removed. She took her seat, her face immobile. The jurors filed in, then the judge.

He asked the jurors if they had reached a decision. They had. The foreman—a homemaker around the age of the defendant—stood to read the verdict.

"In the case of the People versus Nancy Seaman, the jury finds the defendant guilty of murder in the first degree."

The day before, when Lisa Ortlieb had pulled out that hatchet, Nancy Seaman had cried out and then wept. Today, hearing the words that would send her to prison for the rest of her life, she shrugged as her attorney patted her arm. The only change I could detect in her expression was an odd flash of something resembling a smile. Maybe it was a look meant to suggest she'd known it was coming. No big shock. Perhaps just an odd nervous reaction.

Lisa Ortlieb was not the type to gloat, but her joy at the verdict was unmistakable. Larry Kaluzny—a man accustomed to a certain amount of disappointment in the courtroom, shook his head with weary but good-natured resignation and regret. With stunning speed then, Nancy was shackled and led from the courtroom. The whole thing— from the reading of the verdict to Nancy's exit from the courtroom— lasted two minutes at most, though as she was being taken away I thought about how often over the years she would replay this scene, and how much time she would have to do so.

Later, once things calmed down, a small group of jurors appeared back in the courtroom, ready to answer questions from the press. Had there been any major dissent among the jurors as to the verdict? Did they at any point consider the lesser charges of second-degree murder or (the hope of the defense) manslaughter?

"No to both. The verdict was unanimous."

They had not been particularly impressed with the job the defense had done, one of them remarked, but Lisa Ortlieb's theatrical display of the blade cover, in the final moments of her rebuttal to Larry Kaluzny's closing statement, had in no way influenced them, the jurors said.

What had been compelling in the testimony, to bring the jury to its decision? one of the reporters asked.

"Bob had no defense wounds," said a juror named Michael Jezierski. "We didn't think he saw it coming."

"She didn't have defensive injuries either," said Michelle Kenyon, another juror. "I didn't think she was abused. She didn't shed a tear. And Greg—though he looked sincere, I just didn't believe him."

"I thought she was trying to oversell it," said another juror, Tom Rachfal, of Nancy Seaman's testimony. "It came across as rehearsed. She was not a meek woman, waiting for the next beating."

"The toughest thing was the Home Depot trip, to buy something to do what seemed pretty insignificant yard work," said Jezierski.

Juror Patty Bedard added, "I do not believe she was a battered woman." Instead, she said, Seaman had come across as "jealous and hateful"—a mother who caused friction between her husband and sons.

"I think both of these boys were in a horrible position," said the jury foreman, Nini Guindi Couri. "It was very sad to watch. Very disturbing."

"At the end of the day, that's the tragedy," offered Lynn Bronson. "The brothers' relationship is over."

The jurors didn't buy the argument that Nancy Seaman had continued stabbing her husband out of fear that he might get up and kill her, they said. They were shocked by the brutality of the killing—some of them adding that since beginning their jury service, they'd had difficulty sleeping.

But they would not lose sleep over this verdict, they now told the assembled press. They had entered into the trial with minds open, but by the end, no ambivalence remained concerning the guilt of Nancy Seaman or the fact that when she set out to Home Depot that night, it was with the intent to buy a hatchet to kill her husband.

For me it was a little different, contemplating the guilty verdict that day. Heading out into the snowy parking lot of Oakland County Courthouse, I imagined how it would be if I were sent to prison for life. My first thought: how I would miss my children.

I thought about the babies they would have someday, most likely, and all the things I wouldn't get to do with them. Odd pictures came to mind: no more swimming; no more making pies; no more kissing. Good-bye to pretty clothes and riding a bicycle, privacy in the bathroom, the ocean, wine. Thinking about the catalogue of losses a woman faced, heading to prison for life, my head began to ache, and I felt nauseated.

I hadn't murdered anyone, of course, and Nancy Seaman had. Still, I had come to Michigan believing that perhaps this woman had no choice in the matter—or not enough of one, anyway. And although the scraps of testimony I'd picked up so far, combined with what I'd gathered of the case from the two lawyers' summations, had left me with the sense that things were not as simple as how they had been represented to be in that first television report (abusive and unfaithful husband, battered woman, self-defense). Still I was thinking: nobody kills her husband with a hatchet unless he's done something terrible to her first.

I thought about the book I wanted to write. I intended to tell what really happened. But there was another part of the process. I wanted to find out why. If I stuck around this place awhile, I thought, I would find out.

For some reason that I didn't fully understand at the time, I knew as I drove away from the courthouse that day that for a while at least—how long, I didn't know—I would be leaving the life I'd made for myself in my comfortable, sunny California home, for the landscape of suburban Michigan. There was some kind of lesson for me in what had taken place here, though at the time, I couldn't have said what it was.

St. Louis days: Ward and Helen Seaman
with their children, Margie, Bob (front
right), David, and Dennis, summer 1953.

Bob's high school graduation portrait, class of '64 (just before the release of the first Mustang).

Straight-A student Nancy D'Onofrio's senior picture. "A giant step in the pursuit of excellence has already been realized."
—Lincoln Park High School yearbook, 1970.

The young bride, Nancy D'Onofrio, gets her Ford man, summer 1973.

"Smart, single, and short." Bob Seaman admires his new bride, Nancy, at their wedding.

Bob, the new father, holding infant Jeff, approximately six months old.

Jeff and Greg,
September 1981.

Jeff Seaman and his little brother, Greg, dressed up for a
family graduation, May 1985.

Nancy and Greg (hiding his face), August 1995.

Christmas with Bob's family in Missouri: Nancy, Jeff, and Bob (Greg is hiding his face), December 1997.

Jeff Seaman, the spitting image of his father, senior picture, 1997.

Greg Seaman, his mother's boy, senior picture, 1999.

The Seaman home in the Ramblewood subdivision in Farmington Hills, May 2004. Photo by Amy Leang. (Reprinted with permission of the *Detroit Free Press*.)

Bob with Jenna and Dick Dumbleton, when the two men coached the Northville Girls, 2001.

The wedding of Jeff and Becka Seaman in St. Louis—with best
man, Jake Dumbleton, and Jenna Dumbleton, August 2001.

Dick and Julie
Dumbleton, or—as
Nancy Seaman called
them—"The Dumbies."

Nancy and Bob
Seaman at Jeff and
Becka's wedding in
St. Louis, August
2001.

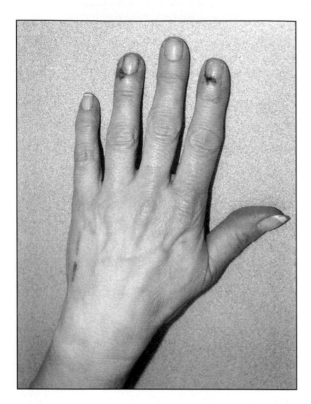

The photograph Nancy Seaman requested after her arrest, to document her injuries.

Bob at the wheel of his Ferrari, in front of the Seaman home on Briarwood Court.

Ward and Helen
Seaman in
Mattoon, Illinois,
in the late
eighties.

Greg's Mustang in the Seaman garage—the place where Bob
was killed.

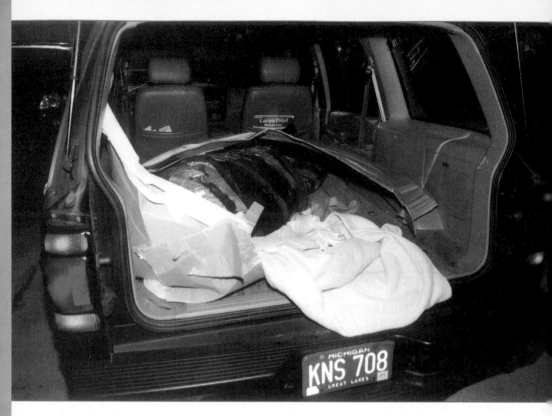

Dangerous cargo: the body of Bob Seaman, wrapped in a
tarp, in the back of his Explorer, as discovered in May 2004.

William Dwyer, Farmington Hills
Chief of Police. (Reprinted with permission of the Farmington Hills
Police Department.)

Larry Kaluzny, for the defense. (Photo
credit: Jose Juarez/ *The Oakland Press.*)

TEACHER KILLS HUSBAND

Woman accused in fatal hatchet attack

COURT TV

Court TV airs Day Two of
the trial. (Reprinted with
permission of Court TV.)

Lisa Ortlieb, for the prosecution. (Photo credit: Jose
Juarez/The Oakland Press.)

Nancy at trial, shackled, but well dressed.
(Photo credit: Jose Juarez/*The Oakland Press.*)

Judge John McDonald presiding over the trial. Photo by Susan
Tusa. (Reprinted with permission of the *Detroit Free Press.*)

Dr. Ljubisa Dragovic takes the stand at the trial. Photo by Susan Tusa. (Reprinted with permission of the *Detroit Free Press*.)

Lisa Ortlieb, wielding the hatchet. Note blade cover circled. Photo by Chip Somodevilla. (Reprinted with permission of the *Detroit Free Press*.)

Nancy Seaman at her sentencing. (Photo credit: Vaughn Gurganian/*The Oakland Press.*)

Greg Seaman at his mother's sentencing. (Photo credit: Vaughn Gurganian/*The Oakland Press.*)

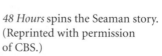

48 Hours spins the Seaman story. (Reprinted with permission of CBS.)

Looking for Answers

CHAPTER 48

Ninety Thousand Burial Sites to Open Shortly

T he recorded announcement callers hear when put on hold at Oakland County Courthouse reminds them that Oakland County is one of the four most affluent counties of its size in the United States, with an average household income of just under $50,000. The place where the murder of Bob Seaman occurred also boasts that it is home to corporate offices of every Fortune 500 company in America, as well as "a dynamic international marketplace."

Over the course of the many months I spent immersed in the Seaman case, I made so many calls to the courthouse that eventually I had most of the message memorized. "Wall Street has rewarded Oakland County for its strong economic performance and prudence with a triple-A rating, the highest rating possible," the tape continues. "Retail sales in Oakland County for the year 2002 surpassed the total retail sales of fourteen states and the District of Columbia."

Days when I was kept on hold a sufficiently long period of time (as frequently occurred, in a county where so much growth and business were reportedly taking place), I was also reminded that in addition to being "home to Automation Alley, the premier technology corridor in America," and to the Chrysler Motor Car Museum, Oakland County boasted the Cranbrook Academy of Art Museum, eighty-nine thousand acres of pristine parkland, and the Woodward Avenue Dream Cruise, attended by over a million visitors every August. With no shift in tone, the soothing female voice on the recording then went on to say that Oakland County also holds the unique distinction of being the site of Michigan's second largest national veterans' cemetery, with ninety thousand burial sites, set to open shortly.

All in all, the voice concluded (before the loop began again), Oakland County "is gaining recognition as one of America's premier locations in which to live, work, and raise a family." (And, based on available cemetery plots, a great place to die—for veterans, anyway.)

The Seamans, residents of the Ramblewood subdivision of Farmington Hills, could have been a prime example of Oakland County prosperity and quality of life—up until Mother's Day weekend of 2004, at any rate. Of course, the cars and boat, the season tickets to ball games, and the ease with which the family went out for restaurant dinners or sent their kids to expensive private colleges did not tell the whole story. The Seamans were surely not the only family whose enviable-looking life was not all it appeared to be, viewed from outside the gates of their exclusive gated community. All up and down Telegraph Road, in the equally comfortable-looking subdivisions of Birmingham, Bloomfield Hills, Southfield, and Grosse Pointe, other families like the Seamans were no doubt hauling around their own forms of uncomfortable baggage, as they made their way from jobs to kids' practices to shopping, at the wheels of their big American SUVs that appeared to be the vehicle of choice, from the looks of the parking lots at the chain stores and supermarkets lining the highway.

The particular bizarre turn that the lives of Nancy and Bob Seaman took may have been unique, but stories of domestic violence, divorce ugliness, and fractured families were hardly unique to Briarwood Court. If most of these families did not end up as ruined as the Seamans, the signs of economic stress and unraveling, at least, were abundantly evident in Oakland County in the summer of 2005— where, despite the upbeat reports on the tape-recorded message at the courthouse, times were tough and getting tougher.

Middle-class families had no doubt endured stress acquiring and then holding on to their "toys," to use the language of the Seamans, for as long as there had been gated communities and subdivisions, Target Stores and charge cards, car payments and divorce attorneys, but the economic picture in Metro Detroit was particularly bleak that summer.

More days than not over the course of those months, when I picked up my copy of the *Detroit News* or the *Free Press,* it would feature a story about trouble in the auto industry: recalls, layoffs, more disturbing signs of business moving overseas, or at least away from Detroit. In July, the *Free Press* ran a story about the Explorer—for many years a key element in the fleet of big-selling Ford vehicles. Sales were way down. Prices had to drop, with longtime Ford loyalists looking toward Japan for their automotive purchases. It was uncertain, the paper reported darkly, whether the traditionally top-selling Explorer line would find much of a buying public out there waiting for the 2006 line of cars.

Reading this story, I tried to imagine any major metropolitan area in the nation—not even Silicon Valley, California, perhaps—where news of a single product's sales would hold such a powerful place in the lives of its inhabitants as to appear not in the business section but the front page. As the fortunes of the Explorer went—and the Mustang, and the Ford F150 truck—so, to a certain degree, went the fortunes of Metro Detroit.

This was bad news, all right. In Dearborn, at least, the sun rose and set over the headquarters of the Ford Motor Company, where Bob and Nancy Seaman met, and where—thirty-two years later—Jeff Seaman held the title of senior calibrator for none other than the Ford Explorer. Jeff's job was not in jeopardy, but the world around him and his coworkers (like that of Greg Seaman, over at the offices of American Axle in Troy) was filled with an unfamiliar brand of uncertainty.

Automobiles matter everywhere these days, of course, but the vehicle a person drives carries a whole other significance in Oakland County, I learned. One of the first things I had done, after settling in there to conduct my research into the story of the Seaman case, was to buy myself a car. As a lifelong believer in used vehicles, I set out to locate the cheapest form of reasonably reliable transportation possible, and found myself a 1997 Pontiac Eagle with 130,000 miles on the engine and enough rust that you could see inside the trunk without opening it. It was Mike, the husband of my new friend Lori Brasier, who had located the car for me. The price was $2,000.

I'd driven older used cars all my life without shame or apology. Now, though, cruising along the highway (and parking outside the many tidy suburban homes and offices where the people lived and worked, with whom it was important to talk in pursuit of my story), I came to understand the way people in Metro Detroit viewed their vehicles, and the way that what you drove colored their attitude about who you might be. A person could go a few miles along Telegraph, or Woodward Avenue that ran parallel to it, without spotting a vehicle manufactured before the year 2000, unless it was something along the lines of a classic Mustang or Thunderbird, a Cadillac convertible, or maybe a Barracuda.

And the cars were not just new. They were American. In California, I hardly ever thought about the makes of cars around me when I drove, but here in Detroit, a BMW or even a Volkswagen would stand out in the sea of American-made products, so many of them sporting yellow "Support Our Troops" decals and flags or—a little further north—gun racks, and it was not entirely impossible that other drivers, spotting an expensive Mercedes or an Audi, would register a certain hostility as they pulled up alongside those vehicles at a stoplight.

Hondas, like the one I drove back home, and Toyotas, and VWs, and Nissans like those in whose design and engineering Dick Dumbleton participated over in Northville—were one reason why the GM plant in Flint, and even Ford, were laying off workers. The glory days of the seventies that people in Oakland County still talked about were long past—days when a high school graduate fresh out of school could get a job on the assembly line and (thanks in part to the man who remained a hero to many here thirty years after his disappearance, Jimmy Hoffa) find himself pulling down $70,000 with benefits before he was twenty-five.

What jobs Japan hadn't stolen, automation and the rising cost of fuel had. It might not be immediately apparent in the comfortable communities like Farmington Hills, but when you drove up and down Telegraph you saw the signs of a fraying economy: real estate that stayed on the market month after month, reduced prices reduced again; empty storefronts; businesses announcing going-out-of-business sales.

The most eerie sign, to me, could be found within a half mile of the Oakland County Courthouse, at the once-bustling Summit Place Mall. The flagship store of the mall—Marshall Fields—remained open, but with only a handful of cars in front, and more than half the retail spaces were vacant, the movie theater not simply closed down but with an actual fallen tree now blocking what had once been the front entrance.

I had stopped by one Sunday afternoon to pick up a pair of running shoes. Inside the deserted mall, women wearing workout suits and pedometers had evidently discovered that the nearly vacant expanses of heated walkways connecting the closed-down stores were the ideal location to get in a quick hour of vigorous cardio without the cold blasts of wind blowing in from the lake or the inconvenience of too many shoppers in the way to slow them down.

Maybe it was the easy availability of vacant mall space or the depressed job market or the general economic climate, but I observed a curious phenomenon at this and other malls (curious to a resident of liberal Marin County, California, anyway): nearly every one of them housed an Army recruitment center. The recruitment centers appeared not to be doing great business either, but they were everywhere, doors open and lights on, waiting for the moment when the young people who could no longer win jobs with the Big Three got desperate enough.

CHAPTER 49

A Letter to Oakland County Jail

T he first thing I'd done back in December of 2004, when I decided to embark on researching the story of the Seaman family, was to send a letter to Nancy herself, explaining my interest in her case, my background as a writer with a particular interest in family relationships, and my hope that by spending time with her and listening to her story, I might be able to understand, and then to help explain, how such a tragedy could have occurred.

In that first letter to Nancy Seaman, I wrote that it seemed reasonable, given that I was asking her to tell me her story, that she have some sense of mine. Rules concerning the mail for inmates in the county jail (and, later, the prison where she was remanded to serve her sentence) made it impossible for me to send Nancy Seaman a copy of any books I'd written, but I filled her in on my background as a writer and what I'd published in the past. (One piece of work I chose not to mention was my novel *To Die For*, loosely based on a real case that had played out in my home state of New Hampshire, in which a wife had conspired with her teenage lover to have her husband killed.)

What I did write in my letter to her was that I too had known unhappiness in my marriage and had lived through a painful divorce. I told her about the years I'd spent writing a newspaper column dealing with the life of a woman at home, raising children—and the letters I'd received from readers over the years, speaking so often of abuse they'd experienced in their marriages. If she gave me a chance to hear her story, I wrote, I felt I could understand.

At the time I first wrote to Nancy Seaman, I had not yet heard all the testimony offered at her trial or read the trial transcript. I had not yet spoken to anyone other than those individuals to whom I'd introduced myself so briefly in the courtroom the day the jury came in with its verdict. I explained to Nancy Seaman that it was my plan to seek out people affected by this story, of both points of view (meaning that I'd be contacting her son Jeff as well as Greg, and Julie Dumbleton and Dennis Seaman).

"No reputable reporter would fail to do this," I wrote, "and were I to neglect contacting those people, nothing I ultimately wrote could be taken seriously." But I added that "the truth of the story should speak for itself," and that if in fact her story of abuse was an authentic one, that would emerge in my telling of her story.

My letter was mailed shortly after the guilty verdict but before the date of Nancy Seaman's sentencing, January 24. I would be back in Oakland County for that day, I wrote. (There was no question what Judge McDonald's sentence would be. No options existed but life without parole. But Nancy would have an opportunity to address the court, and I wanted to be there to hear her.)

I knew that once Nancy Seaman was transferred from Oakland County Jail, where she'd been held since the previous May, to whatever facility was chosen for her to do her time, visitation restrictions would be considerably tighter: no visits for the first several months in prison; only a certain relatively small number after that, and only for the few individuals—the allowed number was ten—whose names she had chosen to place on her list. Even more restrictive: an inmate was allowed only two opportunities in a given year to add or subtract a name from her visitors' list. Even assuming I made the cut, it was unlikely I would be allowed to bring paper and pen into the prison.

For all these reasons, it seemed likely that the majority of our discussions—discussions I imagined were likely to involve many days and months of talk between the two of us, as I sought to understand what had taken place and perhaps befriend this woman—would have to be conducted over the phone. Specifically because this was so, it seemed important that we meet face-to-face at least once, before her transfer from the county jail to the prison, so that she could get to know me (and could decide if she felt comfortable talking with me) and I could get to know her.

I could feel the pressure now of vying for an audience with a woman who, for this brief moment at least, seemed to represent a hot media commodity. The producers of *48 Hours* were now moving forward with their plan to produce a segment on Nancy's case, and *Inside Edition* was talking about a follow-up. Now and then that other elusive and magical name came up too: *Oprah.*

So I made my pitch, the best I knew how. I couldn't offer the glamour of television or a glossy magazine, but I would take the time to understand her story in a way television was unlikely to. I knew too that if Nancy felt comfortable talking with me, it was a sure bet that Greg would do the same, along with Nancy's brother and father, the teachers who had supported her through all these months, and Rick Cox.

The problem as I saw it then lay less with Nancy and Greg than it did with Jeff and Becka Seaman.

I sent letters to both Jeff and Greg, introducing myself, explaining my intentions, and enclosing examples of books I'd written—my recent novels, *The Usual Rules* and *The Cloud Chamber,* and my memoir, *At Home in the World.* I explained to each of them my intention to hear what everyone had to say in the case. I told them what I truly believed: that a person who tells the truth and believes his actions to have been the best he could have undertaken in the circumstances need not be afraid of seeing them reported on or of being quoted expressing what he feels. Not if he's talking with a fair and thoughtful reporter, I said, and I knew myself to be such a person.

"My role here," I wrote, "is to listen to what everyone has to tell me, with an open mind."

I did not hear from either Jeff or Greg at this point, but I understood that they were going through a terrible experience, and figured now was not the time to pressure them.

Then came a call from Larry Kaluzny. "Nancy wants to meet you," he said. As many people as there were wanting to talk with her, he had reserved an hour for me to meet with her on the afternoon of the sentencing, January 24, at Oakland County Jail.

CHAPTER 50

"Your Mom Slept with My Dad"

On January 23, 2005—the day before Nancy Seaman's sentencing in Judge McDonald's courtroom—a monster snowstorm hit the Midwest. Flights were cancelled, and those that landed arrived hours late. Reports on the Weather Channel, and the assessment of my friend Rebecca in Birmingham, suggested that I'd be lucky if I made it to Detroit in time for my scheduled visit with Nancy, let alone the 9 A.M. sentencing. As a woman who had experienced three major winter car accidents in New Hampshire before moving to California, I couldn't face the prospect of heading out to Michigan that day, taking my rental car out on roads far snowier than the ones that had scared me the month before. With great regret, I canceled my flight and my meeting with Nancy Seaman.

So the news of what happened in the courtroom that day came to me through the television cameras again and the transcript of that day's proceedings and the observations of those who were there—chief among them Lori Brasier of the *Detroit Free Press*. I was home in California while the scene unfolded.

The sentencing began with a statement by Lisa Ortlieb explaining that Dennis Seaman had intended to be present but had not been able to get to Detroit. His request that Julie Dumbleton read his Victim Impact Statement was denied by the judge, as was the request of Jeff Seaman (also out of state) that Jenna Dumbleton be allowed to speak on his behalf.

Lisa Ortlieb was allowed to read Dennis Seaman's statement into the record, however. As she did so, Nancy Seaman sat motionless. Whatever Dennis Seaman's words might have meant to her, the expression on her face conveyed no clue.

Nancy, what a fixer you are. You fixed it so Bob could not enjoy the rest of his life away from you. You fixed your boys too. They now won't speak to each other. They get into fistfights and call the police on each other. You have fixed one son so that he is as deceitful and a liar just like you. His bitterness he carries to others will serve him as yours did for you. You fixed it so your ailing father lied and lost his honor when you coached him on the stand. Your other son lost his best friend, his father, his mother, his brother, his grandfather, uncle, aunts and all other family he had loved since birth. You fixed us all, didn't you? . . .

You are a planner and you are a fixer and you have no one to blame but yourself. . . . You could have just left, got a divorce, and gone to your new condo and lived happily ever after enjoying your sons, their wives, and future grandchildren.

Larry Kaluzny then spoke briefly about the letters he'd received since the guilty verdict.

"Unfortunately, this jury did not see the Nancy Seaman that Todd and I saw at the jail," he said. "I had many calls from people who had only good things to say about the compassion that she showed for them as a teacher. How well they loved her, from the parents as well as the students."

Nothing in Nancy Seaman's history or activities to date suggested she had been much of a woman for social causes, but Larry Kaluzny raised the banner now, on behalf of abused women everywhere, speaking not just for himself, he said, but for his client.

"If one person hears what happened and says 'I've got to find the strength to leave a relationship,' then I guess there is some good that comes out of the trial. . . . We wish the law in Michigan was different. We wish the experts could have given their own opinions to the jury as opposed to just the general statement."

Nancy Seaman spoke next. The last time she'd addressed the court, she was wearing one of her smart suits, but now she had on an orange jail jumpsuit. She began not with remarks about her husband or her family, interestingly, but with harsh words of blame suggesting that the whole thing was at least in part Dennis Seaman's fault.

"Perhaps things would have been different that Monday morning if Dennis hadn't worked on Bob and instilled so much hatred in him," she said. "That fueled the rage that caused so much of what happened that morning.

"I am heartbroken," she went on, "not only for myself but for the abused women who suffer verbal, physical and psychological abuse at the hands of their husbands."

She had harsh words for the prosecutor. "It was like being battered one final time," she said. "Only this time by the judicial system."

There were angry words, too, for Chief Dwyer, whose comments to the press had in her view hopelessly prejudiced the jury so that "they had made up their minds before they ever walked in that jury box. I could see it in their eyes. I saw it in their body language."

As many harsh words about Bob Seaman as she'd delivered in this room already, she had a few more of those now too: reminders of the names he'd called her, the affairs he'd had, the cruelty of his treatment of her.

"I loved my husband unconditionally," she added, somewhat incongruously at the end of her recitation of her husband's crimes, as some in attendance struggled to remember a single remark they'd heard from her that seemed to support such a statement. As if repetition might make the idea more convincing, she restated it. She loved Bob Seaman, she told the court, "with all my heart."

Before stepping down, she made a last plea. "Justice has been denied," she said. "I can't fight this battle and right this wrong without the support of the media, community, family and friends. I am asking that you please help me undo this grave injustice."

Now it was Greg Seaman's turn to take the podium. Like his mother, he stood, not in the witness box as he had during the trial, but at the front of the courtroom, inches away from where Lisa Ortlieb sat, and his words, as he began to speak, were spat out directly at her.

"Shame on this prosecutor," he said, almost trembling with rage. "Her entire case she spent . . . dismissing thirty years of spousal abuse. Which I thought was disgusting.

"She did a great injustice to battered women everywhere," he said. "Especially in Oakland County, where this woman is supposed to be in charge of some unit that helps battered women. I can't imagine battered women coming up to her now. I can imagine what this prosecutor may say, 'Here defend yourself with this pamphlet on domestic violence.'"

As he spoke, Lori Brasier told me later, "it looked like he might actually hit Lisa Ortlieb." She was evidently not the only one to entertain that thought. A bailiff, standing guard as they always did, moved closer in, clearly on guard for the possibility of another Seaman attack. It only lasted a second, but a look had come over Greg's face (and it wasn't just a look, either; he was his shaking his fist and advancing toward the prosecutor) that Lori Brasier described as "murderous rage."

"Shame on Jeff, my brother," he went on, "for his shameful lying on the stand under oath. . . . I hope that every coworker and boss of his at Ford Motor Company understands what he did to his own mother, with the intention of lynching her."

Even now, it seemed—with his father dead, his mother going to prison—Greg Seaman's overriding impulse was for vengeance in the most effective form a son of Detroit might envision: to get his brother in trouble with Ford.

He was all over the map then: touching on the moments of the trial (and they were many) in which he'd felt his mother had been wronged. He revisited why he hadn't called back Don O'Chadleus. He went back to the money in the estate account. He went back to Jeff's name being taken off the visitors' list, quoting his brother telling him, "she's fucking guilty." Few might have doubted Jeff Seaman's saying this, but his brother's citing it revealed something else too: beneath the clean-cut appearance, evidently, was a young man who could utter what Julie Dumbleton called "the 'F' word" with surprising ease.

"I lost a father who I loved," he said. But not even now could Greg Seaman leave the court with an expression of affection that wasn't tainted by his quivering rage. His voice was still raised in fury toward his father as he delivered his final words.

"Everything he ever accomplished will forever be overshadowed by the fact that he was a wife beater."

Greg took his seat. Only after he did could those observing exhale fully again.

There was only one thing left that day: Judge McDonald had to hand down the sentence. Before he did so, he made what was, by the account of legal observers as well as the press, a virtually unprecedented move.

"Mrs. Seaman," he began, "this case is undoubtedly the most tragic, troubling and saddest case I've ever had in twelve years as a judge. In a matter of minutes, your entire family has been destroyed. You had two sons, who, because of the positions they took in this case, their relationship is irrevocably destroyed.

"I have my opinions of who was lying in the case," he went on, "and it wasn't your son that testified just now. I don't know whether it would have helped you any if your other son would have told the truth, but I notice he's not even here. His work is too important.

"I don't doubt for a moment that you were both physically and emotionally abused," he said now, addressing Nancy Seaman in a voice of tender understanding.

"What you did is so uncharacteristic and contrary to the type of person you seem to be," Judge McDonald went on. "From all I could gather in reading the pre-sentence report and the many letters supporting you, you were both a loving wife, and a devoted mother and a dedicated teacher. . . . I can't believe that you went out to Home Depot to buy a hatchet to kill your husband. It just doesn't make any sense."

He leaned over the bench. In a voice filled with regret, he told Nancy Seaman, "I have no discretion in imposing the sentence that I have to impose by law. . . . I have to sentence you to life in prison. . . . without possibility of parole."

On the faces of those on the benches that day, there were no looks of joy, only various expressions of sadness and grief. For the Dumbletons, whose son Jake had taken the day off from college to be present, it was a somber moment more than one for rejoicing, but there was relief on their faces.

In a few minutes, Nancy Seaman would be led away again, in shackles—this time, to spend the rest of her life behind bars. First, though, she was allowed to meet with the assembled press for a few minutes, for the purpose of answering their questions. If anyone had supposed they would hear a chastened and repentant Nancy Seaman that day, they were swiftly disabused of the notion. She addressed the assembled media as a teacher might, in a conference with the parents of a child who has grossly misbehaved and needs to be set straight at home. Her words had the ring of having been carefully prepared, and her delivery was firm, almost defiant.

"This is a terrible miscarriage of justice," she said. "I did not commit this crime. I fought like my life depended on it, because it did. The alternative was to have let him kill me."

She was led away as the crowd dispersed.

This next moment, the final one, I would hear about only later, from Lisa Ortlieb, who overheard it from where she was standing nearby, and later still—when he was finally ready to talk about it— from Jake Dumbleton himself: as he walked out of the courtroom, Greg Seaman stopped in front of Jake Dumbleton. After the fury with which he'd addressed the court earlier, his tone appeared calm again, and he spoke in a low voice. Even now, after everything that had happened, it was difficult for Jake Dumbleton to fully grasp that the young man standing before him—someone he had once admired and called by the nickname "Nike"—no longer wished him well.

"Your mom slept with my dad," Greg said, in a voice just barely audible. Then he was gone.

CHAPTER 51

Not Everybody
Loves a Reporter

H aving missed my first appointment to meet Nancy Seaman, I sent her a second letter, reiterating my keen desire to hear her story, as well as my understanding of what a difficult time this had to be for her. I would wait patiently until she sent word that she'd be ready to see me, I said. I gave her my phone number so that she could call collect. Any hour of the day or night, I told her, assuming at this point that I'd be hearing from her within a matter of days.

Meanwhile, back home in California, I figured I'd get to work educating myself about the case.

A call to Greg Seaman's cell phone number elicited no personal greeting—just a message from some anonymous telephone company voice instructing callers to leave a number. Jeff Seaman's home number was answered by a woman's voice—his wife Becka, clearly, her tone making it plain she didn't want to talk and wished I'd go away. A call to Jeff's cell phone got a human voice on the message—Jeff's, instantly recognizable as that of the young man I'd heard briefly on the television news report about the murder.

"The calibrator you are looking for is unavailable," he said, in a voice that made it hard to know if he was intentionally joking or actually referring to himself as something one step removed from being a machine.

I left messages for both Seaman sons, reminding them of the letters and books I'd sent them earlier.

"I'm happy to sit down with you, first, to answer whatever questions you might have about me and the book I'll be writing," I said again. I was clear, in all my communications, that I'd be seeking out the remarks and observations of people from all sides of the case.

Jeff didn't call back. Neither did Greg. I called Larry Kaluzny, who said he felt confident that Greg would want to talk with me—he was "a fine young man," so different from his brother—but right now "the family had a lot on their minds" (though we both knew that what was on the mind of one member of the Seaman family was not at all the same as what might be on the mind of that person's brother).

Meanwhile, the *48 Hours* crew was filming an interview with Nancy. I'd have to wait a little to talk with her now, until things settled down.

Rick Cox was not an easy man to reach either—seemingly always off on a trip, out of town, away from his desk, tied up in a meeting, on the phone, just stepped out.

Finally, though, his secretary put me through to him. He spoke to me now with the blandly calm, almost anesthetized manner of a politician delivering his statement to the press in a potentially sticky situation, the soft, almost reverential tone of a funeral director who recognizes that a group of bereaved individuals may be within earshot.

"This is a tragic situation," he whispered. "It breaks my heart to see that family torn apart this way."

"You and Bob were good friends?" I asked him.

"I was probably his best friend," said Rick. "We knew each other since college days. I was at his wedding."

He was stepping in as a father figure for the boys, he explained. In fact, Rick Cox was the one person in this whole tragic situation who had managed to maintain contact with both Seaman brothers. Whether this had something to do with the fact that Greg and Jeff remained the sole heirs to Bob Seaman's estate—including his far from insignificant 49 percent share in the Waterwheel Building—was a factor that Cox, when asked about it, chose not to discuss. Similarly, he was not about to get into details concerning the future of the real estate, though I knew, from the terms of the partnership agreement with Bob, that

Rick now held license to buy out the Seaman portion of the building. (The question was, at what price, and how would it be arrived at and agreed on by factions so deeply at odds with each other?)

The aspect of his relationship with the Seamans on which Rick preferred to dwell was his role as self-appointed spiritual counselor to the family at a time when such guidance was so clearly needed.

"Jeff's a hotheaded young man like his father," he said, "but you have to feel compassion for him." There was little doubt, as he spoke, that the brother he held in higher regard was Greg. "An outstanding individual," he said. "A comfort to his mother."

As for Nancy, Cox was trying to get in to visit her, he said, with a special dispensation he hoped might be achieved through his role as a lay minister, though so far this had not been possible. He wanted to pray with her. Now was the moment in a person's life when spiritual support was indispensable.

What about the Waterwheel Building, I asked? How would the sale occur?

He was not at liberty to discuss that issue, he told me.

I asked if we could meet at his office to speak about the business partnership with Bob. That would not be possible, he said, "at this point in time"—words that have signaled to me, ever since the Nixon administration invoked them with regularity during the Watergate era, the underlying code that I had entered into forbidden territory and was now being ushered out.

Rick would talk to Greg and Jeff about meeting with me, he said now, in his same smooth, placid manner. He'd get back to me.

On my return to Michigan a few weeks later, Chief Bill Dwyer of the Farmington Hills Police Department was a lot more welcoming to me. Tall and tanned—even in winter—with his white hair forming a perfect wave over his chiseled face, he stepped out from behind a desk piled high with paperwork and file folders with the unmistakable air of a man born to be on television. Standing in shirtsleeves (custom-tailored shirt, monogrammed cuffs) in a spacious office whose bookshelves were lined with photographs of himself with his grandchildren and prominent members of the community, as well as President George W. Bush, he greeted me with a warmth that had been singularly absent in my conversation with Rick Cox.

"I've always had a good relationship with the press," he said. His handshake was the kind that made you feel you were safe—so long as you stayed in the jurisdiction of Chief Bill Dwyer, anyway. And so long as you kept on the right side of the law.

Although he was unquestionably a man of many responsibilities, and much in demand, Bill Dwyer was generous with his time. He'd been in law enforcement for forty-three years, he told me—twenty-three of them in Detroit, where he headed up narcotics enforcement. He'd gotten into this line of work by chance, at age nineteen, when he'd been working as a carpenter and looking for a more reliable job, but the surprise for him was the discovery that he was born for police work. He loved it. You could tell that, meeting the man.

Sitting down behind the broad expanse of his desk now, he reflected over his many years in Farmington Hills, and the highlights of his career there: there was the story of the *Detroit News* sports reporter they'd nabbed, discovered to have had over twelve hundred encounters with young boys; a man named Thompson who'd lost big in Vegas and had come home to Farmington Hills to murder his wife and three kids; a college student named Tina Biggars who'd taken up prostitution and got herself killed. (A paperback crime story was published about that one, in which he appeared, he told me. He'd get me a copy.)

One particularly horrifying case involved a drug dealer in Detroit who got in trouble with the mob and was not only murdered but left with a crucial body part severed and stuck into his own mouth. The image was disconcerting, to put it mildly, but to Chief Bill Dwyer, this was all in a day's work. Only once in all his years of police work, in fact, had Dwyer actually broken down. That was in the Thompson case, the man who murdered his wife and kids. Years later, Chief Dwyer said, it was the memory of those dead children in their beds that haunted him.

Still, Farmington Hills was not what you'd call a crime-ridden community. Far from it. In fact, Farmington Hills was named one of the safest communities to live in Michigan, Chief Dwyer told me. And the Farmington Hills police force was among the reasons why.

Chief Dwyer was proud of his team, that much was clear. "I run a highly professional department here," he said. He was hugely proud of the men and women of his force. Never more so than in the Seaman case.

An expansive, highly personable man, Chief Dwyer also possessed a certain testiness when it came to questions about the way his team had conducted themselves on the Seaman matter—no doubt the result of criticism he'd received not only from Nancy Seaman but from a number of highly vocal supporters in the community, and most particularly Nancy's colleague Rose Christoph, wife of a local magistrate and the one responsible, he believed, for a gag order on his media appearances.

It was true that Chief Dwyer's first impromptu press conference, held outside the Seaman home shortly after the arrest of Nancy Seaman, had incorrectly conveyed the impression that Nancy Seaman might have murdered her husband in the family kitchen and then carried his body out to the garage to dispose of it, but the error had been swiftly corrected.

But in the eyes of the Seaman defense, the damage had been done: they felt that the perception had been indelibly created in the minds of Oakland County residents that Nancy Seaman was a crazed and bloodthirsty ax murderer who had chosen to do in her husband in the very spot where in happier days she had prepared Thanksgiving dinners. The jury pool would be impossibly tainted now. So the order had come down from the city manager, Steve Karp, that Chief Dwyer and his men were not to speak further to the press concerning the Seaman case—a prohibition that may have had something to do with the influence of magistrate Carl Christoph, husband of Rose.

The crew from *48 Hours* had been in town, Chief Dwyer told me, preparing their story on the Seaman case, and of course they'd wanted to interview him, but because of the city manager's orders, neither he nor Detective Al Patterson had been allowed to give interviews for the program. Appearing on national television, describing his successful investigation of a murder, was just the kind of thing Chief Dwyer was born to do, and he knew this. It was plain, talking with him about the missed opportunity of appearing on *48 Hours,* how painful it had been to stay away from the CBS people.

But enough was enough. He'd decided to ignore the city manager's gag order and speak to me. He'd missed out on appearing on camera, but as I reminded him now, sometimes books got made into movies.

He told his secretary to hold all calls for the next hour, and ran a hand through his elegantly waved white hair.

"We had five evidence technicians working twenty-four hours straight, going through the whole house, looking at every piece of evidence, to come up with an understanding of what happened in this case," Chief Dwyer explained. "Every inch of that garage was analyzed, every blood spatter, every article of clothing, before we came up with our assessment. It's unusual for a department of this size to have this level of expertise. We weren't trying to say she was guilty or innocent. Our job was to investigate."

Once the investigation got under way, however, the evidence had pointed clearly to the guilt of Nancy Seaman, he said—and what it suggested was not simply a crime of passion in self-defense, either, but a premeditated attack against Bob Seaman.

"I have no doubt," Chief Dwyer added, "that if we hadn't returned that afternoon to the home and located the body in the back of her vehicle when we did, she would have removed it before the day was over, and we might never have found him.

"He didn't fit the profile of a man who commits domestic violence," Chief Dwyer added of Bob Seaman. "If she'd been a victim, why didn't we have any records of her calling for help? Why didn't anyone report concerns? Why didn't she get out? I've seen domestic violence cases, believe me—and I've seen them cut across all socioeconomic levels. But this woman wasn't the type to sit around and take it. She was the type that gives it out.

"I saw her at the station," he said. "No emotion."

Chief Dwyer was a believer in evidence: blood spatters, the angle of entry of the hatchet blade, tissue samples from the Mustang. But he was also a believer in gut instinct, and his own gut instinct had been pretty well refined, as a man with four decades of exposure to criminal activity under his expensive belt.

"When I watched her testimony in the trial," he said, "her whole demeanor didn't ring true to me. There's this thing you can see in their eyes when a person's not telling the truth. I saw it in hers."

I told Chief Dwyer I'd be around for a while. No doubt we'd be talking. "Let me know anytime you need some help on this," he said, pressing his card into my hand. I told him it was too bad Jimmy Stewart was dead, because Jimmy Stewart—at a certain point in his career—or maybe James Garner, would have been the perfect one to portray Chief Dwyer on the screen.

"Call me anytime," he told me. "I'll fit you into my schedule."

Those were words I had yet to hear from Nancy Seaman—though unlike Chief Dwyer, she definitely had an abundance of time on her hands now.

CHAPTER 52

"Show Me How You Love Me"

Like his mother, Greg Seaman was still not responding to my messages, but I'd heard he was probably tied up with the *48 Hours* people, so with only a few days to be in Michigan on this visit, I headed out to Northville next, to meet with Julie Dumbleton, who had made it plain that because this experience had been so upsetting to her kids, it was best that we talk, for now anyway, at a time when Jenna was at school. Jake was off at Albion College now, an hour's drive away. And Dick, of course, would be at work, but I could catch him later, in the months to come.

The Dumbletons lived in a subdivision just off the main thoroughfare running past a series of shopping malls and chain restaurants (Chevy's, Applebee's, Starbucks), toward downtown Northville. Their subdivision, Northville Commons, though tidy and well groomed, with only new-looking cars in the driveways (SUVs mostly), appeared to be a few steps down in exclusivity from the Ramblewood subdivision where the Seamans had made their home. No gate at the entry, and the houses, though attractive, were considerably smaller. In front of the Dumbletons' home was an American flag, along with a wreath that said "Bless This House."

Opening the door for me—her big, friendly golden retriever–lab mix, Bailey, panting happily at her side—Julie Dumbleton extended a hand, apologizing for the mess, though I could have worked on my own house for a solid day and it still wouldn't look as tidy as the Dumbletons'.

If a woman's attractiveness were a measure of the likelihood that she was having extramarital affairs, Julie Dumbleton would have been ripe for suspicion, all right. Her features were fine and delicate, hair perfectly blown dry, and even now, at a little over fifty, she had the figure of a cheerleader. But nothing about Julie Dumbleton suggested the appearance of a woman inclined to stray from her marriage. Just the opposite. She was one of those women who I figured had probably worn a "Baby on Board" T-shirt during pregnancy, and now— considerably later along—was sporting one that read "Fast Pitch Softball Mom." She was as cute as a fifty-year-old woman can be, and about as unlikely to have been fooling around with Bob Seaman as Laura Bush would be to take up with Michael Moore.

She put on the coffee and gave me a quick tour: pictures of the kids everywhere, and some of Julie and Dick together; on the mantle, softball and baseball trophies; and in the bathroom, a joke mirror with a partially exposed softball in one corner, pressed against the glass like a half grapefruit, as if someone with a particularly powerful throw had just lobbed it into the glass in such a way that it had gone through to the other side.

A framed plaque reminded visitors "Friends are the family we get to choose," and on another wall hung a photograph of Bob Seaman in his baseball cap. All these months after his death, it was apparent from the look on Julie's face as she pointed it out that she could still cry at any moment, thinking about what had happened.

We settled into the tidy eating nook in the kitchen, with its Formica countertops so clean, I got the feeling hernia surgery could safely be performed here, and a fluorescent light over the counter in the shape of a softball. Julie set out the cookies: chocolate chip, fresh from the oven.

It was a cozy scene, though something else besides the smell of cookies hung in the air: a low-level but pervasive sadness and tension. Julie's kindness felt real, and so did her hospitality, but in another way, she was wary and anxious, like a dog who's been hit in the past, or someone who has experienced a near miss of a plane crash or a car wreck in which the passenger in the other seat didn't pull through.

"I'm not sure about talking with you," she said. "What I really want is to put this all behind me. The problem is, I can't."

Just the opposite, in fact. As the months had passed since Bob Seaman's murder, things almost seemed worse instead of better.

"I can't get what happened out of my mind," she said. "My family's not the same anymore."

In spite of the friendly, wholesome atmosphere, I could sense that. It was as if radio waves were being emitted in this place that only dogs could pick up. Or maybe it was more like the feeling you'd get sitting on a front porch on a summer evening, when a mosquito hits the bug zapper and you hear the momentary sizzle of frying insect. Julie Dumbleton was keeping it together here, but she was tightly wound, and might not hold. There was an obsessiveness about the way she had held on to this story. It was eating her up.

"I miss Bob so much," she said, setting a cup of coffee in front of me. "We all do." For long hours, he had sat at this very kitchen table, pouring out his story to Julie. With Bob gone, now she had to be the one to tell it.

"I was his confidante," Julie went on. "He probably told me more over those last years than he'd ever told anybody else before."

She began her story like a woman who'd spent many hours over the course of the last eight months going over everything—in the middle of the night, most likely. She had it all in her head: names, dates, violent or threatening encounters, ball games, meals, trips—events she'd lived through and ones she'd merely heard about. Which meant, of course, that all she could tell me about Bob's life was what Bob himself had told her. I could choose to believe it or not, but it was hard to imagine this woman telling a lie. She seemed to remember everything he'd ever said to her, and she recounted it all with astonishing precision and detail, as if the life she was describing had been her own.

In the world of characters in Bob Seaman's life, Julie Dumbleton stood out like a one-speed bicycle in a parking lot full of Corvettes. From everything I saw of her, she had been a person (as were her husband and her children) who had operated for most of her life up until recently on the principle of honesty and trust. She was not a person who took in what others around her said and did with a measure of skepticism or analysis of motive. She didn't conceal things; she didn't have anything to conceal. She and her family clearly adored and admired Bob Seaman's wit and capacity for drama and playfulness, and laughed at his many stories and jokes, but she herself possessed no particular sense of irony. She was utterly literal and seemed, in the way she approached life, like a throwback to some other era, when a person really did do things like volunteer to work at a friend's batting-cage business without pay, for no other reason than to help him out.

On the surface, Julie and her husband seemed like the least likely of friends for a man like Bob Seaman, a wise guy with a touch of the bad boy about him. But as much as he provided color and drama to the Dumbletons' lives (more than they'd bargained for), they had given him something even more precious and rare: simple, unconditional acceptance and trust—love, even. A renewed faith in goodness, maybe.

But Julie's belief in goodness was precisely what she had lost now. Her world had turned ugly overnight, and she had no tools to deal with the transformation. All she could do was go over and over the events of the last few years, to herself, to the producers at *48 Hours* who would set the record straight with their broadcast (she hoped), and now to me.

Julie Dumbleton had loved Bob Seaman. Just not the way the media made it out. She loved him, it appeared, for all the qualities he possessed that were most different from those of herself and her family. Even at fifty-seven, he had a playfulness about him, and a kind of brashness and bravado. He was risk-taker: a man who could drive 120 miles an hour and put the bulk of his retirement earnings into building a batting cage unlikely ever to earn a profit. But as it turned out, it wasn't any of those gambles that got Bob Seaman into big trouble. The riskiest part of Bob Seaman's life turned out to be his marriage.

Bob had confided to Julie that even before his wedding, there had been evidence that he was making a mistake. He remembered bringing Nancy home to meet his parents and her taking offense that they had neglected to give her a present. At their wedding, driving to the reception with Nancy's father in the car ahead of them, Bob had said "Get out of my way, old man" out loud (not loud enough for anyone to hear but Nancy). She had become so angry she'd started hitting him, he said.

But the episode that Bob described to Julie as one of the defining moments of his life occurred a few years later. This was the infamous coffee-cup episode recounted by Nancy Seaman at her trial, which had culminated in her call to the police, charging her husband with domestic abuse. In Bob's account, to Julie, he had thrown the coffee cup at Nancy in the car, but the circumstances had been different from what Nancy had described.

"They were on a drive with their young sons to visit Bob's parents just outside of St. Louis," he'd told Julie.

It was a trip Nancy had always found distasteful. She had made some critical remark, and he'd thrown his Styrofoam coffee cup at her (empty, in Bob's version). She'd "lunged at him and clawed at him."

"He pushed her and smacked her lip," Julie told me. When they got to his parents' house, Nancy called the police, who showed up a few minutes later. Although he hadn't been arrested, it had been a terrible moment in their marriage and one Bob never forgot.

"He told me, 'Maybe I just don't have the guts to leave,'" Julie added. "He was definitely concerned about losing his house and his cars and his retirement fund, but the main thing for him was his sons. He didn't want a divorce to mess things up for Jeff and Greg. Jeff was out of the house by this time, but Greg was still in high school, and he just wanted so badly for things to be good with him. And Greg was so attached to Nancy."

In Julie's eyes, it was Greg's attachment to his mother and her requirement of loyalty that had begun the sad unraveling of Greg and Bob's relationship.

"Bob told me she used to tell him how she'd make their boys stand in front of the closet in her bedroom when they were little," Julie said, "and point at Bob's clothes. She'd say, 'See, you really do have a father.' As if they didn't know. Trying to give them the impression he was abandoning them when all he was doing was working like a dog to support her in the manner she expected."

In spite of that, Julie said, Bob and his sons had been close while they were growing up. But more and more, as Greg moved into his teenage years, he had taken Nancy's side in their arguments—even, Julie said, "using the same language his mother used, when he complained to his father. Like he was repeating all the things she'd told him. Like he believed it was his job to take her side against his own father."

It was in the context of the breakdown in his own family that Bob Seaman had reached out to the Dumbletons, Julie said.

"He was lonely, that's all. His own home was a miserable place. So he would go to Jenna's band concerts, to Jake's baseball games. It was like we were the family he didn't have."

Julie understood that Nancy resented the time Bob spent with the softball team. "She didn't like him having fun with anyone but her," said Julie. "But he didn't have fun with her."

Julie didn't understand the extent of Nancy's hostility toward herself and her family until Jeff's wedding in St. Louis, in the summer of 2001. The Dumbletons, who had become close with both Seaman sons by now too, had made the five-hour drive to attend, with Jake taking the role of groomsman—a responsibility the groom's own brother, Greg, had not been asked to perform. At the rehearsal dinner the night before, Nancy had ignored Julie.

"That's when we knew," said Julie, "that she didn't just dislike softball. She disliked us."

Two weeks later, on the day of the annual Woodward Avenue Dream Cruise, Dick and Jenna and Julie had gotten together with Bob at his house to prepare the Shelby for Oakland County's biggest annual vintage car event. (The Boss was sometimes taken out for this event too, but the Shelby was the star of Bob's collection.) Then, according to Julie, Nancy came home, opened the door from the house to the garage, saw them there, and slammed the door shut again. She did not attend the Dream Cruise that day. Jake and Jeff rode in the Shelby.

Things went downhill fast after that. In December, Julie said, Nancy had stormed into the office shared by Julie and Bob at the Upper Deck and knocked all of Julie's framed photographs of Jenna off the shelf, replacing them with a photograph of Bob and Nancy taken at Jeff's wedding.

Then came the gift to Greg of the black 1989 Mustang that would ultimately sit in pieces in the driveway on Briarwood Court so long it had to be towed away and was eventually given to Jake. It was the gift of the Mustang that had inspired Nancy's threatening call to Julie and her application for the PPO against Julie in February of 2002.

It was hard to keep everything straight, and I wasn't the only one with the problem, evidently.

"I made a timeline for the producers at *48 Hours*," Julie explained. She'd spent hours with Nancy Kramer, the chief producer on the segment, "to help her understand what had happened," she said. "And because Bob wasn't there to speak up for himself."

Julie got up for a moment. When she came back, she had a sheaf of papers in her hand, typewritten—a timeline based on the notes she'd been keeping over the years of increasingly tense and troubling interaction between the Dumbletons and Nancy Seaman (and, later, Greg).

The timeline was clearly the work of a meticulous person, and one in possession of a strangely prescient understanding of the ominous direction in which the story might unfold, as well as a certain obsessiveness of her own. Reading it over now, in the wholesome environment of the Dumbletons' kitchen, I felt a headache coming on as I made my way through the catalogue of ups and downs (mostly downs) in the marriage and family life of Nancy and Bob Seaman.

Alienation, confrontation, reconciliation, followed by alienation again. Some people might find a certain dark humor in the chronicle of ludicrously petty grievances and childishly bad behavior reflected in Julie Dumbleton's timeline. For anyone (myself, for instance) who had ever lived through the particular variety of madness that may be unique to an angry divorce, however, reading Julie Dumbleton's astonishingly detailed report—filled with names, dates, specific quotations—was a mind-numbing, almost nauseating experience.

The entry describing that summer's Dream Cruise began with the date, "8/16/03."

Dick gave 2 passes (Becka and Jeff) to a complimentary booth. Food and drinks provided.

Bob hurried his family, so not to be late. Becka decided not to go because she didn't feel well. Nancy decided to stay home with Becka.

Bob and Jeff showed up at booth mid afternoon and joined us. Bob wanted to take us for a ride in his Shelby. Jake, his friend and I hop in.

Dick, Jenna and Jeff still at the booth eating and drinking. Bob gets a call from Greg (first time Greg called or talked to Bob since mid-July). Greg wants Bob to drive by his booth to show off Shelby.

We drive by booth. Bob gets an angry call from Greg, upset that we were in the Shelby.

Greg and his friends walk past Dick, Jenna and Jeff very angrily. Dick and Jenna go say "hi" to Greg. Greg walked away. Jeff witnessed this.

Bob and Jeff got home. Greg and Nancy attacked Bob "like mad dogs." Greg called his dad "an 'a hole,' not my father." Greg said "I've hated you for the past two years. Choose between your friends and me."

Greg tried to hit Bob with the pool cue. Bob blocked him.

Greg, Nancy and Kristin and friend all took off to eat and left Bob home.

Nancy accused Bob and Jeff that they conspired to leave her behind so Bob could meet up with us. Cited as evidence: Bob packed extra bottles of water in the car, when booth had all the food and drinks we could possibly want.

The timeline went on to a confrontation with Nancy at a game in Ann Arbor and the confrontation with Nancy at the Upper Deck, leading to the broken fingernail and the assault charges against Julie.

Thanksgiving, 2003: Bob drove to Matoon, Indiana, to bring his parents to Michigan for Thanksgiving ("whether Nancy wanted them or not"). This time, he said, his parents were going to stay at his house, not at a hotel, as Nancy had required in the past. At dinner (with Nancy "playing Miss Perfect Hostess"), a call had come from Greg, wishing everyone a happy Thanksgiving. Nancy's mother, Lenore, had handed the phone to Bob. Greg hung up on him.

December 2003: Lenore died suddenly. Greg made special arrangements for final exams and came home for the funeral. Bob tried to talk with Greg, offered to give him a ride to the funeral. Greg refused to acknowledge him.

Christmas, 2003: Greg came home, bringing his new dog, Shelby (named for the car), and left the dog at his parents' house while he took off for Chicago with his friend. Bob took care of the dog. Greg did not speak to him.

January 2004: Bob discovered that all of Nancy's credit card charges—somewhere around $30,000 worth—had been transferred to his accounts. He closed his credit card account and joint bank account and met with a divorce attorney, J. Robert Rock, who reportedly warned him, after studying his financial reports, to "be careful of what's going on with Rick Cox." If the attorney had offered an amplification of that cryptic remark, Julie did not know about it, and considering the casualness with which Bob appeared to have overseen his financial life, Bob may have been too absorbed in other matters at the time to think much of the caveat.

Valentine's Day, 2004: The anonymous letter arrived at the offices of Compuware, accusing Coach Bob Seaman of being "obsessed with little girls." Bob Seaman had little doubt as to the identity of its author.

"You've put a lot of work into this," I told Julie, when I was done studying the timeline. The experience of reading it left me with a feeling I'd had on the rare occasions I'd gotten sucked into watching reality television.

"I needed to," she told me. "Someone has to understand what this woman did. She tried to portray herself as this helpless victim. I couldn't just stand there and listen to that stuff and not do anything, when our friend's been murdered. He can't speak for himself anymore. So I have to. I have to make sure the television people get the story right."

It wasn't my business, I knew, but I couldn't help interjecting a comment here: "You might not want to get your hopes up too high for this *48 Hours* show. The story might not come across the way you'd like."

Maybe we would have spoken more about this, but just then Jenna Dumbleton walked into the room, home from school and looking for something to eat. She headed straight to the refrigerator.

At age fifteen (she'd just celebrated her birthday), Jenna was immediately recognizable as an athlete—a young woman who looked as if she could step into a ball game with the bases loaded and a full count, and not break a sweat. Her features combined her mother's Korean American heritage with that of her father (German, English)— with the end result of producing an attractive young woman who could have been Native American or Asian or simply unplaceable. She would almost certainly have appeared friendlier to virtually any visitor other than the one she'd just discovered sitting in her family kitchen: a woman who'd come to talk about the single worst thing that ever happened in her life, the murder of her beloved coach. Her parents had clearly raised her to be polite—to call adults Mr. and Mrs. or Miss—so Jenna extended her hand now, but what was almost certainly an uncharacteristic look of distrust was apparent on her face too.

"I don't blame you for not wanting to talk about what happened," I told her, having heard from her mother that she'd been unhappy with the news of my visit. At some point, I said, she and her brother might be willing to talk with me about the man they still spoke of as Mr. Seaman, but I wasn't expecting her to do that now.

She looked only mildly relieved, swung open the refrigerator door in that way teenagers have, when they've just come home from school and they're grazing for a snack. "Someone ate all the yogurt," she said.

"That was me," said Julie.

"I got my paper back," Jenna told her mother, eyeing me a little warily.

"We'll look it over a little later," Julie said. She was one of those mothers who look over homework and probably listen to the lyrics of songs on her kids' CDs to check for inappropriate language. She did not miss one of her children's games, either. Julie and Dick Dumbleton were the most careful and vigilant of parents, the kind who would have supposed, until fairly recently, that if you do your job well enough, raising your children, they would be safe from the worst kinds of trouble the world had to offer.

CHAPTER 53

The Difference Between Alan Trammel and Jose Canseco

I'd made that first visit after the trial in February. In March, with the winter beginning to wind down, I traveled again to Michigan. I wasn't holding out much hope for speaking with Greg Seaman, who had yet to respond in any way to my letters and calls, but I thought it would be easier to convince Jeff to speak with me if I were in town rather than calling from California.

When I reached him at home one night, he said he wasn't going to talk to me.

"What's the point?" he told me on the phone, when I finally got his actual voice and not the recorded message telling me for the hundredth time, "The calibrator you are looking for is unavailable."

"I know who my dad was," Jeff had said. "My dad's friends knew who my dad was. Why should I care what Judge McDonald or some person lying on a couch reading a book thinks about who my dad was? It's not bringing him back. That's one of the things my dad taught me."

It was hard to argue with this. Partly I agreed with him. I asked myself regularly—for the entire year I spent trying to find out about the Seaman story—why I'd felt a need to explore this story myself. Now I attempted to construct a reason, for us both.

"I'm not interested in murders," I said. "I'm interested in families. I want to understand, when things go wrong, where it comes from."

He didn't seem impressed.

"Just meet me one time, so you'll know who this person is that's writing a book about your family that you aren't interested in."

I wasn't expecting him to say yes anymore. He had talked with the *48 Hours* people only at the urging of his uncle Dennis, he told me, and though the segment had not aired yet, he already regretted it.

"Drop by Chevy's in Dearborn," he said. He'd have a beer with me after work.

The day we met, Jose Canseco had just appeared on *60 Minutes*, talking with Mike Wallace about his experience with steroid use in the major leagues and naming names of other well-known players (Mark McGuire among them) who'd taken advantage of the drug. He'd been promoting a book, of course, due out in a few days; so, because it seemed to provide a certain link between us (Jeff loved baseball; I wrote books), I brought up Canseco. I asked Jeff if that was a book he'd be reading. He practically spit out his beer on the table of our booth.

"It's funny," he said. "I always said you could tell a lot about a person by which ball player was their hero. My brother always loved Canseco, which fit. Big flashy star, show-off player, huge ego, huge money contract. Greg was impressed by all that stuff. Now look who his hero turns out to be."

I had to ask who Bob Seaman had admired most, then. Jeff didn't have to hesitate before answering. "Stan Musial," he said. Outfielder for the St. Louis Cardinals, Bob Seaman's hometown team. Quiet man. A player of huge gift and huge modesty. Never a show-off.

And how about himself, I asked. Who was Jeff's guy?

"That would be Alan Trammel," he said. Shortstop (among other positions) for the Detroit Tigers. "Not a big-name star, but a totally dependable player, with a workmanlike attitude."

"To my dad and me," said Jeff, "Alan Trammel was like the Stan Musial of his day."

Jeff had told me on the phone he'd have only a few minutes for me. He was on his way home from a long day at Ford, calibrating the 2007 Explorer, as usual, and it was close to eight o'clock, but Jeff showed no sign of being in a rush to go. He was a short man, stockily built like his father. Maybe because of everything he'd gone through in the last year, but more likely for other reasons besides, he looked a good eight to ten years older than twenty-five.

From the moment he started speaking, it was apparent that Jeff was a man of sharp, almost crackling intelligence, with a gift for language and self-expression you might not expect of a high-level automotive engineer—a young man with a particularly striking talent for selecting the most perfectly apt metaphor to describe situations in his life that most people, thankfully, have never had to describe because they haven't lived through them; a young man who used words like "fisticuffs" and named *The Art of Happiness,* by the Dalai Lama, as his favorite book. Maybe he was trying to impress me, but he wasn't someone who seemed to care about impressing anyone; in fact, he appeared to take a certain perverse pride in rubbing people the wrong way.

It was easy to see why Judge McDonald and plenty of others had taken a dislike to Jeff. He had a brittle quality, a chip-on-the-shoulder "I dare you" attitude, a manner many might regard as cocky, though I interpreted it differently myself. If you studied only his body language—arms folded across the chest, lip curled a little, spine leaned against the back of the booth in a manner that seemed to suggest diffidence—you might easily get your back up. But what struck me were his eyes: about as blue as any I'd seen, and moist as stones in a river. He looked away a lot, as if he knew his eyes gave him away.

"Listen," he said. "I'll tell you how it was."

He had ordered dinner now, without discussion of the change in plans, so I opened my computer on the table and began taking down his words. He spoke in paragraphs then, spoke almost without taking a breath. Unlike his brother, who, as I knew from his appearance on *Inside Edition,* could look right into the camera like a pro, Jeff would be a disaster on television, and he knew it, but he wasn't auditioning to be a game show host or to get picked for *American Idol.*

He was a young man whose mother had evidently said to his brother, on those jailhouse tapes, that Greg was the only person she cared about. He had listened to those tapes and heard his mother say "Jeff would screw you" and that she hoped Jeff would stay away from his brother, that she didn't care if she never saw Jeff again, that she'd never forgive him; he was always a weak person, they'd known that, hadn't they? He was just like his father, she said. Well, that was the good news.

"Have you ever broken a bone, or one of your kids broke a bone, and it still gives you a problem?" he asked me. (Not that I'd brought up my children to Jeff Seaman, but evidently I came across as someone's mother. And of course, I was.)

"That's how this situation is for me. A bad thing happened here, a major problem. But what am I going to do? I have to deal with it. My fatal flaw is probably how analytical I am. I'm not an emotional person. If I get angry, what will that accomplish? If my truck breaks down and I kick the bumper, will that fix it? I look at situations like I'm working on an engine.

"Have you ever watched the show *Married with Children?*" he asked me. I had once, and I hated it. I never found anything remotely humorous in the spectacle of a massively dysfunctional family mistreating each other relentlessly, I told him now.

"My parents argued like that all the time," he said. "It went both ways. He said terrible things to her; she said terrible things to him. I never thought, when I heard them going at each other, 'Yeah, one of them's going to kill the other one.' That was just life for us.

"They both had a very aggressive personality type. They both strove to be successful. They both believed they were right. It wasn't a very good idea for two people like that to get together, and my parents dealt with it poorly. I definitely didn't have any desire to reenact how they were in my own life, with my marriage. I had no desire for any of that, after growing up like I did, and neither did my wife.

"My parents were extremely well off," he said. "Why would two intelligent adults argue over an old Ford Mustang? Not even a good Mustang!"

Only it wasn't about the Mustang, naturally. It was about power. Same as that last fight they had about his mother wanting his dad to lend her his Explorer and his dad saying no wasn't really about the Explorer. His mother knew what his dad's response would be before she asked. It was power again. She wanted him to turn her down so they could start in again.

"Look at the situation with the lawn, nobody mowing it, the whole backyard starting to look like the Everglades, and poor old Mr. Su pushing his lawn mower closer and closer," he said. "Look at what they had going with the trash. You ever hear of *Alice's Restaurant?*" (This was funny. A twenty-five-year-old was asking me if I knew about *Alice's Restaurant*.) Yes, I knew about the trash situation in that one too, I told him. Power struggles again. Some issues were timeless.

As Jeff saw it, his parents had both believed that the other one should carry out the trash, and they were prepared to live with the stink rather than give in. With the idea of the divorce the same stand-off existed: they were staying, or they were leaving. Nobody could decide. They were each still trying to figure out which was the more powerful position, still pulling on the rope from opposite ends. Only in the end, Bob had changed everything by letting it go. He had told Nancy he was getting out. What happens when you're pulling hard on that rope, and all of a sudden, there's no resistance anymore? You wish you'd been the one to let go first.

But this was hardly the first instance of two siblings in a family, faced with the same problem, arriving at radically different ways of dealing with it. To hear him describe it, Jeff had seemingly let the whole experience of growing up in the Seaman household run off his back. As we sat at Chevy's and I picked at my overcooked salmon, the image came to me, crazily, of a big car with a V-8 engine—an SUV probably—gliding through a car wash, getting pummeled with suds and water shooting out from all directions at high pressure, followed by scrubbing brushes and those floppy strips of fabric, sweeping over the hood until it's finally over, and the car glides away, no longer even damp. But glistening.

Maybe Jeff could pull off the car-wash to his parents' marriage, but for Greg it was all too much. His mother's rage or pain or disappointment or sense of betrayal had become his own. He would do whatever he could to make her happy. She rewarded him with the status of the beloved favored child.

"Greg is the anti-me," said Jeff, taking a large bite of burger and laughing as he often did at statements that may or may not have contained humor. "He's a person that, if he wasn't my brother, I wouldn't even know him.

"He had a knack for getting hurt," said Jeff. "And when he did, it was always my fault. He was like a china doll. He needed lots of attention. But it didn't bother me; that's just the way Greg was. Our mom always gave him money for things, gave him cars, paid his charge card bills. It was just one of those things I accepted, but it was OK. I can buy my own Mustangs.

"One of the funny things about how this played out," he said, "was all this insinuation about an affair. Here's how ridiculous that was: my dad and I did stuff together all the time. I mean all the time. I didn't call ahead and set a time. I'd just show up. I'd pop in at the Upper

Deck or someplace, or over at the house, and hang out with him, and he was always easy to locate. All the hours we spent in that basement over at the Waterwheel Building, he didn't have time for an affair. His big passion was working with me on cars.

"You think I could have chosen him for my best friend if he didn't respect women?" Jeff asked me. "You think I would respect him the way I did if he had been a drunken, wife-beating slob? I tend not to associate with people like that."

He adored his father, that was clear, and clearly Bob Seaman had adored him. "My dad was the kind of guy," he said, "that would take up cross-country running so he could run with Greg. My dad—can you picture a person with a worse body type to be a runner? But that's what he did. With me, it was baseball. He didn't want to miss a single game.

"There was this time in Ann Arbor," Jeff said. "My team had come all the way over, and we didn't have enough players. My team was a little on the young side compared to the other guys, due to the fact that I recruited them all from Saturday-morning Hitters Club at the Upper Deck. When all the other guys were going out for beer, my players had homework. And this particular time, a bunch of them had term papers or something and bailed, and we were going to have to forfeit the game.

"So I called up my dad, and he came right over. He showed up with the uniform and everything, like Superman, only Superman on an off day. He was terrible, but he played. He even slid into bases, he had so much heart."

Julie Dumbleton had spoken of Bob as a man of huge intelligence, and even Rick Cox, critical as he'd been of the man, had attested to his brilliance. Jeff described him a little differently:

"My dad wasn't necessarily the sharpest knife in the drawer," he said. "He always had to take a slide rule to class. He graduated with a 2.0. But he had this rare talent as a catalyst. He could inspire average people to do great things. After he left Borg Warner, all of these people just fell off the apple cart. Kids he coached, who started out looking like hopeless cases, and he'd see something in them and they'd turn into these amazing players."

"The Dumbletons," he said, shaking his head and smiling. "There was a family for you. But my dad just loved them. They were nothing like our family. They were just nice, was all. They accepted him without wanting to change him all the time. To them he was a hero, where to my mom he was this total screw-up loser."

Once again, of course, a car had touched off the big trouble. That Mustang. "I truly believe, if my dad could have gone back in time, he would not have given that car away again," Jeff told me, taking a large bite of burger. "He should have junked it and given Jake a different car. It was a mistake, doing that, but he wasn't great at admitting mistakes. He was stubborn, so he held his ground, and look where it got him.

"The only time I thought my mom was truly loony was when she swore that Jake Dumbleton would never drive that car," he said. "She told me she'd blow it up first. At the time I thought it was just an expression, but the more I look back, the more I think she was not kidding. If she could have pushed that car over a cliff, she would have.

"My mom had a lot of obsessive behavior," he said. "Not that I can criticize her for it, because I inherited that trait. Why do you think I had to go to work for Ford? I'm obsessed with Mustangs. When I started to like baseball, I didn't just *like* baseball, I became Mr. Baseball. Ask me the lineup of any major league team from 1987.

"For my mother," he said, "the obsession was that the Dumbletons were ruining her marriage. They were these totally evil people, which is pretty funny when you know them. If you ever read *The Art of Happiness* you understand there are no good or evil people—and even if there were, it wouldn't be the Dumbletons. But to her, that's how it was, and you should have heard her, when I told her I was putting Jake Dumbleton on my wooden bat baseball team in Ann Arbor. Let me tell you, there's nothing like having to keep your shortstop from flipping out when your mom is doing nine rounds with his mother out on the stands, and you're trying to keep the game moving along.

"Finally, last May, she just snapped," Jeff went on. "She went sideways. She lost it. If going out in a rainstorm to buy a hatchet to kill your husband isn't proof of insanity, I don't know what is, and if she'd been able to say yes, I went crazy, admitted she was wrong and pleaded insanity, I would have done everything to help. But she couldn't."

Now was one of those times Jeff Seaman looked away. He was staring off in the direction of the bar, though there was nothing on the television screen but a commercial.

"People think I was against my mom and for my dad, but I never see it that way," he said, brisk again. "The way I lay things out, neither one of them was a saint, and I know that, but they were also great parents. I loved them both. I miss my dad but I miss my mom too. I miss spending time with her. You think I want to see her rot in jail?

"But there are certain characteristics each of us has in life. One of mine is I tell the truth. I can't lie to help someone out, even my mom. Rick Cox kept telling me, 'Listen Jeff, your dad's gone, there's nothing you can do for him, so help your mother now.' Would you betray half your family so the other half could get what they wanted? Even when you knew they'd done something wrong?

"My brother really needs to believe our mom is innocent of everything, and to do that, he's got to tell himself our dad was this terrible monster. I think he stopped talking to me because I made too much sense for him. I tried to force reality on him, and nobody ever said I'm tactful about it."

Of course, it could still be Jeff Seaman who was deluded, I reminded myself. Perhaps, in the same way that Greg needed to believe his mother was a battered woman to excuse her murder of his father, Jeff needed to believe his mother was a murderer, rather than believe his father was a batterer. I would have liked to explore that question with Greg, only Greg still wasn't returning my calls.

It was a stark contrast, all right, and the lines were nothing if not clear: Greg Seaman on one side, Jeff on the other. Nancy Seaman in prison for life, Bob Seaman dead. Jose Canseco, Alan Trammel. A hundred thirty thousand dollar Shelby Mustang, a thirty thousand dollar Boss.

As things worked out, Jeff Seaman and I sat talking in that booth at Chevy's for close to three hours, though he continued to remind me that he wasn't interested in having anything to do with this book of mine. It was close to ten o'clock when we got up from the table.

I thought maybe I'd see the Boss when we walked out to the parking lot together, but no such luck. The car he was driving was an Explorer. The Boss was back at his house, in the garage. That car, he took out only for certain special moments in life. This hadn't been one of them.

"Maybe you can come over to the house some time," Jeff said to me as we parted. "Who knows, maybe I'll read your book and find out something I didn't know." He laughed, though there was a hollow sound to his laughter, I thought, that reminded me of the way some people write "LOL" in an e-mail to indicate they're making a joke, when what they've just written is exactly what, in their heart of hearts, they truly believe. They just have a hard time admitting it.

CHAPTER 54

CBS Comes to Town

W hen I had first arrived in Michigan, by far the most high-profile media presence in town belonged to the crew from the CBS news program, *48 Hours,* which would be airing a one-hour broadcast on the Seaman case sometime in early spring. This was hardly the first time for me, as a journalist, to observe the way the television camera seduces people, the blind faith that otherwise reasonable individuals are capable of investing in the notion that because a camera is involved (and possibly the familiar face of a well-known broadcaster), because the name of a major network is attached and millions of people will be watching the result, the televised product can be trusted to convey the truth of a story. A not particularly glamorous-looking writer, driving around in her rusty Pontiac Eagle, carrying a spiral notebook and a pen, is a less worthwhile repository for one's experiences.

Because in the past I've covered stories where I found myself in reluctant competition with the glitzier television types for interview time, I concluded long ago that this was a losing proposition. So I deliberately waited to get down to serious work in Michigan until the television people left town. You never have to wait that long; television crews are expensive to run, and producers of these programs like to get them put to bed efficiently so that the crew can move on to the next project. No doubt my decision not to hunker down for an extended time in Michigan until the CBS people were finished was assisted by the fact that it was winter at the time, with snow falling regularly and the thermometer registering below freezing every time I hit town in my borrowed coat and boots.

While the television program was still in the works and the people I recognized as important for my story were giving their interviews or in some way cooperating with the project, I tried to get one idea across to them.

"I truly hope I'm wrong," I said, "but if this TV show doesn't work out the way you hope, please don't judge me for the sins of CBS."

Still, Julie Dumbleton remained cautiously optimistic. After months of back-and-forth e-mails, she had decided not to appear on camera in the segment, but she had worked closely with its producer, Nancy Kramer, based in New York   a really nice woman, Julie told me. Julie and Dick had gone out to dinner with Kramer. For a while there, they had exchanged e-mails constantly, Julie told me—not just about the program, but small talk about Jenna and school, how Jake was doing, how good-looking the Dumbleton kids were, and how proud Julie and Dick must be.

Julie had sent Nancy Kramer the timeline, among other things, and carefully selected a bunch of photographs to use in the segment—pictures of Bob coaching the team, driving the Shelby, out on the boat with Jake and Dick. And she had told the producer stories.

Julie was hoping that the program would finally bring a measure of justice to her murdered friend, she said, show what a great guy he'd been, and reveal Nancy Seaman as the ruthless and calculating monster she was, for killing him. Where better to redeem a dead man's ruined reputation than on national television?

CHAPTER 55

How Television Spun It

B ack home, I waited for the snow to melt and the cameras to leave Oakland County. I wrote another couple of letters to Nancy and Greg Seaman. I did some reading on the history of the Ford Mustang and the Explorer, the Detroit race riots of 1967, and studied the work of Dr. Lenore Walker on Battered Woman Syndrome.

On April 9, 2005, CBS's hour-long program about the Seaman case, titled "Blood Feud," was broadcast nationwide. Home in California, I settled in to watch, with anticipation and a certain sense of dread, as the predictable images flashed across the screen: the "Welcome to Farmington Hills" sign, signaling that this would be a story about an affluent, white middle-class family, the familiar Tudor façade of the Seaman home on Briarwood Court, the smiling images of Bob, Nancy, Jeff, and Greg at Tigers' Stadium.

In the fashion of television, the program cut with whiplash speed through images of Bob and Nancy's wedding, the boys on their bicycles and in their Little League uniforms, Nancy collecting her Teacher of the Year award, the Shelby and the Boss, Jeff and Becka's wedding, the Creepy Dumbletons.

Then the smooth tones of the network correspondent laid out the bones of the story—so familiar to me by this point: the secret condo purchase, the Home Depot trip, the discovery of the body in the car, and, most dramatically, the terrible division between the brothers. Both Jeff and Greg appeared on camera—separately of course—offering their opposing perspectives on their family, as snapshots and ominous background music underscored the picture of a father increasingly out of control, a mom trying to hold her family together, a son loyally standing by while his strangely uncomfortable-looking brother joked, "I didn't fall off the turnip truck yesterday, you know."

Cut to: Photographs of Nancy's bruises—faint blue places on her arm and legs. Footage of Nancy dabbing her eyes, speaking of her love for her sons, her effort to protect them from their father's uncontrollable rages, her desire to ensure that they would never know the truth about him, at the risk that they would cease to love him if they did.

Then came footage of the Dumbletons: Jake and Jenna's faces blotted out but Julie's plainly visible, as the voiceover relayed Nancy's suspicions, and those of Greg, that Bob Seaman had been having an affair with her. Perhaps because it would have been confusing to offer two alternative pictures of Bob's alleged sexual indiscretions, no mention was made in the *48 Hours* broadcast of Nancy's other allegation, that her husband harbored inappropriate feelings for young girls, Jenna Dumbleton in particular. The pedophile angle might have done well with the ratings, but selling both stories simultaneously could have presented a challenge.

As I watched the program, I tried to imagine how the story might come across to a viewer unacquainted with the Seaman story. My guess: it would seem like the most clear-cut case—almost boring in its predictability.

A battered woman suffers silently through three decades of abuse out of a desire to keep her family together. A cold and ruthless engineer (pictured unshaven and glowering), embittered by the loss of his high-paying job, spirals into a cycle of escalating violence. Enter: a highly attractive Asian woman—portrayed on the broadcast dancing suggestively at Jeff Seaman's wedding (her husband conveniently out of camera range).

Cut to: a tearful woman led away in chains, uttering as her final words on the tragedy her heartfelt prayer that her sons would one day find their way back to each other.

"Blood Feud" was hardly memorable television, but it was an hour of programming, like so many thousands of others, that would leave a viewer with the sense of knowing the story, with just enough juicy details and none of the troubling complexities to bog a person down. No mention was made in the broadcast of the defensive wounds on Nancy Seaman's body following what she claimed to have been her husband's attack, or the evidence technicians' analysis of the blood spatters on the garage walls suggesting that Nancy had not been cowering on the floor as she claimed, when she struck her husband. The broadcast gave viewers Nancy's tearful hope of reconciliation for her sons, but not her statement to Greg (recorded on tape) to the effect that she never wanted to see Jeff again, or Greg's use of the phrase "your husband" to describe his father.

Measured strictly by standards of television likability, Greg Seaman's performance in the *48 Hours* interview (absent all references to his calling his father "an asshole") won the contest hands down over that of his brother Jeff. Greg, speaking to the reporter, sounded sincere and heartfelt, tender and loving to his mother, incredulous over what he described as his brother's out-and-out lying. Jeff, speaking to the same reporter (seated uncomfortably on a sofa next to Becka) made odd and unsuccessful attempts at humor. Where Greg looked sincere, Jeff came across as wary, suspicious, and untrusting, a young man with a giant chip on his shoulder. (And no doubt he was.)

As for Nancy, she was not a natural winner in the role of lovable victim. Still, the tears that seemed so inauthentic—when juxtaposed with other aspects of the story the producers had not included—seemed reasonably affecting on the program. Viewers of *48 Hours* did not hear about the shoplifted hatchet or Nancy Seaman's shopping trips and cleanup efforts after the murder or the jailhouse tapes with Greg. Neither was the information conveyed concerning Nancy Seaman's assault charges over the broken fingernail, or her comment, when caught in a lie, that "Bob is having a midlife crisis."

The segment ended with footage of the on-camera host—Maureen Maher—walking thoughtfully through what had been, until recently, the Seamans' home on Briarwood Court, standing in the very kitchen where, she suggested, Bob Seaman may first have attacked his wife with the knife, then cutting to the black-and-white tiled garage where Nancy—in desperation, and fearing for her life, as Maher described it—had reached up to grab the hatchet.

The broadcast ended with a poll of viewers, asking that they e-mail their vote on the guilt or innocence of Nancy Seaman. No question that she'd killed Bob, but was she a battered woman, acting in self-defense?

Not surprisingly, given the material included in the program and the way it was edited, CBS viewers voted resoundingly in support of Nancy Seaman and expressed outrage over the verdict and her sentence.

Interestingly, a few weeks later Court TV broadcast four days of its recorded tapes from the Seaman trial, with regular commentary from Court TV hosts and trial commentators like Nancy Grace, the on-air crime-stopper who made Lisa Ortlieb look like a softie. Here, however (though commentators still seemed to accept as fact the notion that Bob Seaman had abused his wife), the poll of viewers as to the guilt or innocence of Nancy Seaman and the appropriateness of the jury's verdict weighed heavily in the opposite direction.

The reason was clear enough: though neither broadcast could have been termed thorough or objective, viewers of Court TV had seen what viewers of *48 Hours* had not: the cool, self-justifying, and frequently querulous testimony of Nancy Seaman. She wasn't likeable. Worse than that, she seemed to be missing a heart.

There was probably no such thing as totally impartial reporting on this case. I knew that, because with every passing day, I felt less impartial myself. Initially Nancy Seaman had been the object of my compassion—a woman with whom, as I had written in my first letter to her, I could identify as someone who had struggled in a difficult marriage and one who'd tried to raise her children the best she knew how. But by the time I too had watched this Court TV broadcast of the trial—some months after it first aired—I was increasingly skeptical that she had ever fallen into the "battered woman" category. From what I now knew of her capacity for rage, however, I could certainly imagine Nancy Seaman striking Bob. And once she did, it was hard to see how he would have refrained from striking back, unless he was quickly rendered incapable.

CHAPTER 56

A Travesty

I had been afraid this would happen, and it did.

After the *48 Hours* broadcast, nobody who cared about Bob Seaman wanted to talk to me. They'd trusted television to tell the story fairly, and now look what had happened: Bob Seaman had come across as an out-of-control wife beater, a man whose own son (the younger one, anyway) held in deep contempt.

Before the airing of *48 Hours*, Dennis Seaman had been enthusiastic about my book project (even suggesting we might collaborate), but now he was rethinking his decision, he told me. Worse yet, Dennis suggested to me that Jeff had serious second thoughts about any future conversations between us.

"The only reason he agreed to talk to *48 Hours* was because my wife Robin begged him to do it, for Bob," he said. "He's feeling pretty burned right now."

But more even than Dennis Seaman, Julie Dumbleton had been deeply traumatized by the *48 Hours* broadcast. Over the phone, alternating between tears and outrage at those misleading shots of her dancing at Jeff's wedding, she asked over and over, "How do I know you won't do another one of these stories about what a victim Nancy was, and what a terrible man Bob was to make her do something like that?" For Julie, the pain of watching that broadcast went beyond her own humiliation on national television; it was seeing what the program had done to her children.

"We raised our kids to trust people and believe they were good," she wept. "Now they can't trust anyone."

"Trust isn't a bad thing for a young person to possess," I said. "It's blind trust, blind faith, that gets us into trouble."

I wasn't sure she got the concept, however. For Julie, it seemed, there were only two modes possible: total trust or total suspicion. Total trust being more her natural mode, even now she reverted to it.

"Are you going to write a smear job about Bob where Nancy comes off looking like the victim?" she asked me. "Are you going to turn out to be just like Nancy Kramer?"

If I were, I reminded her, I probably wouldn't admit to it.

We spent a lot of time talking on the phone about whether or not it was a good idea for her to talk with me. When we spoke, the main topic was the television program. Jake and Jenna Dumbleton had lost their innocence over the events of the last year, she said, and that was one of the saddest things of all.

It seemed to me that Julie had lost plenty too, including her equilibrium. I liked her, but it was hard staying on the phone with her sometimes. There was an obsessive quality to the way she held on to her grief and rage, her recitations of the events, her painstakingly detailed lists of the terrible things done by Nancy Seaman, and now, added to the list, the terrible things done by CBS in putting together what she considered to be not simply an unfair and inaccurate portrayal of the story but "A travesty!" "An outrage!" "A crime!"

I felt sympathy, but there was a part of me that didn't want to hear it anymore. Often, when I got off the phone with Julie, I'd find myself pouring a glass of wine, or wanting to.

She wanted to talk to me. She didn't want to talk to me. She wanted me to write a book. She wanted me to disappear. My presence was reminding her family of the worst thing that ever happened in their lives. But I was unconvinced that my absence would result in their forgetting it, or anything close.

Partly, she said, she wanted her children to talk with me because they weren't talking about this, and maybe it would be a good idea if they did. But she was scared too, and as a woman so unaccustomed to distrusting people (even when she said she'd lost all her faith in human nature), the way she dealt with her distrust of me was to ask again if she should trust me.

"Nancy Kramer started out nice too," she said, speaking of the *48 Hours* producer. "I sent her all these great pictures of Bob—what did she use? The one shot of Bob where he hadn't shaved, and he looks like a convict on death row."

Sometimes, discussing this, Julie Dumbleton would start to cry. She missed Bob, but she also missed her old life—when everything had been so uncomplicated and happy. She missed her children as they used to be, missed the days when the worst thing likely to happen in Jake's day was striking out in a baseball game. And now he wouldn't even play anymore.

Jenna was hurting, but silently. With Jake, it was easy to recognize the signs of pain; they were all over his face.

"He doesn't tell me," she said, "but I know he drives around for hours sometimes, just thinking about Bob." He had called her from school back in the spring, wanting to know if she had kept the recording she'd made of Bob's message on his answering machine down at the Upper Deck. If so, he wanted it. He'd erased it by mistake from his own cell phone. (This was a family, I reminded myself, that still chose as their answering machine message the voice of Jenna at around age six. They were likely to hold on to that recording of Bob Seaman well into the twenty-first century.) And in much the same way, it occurred to me, Julie Dumbleton had created an endlessly repeating loop, on the subject of Nancy Seaman, and the murder, and what it had done to her children.

"You know what Jake did recently?" Julie told me. "He got his ears pierced." I knew when she said it that I was supposed to recognize this as the clearest indication yet of how troubled he'd become over Bob's death and the media's response to Nancy's battered woman story, but as a mother of sons a few years older than Jake, I didn't find this so ominous.

I had seen Jake at the Dumbletons' house, but he was keeping his distance from me, and I wasn't pushing things. He was a tall, athletic young man who wore his baseball cap backwards sometimes and dressed in the slightly baggy shorts that defined him as a jock, not even close to a gangster and the furthest thing from a goth. He wanted to get a tattoo also, Julie told me, but when I asked what symbol he had wanted to put on his arm, it turned out to be his grandparents' initials. If she thought that was what trouble looked like, I told her, she should probably stay away from the state of California. I was trying for a little humor as I said this, but no humor was possible here. Julie was on a tear.

"My children have just been through so much," she said, crying again, though my guess was that nobody in the Dumbleton family had suffered this experience more than Julie herself.

And there was more. Julie had been called "inappropriate" and "creepy" in open court. A relationship she treasured—the one between her daughter, Jenna, and her friend Bob—had been made to look illicit and dirty. Julie had been described on national television as the possible lover of a man she regarded as almost a family member. But the worst for Julie were the things that had been said about Bob on the CBS broadcast, the interviewer's unchallenged assumption that Bob had abused Nancy, and the fact that of all the people interviewed on the program, the one to whom by far the greatest air time had been given was Nancy Seaman herself.

I was still at my home in California that spring, but Julie had forwarded to me well over a dozen e-mails, copies of ones she'd sent to Nancy Kramer, along with copies of letters she and her husband had sent to Lisa Ortlieb, Detective Patterson, Rick Cox, and others, expressing their dismay and anger over the broadcast. They were the kind of letters you pictured a person writing in the middle of a sleepless night that has been preceded by many other sleepless nights, letters filled with words in boldface and exclamation points. Reading them, you practically expected blood to begin dripping off your computer screen. Nancy Kramer and the other CBS producer to whom they had been sent had not responded.

I knew Julie would hate it if I said this, but the woman those letters reminded me of, in their over-the-top tone and choice of language and in the sense of something like hysteria brewing just beneath the surface, was Nancy Seaman herself, in the months leading up to the murder. In Julie's case, the origins of her rage and frustration may have been eminently understandable, but the effect on a reader was similar: it was all just too much. It was hard not tuning her out after a while.

"Heinous crime!" "Cruel and ruthless!" "Bitter shrew!" "Evil murderess!" "Pathological Narcissist!" "Web of Lies!" "Psychotic woman!"

"Queen of Denial!" (For Julie Dumbleton the exclamation point was the favored mark of punctuation.)

"We are creepy?????" she wrote in an e-mail—a shrillness coming through, even on the computer screen.

> Why . . . because we are a loving and caring family, who showed nothing but kindness and compassion to a friend who was in total despair? Now let's see. Here is Nancy, who was no better than a wild animal on a hunt . . . who savagely chops and mutilates a man she "loved" with "all her heart" . . . stuffs his tarped dead body in her car for three days, goes about her daily business as usual and has lied about just about everything and anything for her defense. . . .
>
> Then here's Greg, who considers this monster his "inspiration" . . . who's seen washing the bloody car his father's brutalized body was stuffed in and is driving around in that car . . . who commits perjury to protect this heinous murderer . . . then there is the defense attorney who's fattening his bank account defending this modern day Lizzie Borden while trying to destroy innocent people's reputations and lives . . . now you tell me, WHO is creepy here???? . . .
>
> Bob Seaman, AN INNOCENT DEAD MAN was VICTIMIZED again . . . this time by your CBS/48 Hours.

"How do I know I can trust you?" Julie asked me again.

I wasn't going to do what the television people did, I knew. In another way, though, I understood a darker truth: nothing I could write about what had happened would be enough to make it all right for Julie Dumbleton.

CHAPTER 57

Talk About Stress!

I might have supposed that after the relatively gentle treatment of her story on CBS, Nancy herself (and therefore Greg and all the team of Nancy supporters who had refused to take my calls till now) would have changed their minds and decided to speak with me after all, but they didn't. So now it seemed that neither side was talking: not Greg; not Jeff anymore, for the moment at least; not Nancy or her fellow teachers; not Dennis; not Julie and Dick perhaps, or their children. Given the main players' nearly total unwillingness to participate, I had to ask myself if there was any way to continue or if I should give up on ever telling this story.

For a few reasons, I didn't. I still believed, for one thing, that Nancy Seaman would change her mind. Lori Brasier remarked to me that if ever there was a woman who had to get the last word in, it was Nancy Seaman. She'd come round eventually.

But the other part of my decision to stay with my pursuit of the Seaman story had to do with a certain stubbornness. The view had been expressed to me—and perhaps it was the one thing Greg and Jeff Seaman agreed on—that if nobody talked, I'd have to pack up my bags and leave town. Theirs was not a tale the Seamans wanted told, and although I did not elevate my mission in telling it to the level of global importance, it struck me as a poor idea that journalists limit themselves only to those stories whose key participants give them permission to proceed.

I hadn't given up on speaking with Nancy or Greg or Jeff, but meanwhile I took it as a challenge to see how much I could uncover about what happened, without (for now) the assistance of a single member of the original nuclear Seaman family. I wanted to know if, working with the many fragments offered up by seemingly insignificant sources, I could piece together an understanding of their lives and the tragedy that had occurred. This was certainly a much more labor-intensive way of conducting my research than sitting down with Nancy Seaman and listening to her life story. But it was an interesting question too, whether a cohesive portrait of a family might be assembled from many small scraps rather than from whole cloth.

But my reasons for continuing to pursue the story went deeper, to a place I didn't fully understand myself. Something about the war that had taken place in that household, and the awful place in which it had left the two surviving sons, both repelled and fascinated me. There was hardly a night now when my last thought before sleep (and sleep was now harder to come by than it ever had been) was of those four members of that unhappy family, and what had brought them to the tormented place the three survivors must now inhabit.

I made two more short trips to Michigan that spring—one in April, one in May—but I was waiting until summer to settle in for the extended period I knew my research required.

Between visits, I sent off another communication to Nancy Seaman, who'd been transferred to the Robert Scott Correctional Facility in Plymouth, Michigan. I had learned that a new inmate is not allowed visitors during her first sixty days in prison (the somewhat disturbing idea being that adjustment to incarceration is easier when contact with the outside world is kept to a minimum). Knowing this, I hoped and still believed that Nancy Seaman's continued silence might be attributed to the restrictions at the prison. I could also well imagine that she might simply be overwhelmingly depressed.

This time, to make sure she got my note, I sent it in the form of a telegram, delivered at the cost of $142 by a private business that handled only prison telegrams. Mostly it was all the same stuff I'd told her before, though now a faint edge of quiet threat could be detected in my language, perhaps. "Knowing I'll be writing about what happened," I said, "you might want to make sure your point of view is expressed."

I called Larry Kaluzny too, but—strangely, for a man with a reputation for being so accommodating—heard nothing back.

I continued to make overtures, as well, to the Seaman sons. Greg still had no message on his cell phone—only one of those electronic voices. Rick Cox, when I called him, promised to deliver messages to Greg, but sounded increasingly vague.

Then came good news. Although he continued to express reservations about speaking with me—and, like Dennis Seaman and the Dumbletons, felt burned by CBS—Jeff Seaman said he'd meet me again, so we could at least talk about it. On the basis of that conversation, I booked another flight to Michigan for the last week in April, with the plan of having a good long talk with Jeff, seeing some family videos he'd mentioned, looking at pictures, and taking a ride in the Boss if I was lucky.

"Call me when you get to town," he told me.

When I landed in Detroit, his was the first number I called. Hearing the old familiar cell phone message, I left one myself, and by the end of the day, three more of them on both his cell and home phones.

Over the course of the days I spent in Michigan waiting to hear back from Jeff, I talked with a number of people who knew Bob Seaman—softball parents, mostly—and I spoke briefly again with Julie Dumbleton. I had coffee at the courthouse with Lori Brasier, who filled me in on the current roundup of crimes in Oakland County—a young woman who'd scalded her baby, a young man (good student, never in trouble before) who'd been pulled over for driving under the influence, only to see the police officer who'd stopped him struck by a second vehicle and killed, so now he was up for homicide.

I stopped by the Farmington Hills Police Department and watched the Home Depot surveillance video on the computer of Detective Al Patterson, then stuck my head into the office of Chief Dwyer, who was flying high after a successful sting operation at a suburban home in which the police had broken a drug ring found to be trafficking in hundreds of pounds of marijuana. Chief Dwyer had been on the six o'clock news the night before, he told me. For Bill Dwyer, that was better than courtside seats at a Pistons game.

One afternoon, I drove out to Plymouth and passed by the Robert Scott Correctional Facility, new home to prisoner 520695, Nancy Seaman.

The actual building, hardly an architectural gem, had a blank, characterless appearance that might have suggested a factory or even a school—a long, low, flesh-colored block—except for the curlicues of concertina wire around the perimeter of the grounds. There was a flag outside, and a patch of dirt, not grass, but no sign of human activity.

Just being that close to the place filled me with anxiety and the desire to drive away as swiftly as possible—but not before noticing the baseball field on one side of the prison and, a stone's throw away on the opposite side, a Home Depot.

I drove around some more, still leaving messages for Jeff. After five days of waiting for a call back, I gave up and flew home to San Francisco. I was on the Airporter bus taking me over the Golden Gate Bridge back home to Marin County when my cell phone rang: Jeff Seaman, sounding like a long-lost friend.

"How's it going?" he said, as if there was nothing particularly unusual about the fact that over the course of the last few days he'd received a couple of dozen messages from me, all unanswered.

"Not bad," I told him. "I've just gotten back from your neck of the woods." I wasn't about to give Jeff a hard time about having just flown halfway across the country and back to see him, without success. All I said was, "I was really hoping I'd get a chance to talk with you."

"Oh, right," he said. "Sorry it didn't work out. I've been so busy."

"I understand," I told him, and though it was definitely inconvenient, I actually did. In another three days it would be Mother's Day, the one-year anniversary of his mother's murder of his father.

"I know this must be a stressful time for you, Jeff," I told him. I remembered how hard the anniversary of my parents' deaths had been, the first few years, even without the added element of murder.

"Stressful! You can say that again," he said. "We're talking the start of baseball season."

CHAPTER 58

A Woman out of Control

I wound up not seeing Jeff on that visit, but on the phone we promised to see each other on my next visit, which would be "soon."

Another month passed. I spent most of it tying up loose ends at home, in preparation for my return to Michigan. This time, though, I would settle in for the summer. No more traveling back and forth.

"I'm writing a book about a murder," I said, as I arranged for my mail to be forwarded and paid my last wistful visit to a sushi restaurant. "I'm writing about a wife who killed her husband with a hatchet."

Nervous laughter from the man I was having dinner with. "I hope this doesn't give you any ideas," he told me.

On a trip to New York, I took my younger son, age twenty-one, out for lunch one day. He'd just come back from New Hampshire, a visit with his father, who was in a new relationship now, living in our old house in the country with the mother of his four-year-old son. Over our meal—a get-together I'd been looking forward to for weeks—Willy began to tell me, cautiously, about the little boy he speaks of simply as his brother—not his half brother—and how much he loved him. What a great time they'd all had together, climbing a mountain where we used to hike.

Listening to Willy speak, an old familiar feeling came over me. Five years earlier, when my sons and I were having another too-rare dinner together—same city, different restaurant—and the news about my ex-husband's girlfriend's pregnancy had come up, I had picked up my wine glass and poured what was left of its contents over my head. I didn't do that sort of thing anymore. Years had passed since the full-moon night I'd driven my station wagon to our old house, where he still lived, and went in—when he was away—and (while our children gathered their belongings for the trip back home) picked up the screw gun he used to hang drywall, carried it outside with me into the snow, and flung it as far as I could, into the very field where, when we were young, we'd celebrated our wedding.

I hardly ever thought about those old times anymore, in fact. I lived in California now. New Hampshire days—my marriage and the divorce—seemed like some other woman's life.

But this much was true: I knew plenty about rage. I knew what it was like to be hit with a wave of feeling so huge—part despair, part anger, part hate, and part the memory of love—that I couldn't even see, and all there was in front of my eyes was red. I could have told you that at the exact moment I poured that wine over my head, I knew I'd regret it. Same as I probably knew, as I raised my arm to fling it, that one consequence of throwing my husband's screw gun into the snow would be having to drive the thirty miles back to this place on those same icy roads the next day and spend the better part of an hour tromping through the snow, looking for it.

At the moment I did those things, I was no more able to stop myself than an addict sticking a needle in her vein. That was anger for you. That was what the sorrow of a ruined relationship (or any kind of loss maybe; who knew the origins?) could do to a person.

Now, when my son told me about fun times with his little brother by his father's girlfriend, I was a calmer, more rational woman.

"I'm really glad for you," I told him. "And I know it's a good thing in your life. But sometimes it's hard, seeing you go back to our old house and having all those happy family times with a new family that I'm not part of."

"You took us away from our dad," he told me then—my last-born child, the spitting image of his father at that moment, as he looked at me clear eyed and steady, his voice firm and frighteningly cool. Knife in my heart.

"It was hard for him," he said. "Dad missed out on a lot, when we were young."

Now was the moment I would once have reached for my drinking glass and lifted it. I could feel the room spinning. The table wasn't actually tilting; it just seemed that way.

I didn't scream, or cry or throw my drink this time. I laid a wad of bills on the table and walked out onto the street, away from my son, whom I hadn't seen for months and wouldn't see for many months more. This was going to be a special lunch we were having, but now I raced down the street, breathing deeply, as a woman might in the early stages of labor.

I might not know about homicide, but I knew about uncontrollable emotion, all right.

Before I left California and headed back to Michigan, I told each of my three children I was working on a book about a murder. I said I was interested in why it was these two people stayed married as long as they had, when it was obvious they were miserable together. I told them I wanted to understand how it could be that two brothers, so close in age and growing up under the same roof, could have formed such different ideas about what had been going on between their parents all those years.

"What's so surprising about that?" Charlie had commented. "You and Dad saw everything totally differently. We just decided you were both crazy, and we loved you anyway. But it can be confusing."

CHAPTER 59

A Cottage at Potter Lake

I landed back in Detroit on July 2. Back in the winter, when I'd first befriended Lori Brasier, she'd told me that she and her husband, Mike, had a little cottage up north in Lapeer County at a place called Potter Lake. They came out there most weekends with their kids—Mike's daughter Alex, from his first marriage, and the son they had together, Ben, and now and then Lori's daughter from her first marriage, Courtney, and the children of Mike's first wife's son from her previous marriage (because their parents had taken up with other people), and Mike's fishing buddy, Ken, and usually a group of other friends and their kids.

Lori and Mike tried to get out there every weekend with various members of their family, but on the weekdays, the place sat empty. I was welcome to stay there, Lori told me. It was a fifty-minute drive into Oakland County from the lake, but there might be times when I'd be glad to get that far away from things at the end of the day.

Lori and I had just met that day in the courtroom. She barely knew me. Still, she was offering her house—wouldn't think of collecting rent. The house might get a little crowded on the weekends, but I was welcome then, too, as long as I didn't mind putting up with playing

Marco Polo and a bunch of men (this was Mike and his friends) obsessed with fishing.

Every other weekend, Mike's Aunt Ebby would join them. Ebby had retired from her job as a secretary a while back, but still knew everything there was to know about the Ford Motor Company, where she'd worked for thirty-eight years. She liked to sit on the front porch, crocheting edging around towels she picked up on sale at Target, to make into potholders, while she told us stories about the old days at Ford.

Then there was Chuck, the neighbor—the only other person I'd see at the lake during the week, most likely, because he lived there year round. Chuck had been operated on for a brain tumor when he was a child, and amazingly, had survived. But there was a large dent in his head from where the surgeons had taken a piece of his brain out, and because of that, he couldn't drive, or hold a job, so he mowed lawns and looked after things for people who had cottages, and sometimes, when you stepped out on the porch in the morning or at night, he'd be standing there, not meaning any harm.

I took all this in the pontoon boat, the neighbor, and most of all the prospect of starting and ending every day with a swim in Potter Lake—and told Lori I'd love to take her up on her offer. Now it was Fourth of July weekend, and I was headed, in my rusty maroon Pontiac Eagle, for Potter Lake with a bag of limes for the margaritas on the seat beside me.

In between leaving messages on Jeff Seaman's cell phone ("the calibrator you are looking for . . ."), I spent that weekend with Mike and Lori and their family and friends, putting on a baseball glove for the first time in a dozen years to play catch with their son, Ben. Mike took me out on their pontoon boat and his friend Ken—a reporter with the paper up in Flint—baited a hook for me and helped me cast in my line until finally, after many tries, I reeled in a crappie. That night, after the men cleaned the fish—including the first catch of my life—and cooked them up, along with the tomato and mozzarella salad, and the pie I'd baked, we sat out on the porch watching the fireworks and listening to karaoke from the campground on the other side of the lake, drinking margaritas while the kids played cards, and Aunt Ebby crocheted a pot holder.

I thought about families—the dream of how you imagine one could be, and the nightmare they become when things go wrong. That day at least, on Potter Lake—though the cottage was crowded and the wine was nothing special and the dog was incontinent and the pontoon boat was old, and the plates were plastic and the guest list included a man with a piece of his brain missing, and the little boy I'd played catch with that afternoon had to put on his brace now, the one he slept in every night on account of the scoliosis, and Aunt Ebby's stories went on so long some of us dozed off—I had the sense of being in the midst of a happy family.

I had been leaving messages again for Jeff Seaman. On the Fourth of July, he finally called back.

It was hard making out what he was saying. He was calling from the cell phone store, he told me. He'd come to get a charger and only had a minute, but he figured he'd give me the courtesy of a call to tell me he'd decided not to have anything to do with me and this book I was writing.

"I know you're busy," I said again. "You name a time—whatever hour—and I'll come to where you are."

No, he said. He'd had enough of this. "Here's the deal," he told me. "We've got some serious issues going on at the test facility right now, and I'm flying to Las Vegas tomorrow. If I can't work some of these problems out, we could be looking at a situation where there's just no Ford Explorer anymore."

He said it the way a person might who was imagining no sun, no moon, no stars. No Beatles music. No love.

"I've got a car to take care of," Jeff said. Then he was gone.

I settled into life in Michigan—waking at the cottage early enough to see the mist over the pond before diving in for my swim. I didn't mind the long drive into town; it gave me time to think, and there was plenty to think about. I turned the story over and over in my head— why Bob had stayed, why Greg had turned on his father with so much venom, why Jeff wouldn't talk with me, what Nancy was doing.

Still waiting for word from Nancy Seaman, I started calling teachers she'd worked with at Longacre Elementary, now that they were on summer break. Jeff Rehbine—who had reportedly come down with a painful case of hives shortly after the arrest of his fellow fourth-grade teacher—did not return my call. Neither did Barb Mikel or Tim Lennon or Elaine Gilbert—other teacher colleagues of Nancy's.

When I called the home of Christine Brueck—the other fourth-grade teacher at Longacre—I got her daughter and left a message with my name and number. Brueck called back an hour or so later, unaware of the purpose of my call, but when she heard what I was doing, she lit into me with a level of fury unexpected for a teacher of young children, then slammed down the phone. An hour later, she called again, this time with a warning:

"The nerve of you," she said. "You should be ashamed. If you ever try to call this number again, I'll have you charged with harassment."

In spite of all the years I'd worked as a journalist, the brand of rage and hostility that came at me over the phone from Christine Brueck—and, later, from others among Nancy Seaman's friends and supporters—was unfamiliar to me. I could imagine a person feeling grief and sorrow over what had happened, of course, and reluctance or out-and-out unwillingness to speak with a member of the press about a deeply painful situation. But the righteous indignation that Nancy Seaman's colleagues and friends (or, to use Nancy Seaman's own term, her "close acquaintances") seemed to possess toward the very concept of a journalist's seeking information about a brutally violent crime—a crime for which their friend and colleague had been found guilty by a jury of her peers—was surprising and unnerving.

After Christine Brueck finished berating me—and slammed down the phone for the second time—I set my own phone down and observed, to my surprise, that I was shaking. Not for any fear of the threatened legal action, but from the sheer force of the vitriol my inquiry had evidently inspired. Something about this case touched off strong emotion in everyone associated with it. What Nancy Seaman had done seemed to arouse other people's demons.

William Smith, the former principal of Longacre Elementary School, was more civil, but almost equally withering in his dismissal of my request to speak with him about how the events surrounding the arrest of a teacher at his school had affected the Longacre community. Ron and Ginger Schoenbach had nothing to say to me. Dennis and Paulette Schleuter did not return my calls.

Finally, a teacher who knew Nancy Seaman agreed to speak with me, though with obvious trepidation. As with the others I spoke with, her allegiance to Nancy Seaman was clear, along with her unwillingness to say or do anything that might make more trouble for a woman who, they all agreed, had suffered enough. But Jill Fleming also believed, she said, that if nobody who knew Nancy as a teacher were willing to speak with me, it would be impossible to understand her point of view, or what an outstanding teacher she had been.

So she agreed to meet with me at a Starbucks outside of Farmington Hills, with another former teaching colleague of Nancy's named Sandy, who preferred not to give me her last name. I could tell, from the demeanor of the two women, when I came into the restaurant, that the decision to talk with me had been a difficult one.

Sandy had taught at Longacre for several years with Nancy, she told me, though she had transferred to another school a few years back. Jill Fleming was something called "a reading recovery specialist." She worked in a number of schools, not only Longacre. She had met Nancy while the two of them served on a committee together, having to do with children's writing. They didn't know each other well, she said. Nancy would not have regarded her as a friend. But Jill Fleming had respected Nancy Seaman's dedication and commitment to her work, and initially at least, had been struck by her liveliness, her ready laughter, and energy.

The woman Jill Fleming described was unrecognizable as the same person whose testimony I'd studied, on the Court TV tapes I now studied regularly: the stiff, self-justifying woman whose testimony had come across as so singularly lacking in humility, compassion, or remorse, a woman who had appeared incapable of cracking a smile. But Nancy Seaman, as she'd been when Jill and Sandy knew her, had been a lot of fun. A dynamo, with a love of teaching, a love of her students.

"Always laughing," said Jill.

The previous year, however—fall of 2003, at the outset of the school year that would prove to be the last for Nancy Seaman—Jill Fleming had noticed a dramatic change in her colleague, she told me. The most obvious thing was that Nancy Seaman no longer wore her large diamond ring, but the change went deeper.

"She just seemed so distracted," Jill told me. "She didn't laugh at all anymore. She looked depressed."

Jill Fleming—though she knew nothing of Nancy Seaman's personal life—said she could guess from the look on Nancy's face that she was having problems in her marriage, and she thought about talking with her, asking what was wrong, offering her friendship. She knew plenty about that kind of trouble, she told me, having recently ended a long and unhappy marriage, herself. She also understood the impulse to keep such a story quiet. It had taken Jill a full two years before she'd been able to tell her colleagues about her own divorce.

"As a teacher," she said, "you see children all the time, who have been damaged, very often by divorce. The last thing you want to do is something like that. You care about kids. You feel like a failure.

"Now that I know what she was going through," Jill Fleming continued, "I understand why she was so into our project at school. That was her refuge and escape. No wonder she wanted to work all the time.

When you take care of kids, the focus is on them. That's your safe place. There's no time to think about your life.

"I used to say that as someone who loves children, I could never understand child abuse," she said. "But I was wrong. I have a deaf daughter, and when she was very little, and I was dealing with the frustration of getting through to her, I could sometimes imagine hitting her. You just get so desperate. You lose your mind.

"When I heard about the murder on the radio, and they said the name of the person they'd arrested, at first I didn't know who it was," she went on. "I thought it was a different Nancy. Then I saw the photograph and I said 'Oh no, not her.'"

She picked at her salad a little. I asked her if she'd written to Nancy.

"No," she said. She'd thought about it, but what was there to say?

"After it was over," she said, her voice full of regret, "I asked myself a hundred times, what if I'd talked to her. Could I have made a difference?"

In the end, the ones she'd talked with were the children she worked with. "Kids are amazingly resilient," she said. "Often they accept a simple explanation, if you give them one. It led to a good conversation, about the importance of not holding things in."

The other woman at our table, Sandy, had seemed reluctant to speak much at first, but now she too shared her impressions of Nancy—out of the conviction, she said, that Nancy was a good person who'd gotten a raw deal. Like Jill, Sandy saw Nancy Seaman as the victim of a cruel and abusive man who'd driven her to murder when no other options seemed to exist.

"Nancy was known throughout the district as a model teacher," said Sandy "She was just a very structured kind of person. Now I understand, that was probably how she kept things together. If her life was out of control, she always knew her classroom wouldn't be."

But she was a warm person, too, Sandy was quick to add. "Fourth-graders are still at that stage where their teacher's the most important person in the world to them after their parents," she told me. "Even the boys, though they won't let you know it the way the girls do, sometimes lean up against you and you know when they do, they just need a hug, and Nancy was the type who always gave them one. The children just loved her."

She smiled, remembering what Nancy's classroom looked like. "It was just so bright and cheerful," said Sandy. "She even decorated the Kleenex box with a picture she drew of someone sneezing. There wasn't one inch of that room that didn't have something interesting to look at."

They had a joke between them, in fact, about all the duct tape Nancy used, to stick things on the walls. She'd be teaching a unit, and all of a sudden one of the things she'd duct-taped on the wall would fall down. Finally Nancy and Sandy got fed up, and just glue-gunned everything in place.

"She loved the color red, and it was all around. At some point I told her about these studies that say red is an overstimulating color for elementary school students. The better color, for your classroom, is blue. But she was new. She hadn't figured out some of those things yet."

She met Bob Seaman only once, Sandy said, when he came by for an open house. Walking in Nancy's classroom, with all the decorations, he had made a joke, acting as if the experience made him dizzy. After he'd left, Nancy had made the comment to her, "Isn't he funny?"

"I didn't actually think he was so funny," said Sandy. "He wasn't the type I liked. She thought he was so charming, but he didn't seem particularly charming to me."

Nancy hadn't talked much about her marriage, though one time she had mentioned that everyone in Bob's family—everyone but him—was divorced, and Sandy had made the comment, "I guess you got the pick of the litter."

"I overlook a lot," Nancy told her.

Sandy had recently married and when Nancy had met Sandy's husband, she'd made a point of saying "I always tell Sandy how lucky she is to have you. She says you're always carrying her school things for her." This was a recurrent theme in the conversations between Nancy Seaman and other women, I had come to see: comparisons between their husbands' treatment of them, and that of her own, invariably showing Bob up to have been lacking in consideration, sensitivity, generosity, or appreciation for her.

Sandy had not registered this, however. "I said, 'Oh, I bet your husband does that too,'" she concluded, "but she just looked a little sad."

The last time they'd seen each other was a district Christmas party, in December of 2003. Nancy's mother had just died. She definitely wasn't herself.

"But we still joked around," said Sandy. "We exchanged these joke presents. Considering what happened, after, with the body in the car, I probably shouldn't say what mine was, for her."

But she did tell me, in the end. The gift had been a calendar: *1001 Uses for Duct Tape.*

CHAPTER 60

"Softball Is Our Life"

It was a Saturday in late summer, and I had driven an hour to watch the Compuware Girls Sixteen and Under Fastpitch Softball team compete in a tournament. Many of these were girls Bob Seaman used to coach, back when they were fourteen and unders. I wanted to watch them play, I told Julie, to get a feeling for this game that had meant so much to Bob, and to talk with people who knew him as a coach.

They were devoted, these Compuware fans. Some of them wore shirts that said "I ♥ Fastpitch." They all had special folding chairs and wagons to carry their coolers, and many of them decorated their cars with Silly String and signs that said things like "Number 18 Is Awesome" and "Go Compuware."

"We have jobs in our spare time," one of the fathers of a girl on the team told me, as we discussed the upcoming trip to Lexington. "Softball is our life."

Hearing that I was writing a book about what happened to Bob Seaman, a number of the parents and assistant coaches had come over to introduce themselves to me and tell me what a great guy he had been and what a great coach for their daughters. Every single one who'd heard about it, as many had, expressed the view that the anonymous letter accusing Bob of inappropriate behavior with the players (something everyone in this sport is on the lookout for) was a put-up job. Contrary to the descriptions of him that had come out in the testimony of Rick Cox and Greg Seaman at the trial, those of the parents portrayed Bob as a man of striking patience and calm.

"I never saw him blow up," one of them said. "Even when an umpire made a bad call."

"Girls this age get pretty high-strung and moody," said Sal Agro, grandfather of a player on the team who said he'd been a coach himself for many years. "But Bob was always kind to them. If he had a violent side, we would have seen it. Any man who has a hard time with women wouldn't want to deal with these girls, I'm telling you."

"He even gave pointers to girls on the teams we played against," one mother said. "That's the kind of coach he was. He had a big heart."

Jenna Dumbleton appeared to be having a hard time out on the field, where Dave Brubaker had placed her in her least favorite position, third base. He had said something to her, evidently, though neither Julie nor Dick was sure what.

"She's upset," said Julie, reaching for a Twizzler and handing one to me as well. "You can tell by how she's standing."

Dick looked concerned. Sometimes he was first base coach; sometimes he stayed on the sidelines. Now he was considering whether he should go over to the dugout when she came in and talk with her. This was a family in which, if one person was unhappy, everyone suffered.

"I think it's her shoulder giving her trouble," said Julie. "But she's also thinking about Bob."

"I think it's about Bru," said Dick. "He's too hard on her."

"Bob was so different," said Julie.

In the next inning, Jenna took the mound. Though I was hardly an expert—though this was my first fastpitch softball game ever, in fact—it was apparent as she blasted her first pitch over the plate that getting a hit off Jenna Dumbleton was not an easy task for a batter.

No doubt Bob Seaman, if he were describing this, would have had a few thousand words, minimum, to say about Jenna's motion. My description is a lot more basic and less attuned to the subtleties of the game, but I was struck by the explosiveness of the pitching in this game—the way, following her windup, Jenna released the ball such that it didn't so much leave her hand as it was ejected from it, and fired like a rocket toward the batter (who swung and missed). The follow-through, Dick Dumbleton explained to me, had been an issue for Jenna in the past.

She followed that first strike with a couple more. For a girl with a sore shoulder, she was looking good, and Julie was guessing her speed at somewhere around eighty miles an hour. But this was just a local tournament. She'd do better in Kentucky.

"Jenna's looking good out there," one of the mothers said to Julie.

"Dick's worried about her shoulder," Julie said. "We've been taking her to a physical therapist."

The conversation went like that awhile. I remained silent. Then one of the other mothers, showing signs of wanting to include me, asked what sports my own kids played.

I knew enough not to mention skateboarding and the gymnastics rings at Venice Beach, where my son Will likes to work out. "They used to play soccer," I offered.

In the world of fastpitch softball, that was a conversation stopper too, it turned out.

CHAPTER 61

Three Years' Worth of Valentine Boxes

Michelle Siskowski had crossed paths with Nancy Seaman in a couple of ways. For one thing, her stepdaughter Kristen had been a student teacher at Longacre Elementary school, having completed her teacher certification at Eastern Michigan University in Ann Arbor at the same time Nancy Seaman had gotten her master's degree there.

She was also the mother of a younger daughter, Emily, who'd been a fourth grade student of Mrs. Seaman's the year before the murder took place, and she had been Classroom Mother, volunteering her time for Nancy Seaman with things like photocopying materials out of her belief that if parents helped out that way, teachers would have more energy and time to give their students. Like Julie Dumbleton, Michelle was a stay-at-home mother, who had made it her business to keep her children's lives insulated from the harsher side of life, and up until recently, had largely pulled this off.

The decision to speak with me had not been easy for Michelle, and she told me that her upcoming talk with me had been the source of heated debate that morning, at her daily exercise session at Curves, where a number of women had been critical of her choice. Now, as she opened her door to me (apologizing for the mess, as women seemed to do, wherever I went in Oakland County, though their homes always looked spotless to me) I knew that this friendly, generous woman was also filled with apprehension. This event did that to people.

The way Michelle Siskowski saw it, Nancy Seaman had been a wonderful teacher for her daughter, and she wanted simply to tell me that part of her story. Until fourth grade, she told me, Emily had struggled in school, but once Mrs. Seaman began working with her, "she just blossomed."

"She had a way of finding something nice to say to every child," Michelle told me, taking out a booklet she had, with photographs showing a smiling Nancy Seaman, surrounded by fourth graders. "She had an incredible memory. She kept track of every single thing. She wrote little notes to the children, gave them a big hug when they came in, mornings. Her classroom was so full of life, with a science table full of interesting things to take apart and study under the microscope, pictures all over the walls, bright colors. She made a little book for each of her students, with their picture on the cover, for collecting autographs. Mrs. Seaman was very big on autographs," Michelle said.

Michelle Siskowski and the other classroom mother were around a lot that year, but Nancy Seaman was a private person, she said, not someone it was easy getting close to.

"Mostly we talked about things like gardening," she said. "I certainly never heard anything about trouble in her marriage. But I was in the office that December, the day her mother died suddenly. I wasn't working in Mrs. Seaman's room anymore because Emily had moved on to fifth grade, but I still saw her all the time when I was down at school, and naturally she was broken up that day. The other time I saw her cry, which was more unexpected, was when the principal, Mr. Smith, announced that he was retiring at the end of the school year, and she just sobbed and sobbed."

In May of 2003, Michelle's daughter Kristen was due to get her teaching certificate from Eastern Michigan University, and she had noticed, among the names of those receiving degrees, that of Nancy Seaman. "So I ran out to Costco and got her a cake, and a card, and told the principal about it," she said.

"When I gave her the cake," Michelle went on, "she was just so appreciative. She said 'You did more for me than my family did.'"

It was the kind of remark I was accustomed to hearing attributed to Nancy Seaman, by this point—the observation of a woman who relentlessly compared her life to that of those around her, and found hers lacking.

Really, what she wanted to do in speaking with me, Michelle had said, was to balance all the bad with the good aspects of her daughter's beloved teacher. But Mrs. Seaman did have this one odd trait, Michelle added, a little cautiously.

"She was extremely particular about locking things up. If she stepped out of her room for even a minute, she locked the door, and sometimes it was a problem, because she locked all her cupboards too. She was strict about rules. She didn't like it if you interrupted her when she was in the middle of presenting something to the children. She liked things a certain way, and you knew that about her."

Another thing about Mrs. Seaman: she planned ahead. "I had copies of worksheets made for her, years in advance," she told me. "There were these Valentine boxes she wanted me to put together, out of construction paper and heart-shaped noses and ears glued on the front of every one. I had to cut each one out individually. She wanted fifty for the next year, and another fifty for the year after that."

After word of the murder got out, Michelle was upset of course. Everyone was. "I know there were kids having nightmares, kids whose parents let them watch the news on television, which I personally can't imagine," she said. "Some parents were saying things like 'I never liked her,' but all the way up to the high school, kids who'd been her students over the past seven years that she'd taught at the school were crying. A local radio station was making all kinds of sickening jokes. It was an awful time."

Her daughter was fine now, she said. She didn't talk about Mrs. Seaman anymore. Michelle hoped she'd put the whole mess out of her mind.

"It's still hard for me to understand," she said. "I know this is stupid, but I keep thinking about those Valentine boxes, and all the work it was to make them, and how pointless it turned out to be. I guess someone at the school probably threw them out."

CHAPTER 62

A Heart-to-Heart on a Ballfield

I ran into Jake Dumbleton at one of Jenna's softball games, as I knew I would. (Jake was the kind of brother who still showed up to watch his sister pitch, either because he wanted to be there or because that's what you did in this family. Not a lot of nineteen-year-olds would choose to spend their weekend at a girls' fastpitch softball tournament, but that's how it was for this one.)

Jake was not happy to see me. "Don't take it personally," Julie told me, and I didn't. I knew that my presence simply brought to mind the memory of a terrible experience, though from all I gathered, that experience had been on Jake's mind plenty anyway.

I went over to say hello.

"I know you were upset about the *48 Hours* broadcast," I told him. "And I know you have a lot of concerns about talking with me. How about if we sit down and discuss it. You tell me what's bothering you. I'll tell you what I think. Then make up your mind how you want to handle it, and I'll respect your decision."

We walked to the far end of the playing field, away from the many girls' softball games under way. We sat on the grass—Jake with his baseball cap on backwards, the holes from piercing his ears barely visible, a macramé shell necklace around his neck, and an intense, worried, expression. I could tell he had been thinking quite a lot about the prospect of speaking with me.

"So do you think Mr. Seaman beat Nancy?" he asked me, studying a blade of grass, hard. "Are you going to be telling this like she was this big victim, and he was this terrible guy?" Like his mother, he was a person in possession of so little artifice himself that he had little defense against the potential deception or betrayal of others but to ask if they were going to deceive or betray him.

"It seems as though you may be having a harder time with Bob's murder than Bob's own sons," I told him. "But maybe it's just that you're more willing to acknowledge how rough this was." I was thinking about my recent conversation with Jeff Seaman—his remark to me that he was "moving on."

"So what's the point?" he asked me. "What good does it do having a book about any of this?

"I drove past the prison," he went on. "I wanted to curse at her.

"I heard you wanted to talk to her," he said. "I heard you were going to talk to Greg too."

I replied, "What I want is to get the best picture I can of what Bob was like. I figured you'd have a lot to say about that."

He told me he'd think about it. Jake was not a person who could easily behave rudely, and he didn't now. He shook my hand as we walked back to the game together, though for the moment he had nothing more to say to me or anyone, it would appear. He disappeared after that—a fact his mother noted, immediately after our return. She wanted to know how it had gone, how Jake seemed. She was worried that he hadn't eaten anything.

CHAPTER 63

The Nancy Crap File

From the prosecutors' office and Chief Dwyer, I'd assembled a mountain of paperwork about the Seaman case. Slowly I made my way through it all: the highly technical reports of the evidence technicians on the Farmington Hills police force; the body map compiled by the nurse who'd examined Nancy Seaman after her arrest, detailing the bruises on her body. (None on her face, and this was curious. The face was where batterers struck first and hardest, Chief Dwyer told me.)

Buried in the stack was a photocopy of a letter written by Nancy to Bob sometime early in 2004 and left—as was her habit—on the kitchen counter in what substituted for normal communication in that household. (His half of the dialogue appeared to have been supplied largely in the form of angry or sarcastic messages on Post-it notes.)

Bob had evidently placed the letter in the "Nancy Crap File" he kept at the office, that Julie had rescued. Now I was making my way through its contents.

"You're losing both your sons," the letter began.

Not because of anything I say, but because of your actions. They're not little boys any more. They see quite clearly that you are the one breaking up this family and how hard I have tried to keep it together. I can't shield them from your behavior any more. . . .

Marriage and family are important to both of them. Greg has told me on more than one occasion that he doesn't believe in divorce. That's how I raised them: to know that marriage and family is sacred and you fix it if it is broken. We're supposed to be setting the example. Nice example. . . . The irony is that you had it all. I used to watch the faces of people when the two of us would walk into a room. We were a handsome couple. . . .They envied what you had—a beautiful wife who valued homemaking and hearth, two handsome, smart, successful sons, a business, a beautiful home, toys most men would die for. For whatever reason you have decided to trash it all. Now instead of envy, they'll pity you for the choices you're making. . . .

Toys most men would die for, Nancy Seaman had written. And it could be said he had died for them, as things turned out.

I know that you think the Dumbies had nothing to do with this, but you're wrong. Friends do not come between a man and his wife and family. Do the math, you have spent more hours with them than with your own family these past three years. . . .

We all want you to come back to us. You say you love your sons but that is such a lie. A man who loves his sons would not do what you are doing to this family. That is what your sons see. The only person turning your sons against you is you. . . .

It is time for you to step up to the plate and do what is right.

Put the Dumbies out of your life and make your family and life a priority. They shouldn't be working at the Upper Deck; you need to put some space in that relationship so that you can start to see things clearly and fix your family.

What you don't understand is that we are a family. You can't pick and choose who you love. We are one; a unit. The boys love you and me. They are a part of us both. . . .

Let me know by Wednesday whether or not you want to fix this family. You decide. If the Dumbie friendship is more important than 30 years of marriage and your sons. The choices have always been yours; so stop trying to blame me for your fucked up life.

The letter evidently didn't succeed in convincing Bob Seaman to cut off all contact with the friends who valued him, and to come on home to the wife who thought he was fucked up, for the purpose of fixing his family. It would appear, from the history of his final months of marriage to Nancy, that Wednesday—whatever Wednesday it had been—came and went without any fixing having taken place.

CHAPTER 64

A Seventeen-Cent Charge at Kinko's

—~~~—

Another item in the Nancy Crap File that I now read and studied was the anonymous letter sent to the Compuware Softball Association concerning Bob Seaman's alleged sexual interest in his players—a letter Bob had believed to have been written by Nancy. Since my arrival in Michigan for the summer, I'd made a practice of dropping in on Jenna Dumbleton's softball practices with the Compuware girls' team. Shortly after reading the contents of the Nancy Crap File (including the anonymous letter), I was once again attending a game with Julie Dumbleton. She pointed out to me that several members of the Compuware Software advisory board were in attendance that day, so I made my way over to the spot on the sidelines where they had gathered, to ask them about the letter.

"Those were serious charges we received. We have a policy here not to respond to anonymous letters," said Ron Repicky, director of the board, and a coach who had worked with Bob in the past. "But the letter also just didn't ring true to us. We knew Bob, and we'd seen him working with our players. The person who wrote the letter hadn't even gotten the age group right for the team Bob had been coaching, which was fourteen and under, not twelve and under. And whoever it was that wrote the letter wouldn't even sign their name.

"If they knew anything about the Compuware team, they'd know it's not unusual for a guy to coach who doesn't have a daughter on the team. Hardly any of the coaches did have a daughter on the team, in fact."

All in all, though they acknowledged the importance of watching out for any sign of inappropriate behavior toward players on the part of coaches, nothing about this particular warning made sense to the board.

"We didn't even want to show it to Bob," said Repicky. "But we talked about it, and in the end we figured he should know."

When they had called Bob in to discuss the letter, he'd said he knew right off who must have written it.

"He told us, 'I'm going through a divorce, guys,'" said Tom Hillsey, another coach on the board who also knew Bob. "He was the kind of guy who never even made a comment about the waitress when we went out for pizza and beer, he was so focused on the game."

"If Bob was ever guilty of looking at a little girl's fanny, there was only one reason he'd do it," said Newt Barefoot, another coach, "and that was to see if her hips were rotating properly when she swung the bat."

Because its origin had never been definitively established, the letter to Compuware had not been admissible as evidence during the trial, but to many people familiar with Bob Seaman's story there had seemed little doubt who'd written it, and that the charges alluded to were groundless.

Another odd thing about the letter was its timing. The letter had been postmarked on February 14, 2004. It would seem odd that a genuinely concerned individual would have chosen a month when nothing was happening in the world of girls' softball to send such a letter. It was less hard to imagine an angry woman, feeling particularly slighted by her husband's lack of attention on this day of all days, choosing February 14 to compose and mail it.

For whatever it was worth, I later learned from the records of Bob Seaman's charge cards that on the day the letter was mailed, a charge appeared on the card that had been carried by Nancy. It was a printing and copying charge from Kinko's, for seventeen cents.

CHAPTER 65

Black and White

I spent my days now talking to people in the mostly affluent suburbs and gated communities that branched off of Telegraph along the stretch north of 12 Mile Road—places with names like Rolling Oaks and Timbers Edge and Chelsea Park and Camelot, whose citizens (for now, anyway) appeared unscathed by the well-known hard times in the automotive industry—people Nancy Seaman would have regarded as "handsome couples" of the sort who might inspire envy, perhaps.

By day, I drove around gated communities and attended softball practices, sipped cappuccinos at Starbucks and pored over documents at the Oakland County Courthouse—a place where it was striking to observe that while a vast proportion of those charged with crimes, and on trial, were black, nearly every judge, every juror, and every single employee I spotted among the dozens working in the office of the County Clerk, was white.

But I headed north every night. The cottage where I was staying in Lapeer was ten minutes from Flint and a forty-mile drive on M15 and the Dixie Highway from Oakland County. I liked it that in the evenings, when I put away my notebook and computer, I could have my beer on the porch, looking out at Potter Lake and sometimes watch the heat lightning over the water, and sometimes watch the rain, which I had missed in my last ten Northern California summers, where the evenings were never quite warm enough.

Friday nights at Potter Lake, Lori and Mike would drive up with Ben and sometimes Alex, and their two dogs, the same way so many other families did, who had cottages around the lake, and ten minutes after they pulled up, you could see the children dropping their fishing lines off the end of their docks, and teenagers on jet skis and the men heading out on the pontoon boats to fish some more or just get off and kill a six pack, and a little later would come the smell of the barbecues. Fish, if the men had been lucky. Burgers, if not.

Sunday nights, everyone packed up and took off for home again— except for me and Chuck. I might spot him later that night, on the porch, or outside one of my windows, where, if I asked what he was doing, he'd say he was just checking up on me.

It bothered me less than a person might have thought. Friends back home, hearing about this man, expressed concern, but I knew I had nothing to worry about there—that just when you think it's the unshaven man taking a quick look in your window you should be worried about, with the fishing knife in his belt and the dent in his skull from where doctors had cut out a piece of his brain a few decades back, it turns out the really scary person is the fourth-grade teacher in the Talbot's suit. When I had nightmares at Potter Lake, she was the only one who appeared in them.

Here was the one bad thing that started happening to me, at Potter Lake. I started having bad dreams—dreams so unsettling, I'd wake up in a bad mood, and not realize until later the thing clouding my day wasn't real, only images that had come to me in the night.

I dreamed about prison sometimes, and being on trial for some crime I never could identify. I dreamed I killed someone, and that I was caught on a surveillance video. One awful night, I dreamed I'd somehow killed my own children by mistake.

Still I liked it that I woke to the sound of fish jumping in the lake, and that I started my day swimming there. Then I'd drive into Oakland County once more, past the previous night's road kill, the Support our Troops and Save the Babies signs (both on the same lawn in one instance), the bait and tackle shops, the package stores displaying Day-Glo offers on beer and party mixers, the Curves salons, the Chinese take-out joint called Takee Outee, the perpetual yard sales whose merchandise hadn't seemed to change or be depleted for all the weeks I'd passed them by, the church with the sign out front that read "You Think It's Hot *Here*?" (And it was.)

Although my Pontiac had no radio, I didn't mind the drive. It gave me time to think. I found a certain comfortable familiarity with the people of Lapeer County and the places I passed through, on my way to the more affluent and gentrified communities of Birmingham and Southfield, Farmington Hills and Northville. People in Lapeer County drove trucks with tools in the back and jumper cables; they had gun racks and fishing licenses and even bow hunting licenses, and bumper stickers that said "One Day at a Time," and when you pulled your car up alongside theirs at a stop light, the music you heard blasting was often country.

I liked it that people here said "Hot enough for you?" when you ran into the store for a dozen eggs, that they could clean a blue gill in three minutes, or crochet edging around a handmade pot holder. I loved the green and gold of the rolling fields I passed along my drive, the early morning mist on the lakes—and in Michigan, there were so many of those, which caused me to reflect (immersed as I was in the Seaman story) of how easy it would be to dump a body here.

One of the things I found myself thinking about a lot, on those long drives between Oakland County and Lapeer, was families. Not only the Seamans, and the Dumbletons, and the family Lori and Mike had made of their combined friends and children (children of their ex-spouses' children, even). I thought about how their family had taken me in that summer—in a manner not wholly unlike the way the Dumbletons had taken in Bob Seaman, it occurred to me now, though in my case I wasn't escaping anything, I reminded myself.

I thought a surprising amount about cars, on my drives from Lapeer to Oakland County, and not just because the performance of the Pontiac was iffy, and getting worse all the time. There was an old Cadillac convertible I liked for sale in Goodrich, and a beauty of a Chevrolet Bel Air for $3500 just outside of Clarkston, that had no takers all summer, which struck me as odd. I liked it that people here grew tomatoes and corn, whose progress I followed over the course of the summer, waiting for August and September, the harvest. There was no corn to be found like this in California, and though in Marin County you could buy what they called "heirloom tomatoes" for $3.89 a pound, they wouldn't taste as good as what the farmstand outside Lapeer would have to offer soon, at five dollars a bushel.

I always knew I was getting close to my destination, on my morning drive back into Metro Detroit, when I passed the used car lot on the Dixie Highway with the fountain in front, whose water had been colored pink. (It brought to mind the cleanup project at the Seaman garage after the murder.) Then came the giant Dixie Flea Market, right where the Dixie Highway intersected with Telegraph Road—a place where you could pick up a Harley Davidson mirror or a lamp base made out of a Barbie doll, or a set of Topps baseball cards from 1997, or a Pam Dawber "Mindy" collectible doll, or a hub cap.

For a few miles then, you'd pass through Pontiac and the beginnings of Waterford—home of the nearly empty Summit Place Mall. After that though, you crossed into the prosperous part of Oakland County, where whatever bad things were going on in the American automotive industry had not yet seeped through the gates of the gated communities, or not much anyway.

I had learned from Lori and Mike that it was inaccurate to speak of where I was spending my time as "Detroit." Detroit proper (if that's what it was, and opinions varied here) was a very different place from either Lapeer or Oakland County. You could get there easily enough by driving down Telegraph Road, past the car dealerships and shopping centers, the chain restaurants and perfectly landscaped golf courses, the private schools and churches and houses with rolling and weed-free lawns and heated driveways and glassed-in porches that people here spoke of as Florida rooms—a stretch of thoroughfare where the only way to make a left turn is to make what they call a Michigan Turn, meaning first you turned left to reverse direction, then right.

If you kept going straight, heading south, you got to the highway known as 8 Mile Road, and the landscape changed, but not in the same way that it changes when you drive north, to Lapeer. There was a place at 8 Mile Road where you could see it all: Grosse Pointe and its multimillion-dollar homes in one direction; pawn shops and gun shops and signs for cashing checks and selling blood, just over the line. For people in Metro Detroit, 8 Mile Road (and which side of it you lived on) defined the world.

Driving south, what you saw were fried chicken establishments and Baptist churches and little beauty salons offering cornrows, and pretty soon you hit Detroit, or it hit you. Detroit was a bombed-out looking place, where I was told people lived only if they had nowhere else to go. Detroit was where a giant sculpture of a clenched fist punched out in the direction the Detroit River on the corner of Woodward and

Jefferson in honor of its native son, Joe Louis. Detroit was where the black people were, but the black people didn't want to be there either, and if you were white, from Oakland County, you weren't likely to pay a visit any time soon.

There was no other city in the country, I learned, in which the population was more uniformly black than Detroit. The suburbs were a different story: more and more racial diversity could be seen in the suburbs of Oakland County, but not a lot of the influx was coming from the African American population of Detroit itself. Whatever changes had been taking place in Oakland County, the lines between black and white still appeared as starkly drawn as the tiles on the Seamans' garage floor.

I had been spending my summer in the white world, of course, but I was thinking about what lay beyond 8 Mile Road, and what the relationship might be between the one side of that line and the other. Which led me to cross it.

Detroit was, after all, the home of Motown. I couldn't see spending all this time so close to the city where so much of the best American music made in my lifetime had originated, and not going there and taking in some part of that history. It baffled me that as close as we were to the very spot where the Temptations, Smokey Robinson, Gladys Knight, Martha Reeves, the Four Tops, Stevie Wonder, Diana Ross, and Marvin Gaye got their start—and as many songs as I heard blasting from car radios as I drove along Telegraph—I hardly ever heard Motown music playing. Rap maybe, but you'd hear more R and B a thousand miles away than here, a twenty-minute drive from Berry Gordy's studio, where the Supremes had laid down the tracks for "Baby Love."

Driving as much as I did now—in a car whose radio no longer functioned—I thought about the pleasure I always found in choosing a soundtrack for whatever stretch of road I traveled on. Back when Jeff Seaman was still talking to me, I asked him what music his father listened to when he drove the Shelby or the Boss.

"He liked to listen to the engine," Jeff said. This was a new idea to me: that for a certain kind of person, an engine might itself possess its own kind of music.

Cars and music. Music and cars. It was odd how two such different cultures had formed the basis of two industries—one started by Henry Ford, one by Berry Gordy—that grew out of the same midwestern soil alongside the Rouge River.

There was a connection, of course. The reason black people came to Detroit from the South in such numbers in the first place, during the Depression, lay in the death of rural farming, the end of the cotton industry, and the promise of jobs in factories up north. But if they came to work in factories, they laid down musical tracks once they got there. They might have worked on the assembly line by day, but Sundays they went to church and belted out gospel music, and at night they danced and sang in perfect close harmony.

And still, the automotive industry had kept its distance from the music of the Motor City. The Gadjits had recorded "Mustang Sally" in 1965, but Ford never made use of the song in its advertising, and when Chevrolet was looking for a soundtrack for its truck commercials, the choice (as it always seemed to be) was a white artist from Detroit: Bob Seger. "Like a Rock."

Julie Dumbleton had told me about a remark of Nancy Seaman's that I couldn't get out of my head. At one point, when Nancy was after Bob to do some chores he didn't feel like tackling, he had suggested hiring a yard worker. According to Julie (who'd heard this from Bob), Nancy had said, "Why would I do that, when I have my own nigger right here?"

Back where I came from, whatever prejudice and racism people harbored, they kept it more concealed, by and large. I had never known anyone to speak as Nancy supposedly had, and I would have had trouble believing the story if Jake Dumbleton hadn't reported a similar experience. He too had been referred to by Nancy as "a nigger" one time, when he was doing some kind of particularly menial work on Bob's boat. As it was, the word—and that it had allegedly been uttered by a fourth-grade teacher once presented with the Rainbow Award for promoting an understanding of diversity—was haunting me.

Then there was another story, also reported by Julie: of a time when Nancy's charge card was rejected at the pump, and she became so incensed at the black gas station attendant that Bob had to come down to the station to iron things out. If it did indeed exist, this was a side of Nancy Seaman that would have been unrecognizable to her teacher friends over at Longacre Elementary. But given the other aspects of the woman I had begun learning about, it was no longer totally unfathomable to me.

I was trying to understand the culture of a place responsible for the American automobile and Motown music. A place whose demographics had been transformed by the race riots of 1967 and the years that followed.

Forty years later, there was still plenty of black rage in Detroit. You knew it from graffiti on the walls and from rap lyrics on the radio and from crime rates and unemployment rates, and you knew it when you looked at the nearly all-white juries in Oakland County Courthouse and the benches filled with black defendants.

This was an old story, and everyone knew it here. Maybe that was why people were so fascinated by the story that had brought me to this place: this was the story of a white person's rage. The criminal this time had been a middle-class woman. What Nancy Seaman had done wasn't supposed to occur in places like the Ramblewood subdivision, and as easy as it might be to see why crimes happened on one side of the line at 8 Mile Road, it was that hard to understand how they took place on the other.

You didn't have to be poor or unemployed to be murderously angry, evidently. That was part of what I came here to understand.

CHAPTER 66

The Bass Line

It was just around this time that I opened my *Detroit News* and read that Renaldo ("Obie") Benson, who sang bass for the Four Tops, had died at a Detroit hospital, at the age of sixty-nine, from complications of lung cancer. (He died the same day as Luther Vandross, in New York.)

The funeral was set for late that week, at a church in Detroit. I knew there'd be great music and a great preacher. If ever there was an event that would give me a glimpse of Motown and Motown history, I figured, this was one. I dismissed the warnings of a couple of Oakland County residents, who asked me if I felt safe doing this, and made my way down Woodward Avenue. Only this time, instead of looping around as a person does if she's just doing a little shopping in Birmingham before heading back to Bloomfield Hills, or attending the Dream Cruise, I kept on going to the Tabernacle Missionary Baptist Church on West Grand Boulevard in Detroit.

Car conscious as I'd become, I was struck first by the sight of the vehicles pulled up in front of the church: a line of identical luxury sedans, all of them a distinctively designed model of Plymouth, the

Magnum, all of them white. I had worn a skirt and high-heeled sandals for this occasion, but as mourners emerged from the vehicles, I realized that I was underdressed. Nearly every one of the women in attendance wore a brilliantly colored suit and a hat, many with feathers, and the men wore suits almost as colorful, with shoes to match, and hats, their gold jewelry glinting in the sun.

A music writer I knew from the *Detroit News,* Susan Whitall—one of the half dozen other white faces in the crowd of several hundred—pointed out to me a number of the more prominent guests: Otis Williams of the Temptations; Smokey Robinson—still looking good—and his ex-wife, from the original Miracles; Eddie Holland and Brian Dozier, of the Holland-Dozier-Holland team responsible for writing most of the Supremes' biggest hits; Sir Mack Rice, who wrote "Mustang Sally" and "Respect Yourself"; and the two surviving Tops, Levi Stubbs and Duke Fakir.

Inside the church, several nurses—all wearing white uniforms and the kind of headgear I associated with nurses of the World War II era—were stationed around the vast room, evidently looking out for mourners who might be so overcome that they'd faint. Once the service got under way, I could understand the need for them. It was hot in the church, for one thing, but more than that, the emotion in the place seemed almost to vibrate through the benches, and particularly for a person who'd been spending the majority of her time among those whose emotional expression was far more contained (Julie Dumbleton and the fans of the Compuware girls' softball teams excluded), the contrast was striking.

A series of moving testimonials was delivered—stories about Obie Benson's famous good humor, his smile, his kindness, his love of singing with the Four Tops. Eddie Holland read a letter from Berry Gordy, calling Obie Benson "a shining light." Smokey Robinson said "my brother isn't in the casket anymore." He was "somewhere having a good time like he always did."

Duke Fakir, looking a little fragile, pushed the wheelchair of Levi Stubbs to the casket to give his respects. Obie Benson's daughter Eboni called him "the absolute best father ever."

There was a sermon, of course—a rousing reminder that death need not be a time for grieving, when the departed loved one was sitting at the right hand of God, as Obie Benson surely would be now. Ollie Woodson, a former singer with the Temptations, sang "Walk Around Heaven One Day" so powerfully that when it was over, I wished the room could have stayed silent for a long time, just to let the sound of his huge, clear voice hang in the air awhile.

The church was filled with floral displays of a kind I'd never seen before—a treble clef five feet high; a cross as tall as a man, made out of yellow chrysanthemums, with red carnations shooting out on all sides like a corona; a heart; a star; a gold record all in flowers.

The service ended with the mourners pouring down the center aisle, one by one, row after row, past the casket, in a colorful parade of hats and suits, silk dresses and gold. Some of them picked up one of the floral displays as they passed, creating a glorious procession of flowers, moving like a river down the center of the church and out the door, where they would be transported to the cemetery, no doubt.

The mood outside the church was in no way somber. It would not have surprised me if someone among the many mourners assembled had burst into song there on the sidewalk, or joined together in some kind of impromptu a cappella harmony—as so many here were no doubt equipped to do. They were laughing and talking, hugging each other and waving, calling out, kissing. It was nothing like any funeral I'd attended. It was the kind of funeral that leaves you thinking you should attend funerals more often—but then they wouldn't be like this one.

Not right away, but eventually, the mourners (if that's what they were) climbed into their big white cars and glided out of the parking lot, flowers everywhere, as if this were the Rose Parade or Mardi Gras. Once they were gone, the street seemed suddenly bleak, and I realized that West Grand Boulevard was actually a gray and broken-down place, not even close to grand, or much of a boulevard. So long as the stars of Motown and their friends and family had been assembled, I hadn't even noticed.

The only disappointing aspect to the Obie Benson funeral had been the absence, in the hall, of a single note of music from the Four Tops. I was in the mood now to hear "I Can't Help Myself" or "Standing in the Shadows of Love" or "Bernadette." As it happened, less than a mile down West Grand Boulevard I spotted a sign in front of a not particularly distinctive house, announcing it was the home of the Motown Museum, so I pulled over. (Here, finally, was a place my Pontiac fit in. Everyone in Detroit drove vehicles like mine, unless they were riding a bicycle or on foot. Unless they were a star of Motown.)

After a quick tour of the museum—including a walk through the studio where the Supremes had recorded all their early hits, with the wood floor visibly worn where early Motown recording artists had danced—I was able to pick up a CD of Motown hits from the sixties, featuring the Four Tops. Because my car had no CD player, I would not be able to hear the low, soulful voice of Obie Benson until later that night, when I was back in Lapeer, at the cottage on the lake.

It was late when I put the music on and turned up the volume. No worries about disturbing the neighbors, because nobody was there to hear but me.

It occurred to me, sitting on the porch, listening to that mix of perfectly harmonizing male voices recorded almost fifty years before, that except perhaps for some painful karaoke night where some white person at the campground was drunk enough to think he could tackle it, this song might not have been heard over these waters for a very long time, and it might be a long time yet, before it would be heard again. *Baby, I need your loving. Got to have all your loving.*

CHAPTER 67

"Now You Want to Bludgeon Me"

Still working my way through the file of paperwork on the Seaman case, I lifted out several pages of letters written by Bob Seaman to Nancy.

"I am so callous and insensitive to your paperwork burden," one of the letters began.

> After all, how would I know about paperwork? I don't pay the bills around here (remember I NEVER do ANYTHING around here). And there is no paperwork burden with running The Upper Deck. . . . As Greg would say, "I'm such an asshole." Your burdens are so much greater than mine.

There were more:

> Any normal husband would be grateful to a wife who is so willing to spend time with him helping him understand how lucky he is to have a family so willing to take time and financial support. Even my youngest son has graciously offered his heartfilled advice that I am squandering my life with such foolish, wasteful pursuits as "personal

pleasures" like coaching softball (come on, Greg doesn't play softball) and the most despicable self indulgence, FRIENDS!! ARG!!! Greg is right, "I'm just an old fool" and for me not to appreciate him pointing that out. How ungrateful of me.

How dare I not want to spend more time with you. How can you possibly explain to me what a failure I am as a husband and father if I don't spend time listening to you? How can I possibly be cured of the blatant character flaws if I don't spend "Quality Time" with you.

The picture of Bob Seaman that emerged from reading these letters revealed Bob Seaman to have been an angry man, all right. It was not hard to imagine that the person who wrote them would have spoken of his wife as a bitch or called her one to her face. But it was also easy to see, reading Bob's words, that what he wrote was only half of a two-way war of hateful accusation.

Another letter (also too long for Bob Seaman's favored form of stationery, a Post-it) came as a clear response to a series of demands Nancy had made in an earlier letter to him. Printed in longhand, on stationery with the words "From the Office of the Superintendent" on the top of the page, that letter began with the instruction that Nancy should reread two earlier letters—one from him to her, apparently, and one from her to him, in response.

You want me to turn on my friends and return to a son who disrespects me and a wife who has contempt for me?

Please read each of your (19) paragraphs one by one and ask 1) is there any statement of complicity on your part or Greg's part on how this situation came to be? Is it all my fault? And 2) What in any paragraph would convince me that I should want to spend time with you or that would make me attracted to you. (Unless that is, I'm a masochist who craves being told how "fucked up" he is.)

You have always tried to rule the roost, and attempted to neuter me. . . .

I have lived with you for the last 20 years without love for the sake of my sons.

The next line was the most chilling. Speaking of Nancy's threat to "turn Jeff against me as you have with Greg," he wrote, "Now you want to bludgeon me. . . ."

CHAPTER 68

Prisoner 520695

F rom Lori Brasier I learned that in Michigan, a person can go online to the Web site of the Michigan Department of Corrections, type in the name of a specific prison facility and a prisoner's name, and see her most current prison photograph. So I typed in Nancy Seaman's name. This brought up on the screen her prisoner ID number and the mug shot of her taken on the day of her admission to the Robert Scott facility.

Gone now was any trace of the attractive woman bent over the desk of a fourth grader, as shown in the Longacre yearbook of the year before. Her face, on January 26, 2005, could have been that of a drug smuggler or a bunko artist, an armed robber or a murderer, which it was. Below her name, a few lines of basic information told the story. Height, weight, hair and eye color, birth date. *Conviction: First degree murder. Status: Life.*

Some months earlier, shortly after the guilty verdict, the *Detroit Free Press* had run a story by Lori describing the life Nancy Seaman was likely to encounter when she began serving her term at the Robert Scott Correctional Facility.

Nancy Seaman would be housed in a seven-by-eleven-foot cell shared with another woman, also a high-security prisoner, the article explained. They would sleep in bunk beds and share an open toilet, a sink, and a desk. At those times when she left her cell for meals and showers and work, she'd be escorted as part of a group of other high-security prisoners. Although jobs existed at the prison that involved teaching, or work in the library, it would take Nancy Seaman a while before she earned the privilege of one of those assignments. She'd most likely begin as a dishwasher or janitor, at the rate of seventeen-and-a-half cents an hour.

At four-thirty, the workday would end, at which point she could mingle in the common room with other prisoners watching television or playing checkers. Dinner—meatloaf and gravy, corn, and potatoes, and similar fare—was served at six. Twice a week, she'd be allowed to go outdoors in the small recreation courtyard. With rare exceptions, the women with whom she would rub shoulders now were a very different kind from the ones she'd associated with in her former life: younger, for the most part, and far less well educated, though unlike herself, most of them would have legitimate hopes of walking free at some point in the future. Perhaps it was significant, given what I was beginning to hear about Nancy Seaman's attitudes to race, that the vast majority of the inmates at Robert Scott Correctional Facility were black.

She would wear a blue cotton jumpsuit in prison. No jewelry. No makeup other than an eyebrow pencil.

Lori Brasier's story quoted Merry Morash, a professor in the School of Criminal Justice at Michigan State University, who had studied women in prison. "She is probably still feeling stunned by what has taken place," Morash said. "Most women are very oriented toward maintaining relationships, and in prison, you lose those connections."

As Lori's article described it, women in prison tend to focus all their energy on counting the days, months, years, till they get out. For Nancy, there was no such number to hold on to, only the dim prospect of an appeal, and from what I'd gathered from experienced observers in the Oakland County legal community, no grounds existed to pursue one.

Still, because any case in which the verdict is guilty in the first degree is subject to automatic appeal, an attorney had been assigned to handle the case from here. (Unlike Larry Kaluzny, whose defense had carried a six-figure price tag, this one was evidently court appointed.) Now I placed a call to Nancy Seaman's recently appointed appeals lawyer.

Attorney Michael Farraone said little about his client's position on the matter of an interview, but offered the opinion that it didn't seem there was much to lose by speaking with me if she wanted to at this point. He was working on the appeal, of course, though it would be a year, minimum, before they had anything to go forward with. Concerning possible grounds for appeal, he mentioned Larry Kaluzny's failure to pursue a change of venue, on the grounds of excessive and unfair pretrial publicity.

"There was way too much hyperbole getting thrown around about this case," Farraone volunteered. He pronounced *hyperbole* as if it were a holiday football game: the Hyper Bowl (coming somewhere after the Rose Bowl, maybe, and before the Cotton Bowl).

Meanwhile, he suggested I write to Nancy again, making my case once more, but this time offering some examples of specific questions I might have for her. Aware that his client might not want to be quoted on the record making statements that could be used against her in the appeal, I suggested to him that perhaps she'd be more comfortable responding to my questions in writing, which would give him the opportunity to review her remarks before handing them on to me.

The next day I drew up and submitted a list of questions for Nancy Seaman. By now, I held out little expectation that I'd hear back from her. But where all my efforts had been focused on getting Nancy Seaman to talk with me (and if Nancy did, so would Greg), I saw now that my attitude was changing. If a collect call came now from the prison, to say that Nancy had put me on her visitors' list and wanted to see me, I would go, but with a certain amount of anxiety.

I had been reading a book by Janet Malcolm, *The Journalist and the Murderer,* in which she explored the relationship formed between the writer Joe McGinniss and Jeffrey MacDonald, the subject of McGinniss's best-selling book, *Fatal Vision.* Over the course of MacDonald's trial for the murder of his pregnant wife and children, McGinniss had worked closely with MacDonald (even becoming a member of his defense team) and ingratiated himself with his subject. After MacDonald was found guilty of the murders, the writer had continued to correspond with him, enlisting his trust, expressing the view that he "wouldn't rest" until he'd seen Jeffrey MacDonald receive the justice he had been denied.

All this time, McGinniss had withheld from MacDonald his true belief: that despite MacDonald's claims to the contrary, he thought he was a monster and a narcissist, guilty of the crimes for which he was now serving his sentence. Later, MacDonald sued McGinniss for fraud, and—though incarcerated—won a large settlement. Now, in her book, Janet Malcolm explored the ethics of what McGinniss had engaged in, and more than that, explored the very nature of being a journalist. The issues she wrote about spoke to everything I was grappling with now in my own work. The story she told was as gripping as a thriller, in which I could easily enough imagine myself as a central character, in peril.

But it wasn't some legal risk that alarmed me. It was the moral one. The phrase that came to mind was one someone had uttered to me years before, in reference to my novel *To Die For* and my choice to invent the character of a woman who'd arranged the murder of her husband, rather than interviewing the actual woman, Pamela Smart, on whom the character was based.

"That way you don't have to get into bed with a murderer," he'd said to me.

Right you are, I answered. I don't make friends with murderers. And I don't pretend to, either.

Getting into bed with this murderer, or sitting across a table in a prison visiting room, anyway, turned out to be a moot point. I received no response to my list of questions. Nancy Seaman still had nothing to say to me, and I was minding it less and less that this was so.

CHAPTER 69

Every Corpse Tells a Story

—◦◦◦—

At the offices of Oakland County's chief medical examiner, Dr. Ljubisa Dragovic, a plaque in the entryway greets a visitor first: "Show me the manner in which a nation or a community cares for its dead," read the words of someone named William Gladstone, writing in the late nineteenth century, "and I will measure with mathematical exactness the tender mercy of its people, their respect for the laws of the land, and their loyalty to high ideals."

Here in this place, the bodies of the dead might be treated with tender mercy and respect, but all around was evidence of how often that standard went unmet when they were living. One glass case featured skulls of individuals murdered in Oakland County, sometimes by blows to the head. Another case displayed a couple of nooses used in suicides ("67 year old white male, depressed over the death of his mother," "26 year old white male, distraught over the end of a relationship"), as well as a couple of homemade electrocution devices. There was a fetus in a jar—no explanation given for that one—and a variety of knives, bullets, guns, and blunt instruments, displayed in some instances next to the skulls of the individuals on whom they had been used.

One particularly gruesome display, directly across from the lunch-room, told the story of a forty-seven-year-old female who had main-tained a family-owned restaurant with her husband. When reports of her disappearance finally led the police to pay a visit to the restaurant, they found the husband carrying out a large plastic tub, heading toward the garbage.

"Inspection and search of kitchen revealed plastic containers of taco filling believed to be from human flesh," read the information ac-companying photographs of the tub and its contents. "Human bones cooked two days. Burnt bones." Photographs showing those were also part of the display.

I was still standing, transfixed, in front of that case when the re-ceptionist found me to let me know that Dr. Dragovic was ready for me now. She led me into a sunny room—not an actual autopsy lab. A moment later, in came a man I recognized from the Court TV tapes: trim, perfectly groomed, with white hair and a neat moustache. He was dressed in shirtsleeves and suspenders and white pants, and he was wearing one of his trademark bow ties. As I shook his hand the thought flashed through my mind: how many interesting and dis-turbing places those fingers had touched.

I asked him about the profession of medical examiner, the link be-tween medicine and detective work, and the fascinating way in which a body—bones, blood, organs, tissue—tells a story, even after death, that the victim himself is no longer able to recount. It was a notion that spoke to the heart of Dr. Dragovic's passion, clearly—his twin loves of medicine and sleuthing. He spoke now in a voice thick not only with the accent of his native Transylvania but with undisguised love of his work.

"Absolutely," he said, practically pouncing on the concept. "The in-dividual can no longer tell his story, but the body does."

And what had Bob Seaman's body told Dr. Dragovic about the events that took place in the garage on Briarwood Court on Mother's Day night (or, if a person were to believe Nancy Seaman's version, the morning after)?

"The ax or hatchet was used first," he began. "Those blows led to incapacitation, a fracturing of the skull, invasion of the cortex. The level of incapacitation led to a safe approach for the injuries that fol-lowed—additional blows to the head, followed by slashing of the throat and stabbing of the back. Sequence defined by logic."

At this point, Dr. Dragovic called out to a colleague to join us, for the purpose of acting out for me—almost as a choreographer would a dance—the sequence of events and actions he had extrapolated as having taken place between Nancy and Bob Seaman over the course of the minutes in which the murder occurred.

A fellow physician introduced to me as Bernie took his place in the room, assuming the role and position of Bob Seaman, while Dr. Dragovic played Nancy. A stick was used to simulate the hatchet.

"Her testimony revealed many inconsistencies," said Dr. Dragovic, holding the stick aloft over Bernie's head as he spoke. "Supposedly, she was being held by the lower legs, by the knees. She described herself as on the ground with the hatchet in her hands. This doesn't make sense. After any one of those blows, any individual is going to let go and protect himself, fend off his attacker, not hang onto her legs.

"They did not have that level of relationship that he would be attaching himself to her body," he said, dryly.

As Dr. Dragovic spoke, Bernie—still playing the Bob Seaman part—appeared to bend over, as if struck. Dr. Dragovic lowered the stick representing the hatchet in the direction of Bernie's skull.

"It's illogical that she was swinging wildly with her eyes closed, as she testified," he said. "She would have injured herself. People who are in rage have a tendency to cut themselves. It is a more reasonable scenario that she approached from behind and hit him."

The demonstration continued. Sixteen swings of the hatchet/stick, with Bernie keeling over gradually onto the tile floor of the medical examiner's conference room. This was clearly not the first time these two men had acted out a murder here. As they did so, Dr. Dragovic continued to offer helpful commentary.

"The blows appeared to be sustained in relatively fast sequence," he said.

"He would certainly be disoriented. There would be interference of cortical function." Here, Bernie lolled his head, to indicate the effects of impaired cortical function.

"To accomplish this," he said, swinging, "you have to have a relatively stationary target." At this point, Bernie was one. He no longer moved at all.

"And keep in mind," said Dr. Dragovic. "This was a fairly well-nourished guy. Had he been able to respond, he would have offered a significant capacity to overpower his assailant."

Bernie was on the floor now. Dr. Dragovic knelt over him. He had set down the stick representing the hatchet and moved on to a stick representing the knife.

"In order to accomplish the slashing of the neck," he said, his voice level as ever, "she had to be above him. I am left with the impression that she enjoyed total physical control. The knife slashes were grouped in one localized area. In order for that to happen, one has to be immobile. This is not something where we're chasing each other around a car."

Bernie was finished. (Dead, or representing death at least. Or the act of dying.) Dr. Dragovic excused him. Bernie lifted himself up off the floor, shook my hand briefly, and exited the conference room, as Dr. Dragovic, returning to his seat, continued his discourse.

"Here's the crux of my assessment of this case," he said, folding his hands on his chest. "You don't inflict all these injuries, using two separate weapons, without being pretty upset about things. These were not blows incurred to fend off some immediate threat. You have to have your own motivator inside to inflict and reinflict."

Nancy Seaman's big mistake, in Dr. Dragovic's eyes (that is to say, her other mistake, besides killing her husband) lay in her inability to substantiate her statements concerning the circumstances of the attack, and the sense she left, in the eyes of the jury, of untruthfulness.

"That serves as a direct insult to the intellect of the jurors," he told me. "If someone is telling them something that makes no sense, they don't take it lightly.

"This was an emotionally charged killing," he went on. "Some murders seem to come out of nowhere, like thunder in the sky. This one was years in the making. Vengeance does not develop from no feeling."

Dr. Dragovic did not believe that Nancy Seaman struck her husband in self-defense. "The perpetrator would have significant injuries," he said flatly.

"It was a blood bath," he concluded. "There would have been no place in that garage not covered with blood," he said, shaking his head. "No place."

We got up from the table and made our way back out to the lobby. On our way out, Dr. Dragovic picked up the stick—the ax substitute used for demonstration purposes—and hefted it a final time, no longer for the purposes of demonstration, it appeared, but only in reflection.

He clasped the stick in his fine doctor's hands a moment. Then, gripping it around the base, he swung it cleanly through the air, with no target in range. It could almost have been a golf club he was swinging, I thought for a moment. But what his motion most strongly evoked, it came to me, was the swing of a baseball bat.

CHAPTER 70

Memorabilia

ust down the road from Dr. Dragovic's office on County
Drive were the offices of David Gorcyca and his team of prosecutors,
including Lisa Ortlieb. I had stopped by here to introduce myself to
Ortlieb briefly, on one of my short visits to Michigan during the
spring, but at the time I'd believed it was best to hold off on speaking
with Lisa at any length until I'd met with Nancy Seaman or at least
heard from her.

In the time since, I'd checked in with Lisa occasionally, looking for
some piece of information on the case, but now that I was back in
Michigan for the summer, with Nancy Seaman still incommunicado,
I decided to seek her out for an extended conversation about the case.
To my surprise—given the busyness of her schedule—she cleared her
afternoon for me.

One thing about Oakland County prosecutors: no grass grows
under their feet. In California, a person accused of a crime (Scott
Peterson, say, or Michael Jackson) may wait in jail, or out on bail, a
couple of years before seeing the inside of a courtroom for anything
more than arraignment and preliminary hearings. In Michigan, less

than seven months separated the day of Bob Seaman's murder from the opening of Nancy Seaman's trial, and that was typical.

Now, only a few months after the verdict, I knew from Lori Brasier that Lisa Ortlieb was already deep in another case—a teenage boy charged with the murder of his mother. (Her eyes had also been cut out, once she was dead.) If you wanted to talk about psychology, the scars of a traumatic childhood, chemical imbalances, bullying, or sexual abuse as the reason why such a crime could have occurred, you would do well to try out your theories somewhere other than the offices of Lisa Ortlieb. As personable and downright kind a woman as everyone agreed she was, when it came to murder—never mind if the perpetrator was a fifteen-year-old from a broken home—she had no sympathy.

For instance, Lisa had seen to it that the boy accused of murdering his mother and mutilating her body would be tried as an adult. Her goal in this most recent case (also high profile, with the victim and perpetrator once again from an affluent community) was very simple: *let him fry.*

The woman who met me at the main waiting area of the district attorney's office and led me to her cubicle, however, showed no indication of being a ruthless, take-no-prisoners kind of prosecutor. She greeted me warmly, asking how things were going.

"I love your outfit," she said to me.

It was sometimes hard, talking with Lisa, to forget that she wasn't just a girlfriend and you weren't having coffee somewhere, on the way to having your hair highlighted or checking out a sale at Victoria's Secret. She was dressed, as usual, in one of her smart but totally unflashy suits, with her hair down and (even though she had no court appearances today) heels. Her desk was piled high with papers and files, and all around her on the floor were more files, but interspersed with reminders of her work were photographs of her stepchildren, Dave Gorcyca's twins, and of Dave himself. Lori Brasier had told me that Lisa was longing for a baby of her own and hearing the ticking of the clock, but meanwhile, she appeared to be a doting stepmother.

There was another category of item scattered around Lisa Ortlieb's jumbled, but subtly well-organized, office. Mementos of past cases were everywhere: a flag, a samurai sword, an oversized replica of a super hero, exhibits and keepsakes from days gone by, photographs of injuries and crime scenes, a knife in a Tupperware container.

Propped against a file cabinet was a framed photograph of a good-looking man—a former Oakland County attorney named Michael Fletcher—who had murdered his pregnant wife immediately following the act of making love to her, and tried to make the whole thing look like a suicide.

He'd taken her to a firing range earlier in the day, evidently so there'd be gunpowder on her trigger finger. The idea was that after a suitable period of mourning, Michael Fletcher could move on to a happy new life with his girlfriend, an attractive local judge, but Lisa and her fellow prosecutor on the case had foiled that plan.

Here was a curious thing about Lisa Ortlieb: one minute she could be showing you snapshots of the kids at a Pistons game with her and Dave, and the next minute it was the horribly bruised and bloodied body of the woman with the tuna casserole she had prosecuted a few years back (but with a certain compassion) for murdering her abuser.

"Another rat bastard," she commented.

The term appeared to be one of her favorites, and she used it with relish.

She had boxes of this stuff: pictures of corpses, bloody crime scenes, blood-soaked mattresses, severed body parts. And still she possessed this unshakably sunny, all-American-girl quality.

"I'm for victims," she commented.

The ugliness of the stories in which she immersed herself, day in, day out, seemed to roll off her long, elegant back. The idealism with which she fueled herself—her love of the law—radiated like a halo.

On top of the file cabinet in Lisa's office was an item I recognized from the Seaman trial: a life-size Styrofoam head that Dr. Dragovic had used to show the jury where and how, in his assessment, Nancy Seaman had struck her husband's head.

Talking over the case as we did now, I was impressed by how well Lisa Ortlieb retained the details from months before. We talked about that broken window in the basement at Briarwood Court, and my theory (hers too, but they were theories and nothing more) that Nancy herself had broken the glass on the night of the murder as a way of getting Bob to emerge from the basement for what would prove to be the final confrontation between them.

"She couldn't stand it that he was ignoring her," Lisa speculated. "So she had to goad him to come out."

"What about the ice cream poisoning story?" I asked her. "Why didn't that come up in the trial?"

"That was tough," Lisa said, stretching a long leg out and slipping off a shoe. "But Larry would have got me for hearsay."

There were other tantalizing elements of the case that had to be left out: a woman who'd met Nancy Seaman at a neighborhood card party the fall before the murder (a rare social outing for Nancy) who reported that Nancy had actually discussed with her a particular brand of poison she'd been researching. Another woman in the neighborhood spoke of seeing a man outside the Seaman house at Briarwood Court two days after the murder, at an hour that had briefly raised, in Lisa, the hope that she might have found evidence to suggest that someone had helped the defendant put Bob Seaman's body in the Explorer. But once again, there had been no way to substantiate the sighting, so, with deep regret, she'd had to let it go—though the question of how Nancy had gotten the body in the car still nagged at Lisa on occasion.

"As a prosecutor," she said, "it's my job to avoid those gray areas. You've got to leave the jury with a clear picture. No questions."

Unlike many people with passing knowledge of the family, Lisa Ortlieb remained unimpressed by Greg Seaman ("He's a liar") and unconvinced that any battering had actually occurred in the Seaman household.

"Lenore Walker did a good job of describing an abuse victim," she said. "The only problem being, she wasn't describing Nancy. It was Bob."

Lisa was not inclined to criticize Larry Kaluzny's defense of Nancy Seaman. "It's easy to be a Monday morning quarterback," she said. "He tried the case the way he felt best."

But as always, she had withering words for Nancy Seaman.

"She makes a mockery of the plight of women who've been genuinely abused," said Lisa. "There was no evidence that she was a victim of abuse, besides the carefully rehearsed testimony of her father and brother, that they'd seen bruises, and a son who was pathologically attached to his mother." Greg was a young man so filled with rage, she said, that like Lori Brasier, she had considered the possibility, during his remarks at the sentencing, that he might actually strike her.

Jeff might have behaved differently in court from how you or I would think a person should, whose father has been murdered, she conceded. "But who's to say how you act at a moment like that?" she said. "Bob Seaman was Jeff's best friend. He loved his dad so much.

Life as he knew it before Bob's murder is over for Jeff. And Judge McDonald thinks he can tell us how a person should act under those circumstances, or what makes for inappropriate behavior?"

As for the cleanup in the garage: "Innocent people don't cover up their innocence. If this was legitimate lawful self-defense, she would have dialed 911 after it happened. And I'd have had to grant her the benefit of the doubt."

Given the cover-up, Lisa would grant Nancy Seaman nothing, because that, in her opinion, was all Nancy Seaman deserved. There had been no offer made for a plea bargain, no reduction to lesser charges in exchange for admission of guilt.

"We had those tapes," she said. "Those tapes were huge. They showed the jury a side of Nancy that was not rehearsed, and it wasn't pretty."

She was gone a moment then. When she came back, she had a package with a bunch of cassettes for me. It was the complete collection of Nancy and Greg Seaman's recorded telephone conversations while Nancy was in Oakland County Jail awaiting trial. Many more than were played in the courtroom.

Lisa reminded me of the protocol for jailhouse telephone conversations: Because the contents of these conversations sometimes constitute a crucial part of the prosecution's case, as they had at the Seaman trial, a voice always came on the line, early on in the visit, in which the announcement was made to both parties that they should be aware of the state's right to tape-record their conversation. It was therefore surprising that Nancy and Greg Seaman had revealed so much, despite knowing this. It was as if they didn't understand, themselves, how bizarre their attitudes were.

"You'll get a kick out of these," Lisa said, handing me the tapes as if they were a collection of *Friends* episodes or a couple of the latest CDs from Faith Hill.

CHAPTER 71

This Conversation
Is Being Recorded

ecause I had not been present in the courtroom when the tapes were played, and the Court TV excerpts of the trial had not included them, my only experience of Nancy or Greg Seaman's voice, to date, had been the *48 Hours* broadcast and her actual trial testimony. This would be a different Nancy, I knew: speaking with the person she loved and trusted most in the world.

There was no cassette player in the Pontiac, so I had to wait until I was back at the cottage at Potter Lake to listen to the tapes. The sun was already down when I got there, the lake nearly abandoned, except for a few campers on the other side.

It was a hot night. I sat on the porch. A little way off, on the dock where the pontoon boat was moored, Chuck, my neighbor, stood motionless, staring out at the water. From across the lake, a karaoke singer tackled "Our Love Will Go On." I pushed the Play button, and there in the darkness came the voice of Nancy Seaman, speaking from Oakland County Jail to Greg at 10:06 P.M. on May 14, 2004—the first words the two had been able to exchange since Nancy's arrest and Greg's discovery of the murder.

"Hi," she said. "I just want to let you know I'm all right."

"OK," said Greg.

"I just wanted to let you know that you can let the lawyer know that . . . I did not buy cleaning solvent at Home Depot, and the ax that I bought was not the one that was used when I hit your dad. It was returned. I have the return slip, stapled to the purchase slip. . . ."

"How long after you bought it did you return it?"

"Two days later."

"Was it there at the time?"

"Yes, but . . . it's not connected at all with the crime because it's not what I used . . ."

The conversation continued. Perhaps because Nancy and Greg were aware of being recorded, certain portions of their exchanges had the faintly artificial tone of poorly written soap opera dialogue: those moments in which the listener can sense that one of the characters, anxious to get certain information across, resorts to remarks like "remember when Trevor had that quadruple bypass surgery, right after Veronica ran off to South America with her illegitimate son by Phillip?"

"I used to tell him please don't hurt me," Nancy said to her son. "And he'd beat the hell out of me, and I'd go to work every day in tears. It was icepacks and it was X rays. . . . He just wouldn't let it go. He would never let me be free."

More than the expository information Nancy Seaman appeared to be inserting in the conversation, it was the tone of voice in which the two of them spoke that struck me as I listened to the tape—the crudeness of the language they both employed (the ease with which they spoke the words "bastard" and "shit" and "fucking"). The detachment with which these two approached the subject of Bob Seaman's murder was bone chilling.

They said almost nothing about Bob himself or the fact that he was dead, but a great deal about the weapon used to kill him.

"I just wanted to let you know . . . ," Nancy said all over again, ". . . the ax I bought was not the one that was used when I hit your dad. It was returned. I have the—I had a return slip stapled to the purchase slip in my purse. The ax that I used was a different ax in the house, and they have that in their custody. But I returned the ax . . . that they saw me at Home Depot with."

It was a crucial point for her defense, this business of the hatchet. If the hatchet purchased by Nancy Seaman just hours before the murder proved to be the actual murder weapon, that would go a long way toward supporting premeditation and a charge of first-degree murder. Much better for the defense was to suggest that the murder weapon had been a different hatchet, one that had been lying around the garage, picked up in a moment of fear for the purpose of self-defense.

Greg asked his mother why she went to Home Depot to buy that hatchet on Sunday night.

"For the stumps in the backyard, cause our chainsaw does not work. . . .

"When I took the small one back to Home Depot, I told the gal, I said this is too short. I've got two stumps that I can't use this on. She wrote up a receipt. . . ."

The question came up: was the weapon Nancy had used to kill Bob an ax or a hatchet? She wasn't sure about that.

"Did you use two hands or one?" Greg asked.

"One."

"Then that's a hatchet."

To an outside ear, a couple of surprising elements emerged here. One was that Nancy Seaman (who did not yet know about the police officers' discovery of the surveillance video revealing the shoplifting) was lying to her son, even as he begged her to tell him and the lawyer the truth, no matter what. But even more notable was not so much what the two of them said—the talk of hatchets and axes, receipts, stumps, lawyers. It was what they did not talk about.

The mother had just murdered the father. Maybe she used a hatchet, maybe it was an ax. Either way, the man was dead. The son had learned this information just twenty-four hours earlier. He knew that down the road, in the morgue at the county medical examiner's office, lay the corpse of his father, with thirty-seven chop and knife wounds in his face, skull, back, and throat. And yet never in the eight or nine minutes of this conversation did either Nancy or Greg Seaman speak of loss, grief, sadness, horror, or regret.

One thing they did talk about was money.

"They seized your purse," said Greg. "They seized $347 in cash. There's no cash upstairs. There's no cash—"

"They took all our cash?"

"They took all of it big-time."

"Why?"

"They felt they needed it."

"They took my money?"

"They took all of your money. They took your credit cards, all of that stuff. Just calm down. . . ."

Nancy Seaman made sounds here of being upset. For the first time in the conversation it appeared she might be crying. Her son tried to comfort her. "But that was money I was going to give to you," she said.

"I know, Mom," he told her. "We're gonna get it."

I listened with a sick feeling; as the conversation continued, I doubted that listening in on an obscene phone call would have left me any more repulsed.

Nancy and Greg expressed a certain irritation with Bob Seaman for his failure to leave a will, with the regrettable result that his estate would end up in probate court, which would require them to pay all kinds of taxes and slow down the release of the cash. Nancy talked about how much money they might get for the house and the boat, though Greg said Jeff seemed to want that, for the sentimental value— a further source of irritation.

For a moment then, Nancy Seaman appeared to register despair. "I just want to be dead, that's all," she told Greg. "I just want to go to sleep and not wake up, that's all."

"Please don't say that," he told her.

"I just wish he would have killed me and been done with it."

"Hey. Come on. I'm gonna hang up. . . . You have a good case. This weapon is a twist. We can work it out all right. You need . . . hey, if it was the one you returned, you got to let us know. I don't care how bad it looks, you got to let us know."

"No, it's the one they have in custody. See, when I put your dad in the car, I threw the ax with it or the hatchet, whatever. . . ."

"And that was the one . . ."

"That I used."

"That we owned for a while."

"Yeah."

"That's all I want to know."

Greg spoke of his uncle Dennis—"that worm." Dennis was going to try to screw her out of her assets, Greg told his mother. But Greg was getting the locks on the house changed.

And then there was the problem of Jeff.

"Jeff, you know, he said he wanted to come visit you," said Greg. "You know he said, 'let me know about visitation.'"

"I don't want to see him," Nancy said.

"I know," said Greg. "Just don't say anything to him and Becka."

"I was shocked at the hearing today because he has been at the house and seen bruises all over me within the last six months."

"I know, I know."

"He saw bruises."

"Do not say anything, anything, anything about the case at all to Jeff and Becka, OK?" (Greg again, instructing his mother.)

"Yeah," said Nancy. "They screwed me over."

Greg was going to find that receipt, he told her. He'd handle it.

She loved him, she said. "Tell Grandpa if he would give you $30," she told him, signing off. "Anything you want from the house. I want you to have those leather-bound books."

It was late now, but I couldn't stop listening to the tapes.

"Just for my own curiosity. Tell me about the knife Dad cut you with," said Greg. (He called his father "Dad" this time. Old habit, most likely.)

"I don't know."

"We've got a winner here." Greg this time, speaking of their case. Reassuring his mother with the air of a broker delivering a stock tip.

Jeff was talking to the press, he told his mother. "He's enjoying his fifteen minutes of fame."

Nancy: "Do you understand how screwed I am because of that?"

She remarked, during a call to her father this time, "The bastard would never draw up a will. He wouldn't do any estate planning with me. He was such a greedy son of a bitch."

"Yeah, right."

"I just want Jeff to leave Greg alone. Greg's got enough on his shoulders . . . and you don't need that Greedy Bastard Number Two trying to give him any trouble."

"Oh yeah."

"[Jeff's] a lot like Bob, unfortunately."

A later conversation now. This one concerning the sale of the house on Briarwood Court.

"Don't you worry about it," Greg told his mother. "All you got to think about, Mom, is that you got half a house which I did a pretty damn good job at selling and negotiating and you ended up getting about a buck-fifty."

His voice, describing this, carried the air of a young man in possession of a certain newly acquired sense of power and importance. (He'd been a smart negotiator. He'd cleared—not $150,000 but "a buck-fifty.")

"It's $2,000 a day for the trial." Nancy again. Still sounding worried.

Then Greg, the voice of calm reassurance: ". . . You'll probably end up with a hundred. You'll have enough, don't worry."

"And all of the . . . if it doesn't go to me, it goes to you boys, right?"

"For what?"

"The estate."

"Yeah. If you're convicted of anything then it gets split between Jeff and I."

"Between Jeff and you."

"Now, if you're not convicted of anything then you automatically get 50 percent. Jeff will get 25 percent, and I get 25 percent. Which is, to tell you the truth, as sick as it sounds, why I think partly why Jeff is going crazy. Because he knows if you're out of the picture he's gonna get twice as much."

Sounds of disgust on either side of the phone line. It was not news to either of them by now that the only person either of them could trust completely in this family was each other.

"I really love you, darling," Nancy reminded Greg. "I really love you so much, and I pray every day that this works out OK.

"You're the only person in my whole life that I worry about," she told him. "I don't worry about anybody else. It's just you."

In fact—as the next tape made clear—Nancy was also deeply worried about Jeff, but only, it appeared, because he was cooperating with the prosecution and refusing to support her allegations of abuse. He was giving interviews to the press, saying nice things about Bob. It was sickening, she told her father, Eugene.

"I'm hoping when Kaluzny gets him on the stand he breaks him down good," said Eugene, with the tone of a man happily anticipating a boxing match that could, if he were lucky, get bloody.

"Well, he's going to have to, because I'm in deep shit because he knew everything I told him, everything, so he's got to pull it out of him . . . ," said Nancy.

"If Jeff don't tell the truth, that's perjury. He'll go to jail," Eugene reminded her.

There it was again, the old terrible irony. You could kill the father, and the next thing you knew, along came his older son, the spitting image of the guy, coming back in your face to ruin everything. "He's so much like Bob it just scares the hell out of me," she said.

Bob was "an asshole," was the thing, Nancy told her father. He'd made her miss that graduation, ruined everything. All she wanted now was to be home for the holidays.

"Son of a bitch," she said. "Son of a bitchin' bitch. . . . I hope he's burning."

CHAPTER 72

A Touch of Hyper Bowl

L istening to the conversations between Nancy and Greg Seaman brought about a fundamental change in my attitude about the case. Until then I'd worked hard to remain as open as I could to the possibility that Nancy Seaman had been the helpless victim of a controlling and ruthless man, as she claimed. Now, with the sound of her voice in my head, I was having a hard time imagining how it would be to sit across from her in a prison visiting room (assuming she ever agreed to meet with me) or accepting her collect call, and talking as if we were just two women of a similar age—one of whom having divorced her husband, the other one having murdered hers. I could no longer claim objectivity or impartiality where Nancy Seaman was concerned. The woman with whom I had identified six months earlier—a woman my age, a mother of sons, a woman struggling to keep her family together in the face of marital trouble—no longer seemed like someone with whom I shared a single thing.

But as critically as I now viewed Nancy Seaman, I continued to seek out the perspective of others who saw her differently. The less I found myself able to feel sympathy for her, the harder I tried to locate someone who did, to help me balance the scales. I kept looking for a teacher willing to speak with me about the kind of teacher Nancy had been, and her life at the school, but it seemed as if the ranks had closed around her, to the point where nobody I contacted even returned my calls.

Then someone did: Rose Christoph.

Rose Christoph—the same woman who had suggested that Nancy Seaman hire Larry Kaluzny—went through a certain amount of inner struggle about discussing her friend with me, but in the end she decided to meet, she said, just to set the record straight. We met at Einstein's Bagels in Farmington Hills, just down the highway from the condominium community she and her husband had recently moved into following her retirement from the school system. It was midsummer, a few days after I'd listened to the tapes of Nancy Seaman talking with her father and her son.

Rose explained to me that because she was married to a magistrate—Carl Christoph—she had a better understanding than the average person of what went on behind the scenes in the politics of Farmington Hills. If there was one person who had practically singlehandedly put Nancy Seaman in that cell over at Robert Scott Correctional Facility, she now confided, it was that egomaniac Bill Dwyer, who had got things off to such a terrible start for her friend Nancy with that press conference of his, where he talked about her killing Bob in the kitchen. As if Nancy would ever have done such a thing.

"Nancy loved to cook Northern Italian, her specialty," Rose told me.

Sometimes she'd come to school (where Rose had worked as a reading specialist, up until her recent retirement), and all she could talk about was some new cookbook she had. She'd had to give up a lot of her old recipes after her husband had those heart problems, but even then, what had she done? Adapted the recipes to make them more heart-friendly. *Arrivaderci ricotta cheese.*

Rose had served on several committees with Nancy, and of course they'd talked in the teachers' room.

"All we ever heard about was her family," said Rose. "We had no idea her husband was a wife beater. But looking back on it now, of course the whole thing's pretty clear.

"How many times can one person walk into the same car door like she said?" Rose offered. "I should have known, seeing her walking with a cast, using a cane—"

This was the first anyone had mentioned of Nancy Seaman's suffering a broken leg or using a cane, and something told me that if she had in fact ever been injured to that extent, it would have come up before now. But I began to realize that Rose was a somewhat dramatic individual. I chalked this up to what attorney Mike Farraone would have called "hyper bowl."

"One problem was that first attorney," Rose reflected. "The one from Ann Arbor with the patches on his sleeves, like some professor. He should have gotten her out on bail instead of letting her rot in jail. That got things off to a bad start too.

"It was a conspiracy," she said. "Dwyer and the rest of them. They weren't going to grant her an inch."

The fact that she was married to a lawyer, she said, gave Rose an insight into the case beyond that of the average person. For instance, it wasn't a regular murder. It was, she said, "*a massacre.*"

I begged her pardon. I didn't understand the distinction.

"It was a *massacre,*" Rose repeated, leaning in close so as not to attract attention in the bagel shop. "It wasn't like she set out to do this thing; she just had to, when the time came. That's the difference. It wasn't a murder. It was a massacre."

Now Rose Christoph was leaning in closer. She was speaking in a low tone of voice now, and wanted to be sure I heard.

"I heard her husband was Caldean," she said, referring to the ethnic group who had settled in surprisingly high numbers in the area—Iraqi Christians. I knew from my Sunday mornings on the porch at Potter Lake hearing Lori Brasier's stories about crimes she'd covered over the years that a few years earlier a Caldean man had brutally murdered and then dismembered his wife over in Royal Oak. This had not done anything to improve the image of Caldeans among certain residents of Oakland County—Rose among them, perhaps.

"Caldean?" I said. "I never heard that before. I thought his family hailed from Illinois."

CHAPTER 73

No Need for Housewares

With what was left of the Seaman family incommunicado—and most of their friends following their lead by refusing to speak with me, I continued the task of piecing together what I could from a hundred alternative sources.

Dennis Seaman's first wife, Lynn Corneilison, the mother of their children, Tiffany and Christopher—lived in St. Louis with her second husband. Nearly twenty years after her divorce from Dennis, she still called Ward and Helen Seaman "Mom" and "Dad," as did her current husband. I had gotten her number from Dennis, with whom she maintained a friendly relationship, despite the difficult circumstances of their divorce.

"Those two are the kindest, most loving people," she said of Ward and Helen Seaman. "They took in kids, runaways, anyone who needed a home." If you were setting out to find the best in-laws in the world, she told me, those two would top the list.

But one person who never warmed to Bob Seaman's parents was Nancy. "It was like she was better than everybody else," said Lynn.

"She'd have her brand-name clothes and her talk of all Bob's success. She loved that. She didn't show any big love for her nieces and nephews, but you could tell her boys meant everything to her. One time one of them got hurt, playing with Chris and Tiffany, and she just went nuts. I could tell Bob felt bad. We heard them arguing after. Of course, we heard them arguing a lot. There were times I told Dennis, 'I think we'd better leave,' the fighting got that bad.

"Another time, Greg fell down, and Nancy just came unglued," she said. She was going to call 911, but Bob calmed her down. Those children just consumed her life.

"Nancy never liked me," Lynn added. Then Lynn and Dennis had gotten a divorce, and Nancy wrote her a letter.

"All of a sudden, she was my friend," said Lynn. "Mostly just because she hated Dennis more, probably."

One memory of Bob and Nancy stood out for Lynn. "We were all down in the basement, a canning kitchen," she said. "They had a second kitchen downstairs, and Mom needed something from the kitchen upstairs, so I went to get it. I was just opening a cabinet when I saw Bob and Nancy in the hallway. I saw Nancy hit Bob's arm. I couldn't leave the room or they'd know I saw. I was stuck. I just stood there. I'll never forget it."

Later, though, when people were around, it would be different. "She'd come out with this big laughter and put an arm around Bob. She'd act all loving, when Mom and Dad Seaman were in the room. When they left, she got up off Bob's lap and took her arm off his shoulder."

Searching for friends of Greg Seaman, I pored over the yearbooks of North Farmington High, class of 1999. I tracked down a former cross-country teammate of Greg Seaman's named Oz Perlman—now a magician living in New York—who told me Greg was getting married in the fall to Kristin Sears. He was standing up for Greg, in fact, and appeared happy to talk with me, until he checked with Greg. That put the kibosh on our conversation.

I happened to mention this to a friend of Julie Dumbleton's—Mary De Paolo, a therapist in Northville Julie had called shortly after the murder, in an attempt to locate someone for Jenna to talk with. A very different type from Julie, Mary was outspoken, highly expressive, and fascinated by the Seaman story.

"It would be interesting to talk with that girl," said Mary, referring to the bride-to-be. "I wouldn't be too happy if it was my daughter, marrying into a situation like that one."

As the mother of a daughter about the same age, I agreed. Greg Seaman might have a good job and an apartment in a pleasant suburb, not to mention an impressive car collection, but we both knew (as twenty-four-year-olds might not) the ways a troubled family history can haunt a marriage, and doom it. Eugene D'Onofrio had speculated, in one of the taped conversations with Nancy in jail, that Jeff Seaman might inherit the mantle of an abuser. But if, as Nancy alleged, domestic violence had cast its shadow over life on Briarwood Court, there was another son from that household who might also be a candidate for repeating old patterns. Whatever the truth might be there, one thing remained clear: Kristin Sears was not marrying into a happy family.

Another thing about Mary De Paolo: she was a lot more clued-in than I about the way young couples did things in a place like Farmington Hills. So when I mentioned that I wondered where the wedding would take place, she had an idea for me.

"You should check the bridal registry at Marshall Fields," she said. So one day I swung into the nearly vacant parking lot at Summit Place Mall and made my way through the nearly empty Marshall Fields branch there, to the second floor, where the computer was, with the bridal registry, and punched in the names of Sears and Seaman.

Mostly, I think, I wanted some confirmation (given that he had never in any way acknowledged my letters, books, and phone messages) that Greg Seaman did in fact exist. I had almost started to wonder.

Sure enough, there was the information I'd been looking for: the wedding was scheduled for September 24, 2005, in Indianapolis. From the list of items the couple were requesting, it appeared the event would be a relatively small one, though the desired gifts were not the type some twenty-four-year-olds (my children, for instance) would covet: Waterford crystal goblets, Waterford crystal wine glasses, iced beverage glasses (Waterford), champagne flutes (ditto), and a dinner service in a pattern called Waterford Baron, for which a five-piece place setting ran $119.00. Other than that, all the couple asked for was a set of Hampton Savoy Frost flatware, a Copco Fusion pewter teakettle, and a stainless steel potato masher with a nylon end. No Kitchen Aid mixer on the list. No Cuisinart. No set of knives or cookware.

I am not sure if I learned anything about Kristin and Greg from the list, except perhaps that they appeared to be more interested in fine dinnerware than the nuts and bolts of food preparation. Or maybe it was that with Nancy Seaman in prison for life and her possessions not in use, they had plenty of housewares already.

I carried on with my quest, driving my old Pontiac up and down Telegraph Road. The car had been giving me trouble, however. On the hottest week of the summer, the air conditioning quit. Then the steering started feeling odd. Now and then I needed a jump-start.

Having lunch one day at Ginnopolis, where Bob Seaman liked to go for a drink sometimes, I ran into Chief Dwyer having his weekly Monday lunch with the police chiefs of Oakland County—one of whom, he suggested when he stopped by my table, he could set me up with if I were interested. This other police chief—recently divorced—had a cottage up north.

"He's got a couple of jet skis," Chief Dwyer told me. "Also two terrific golden retrievers."

"Till We Dance Away"

I learned from his high school yearbook that Greg Seaman had not held school office or won awards. A single photograph of him appeared, however, from the North Farmington High prom of the year 2000, escorting Heidi Frank, a cute young woman with neat bangs and a gown trimmed with feathers. She had graduated a year after Greg, with the class of 2000, and had gone to college in Hawaii, but as luck would have it, she was home for a visit with her parents when I tracked her down that July. Unlike Greg's other friends, she agreed to talk with me, though I felt it was only fair to tell her that Greg himself had chosen not to meet with me.

But Heidi Frank surprised me by saying she would. "I figure someone who knows him should say what he's like," she told me. "Because he's a great guy. And I liked his mom a lot too."

An hour later, I was knocking at the door of the Frank family's home, a spacious colonial in a subdivision a mile or two from where the Seamans had lived. I was greeted at the door by Heidi, a petite young woman with blonde hair and an easy smile. Behind her stood her father, Bill. He was the kind of father, I realized, who would want to be with his daughter while she met with a stranger like me, just to be sure she was all right, and as I told him, who could fault a parent for looking out for his daughter that way? So the three of us sat down at the Franks's dining room table to talk, though in Bill's case it was mostly about being there to look out for his daughter and listen.

Their family had moved to Farmington Hills in her sophomore year, Heidi told me, and because she also ran cross-country, she'd met Greg within weeks of her arrival in town. He was a year older than she was (though from the photographs in the yearbook, an exceedingly young and skinny-looking seventeen). They started going out, and pretty soon Heidi was spending almost every afternoon at the Seamans' after school got out.

"Greg's mom was always there when I came over," Heidi said. "She was awesome. Very motherly. Greg was her baby, and you could tell that. She'd get us everything. If we were hungry, she'd make cookies. If we were thirsty, she brought us drinks. Sometimes, if Greg wanted to watch a sporting event or something, it would be just the two of us, his mom and me, just chilling. She was easy to talk to. Just so cheerful and bubbly all the time, cute and upbeat. I never saw her when she wasn't happy."

Heidi remembered Bob Seaman too, but with less affection. "He pretty much stayed in the basement," she said. "You never saw him talking to Greg's mom, or in the same room even. The only thing I remember him ever saying to me was the night we went to the prom—he got to drive the Ferrari—and Greg brought me over to their house so his mom could take pictures. He told me I looked like a movie star.

"I never liked Jeff," she said, with unexpected fervor. "I couldn't stand him, actually. He was nothing like Greg. He'd be down in the basement with his dad, watching TV, and you could tell they had the same personality. Greg was the more personable one, definitely."

Greg didn't get along with his father, Heidi said. The only thing they had in common, he told Heidi, was working on cars. He told her there was this other family his dad took a big interest in.

"I remember Greg saying his dad cared more about this other family than he did about his own kid," Heidi added.

"Greg was obsessed with cars. He had an '87 Mustang, and one time I hit his car. Just tapped it, in the parking lot at school, but you could tell he was furious. He didn't say anything, just got in the car and drove away, and of course I felt terrible about that."

She had driven over to the Upper Deck, looking for him. Who she found was Bob, and so, with trepidation, she'd told him what had happened with the car. The surprising thing was that Bob Seaman hadn't taken it as hard as his son. All he said was, "Oh, that was you?"

Other than that one time Greg got mad, though, Heidi described him as "the nicest boyfriend I ever had." Always fun-loving. Always happy. "Nothing too heavy or complicated," she said, "just nice all the time." He took her to Chicago sometimes, and to the Cedar Point amusement park. His mom was so generous; she was always giving him money to take Heidi out to dinner. And he bought her gifts, too. One time he bought her a pillow, and he embroidered the words of a song they both loved, "Till we dance away."

She still had it. She went upstairs and came down to show me. Cross-stitching, hand done. That was Greg Seaman for you. All around, he was your dream of how a boyfriend should be.

It was an agreeable picture: a boy so attentive, he brought flowers for no particular reason, just to say he cared about you; a boy who presented his girlfriend with handmade crafts, a picture frame with a picture of the two of them in it. Things you might expect an unusually sensitive girl to do for a boyfriend, maybe, but hardly likely behavior for a boy of that or any age, I thought. (Her story brought to mind an image of my own two sons in high school. They had adored their girlfriends, but neither one was remotely inclined to make them pillows or embroider anything for them.)

This was what I thought about, as I held Heidi Frank's pillow. I studied the cross-stitch: the evenness of the threads, the skillfulness of the handiwork.

"Maybe his mom had something to do with it," said Heidi, as if she'd read my mind. "Her being a teacher."

In the end, they didn't break up so much as they had just drifted apart. Greg was a year older than she was, so he'd taken off for college, and though she'd gone along for the ride to drop him off freshman year (a trip she'd made with Bob Seaman, come to think of it), Heidi and Greg didn't go out after that.

Now and then over the years, they'd called each other up. Shortly after the murder, Heidi's mother had called her in Hawaii to give her the news, and Heidi had left a message for Greg to say how sorry she was.

"He called me back to thank me," she said. "He was pretty open as far as his opinion went. One thing I remember, he didn't speak of his father as 'Dad.' He called him by his first name, like he was just this person that died."

They had spoken one more time after that, not so long ago, actually. Heidi's brother had died a few months earlier, she said quietly. And this time it had been Greg to call, to say how sorry he was. Which was like him, she said. Always thoughtful and considerate.

A silence came over the three of us for a moment: Heidi, her father, and me. It was the kind of news you needed to acknowledge, but you also didn't want to interfere in a family's grief.

I said nothing for a moment, then asked what happened.

"Accident. A car," said Bill.

We were pretty much finished by this point. There wasn't all that much to say, although suddenly the photograph of the two kids at their prom—Heidi looking "like a movie star," Greg looking simply very young—took on a whole new cast, viewed as it had to be now, with the knowledge that both of those two young people smiling hopefully out at the world, about to head off in a red Ferrari, would within a matter of years lose a member of their immediate family to sudden, violent death.

We had said our good-byes and shaken hands, and the door to their house was all the way shut when I saw it on the outside, facing the street: a gold star. I'd never seen one before, and now, having done so, it seemed important to acknowledge what that star meant to the people who'd put it there. Driving away down their street and back out to the highway, I dialed the Franks' number from my cell phone.

Bill answered—the good, protective father. "I just wanted to say I saw the star and how sorry I am," I told him.

"Our son was killed by a car bomb," he told me. "Iraq. He was twenty-eight years old."

Ever since the night I listened to the tapes of Nancy and Greg Seaman, I'd been aware of a growing distaste for the woman for whom I had sought understanding and compassion.

At first, I supposed that what repelled me was the utter coldness with which she spoke of her husband, the father of her children. But it went deeper, I saw now. What disturbed me was the relationship of

Nancy to her son Greg, as revealed on those tapes and now, in an odd way, by my visit with Heidi Frank.

I thought a lot about it, driving back to Potter Lake that night. What I registered between the mother and son that left me so uneasy might not have entered into the territory of Norman Bates and his mother in *Psycho,* or Lawrence Harvey and Angela Lansbury's characters in *The Manchurian Candidate,* but I registered a queasy-making level of intimacy between these two—Nancy and Greg—that seemed to override all other relationships, if not in his life, certainly in hers. There was a conspiratorial element, certainly, in the way the two of them discussed not only Greg's father but also his brother—the whole world, in fact, apart from the two of them.

"We always knew that, didn't we?" Greg had said to Nancy, confirming her observation of his brother's weakness of character.

"You're the only person in my whole life I worry about," Nancy had reminded Greg.

Whether to call it an Oedipal relationship gone haywire or simply overinvolved mothering, I was not equipped to judge. But it seemed clear to me that in assisting as much as she had in orchestrating the perfect boyfriend-girlfriend relationship between Greg and Heidi, Nancy had managed to experience vicariously the kind of idealized relationship she herself had been denied in her apparently miserable marriage to Bob Seaman. He was not the prince she had hoped for, but Greg would provide, for Heidi, what Bob had withheld.

"Till we dance away" were the words stitched on the pillow.

Those were words Nancy would have loved to have someone—Bob, no doubt—whisper in her ear, I believed. Of course he never did, so she recruited her youngest son to tell them to someone else.

"Creepy" was not a word I'd used before, but I might have applied it now to Greg Seaman. I saw him as tragic, too—as the son who may from infancy have had little choice but to endlessly provide whatever his mother required of him.

It had been getting harder in recent weeks to summon compassion for Nancy Seaman, but I could still feel compassion for Greg, just as I did even for the fifteen-year-old boy who'd recently been arrested in Oakland County for the murder of his mother.

That young man had killed his mother and cut out her eyes. What Greg Seaman had done, it seemed to me, was to cut out his own instead. Unable to stand looking at what his mother had done, he had blinded himself.

It was a terrible thing for a woman to do to her son, I thought. I might have said I would never have left my children feeling responsible for my happiness, but as the mother, myself, of much-loved children of a much-resented ex-husband, I recognized, in the picture of Greg's relationship with Nancy, a certain kind of manipulation of the child, by the parent, that resonated with me. Along with her undying love, Nancy Seaman appeared to have bestowed on Greg the overwhelming responsibility for becoming the man her husband—his father—had failed to be, at least for her. Like a lot of divorced parents I knew, I recognized the behavior, as one who'd been guilty of it on occasion, myself.

CHAPTER 75

Even Her Dentist
Knew It Was Bad

⟨∾⟩ Meanwhile, there was another mother worrying about another son, for different reasons: Julie Dumbleton. We were still talking on the phone a great deal about Jake, his anxiety over talking with me—his anxiety, period. He was brooding all the time. He'd joined up with a baseball team that summer, but dropped out after a single game. All Julie could do now was worry.

Of course it wasn't just Jake who'd experienced trauma. It was Julie herself, as I was understanding better all the time.

Back when I first spoke with Julie Dumbleton and studied her timeline, I'd already been aware of the application for a PPO against her, filed by Nancy Seaman in Oakland County Court, back in February of 2002. In fact, it had been Marcia Low's story in the *Free Press* about the PPO application that had first brought attention to Julie Dumbleton's connection to the Seaman case and touched off the rumor of her alleged affair with Bob Seaman. But the actual language of the application had not become public, and the application had not been entered into evidence during the trial. Only now, months later, did I procure from Oakland County Courthouse a copy of Nancy Seaman's actual statement concerning the danger she perceived coming from Julie Dumbleton.

The application had been made in the aftermath of the incident involving Bob's gift to Jake Dumbleton of the '89 Mustang—Nancy's threatening call to Julie allegedly warning her that Jake had better stay away from the Mustang or he'd regret it, followed by Bob's angry ultimatum to Nancy, warning her to lay off the Dumbletons. One day later, Nancy Seaman had made a trip to the courthouse to file her complaint.

On the form provided by the county, listing her concerns, Nancy had checked the box indicating "threatening to kill or physically injure me." She had crossed out the words "kill or physically injure me" and substituted language of her own: "destroy my career" and "ruin my life."

In the addendum to the petition, Nancy provided an amplified account of her concerns:

"Whenever she knows that my husband and I have plans for dinner or lunch, she makes sure that she interferes or prevents him from fulfilling his obligation to his wife and family," she wrote.

And though, in her communication with Bob, she had expressed anger toward him about his friendship with the Dumbletons, here she placed blame squarely at the feet of Julie alone—portraying her husband as little more than a hapless pawn. "My husband has been so lied to and manipulated that he can't see what is happening," she wrote.

She described herself as "under extreme stress," to the point, she said, where her dentist had recently advised her that her upper teeth were loosening "due to severe grinding." (And from the level of anxiety and possible hysteria conveyed in Nancy's letter, this at least seemed highly likely to be true.) She wanted this woman "put on notice" she wrote, adding (in what some might view as a nearly classic example of projection) that Julie's behavior "borders on obsession."

"The last two years she has systematically tried to destroy my marriage and the relationship between my husband and his family," she wrote of Julie Dumbleton. "She has tried to move into my life. . . . She is trying to take my place and [here she underlined her words for additional emphasis] thinks if she keeps working at it I will cease to exist."

The last phrase, in particular, possessed a chilling ring. Some women, contemplating the possibility of a life without their husband, might speak of heartbreak or sadness, confusion, depression, loss, or rage. But for Nancy Seaman, the idea (accurate or not) that another woman might be trying to displace her—never mind that it was a woman who'd been married twenty-five years to a husband of whom she gave all the indications of being extremely fond, and one who himself seemed unconcerned about alienation of affection—the prospect conjured a very different picture. No picture at all, in fact—just a blank screen. For Nancy Seaman, it was as if Bob Seaman's exit from the long-running performance that was their marriage would make the whole stage go dark. If Julie Dumbleton were truly to leave her husband and take Nancy Seaman's place at Bob Seaman's side, Nancy suggested, Nancy herself would disappear. She would *cease to exist.*

According to court records, I now learned, Nancy Seaman's emergency application for the PPO against Julie Dumbleton had been heard by Judge Rae Lee Chabot on February 22, 2002—more than two years before the murder. The application had been denied, for insufficient indication of imminent danger. But of course, the one in danger hadn't been Nancy Seaman at all.

CHAPTER 76

Brothers

W hen I'd first contacted Dennis Seaman back in spring of 2004, to say I was writing a book about his brother's murder, he had expressed an eagerness to talk with me. It was important, he said—in the face of all the negative things that had been put out there about Bob—that the story of what really happened be told. Maybe, he said, we could even collaborate on a book.

Then *48 Hours* was broadcast, and Dennis felt burned. Having trusted television to set the record straight and finding instead that the producers had put forth little more than a sob story portraying Nancy Seaman as a battered wife, he said he was done talking with the press, placing a substantial portion of the wrath he felt toward the producers of that program at my feet.

I wrote him a letter, sent him a book of mine I thought his daughter would like (*The Usual Rules*), and called him up. After many weeks, he concluded—warily—that I could come to see him in Phoenix, where he lived with his second wife, Robin, and their two teenage kids.

The night before I was due to fly to Arizona, I called Dennis to get directions to his house.

"I've been thinking some more about this," he said, "and I decided it's not a good idea."

I stood in my kitchen, looking out over the redwoods—ticket in hand—a little stunned. What had brought about the change?

"Someone told me you were a feminist," he said. "I heard you were divorced."

I was definitely divorced, same as he had been at one time, I reminded him. And I certainly supported equal rights for women. Why this should affect my ability to tell his brother's story mystified me.

"I heard you were a battered wife," he told me.

It wasn't funny, of course, but I almost laughed. Of the many reasons I might have given as to why my own marriage had failed, physical abuse was never a factor. (Emotional anguish—there's another story.)

"I was not a battered wife," I told Dennis. But his question revealed an interesting notion, and a troubling one. Suppose I had been a victim of domestic violence. Would that automatically have left me sympathetic to any woman who claimed to be a fellow victim and invoked the battered woman defense as justification for the murder of her husband?

"The fact that I wasn't a battered wife isn't the reason why you should trust me to tell a fair story," I told Dennis, "any more than my being one, if I had been, should have been reason for you not to trust me. You should trust me because I'm a fair person who doesn't make automatic assumptions, one way or the other."

"I don't know," he said. "I just can't see any reason for talking to you."

"How about this?" I offered. "My ticket to Phoenix is nonrefundable, so I might as well fly out there anyway. Just meet me for a cup of coffee close to the airport, so you can get a better sense of who I am. If you don't feel good about me, I'll get on the next plane to California."

So we met first at a coffee shop near the airport in Phoenix—a city whose topography, climate, vegetation, and atmosphere could hardly have borne less similarity to that of St. Louis, where Dennis came from, or to any other part of the Midwest. Cactus and desert all around. No need for Florida rooms on the houses, except maybe as places to cool off.

Where Bob Seaman had been a short man—solidly built but only five foot seven or eight in stature—Dennis was tall, and probably had a good fifty pounds on his brother. At age fifty-three, he referred to himself as retired, though he seemed to have a lot of business deals going on most of the time, and had been involved in a surprising number of ventures over the years: car dealer, real estate investor. He greeted me with a firm handshake and a decided attitude of wariness, but I also felt, as we faced each other in the coffee shop booth, that he was longing to tell this story and fighting the impulse to do so.

"Those producers from CBS," he said. "My wife and I spent seven hours talking to them. They took us out to dinner. They said they weren't interested in the sensational aspect. They told me they wanted to get across what kind of person Bob really was."

In the end, only about ten seconds of Dennis Seaman's long interview with *48 Hours* had appeared in the broadcast. There was nothing of what Dennis had told them about what he and his wife had observed over the years of Nancy's behavior toward Bob and the rest of the family, or the things Bob had told him during the last week of his life, that he'd spent in Arizona with Dennis and his family. Nothing about what a great guy Bob had been, all the things he'd done for his sons over the years, the ways—Dennis believed—that Nancy had manipulated Greg.

"You know what they used?" said Dennis. "One remark I made, where I said I felt guilty about telling my brother he was entitled to half the value of that condo."

He had warned me that he wouldn't be talking, but within ten minutes of our meeting, he was. In the fourteen months since the murder, he hadn't been able to stop thinking about it, he told me. It had been a blessing and a curse, he said, the way—after all those years of barely seeing his brother—Bob had finally paid a visit to him and his family, and they'd had such a great time. Then, just when they'd found each other again, he was dead. If they hadn't had that week together, his kids probably wouldn't have taken it so hard. On the other hand, if they hadn't spent that week together, they never would have known their uncle.

"Nancy hated me," Dennis said. "From way back, when we were all first married. She hated it that my first wife and I got married three weeks after her and Bob, for one thing, because it kind of stole her thunder. She wanted to play the bride role a lot longer. She liked being the center of attention, and then at our wedding, naturally, it was

Lynn, not her, that everyone was thinking about. And you could tell that bothered her."

He described his brief glimpses of Nancy over the years that followed, mostly confined to the few days of the annual Christmas visit to Missouri, when the Seaman family would gather at Ward and Helen's house. It had been on one of those visits, during the early years when the boys were small, that the incident of the coffee cup had occurred, leading Nancy to file the police report charging her husband with abuse, and resulting in a visit by a police officer to Ward and Helen's home—with all the relatives present.

"I don't think my brother ever got over that," said Dennis.

Still, they had continued to visit for the holidays, and—as Bob and Dennis's sister, Margie, and others had told me—the pattern was always the same. "Nancy would take the kids upstairs to one of the bedrooms and mostly stay there," he said.

"She hated spending time with our family," said Dennis. "When they'd come to my folks' place in St. Louis for a day or two at Christmas, you could tell she felt like she was in the low-rent district," he said. "She would have picked up a couple of cheap toys at a drugstore or someplace, on the way, that she handed over to our kids. Then she'd take her own kids—Greg, anyway; Jeff didn't go for it after a while—and hole up in an upstairs bedroom most of the weekend, playing card games with him. Like she and her sons were too good for the rest of us. After a while, Nancy and Bob didn't even show up for family gatherings anymore a lot of the time. Bob's attitude was, if it made her so mad, he was better off staying home and keeping the peace.

"My brother didn't make waves," said Dennis. "Some of the most intelligent people you meet are lacking in life skills, and Bob was one of them. He was an engineer. He understood cars, not necessarily people.

"He never talked about what was going on with her," said Dennis. "I think it was a pride thing for him. What kind of a strong, upstanding, virile businessman wants to be known as a pussy-whipped husband?"

We drove back to Dennis's house—the place where Bob Seaman had spent the last week of his life. It was a stark contrast from the sterile environment of the house on Briarwood Court—a big, sprawling place with knickknacks all around, a pool with a bar, cactus gardens and comfortable chairs, and lots of evidence of a family who hung out together a lot: school pictures, sayings on the wall like the one reading "Palacio de Jugar" (palace of play). Dennis had described himself as semiretired, and it was a little hard to get clear what he did for a living exactly, though evidently it involved making deals and being on the phone a lot. But he worked from home and spent most of his time with his wife, Robin, fifteen years his junior and still clearly crazy about him.

"When Bob first got here that week, he was all uptight and stressed out," said Dennis. "But he unwound. We spent all day just hanging out by the pool, playing gin rummy, talking. He said he couldn't believe it, watching Robin and me with each other. He'd never had anything like that. Until he met up with the Dumbletons, I don't think he'd known what it was like to be in a happy home. Not since being a kid anyway. With our parents."

They talked a lot that week. Bob told Dennis he was uneasy about his partnership with Rick Cox and the arrangement they'd made over the Waterwheel Building. "He didn't trust Rick at all," Dennis said. "He told me Rick would stab you in the back. Same with Dennis Schleuter: the guy was a weasel."

It was over the course of that week, Dennis told me, that his children got to know their Uncle Bob for the first time, in any meaningful way. "He and Kyle spent hours talking about things like the U.S. Constitution, history, politics. And cars. Kyle loved hearing all Bob's stories about the cars he'd souped up over the years."

Dennis and Robin's daughter was off on a school trip the day of my visit, but Kyle—age fifteen—had joined us by now, for this part of the conversation. With some experience now of the perspective of children from an auto industry background, I asked Kyle to describe for me his dream vehicle. He disappeared for a moment and came back with a stack of car magazines. Word for word, this is what he told me:

"Possibly an Explorer with the security control microchip and a three-valve piston cylinder to give it more acceleration. Either that or a new Ford Focus, SVT. Or a Nissan Skyline, GTR 34. And of course, a Cobra kit car."

The boy was a Seaman, after all.

Dennis and Robin took Bob to the airport on Saturday evening, May 8, the night before Mother's Day. "He wasn't usually the type for a lot of hugging, but that day he kept holding on to me even after I started to let go," said Dennis.

"I lost you once," he said, referring to the many years in which the brothers had barely seen each other, as part of Bob's effort not to rock the boat with Nancy. "I'm not letting it happen anymore."

"I kept telling Bob, 'Why are you going back? Don't go back to your house. Go get a motel room, or go stay at the Dumbletons while you look for an apartment.' He told us he could take care of himself."

Dennis didn't hear anything after that, until the call came from Julie Dumbleton to say that Bob hadn't shown up for practice with Jenna. He called Jeff, but Jeff didn't know anything. Then, like Julie, Dennis called the police.

Asked by the police investigator to explain why his brother's wife would not have filed a missing person report herself, Dennis Seaman told him, "Probably because she wishes he was dead."

As it turned out, I spent most of the day at Dennis and Robin Seaman's house. At one point in the afternoon, while we were sitting by the pool having a cold drink, the phone rang. It was Jeff Seaman, checking in with his uncle as he had begun doing now and then in the year since his father's murder. When the call was over, Dennis returned to our conversation.

"Darnedest thing," he said. "Jeff just got a call from Greg." This was major news, of course. The brothers no longer spoke, and hadn't for months, and for a moment there, I thought Dennis was about to tell me about a breakthrough in their relationship.

"What brought that about?" I asked him.

"Greg was having trouble getting the Shelby started," Dennis said. "He knew Jeff would have the answer, which he did."

"You mean Jeff helped him with the car?"

"Oh, sure. He knows everything there is about that engine."

Had they spoken, then? Was some kind of reconnection taking place between the brothers?

"Oh no," said Dennis. "All they talked about was car trouble."

Also that day, Dennis and Robin called Hap, a longtime friend of Bob's who lived in the area, to say I was in town and that I'd like to meet him. But Hap had run a Google check on me, saw that I'd raised money for the Kerry campaign the year before, and decided not to talk with me.

"He thinks you're a liberal," Dennis said.

"Well, sure," I said. "But what happened to your brother wasn't about politics. People don't have to agree about the war in Iraq or taxes to agree that murder's a bad thing."

Still, Hap held his ground. He wasn't talking to any Democrat about his old friend Bob Seaman. I probably had some feminist agenda.

Dinnertime rolled around. Dennis and Robin invited me to stay for pizza, but I had a plane to catch. They walked me out to my rental car—Dennis, Robin, Kyle, and their dog. A man of surprising warmth, for one who had so recently distrusted me, Dennis gave me a bear hug. Robin said I was welcome any time.

The sun was just going down as I drove back to the Phoenix airport—the same route, I realized, that Bob Seaman would have taken on what had proved to be the last few hours of his life. Making my way across the vast expanse of desert in the dry Arizona heat, with the western sky on fire overhead, I thought about how strange it was to find myself in this place. At this point I had given over the better part of six months to the story of a woman for whom I was feeling something close to revulsion now.

I figured I would probably spend another six months trying to learn everything I could about this woman. And about her husband too, of course—a man who listened to Rush Limbaugh, whose friends regarded me as suspect for being "a feminist" and "a liberal." Of all the people in whose lives I might have chosen to immerse myself, all the situations I might have elected to explore, the story of what happened to Bob Seaman—Mustang aficionado, fastpitch softball coach, Rush Limbaugh fan—seemed an unlikely choice to move my heart or incite my sense of injustice. Never mind that his brother—my new friend—had chosen to name his dog ("a black bitch," he said) "Oprah."

What was I doing here?

CHAPTER 77

The Other Suspect

There had been a loose end in one small aspect of Bob Seaman's story, and it had been bothering me. In his report on the initial interview he conducted with Nancy Seaman prior to her arrest, Detective Al Patterson quoted Nancy as having referred to an employee at the Upper Deck who had allegedly embezzled money from her husband—the implication being that this person might be a suspect in Bob's disappearance.

Although Nancy Seaman had been caught in many lies since then, this particular remark had a certain ring of truth to it, so I asked Julie Dumbleton about it. Because she had worked at the Upper Deck herself, I figured she might know what Nancy had been referring to. (Even if she hadn't worked there, it was plain to me by now that Julie was a virtually inexhaustible repository of facts on the life of Bob Seaman. There was almost nothing I asked her about him that she had been unable to answer.)

Hearing my question, she had looked briefly troubled, then sad. "I'd rather not tell you," she said. "But there's a person you should see. I think he'll explain to you himself if you give him a chance." Then she gave me the telephone number for Scott Gardner, the batting coach at the Upper Deck.

We met for coffee. He was probably in his late thirties—tall, baseball player build, with a few extra pounds on him now. Scott Gardner was dressed for golf, having just come in from playing a round. I sensed in him a certain quality of sadness—maybe this was present in all ball players who'd harbored the dream of playing in the major leagues but had never quite made it there. But he had a friendly face—not handsome or particularly animated, but with the kind of features that probably came alive during an athletic event. Particularly if he was among those playing.

As a young man fresh out of junior college, Scott Gardner had been drafted by the Chicago Cubs. He pitched in the minor leagues for nine years, always looking for the big break that never came. Bob Seaman had heard about him around the time he opened the Upper Deck and offered Scott a job as an instructor. Scott took it.

"I'd worked in some batting cages before," Scott told me. "But nothing like Bob's setup. The ball machines were state-of-the-art, for one thing, but there was more. It was the atmosphere of the place that mattered to Bob. He'd made a real dirt pitching mound inside, and that mural. He said it was so kids could get the feeling of hitting in a real major league ballpark. He was hoping that someday he'd make the place into someplace kids from Detroit could come—inner-city kids who didn't have a place to go or anyone to work with on their baseball. That was a dream of his."

After hours, Bob and Scott liked to hang out together. Mostly they talked about favorite players, great moments in baseball history.

"Bob was a great storyteller, and a total historian of the game," Scott told me. "You could have a conversation that was supposed to be ten minutes long, and three or four hours would go by, and you'd still be talking.

"He was a Stan Musial man. It bothered Bob that when people talked about the all-time greats, Stan's name didn't usually come up, unless they were from St. Louis. But if you looked at his numbers, man, he was there. He was just so modest and soft spoken, he never got the credit he deserved."

They had spent a lot of time talking about the kids they worked with too, Scott told me.

"Bob just loved those kids," he said. "Sometimes, going over something one of them did, he'd get tears in his eyes. That's how he was about Jake, for sure. And Jenna. When he watched her pitch, he just beamed."

The batting cage never made any real money, Scott went on. "I always used to assume he was some millionaire, doing it as a tax write-off," he said. "Then it turned out he wasn't all that loaded after all. His wife was giving him a lot of grief, actually. She was always coming over with some complaint or other. You could tell, the Upper Deck was like his escape, only it wasn't really, because she kept dropping in."

A couple of years into their friendship, Scott went through a rough divorce. He found a sympathetic ear in Bob.

"He gave me financial help when I needed it. But mostly we'd just talk. He told me about the woman who kind of broke his heart, I guess—a girl he fell in love with back before he was married. He was getting ready to propose to her, only he found out she was cheating on him. He told me he'd met Nancy shortly after that, on the rebound I guess. But even on their wedding day, she started screaming at him about some remark he'd made. They didn't get off to a good start."

By the time Scott met Bob, he said, "there didn't seem to be much left between him and his wife. Sometimes I'd hear the two of them going at each other, and one time, when I was taking a nap in the parking lot, I woke up to the sound of her screaming at Julie Dumbleton. Nancy was yelling that she'd got a broken fingernail.

"Bob complained there wasn't a lot of intimacy or passion in their relationship. Whenever something nice happened at home, it was like a big headline at the Upper Deck. He told me she had sex mostly to get something from him. Like right before Jeff got married, when she wanted everything to be nice at the wedding.

"But all this stuff about Bob being interested in young girls," Scott continued. "That's so not true. I won't tell you he didn't express an interest in women, but it was the farthest thing from little girls. Bob liked women that matured gracefully, he said. I remember one time, after he'd seen Sophia Loren on television, at the Oscars or something. He couldn't stop talking about how gorgeous and classy she was."

I asked Scott about Nancy's allegations concerning abuse, of course.

"Listen," he said. "I always pride myself on trying to see both sides of a situation, and I'm not saying those two didn't yell at each other. But I could never imagine Bob as an abuser. No way. His type of anger was cursing out loud, then he was done with it. Where Nancy, it seemed like she got mad and stayed mad forever. He'd come in, mornings, and say, 'She went psycho on me again last night.'"

Scott had nothing bad to say about Greg Seaman. As far as he was concerned, Greg was just trying to be a good son when he testified the way he had. "He was trying to protect his mom. Though I might not have gone to the extremes he did."

Bob was the type who always gave people a second chance, Scott said. I asked him if that had included himself.

A change came over his face then. "Julie didn't tell you?" he asked me.

"She said you'd tell me yourself," I said.

Scott was quiet for a moment. He stirred his coffee.

"I was going through my divorce, having trouble coming up with child support," he said. "There was some money I got for pitching lessons at the Upper Deck. I didn't report it. Bob found out."

This was embezzlement, when you got right down to it. But Bob Seaman had chosen not to press charges.

"I told him how much money I thought I'd taken," Scott said. "He forgave me. He told me he looked at me like a son, and let me pay it back over time. It was a tearful moment for both of us."

This was the event Nancy Seaman had been alluding to, evidently, when she'd told Detective Patterson—that there was someone out there who'd stolen money from Bob. As if Scott Gardner might be a murder suspect.

Scott had heard on the radio about the discovery of the body, he said. He was the one who told Jeff. It was an awful day. Worst of his life. Though the day they'd gutted the Upper Deck was a close second—seeing the men on Bobcats ramming through the wall with the mural of Tigers' Stadium on it.

There was, he said, one other thing that really bothered him. He couldn't stop thinking about how Nancy had gotten the body in the Explorer. He just didn't see how this was possible.

He kept remembering this time when he was still playing in the minors, and it was his birthday; he'd gotten so drunk that he was dead weight, same as Bob would have been.

"It took four guys to carry me out," Scott told me. "Granted, I'm bigger than Bob was. But *four guys*. And I'm talking ball players."

There was no resolution for that question on Scott Gardner's mind. Either Nancy Seaman had help or she didn't. Either way, Bob was dead. Either way, the Upper Deck was gone.

"He was a great guy," Scott said. "I never knew anyone to love the game of baseball more than Bob."

CHAPTER 78

Possibly the Nicest Guy
in Bloomfield Hills

—◦◦◦— With the end of the summer approaching, I figured it was time to pay a visit to Larry Kaluzny—the blandly almost-handsome attorney responsible, with his son Todd, for the unsuccessful defense of Nancy Seaman.

Months had passed since that call, not long after the verdict had come down, informing me of his client's decision to meet with me on the day of the sentencing—a meeting that never took place, of course, on account of that snowstorm.

"I don't know why Nancy decided not to talk to you," he said to me now, shaking his head. "I can't see what she's got to lose at this point."

Of course, Larry himself had appeared to be avoiding me for a while there, I noted now. But he explained. Though nothing about Larry Kaluzny would suggest a man prone to depression, the guilty verdict in the Seaman case bothered him, he admitted to me now, "more than any other verdict I ever had."

"I was really depressed," he explained as we sat in the Bloomfield Hills office he shared with Todd. "Normally I'd go out and play a round of golf when a case didn't go my way. After Nancy was found guilty, I couldn't even play golf for a while there."

Not that Larry Kaluzny felt guilty over his own performance in the trial. "I can't think of a single thing I'd do differently," he said. "There were times I wished I did something wrong so my client would have grounds for a new trial. But in this case, it was just one of those things. Even now I still feel bad about it."

They had a tough jury; that was one issue. He and Todd could sense that early on, from their body language. "They just didn't seem very sympathetic," he said.

Then there was the case itself. Certain elements were going to be a tough sell, and Larry Kaluzny understood that from the get-go. "There were basically three things that bothered me in this case," he said. "The buying of the hatchet, the brutality of the murder, and the covering up."

Three rather substantial problems, when you thought about it.

Like Nancy and Greg, Larry Kaluzny still had a bone to pick with Chief Dwyer for what he viewed as overly sensational and inaccurate publicity about the case. And of course, the Michigan law that disallowed Dr. Lenore Walker from offering her assessment of Nancy Seaman's case and only permitted her to provide a general overview of Battered Woman Syndrome had cost them big-time.

But the most significant obstacle to winning that not guilty verdict had been presented by his client herself.

"She was just such a bad witness," he said. "The woman I came to know in jail over the months we prepared for this case was not the same one I saw in court. She came across as controlling and deceptive. The jury didn't like her.

"It's so hard to testify," he went on. "It's the first chance a person has to tell their whole story. But no matter how much we tried to tell her, 'Just answer the questions, yes, no,' she couldn't do what we'd recommended. She wanted to explain everything, and it didn't work. All I can say is, it's a common problem. I've tried six hundred cases, and maybe half my clients have testified. Of those, maybe four or five actually helped themselves."

"Did you ever consider an insanity plea?" I asked him. This had been Jeff's idea—the one defense position, he had told me that night we met at Chevy's, that he could have wholeheartedly supported.

Meeting the standard for an insanity plea would have been tough, no question, but perhaps her behavior over the months leading up to the murder might have suggested to a jury that Nancy Seaman was a sick woman.

What about that line in her application for the PPO against Julie
Dumbleton, "I will cease to exist"? I asked. What about her idea that
"You can't pick and choose who you love"? Were these the words of a
rational woman?

Larry Kaluzny looked at me pleasantly, but without apparent recognition. He did not remember that document or those words, he said.
They hadn't made a particular impression on him. The psychological
theories that occupied him more, in this case, concerned his "fixer" hy-
pothesis, (one he began to expound on again, lest I might have forgotten) and the notion he'd tried to sell in court (with no takers, it
appeared) that what had set off Nancy Seaman's final horrifying burst
of violence with the knife had been the experience of feeling Bob Seaman's body on her skin and being reminded, as a result, of the violence
his touch had brought about in the past. It sounded a little too neat for
me, but on swift reflection, it seemed pointless to enter into an exploration of the workings of human pathology with Larry Kaluzny.

He was—as longtime observers of the legal world in Oakland
County invariably said—"a nice guy." He was a decent man, probably
a loyal husband and a loving dad, and he meant well. But though he
was a man who'd spent the better part of the last twenty years defending murderers, serial killers, and rapists, among others, it seemed
to me (and perhaps this was Larry Kaluzny's great good fortune) that
he might also be a person with limited first-hand experience of the
dark side of human behavior. Perhaps his understanding of how men
and women might behave in truly stressful situations outside the con-
fines of Bloomfield Hills remained strictly theoretical. He hadn't been
there.

Larry Kaluzny seemed to have developed little awareness of the true
nature of madness or of the depths a troubled human being was capable of descending to within the territory of her own mind. To Larry,
the story really was a relatively simple one. Bob beat Nancy. Nancy
fought back. Greg was the good son. Jeff was the bad.

"That young man's behavior on the stand," Larry said of Jeff, shaking his head. "It was just so . . . inappropriate."

It was a bizarre picture, to someone like Larry Kaluzny (as it probably would have been for his son Todd) that a husband and wife—or
a father and a mother—might communicate with so much vitriol, by
Post-it notes. That you'd make jokes on the witness stand, recounting
it. But there was another sort of individual—one with a different kind

of family history—for whom the image of Nancy and Bob Seaman's ongoing battles would have seemed instantly recognizable, if more dramatic and extreme, and sitting with him now, in his pleasant, sunny office, filled with golf memorabilia and plaques for community service, I thought of three people I knew who would understand better. My own children.

The kind of individual who might have recognized best the particular tone of weariness, masked by brittle sarcasm, displayed by Jeff Seaman on the witness stand, was any young person who had personally lived through the war between two parents for whom any residue of affection or goodwill toward their former partners had long since been replaced by contempt, bitterness, and rage. And though in my own life—and, thankfully, in those of my children—nothing as terrible as what occurred in the Seaman family had ever taken place, my own wisecracking sons would understand the impulse to laugh at the absurdity of two parents making total fools of themselves in a bad marriage, or a bad divorce.

Jeff Seaman was a young man so well acquainted with how things went between his parents that he had anticipated the fight over the Explorer, before it even began. He didn't pick up the ringing cell phone on Mother's Day night, not just because there was a driving rain storm outside but because he knew that it would be one of his parents, doing the post mortem on the most recent of a long line of battles. No need to recite the words anymore; "*dat . . . dat . . . dat . . .*" (his way, in court, of describing his parents, arguing) was enough. A sound, like gunfire, that left any person with a little sense of self-preservation heading out the door to the safety of the Tigers Game on ESPN, where the worst that could happen was your team might lose, followed by a day at the Ford Motor Company, where the problems—all having to do with engine calibration—might be hugely complex, but they were solvable.

To Larry Kaluzny, Jeff Seaman was "inappropriate," but to a child of battling parents, what is most inappropriate is how they behave to each other, and it was no surprise to me now that the Seaman sons had found theirs: the invention of a new story, for Greg. Making jokes and keeping busy, in Jeff's case.

"Maybe if you look at some individual issues, like Nancy driving around with the body in the back, you could think there was some type of mental illness," he said. "But I never saw any trace of that type of problem. She was a normal woman. Very nice. Very pleasant. Very appreciative of everything we did for her. I can't see a good mother like her missing her son's graduation. I just don't see a person of her caliber saying, 'I think I'll go buy a hatchet and kill my husband.'"

She had bought the hatchet to get rid of a stump. He really believed that, I saw, and I almost envied him, for being able to suppose things were as simple as that.

CHAPTER 79

Back to Briarwood Court

N early finished with my research now, I paid a visit to the Oakland County Registry of Deeds, where I located the name of the family who had purchased the Seaman home on Briarwood Court the previous November: David and Susan S. At a selling price of $380,000—around the going rate for a condominium in a community like this one, and probably a good $200,000 below market value for the property—the S's had probably gotten one of the better Oakland County real estate deals of the decade, though not one that every family would have been willing to accept. It would be a long time before residents of Farmington Hills would forget what had taken place in that three-car garage, or pass the driveway there without remembering the body in the back of the Explorer.

It was one of my least favorite kinds of moments in the work I do: calling up Mrs. S to ask if I could see her house. I took the tell-it-like-it-is approach:

"There's not a single benefit to you in doing this," I said, "but I'd be grateful if you'd let me walk through your home for a few moments, just to get a feeling for the place where the story happened that I'm trying to understand."

I knew from watching the *48 Hours* broadcast that the correspondent who had hosted the segment had been filmed walking through the former Seaman home and into the garage. There had been footage of the well-known black-and-white tile floor, the Tudor façade, the kitchen where Nancy Seaman reportedly fixed herself a submarine sandwich while her husband told her he was divorcing her. But my strong guess was that CBS—unlike myself—had probably paid a hefty fee for the right to shoot on the premises. All I could offer Susan S by way of incentive (when I discovered she had a daughter of the appropriate age) was a signed copy of *The Usual Rules,* a novel of mine that young girls often seemed to like.

Still, Susan S was surprisingly friendly, considering. She didn't tell me right away that I could come by. She said she'd think about it. "I'll discuss it with my husband," she said—words that made my heart sink. A woman might find herself intrigued, and a woman at home with young children might simply be happy for a little momentary diversion. But a husband—if he was sensible—was likely to say "What in God's name are you thinking of?"

He did, evidently. Or offered some variation on no, anyway, and who could blame him?

It was a gated community, or I would simply have driven past the house like rubberneckers everywhere. When I thought about it, it occurred to me that this was the very kind of situation that inspires people to live in gated communities in the first place: to avoid people like me nosing into their business, showing up at their door unannounced.

Still, I called Susan S back with a second proposition. "I won't come to your door," I said. "But would you consider leaving my name at the gate of Ramblewood, so I could drive my car inside and just get a feel for where they lived?"

(My car, of course, was the kind of vehicle likely to set off an all-points bulletin or a frantic message to Homeland Security. People in rusty ten-year-old Pontiacs didn't drive into places like the Ramblewood subdivision.)

But Susan S's response, when I put my question to her, was a surprising one. "I'm happy to leave you permission to come in the gate," she said, "but the truth is, they hardly ever stop anyone anyway.

"And once you're coming over," she said, "you might as well stop by and say hello."

So much for the security of gated communities.

So in the end, I did get to walk through the S's home, and Susan S was so nice about it, I hoped I wasn't going to make for any marital trouble when my book was published and her husband found out.

I don't know what I expected, but after all this time spent thinking about an event that had taken place here, the house on Briarwood Court had taken on a kind of mythic status for me. Now, as Susan S walked me through the rooms—pleasant, airy, not particularly distinctive in any way—I might as well have been at one of those staged real estate open houses.

In the office where Bob Seaman used to work, before he decamped to the Upper Deck, sat the S's youngest child, J, a five-year-old girl who was currently engrossed in a Web site called Paperdoll.com that allowed a person (thrillingly, for any age, if you asked me) to select a particular celebrity, see a paper doll of her appear on the screen, and then drag any of a few hundred jazzy mix-and-match outfits across the screen in such a way that you could see what they'd look like on her. I had selected Hillary Duff and put her in a pair of cute culottes and a tank top. I scanned the list, in search of a positive middle-aged role model with a more realistic body type, but all I came up with was Camilla Parker Bowles, who definitely wouldn't have been J's pick.

We moved through the rest of the house: the carpeted living room, the hallway. Susan reported that although they'd done a fair amount of work on the place, she and her husband had not yet gotten around to replacing the one door upstairs (leading to the room that had been Jeff's) where, according to Nancy's and Greg's trial testimony, Bob had damaged the wood.

She took me into the kitchen, with its expanse of Formica and tile, and the eating island where, according to Nancy Seaman, Bob Seaman had sat on the morning she said the murder took place, threatening her as she made a submarine sandwich for work.

Although I had never set foot in this house before, Julie Dumbleton—in her relentless quest to clear her friend's name, and with her seemingly inexhaustible inclination replay the scenario—had drawn out for me a diagram showing the layout of the kitchen—the placement of the refrigerator, the eating island, the chopping block. As with every other aspect of the case, Julie had given abundant thought to the story Nancy had told, of making that submarine sandwich, and Bob's allegedly having drawn a knife blade across her hand as she did so, while seated at the eating island. Standing in the kitchen now, and seeing the layout of the room in real space, I was as baffled as Julie had been as to why Nancy would have wanted to move all the food products necessary to construct that sandwich (mayonnaise, lettuce, cheese, lunch meat) all the way from the refrigerator to the island, rather than making the sandwich at the other end of the room. Particularly given what had been described, in court, as the highly threatening behavior of Bob Seaman at the time, and the fact that, according to his wife, he was playing with a knife as he spoke to her.

I felt no impulse to share any of this with Susan S, however. From all appearances, she was living a happy life in this place, unclouded by undue attention to the activities of its previous occupants. She didn't need to hear any of this, and I felt no need to share it with her.

Our last stop on the tour was the garage. A person might have supposed that, impressive as it was to have a black-and-white checked tile floor in one's garage, the new occupants might have preferred to remove the tiles, but it seemed to me an indication of a fundamentally positive attitude about the whole situation that the S's had done no such thing, although Susan did tell me that they were meaning to get around to replacing one tile that had been taken up at some point (probably, though again I didn't say this, in the course of the police work, to check for blood).

It was a great garage, actually—spacious and well organized, with plenty of room for the S kids' helmets and bikes. Not every family had its own generator, either, or track lighting over their car.

When we were done in the garage, I told Susan that I didn't want to keep her any longer. It looked as though she had something cooking on the stove, and her son was coming home from camp that afternoon, not to mention that her little girl was calling out to show her an outfit she'd put on the Mary-Kate Olsen paper doll—the only celebrity paper doll in the collection, perhaps, who had been made to look heavier than in real life.

Back in the kitchen, I signed a copy of my novel for Susan's older daughter, thanked Susan again for her willingness to show me the house, and commented on the friendliness of her strikingly talkative and outgoing five-year-old, the paper-doll lover.

"She's adopted," Susan told me, not because I'd asked any questions. "I went over to Russia on a church trip two years ago and fell in love with her at an orphanage. We weren't planning on anything like that; it just happened. And now of course, we can't imagine life without her."

J, the five-year-old, showed me a picture then, of herself in a crib at the orphanage. She knew the whole story, though she no longer remembered how to speak Russian.

"Here's where I used to live before my mommy found me," she told me.

Sitting with J, studying the photograph, I thought to myself that the S's were right to buy this house, to seize on the great real estate deal with no fear that whatever terrible history had occurred under this roof before their arrival would in any way contaminate their own young family, as other prospective buyers might have feared.

It wasn't the house that determined a family's well-being, so much as the people who lived there and the relationships between them, I reflected. Pulling out of the driveway that had once had a car parked in it with a body in the back, I had the feeling that in spite of all that had happened in this place, the S family would be fine here.

CHAPTER 80

"She Was Going Through
a Lifestyle Change"

—◦◦◦— Having now visited the house in which the Seamans had lived out their last days as what is known as "an intact family" I wanted to visit the famous condominium—the one that, according to Nancy Seaman at least, had touched off the final round of bitterness between Bob and Nancy that had ended with the murder.

Considering that Nancy Seaman's job was at Longacre Elementary School, in Farmington Hills, it was a little odd that she'd chosen to purchase a condominium in a town downriver which, though close to her father and to Jeff and Becka, would have required almost an hour's drive to work.

I was surprised, as I made my way along the highway toward the condo development to see the kind of homes and stores in the area, and the contrast between this community and the one Nancy Seaman had lived in with Bob. Although King's Crossing was billed as a luxury development, the area immediately surrounding it looked a little dreary, particularly for a person accustomed to the lush landscaping of Farmington Hills and the tasteful boutique shopping there.

I was met at the rental office by Margie Wright, the agent who had sold Nancy Seaman the condo, as I'd learned from Detective Patterson's notes. She remembered Nancy, and how she'd come to look at a number of units with her two sons, as well as her father and Jeff's wife.

"She was very organized," said Wright. "She had all her papers in perfect order."

As I walked through a unit described as "the Jefferson," the layout chosen by Nancy Seaman, Wright filled me in on the particulars. As Lisa Ortlieb had pointed out at the trial, there had been a different but similar unit available immediately, when Nancy came to look, but she had opted for one that was still under construction and would not be ready to move into until the following August—a choice that, at the trial, had seemed to undercut her claim that she feared for her life, living under the same roof with Bob Seaman.

"She requested that we call her at work with any questions concerning the financing," Margie Wright added. And in fact, there had been questions. Evidently because of Bob Seaman's failure to pay their mortgage for the last few months, the Seaman's credit score had plummeted, which had led to Nancy's needing to take out a higher-interest loan than she would have otherwise. (An event that had evidently inspired her to remark to Jeff, "I could kill your father." It was just an expression, however, he said.)

Higher interest rate notwithstanding, the deal had gone through. The papers were signed. That's when they'd been mailed to the Seaman home on Briarwood Court, where Bob had seen them and found out about the plan. For a woman as organized and detail oriented as Nancy to allow such a slip-up seemed surprising, but maybe someone in the King's Crossing offices was not as good at this type of thing as Nancy would have been.

"They were a super group," said Wright. "A super family. They all seemed to get along so well. They were all getting into things like choosing the colors.

"She wasn't the type to wear her heart on her sleeve," Wright continued. "She certainly didn't tell me any details about what was going on in her personal life. But you got a feeling, looking at her, that she was going through a lifestyle change."

Or not. Because I had gotten the strangest feeling, walking through the King's Crossing development and the model unit whose layout matched that of the one Nancy Seaman had purchased. It was just a feeling, of course—without a shred of evidence to back me up, other than how long the drive took, back to Farmington Hills from the condo that day.

Never mind the long drive to work, even, or the fact that Nancy Seaman was the kind of teacher who liked to get to school even earlier than most. Nothing I'd heard of Nancy Seaman over the months—how important it had been for her to drive that Lincoln Town Car, have a good diamond on her finger, and wear a mink, and to present the appearance of being part of a "handsome couple"—fit with the idea that she would choose to return to an unglamorous, out-of-the-way downriver town, to a condo development just off the highway.

Driving back to Oakland County now, in the fading hours of a hot summer day, I found myself wondering if Nancy Seaman ever really intended to live in that condo. Or if the condo purchase and the elaborate drama surrounding it had been an extravagant message to get Bob Seaman's attention. Not wholly unlike the way a person might, in a moment of despair in her marriage, hold a pair of scissors to her hair or threaten to jump out of a moving car (both of which I had done, many years before, in the last days of my own dying marriage) when all she really meant to say was *"Look at me. Pay attention, for once in your life."*

CHAPTER 81

A Fastpitch
Softball Lesson

I'd been waiting all summer long for Jake Dumbleton to make his decision about talking with me. Now the date of my departure was approaching, and we had only shared those few words at the softball game that one day, when he'd asked if I was going to do another crummy smear job on Mr. Seaman, like the one on *48 Hours*.

With no word from Jake, I made a suggestion to Jenna. It had occurred to me that one way I might gain a glimpse into the coaching side of Bob Seaman's life and the way he had inspired the kids he worked with (Jenna and Jake top of the list) would be to partake of a little softball coaching myself. I asked Jenna if she'd be willing to spend a little time with me, analyzing my motion. Maybe she'd have some suggestions.

I wasn't fooling her, of course. She knew I hadn't come to Michigan to work on my hitting and fielding. Still, she seemed relieved that at least I wasn't asking her about Mr. Seaman. She agreed to see me, and we headed to the field—Jenna at the wheel of the family car, courtesy of her newly acquired learners' permit (she'd gotten it the day before), which allowed her to drive with a licensed adult. Had things gone differently, this would have been precisely the kind of moment she might have shared with Bob Seaman, who—even when she was just thirteen—had begun instructing her in driving, in the parking lot of the Waterwheel Building, same as he'd done a few years earlier with her brother. As it was, we listened to country radio for the block-long drive between the Dumbletons' house and the ball field.

Now, as the two of us faced each other on the field—Jenna calling out instructions I could imagine Bob Seaman delivering to her in years past—she displayed no trace of the anxiety her mother had told me Jenna had expressed privately about my interest in finding out about the single most painful event of her young life, and the one about which she least wanted reminders. Except for the fact that no ordinary circumstances would have put Jenna Dumbleton—star fifteen-year-old fastpitch softball player—in the company of a fifty-one-year-old nonathlete from California, this could have been an ordinary afternoon for Jenna, doing something she did with more ease and efficiency than almost any other activity. She picked up her glove with the offhand ease I might have displayed cracking an egg in a bowl or peeling an apple. This girl was at home here.

"You want to follow through with your throw," she pointed out. Then she told me how Mr. Seaman got that idea across: as part of the follow-through, he would perform a somersault. At one particularly memorable practice, he had all the girls out doing somersaults, just to get the idea across: put your whole body into the motion. Don't stop with just the arm.

"Point your glove at the target," she said. "After you've completed the throw, bring your arm down like you're swimming. Finish with your glove arm down."

"When you hit," she said, "you want your weight on the back foot.

"Bru would tell me to keep my elbow against my side and the bat on my shoulder, but Mr. Seaman told me to keep my elbow up and the bat off my shoulder."

She did it Bru's way now, but it was Mr. Seaman's advice she liked better.

Sometimes, she told me, when he was catching her pitches, he'd have her count out the throws in Spanish, or work on her times tables. One thing they'd worked on particularly hard was her change-up.

"We had to do twenty-five good change-ups before we were done, every practice," she said.

He took her Christmas shopping, to get presents for her family. She still had the glove he bought her, but it was stretched out now, she'd used it so much. As she told me this, I got the feeling that as reluctant as Jenna had been to speak with me about Bob Seaman, she also wanted to tell me some things, and now she did.

After Nancy Seaman's arrest, Jenna said, she knew what people were going to say. It was no big surprise that they'd start speculating that her mother and Mr. Seaman had an affair. The surprise was the other part: the things Nancy had implied about Mr. Seaman having some kind of thing for teenage girls.

"He was like a member of our family," she said. "Why did Mrs. Seaman have to say something that sickening?"

As if murdering him weren't bad enough.

I could tell that Jenna wasn't the sort of girl who was used to speaking critically of people, particularly adults, but she said now that she remembered the day she was at the Upper Deck for her lesson when Nancy Seaman came by, supposedly to borrow Mr. Seaman's car.

She was acting crazy, Jenna said. "She was doing all this stuff. Grabbing onto the netting. She made this ugly face."

For a while there, after the murder, Jenna had worked at the Waterwheel Building. Even after the Upper Deck closed down, she'd kept showing up for her job, cleaning for the Coxes.

One day, she told me, "I asked for the metal sign they had in the hallway, that said Put One in the Upper Deck." She figured they wouldn't want that anymore, because Mr. Seaman's business was closed down now.

"Mrs. Cox said the metal was expensive. She said it had been cut a special way or something. I would have paid for it, but she said no.

"I wanted to remember," Jenna went on. "It just seemed like something I would have liked to have in my room."

I asked her then what it was she had liked best about Mr. Seaman. He didn't treat her like a kid, for one thing, she told me. He was funny. He thought up good ideas, even if they seemed a little crazy sometimes. He paid attention to things. He let her shift the car.

"I'm always going to think of him when I drive," she said.

CHAPTER 82

"Why Did You Get Divorced?"

A long time had passed in which I had not seen or spoken with Jake Dumbleton. (I'd sent him a book of mine, though: my memoir, *At Home in the World*. It was an unlikely choice for an almost twenty-year-old guy who considered himself a jock, but he said he wanted to know who I was, and that book was mostly likely to tell him.)

It was nearing the end of my time in Michigan when I heard from Jake again. He called to say he'd like to meet with me. He had been thinking about our conversation at the ball field that day, and he might be up for talking with me about Mr. Seaman, but he had some questions to ask me first.

We met at a restaurant in Northville on his lunch hour from Nissan. He had a briefcase with him—one that used to be his father's, I was guessing. Now he removed a file folder from it and set the folder on the table, along with a mini tape recorder. "Is it OK if I record this?" he said.

No problem.

I had told him, when we spoke at the ball game, that given his anxiety about the media and his previous experience with *48 Hours*, I'd be happy to answer any questions he might have about what I was doing and who I was. I had been expecting him to ask about my credentials as a journalist, books I'd written, or maybe how I planned to write this one. Now, like a lawyer approaching a witness—or maybe more like a nineteen-year-old boy playing the part of one—he began.

"Do you have any kids?" he asked me.

"Three," I told him.

He asked if I had any pictures on me. I turned on my computer, brought up a file of family photographs, and showed him. Me and my daughter on a trip to Mexico together. My son Willy and me at his high school graduation. Charlie and me, in the kitchen at home. Our dog, Opie. I felt glad to have these pictures, and I could tell that the faces of my smiling sons—two strong, athletic-looking young men who appeared to love their mother—were reassuring to Jake.

In truth, my sons were very different types of young men from the one now sitting across from me. Unlike Jake, they had discovered, long before their teens, that bad things happen even in the supposed safety of your own home, and that events are often out of your control. Like many children of divorced families, they had learned to locate their sense of security within themselves and not in the homes of their parents.

It was not news to any of my three children that husbands and wives could do terrible things to each other, and that children would suffer for them. This may have accounted for why it was that—as confident as I was of their love for me—my sons and daughter appeared happier and more at peace with the world they'd created for themselves, away from their parents, than they did on their rare visits home.

Maybe the absence of that kind of early stability was what had allowed my children to leave home as they'd done, early and often, in a way Jake Dumbleton never had. When my son Will was Jake's age—or a little younger—he'd set off for Africa for eight months, in much the way that his sister had ventured to the Dominican Republic and Haiti for the better part of a year once. When he was Jake's age and living in New York City, going to school, Charlie had made a painting with the image of a woman—as fractured and nonrepresentational as a de Kooning—with slashes of red across her face and one hand raised in a fist. *My Mom on a Bad Day,* he called it, though I'd taken some comfort from that *on a Bad Day* part. Family upheaval wasn't our whole story, just a part of it.

Now Jake was taking a sheaf of papers from the file folder. He had evidently looked up my name using Google. What he would have found there, I knew, would mostly have been reviews and columns written about the controversy surrounding my 1998 memoir, *At Home in the World,* the book I'd sent him. A lot of nasty and sniping columns had been written about me at the time, and even from across the table, I could recognize that what he had in hand was one of the ugliest, a piece from *Slate.*

I knew that even in his role as interrogator, Jake Dumbleton would be way too polite to bring up any of this, so I did.

"Pretty nasty stuff," I observed.

He didn't say anything, but he was looking at the paper in front of him.

"Maybe your own recent experience has taught you to be a little skeptical of how the media report on things," I told him.

When that book of mine was published, my sons were just a little younger than he was now, I told him. "I guess you're familiar with seeing embarrassing personal things written about your mom in the press," I said. "Whether or not they're true, they still hurt."

I had not expected to get into this with Jake, but now I found myself telling him a little of the story of some hard things that had happened to me when I was eighteen years old, and how they had altered my life and outlook. Not that our experiences had been similar, but I could still remember what it was like, as a young person, to believe that life would never be all right anymore, ever again.

Jake put away the article and the folder, which appeared to be filled with many others. He had only one other question for me, and it took me aback for its simplicity. What he was probably trying to get at was whether I had some kind of ax to grind against husbands in bad marriages, or whether I might be coming to this story with the perspective of a formerly battered wife. Still, I was struck, hearing his question and looking into his sweet, open face as he asked it, by the fact that in the sixteen years since my divorce from my children's father, not one person had ever asked me this.

"Why did you and your husband get divorced?" he asked me.

Sixteen years after it happened, I could feel my eyes grow damp. I would have answered if I could, but no words came.

In the end, he agreed to talk with me. Not that same day; his lunch hour was over. (Before heading out to the parking lot, however, he insisted on picking up the check.) But a few days later, we met again, this time at a Starbucks in Northville. He was ready, he said, to tell me about Mr. Seaman.

He went over the familiar history: meeting Bob at the batting cage; getting his treasured Upper Deck membership card that entitled him to unlimited use of the ball machines; joining the Hitters' Club; getting to know Jeff and Greg. (Who used to be his friend, he said. Who sometimes, for fun, plucked Jake's baseball hat from his head and stuck it up in the nets. Jake wasn't a person who had enemies, and he certainly never expected Greg to become one.)

Then Mr. Seaman had started coaching with Jake's dad, and they'd worked on the Shelby together. He started hanging out at the house. In Jake's book, Mr. Seaman had been a family friend, like an uncle, who helped his dad with the basement renovation and hung around for pizza with the family after, and sometimes took them to ball games or just sat around in the family room, talking about baseball.

But he was also somebody who offered an alternative approach to that of Jake's own parents: looser, a little more liberal where things like curfews were concerned. When Jake and his parents were having arguments a couple of years back about Jake getting home after his curfew, and they grounded him, it had been Bob who suggested to the Dumbletons that they ease up on their son. Bob was the one who convinced Jake's parents to lift the curfew, and after that, Jake was nearly always home by midnight or a few minutes after. He didn't get drunk. Didn't do drugs. "You've got a good kid here," Bob had told Dick and Julie, and they'd come around.

Jake's father worked with him on his driving, naturally, but Mr. Seaman had been the one who taught him how to drive a manual shift. And then came the gift of the Mustang that had been Greg's.

"I asked Greg if it was OK with him," Jake told me. "He said no problem. He had a different Mustang, a lot newer. The one Mr. Seaman gave me wasn't even driveable at this point.

"Mr. Seaman thought every fifteen-year-old kid should know how to fix a car," he told me. "He used to say that's what his dad did with him when he was growing up."

So they had taken on the job of putting the Mustang back together. "He taught me how to look up torque specs, things like that," said Jake. "Until I met Mr. Seaman, I didn't have a clue."

There was this funny thing about the way he worked on an engine, Jake told me. "Mr. Seaman's dad was missing two fingers from an accident—the pointer on each hand. So when Mr. Seaman tightened a bolt, he didn't use those fingers either. It was like he didn't have them, even though he did, just because that's how he saw his dad doing things."

He told me about a time when he and Mr. Seaman were in the basement of the Upper Deck, working on the Mustang as they often did together, and Nancy Seaman had burst into the place. She'd opened the passenger-side door, removed some papers from the glove compartment, and stalked out. After she'd gone, Bob had told Jake, "She probably thought she was getting the title and registration, but those papers weren't in the car."

Times like that, and after the Dream Cruise, when Greg had called him an asshole, Bob sometimes talked about his family, his screwed-up relationships with his wife and younger son. At age fifteen, son of two parents who never raised their voices at each other, Jake hadn't known what to say.

"I felt bad for him," said Jake. "Seeing him like that. Knowing he just wanted someone to talk to. He just looked so sad."

Between ball games, and nights at the Dumbletons, and times at the Upper Deck, when he would be doing his job or hanging out, Jake figured he probably saw Bob Seaman practically every day of his life for the last eight years, up until the day of his death. Jake loved his own dad and was close to him, but the relationship with Bob was different. He treated Jake more like a pal: talked with him about politics, what was going on in the world. He was funny—not in a joke-telling way, just a little outrageous, in a way his own parents never were. He made things happen, interesting things. You never knew with Mr. Seaman when you were going to have some unexpected adventure.

None of this meant that Jake hadn't experienced Bob Seaman's temper, he told me. There was one time, for instance, when Jake's family was going on a vacation to Aruba, and he was upset because his parents had nixed his request to bring a friend along.

"He really let me have it about being too spoiled to appreciate the trip," said Jake. "But one thing was: he might get mad at you sometimes, but once it was over, it was over. He was the type that would let you know you pissed him off, but then he'd drop it."

One time, when Jake was sick, Mr. Seaman had brought him a bunch of movies to watch: "There was this movie called *'61* about

Roger Maris and Mickey Mantle. He brought me *L.A. Confidential* and *Gone in Sixty Seconds,* because it had a Boss in it, and *Bullitt,* with Steve McQueen, because it had the original Shelby Mustang in it.

"Anything with a Mustang, he loved it," said Jake.

The hard part of our conversation came when I asked Jake about how it had been for him after Bob's murder, starting with the night he found out (though he already sensed it, even before he got the news). "I just left the house and drove," he told me. "I went over to the batting cage and talked to Mr. Gardner. I just drove around."

The experience had changed him, he told me. Before this, "the only bad thing that ever happened to me was my grandparents dying." Now, he said, "I watch my relationships with everybody. It's like it could happen at any minute: you could be driving down the street and get hit by a car."

He stopped playing baseball, he said, "because it's just not fun anymore." His head just wasn't there, he said.

Many things bothered him now, he told me: the way they made Mr. Seaman look like some kind of bully, when really it was his wife; the way, on that show *48 Hours,* they had made it look as if his mom was dancing with Mr. Seaman, when really his dad was right there on the dance floor, just out of camera range. The one she'd actually been dancing with, he said, was Greg.

"The thing that made me the maddest was the way the press made it out like Mr. Seaman had some kind of weird attitude toward twelve-year-old softball players, just because he coached them," he said. "Like, Nancy Seaman was teaching young kids too. Does that make her a pedophile?"

Sometimes during our conversation, Jake just sounded angry, and frustrated. But there came a moment, when the two of us had been sitting talking for a while—at the point where he was describing how it is for him now—when he started to cry. He was not a person you'd expect to start crying in Starbucks, but he made no effort to conceal it—just wiped his eyes with a napkin and kept talking.

"Everyone keeps telling me I should move on," he said. "Everything else has changed, and everyone's going ahead with their lives, and it's like I'm stuck back in this other time, and I can't get it out of my mind. I hear people complaining about things, like they've got some paper to write or they don't have any beer, and I just look at them and think, they don't know anything about life. I want to tell them, 'You're going to have a rude awakening someday.'"

He might like to go to Iraq and fight someday, he told me. That would be something real, something that mattered, and right now it felt like nothing did anymore. Not that he followed the news that much.

"The only news I watch is sports," said Jake. "You know what I like about sports? It's not a situation where people can make up stuff. It's not like one Web site is going to tell you the Red Sox won and the other one's going to say, no, it was the Yankees. There's facts, and you can't get around them. You can't bullshit with sports."

CHAPTER 83

Dream Cruise

Rain fell on the day of the Woodward Avenue Dream Cruise that August, making turnout low, the broadcaster from 104.3 reported, but you wouldn't have known it if you were standing on the sidewalk in Royal Oak, surveying bumper-to-bumper traffic in which not a single vehicle had been manufactured after the year 1970.

From speakers mounted along the roadway, music of the appropriate eras blasted: "Little Deuce Coupe," "Little Old Lady from Pasadena," "Born to Be Wild." There was a scent in the air of hotdogs and kerosene and carnival food (elephant ears, cotton candy) but even in those moments when the rain would stop for a while, the sky remained a dark, dull gray. You had to be a hard-core car person to set out your folding chair along Woodward on a day like this one, although amazingly, many had done so. All up and down the street, for as far as a person could see, stretched a sea of umbrellas and folding chairs and rain ponchos.

Just two years earlier, Bob Seaman had ridden this stretch of Woodward Avenue in the Shelby, with the Dumbletons on board. (This was the day Greg Seaman had called him an asshole and told him, "You're not my father anymore" and swung the pool cue at him.) The Dream

Cruise had been a big day in Bob Seaman's year, though it also marked at least two of the more bitter battles between Bob and Nancy, both times involving Bob's attempt to let the Dumbletons ride in the Shelby.

Now the Shelby was Greg's. The Boss belonged to Jeff. Though neither of them was communicating with me, and I'd been told that neither was likely to show up here, it seemed like a good idea to be on the lookout for their vehicles. A lot of Bosses were out that day, too—a mustard yellow '70, and one like Jeff's: Grabber Orange (same color, too, as the one Parnelli Jones had driven at Laguna Seca that year, 1970).

Only once in my life had I owned a car that provided anything more than transportation: a fairly beat-up 1982 Mercedes 380 SL convertible. That one, I'd been told, was a woman's car, but looking at the Boss, the first thing you felt was that this was a man's—with its loud engine and aggressive fastback, the racing stripe along the hood, its body low to the ground. A woman might like to ride in a Mustang, but with a man behind the wheel.

A Plymouth Duster passed. A Buick Skylark. A Model A. Then there it was: a 1969 Shelby, Acapulco blue with a white interior, lined up along the side of the street—two gill-like protuberances that turned out to be something called "break vents" on the sides, waxed so well that the rain beaded up. For a second the thought occurred: maybe this would be, at last, a sighting of Greg Seaman.

But no. The owner of the Shelby was a man named John Harris, from St. Louis. He'd had his Shelby for thirty years, bought from the original owner. It was the car in which he'd brought his daughter home from the hospital, he said, a big-block 428 GT 500 automatic. Some people might trailer their cars when they brought them to the Dream Cruise, but John had driven his all the way from St. Louis.

"It's the mystique," he said.

Talk turned to Carroll Shelby, the legendary race-car driver and designer of the Shelby Mustangs, now in his eighties but still going strong, according to his Web site. (Where, visitors learn, they can not only learn more about the astonishing career of Carroll Shelby but also purchase his hot sauce or a vial of sperm from his champion breeding bulls.)

It was a Shelby Cobra—"a Ford product"—that Agent Maxwell Smart had driven in the show *Get Smart*. Steve McQueen drove a Shelby in *Bullitt*. "You want to know a really beautiful Shelby?" someone else said. "The one Nic Cage drove in *Gone in 60 Seconds*. There was a car."

The cars kept cruising by. Sometimes a driver would let the car in front get a ways ahead so he could rev his motor and get up a little speed. The air smelled of engine oil and rubber. Standing there made you a little light-headed from the exhaust.

The route out from the Dream Cruise led down a stretch of Woodward Avenue, at Highway 75, where high concrete walls rose up at least forty feet on either side. It was hard not feeling trapped, with nothing to see in front or back but cars and nothing to hear but the roar of their engines. To a certain kind of person—and Bob Seaman had been one—there would be no better place to be on a hot August afternoon, or even a rainy one, than here, and it struck me that if you had to think of a place where Bob Seaman would want his ashes scattered, Woodward Avenue might have been on top of the list, right after home plate at Busch Stadium in St. Louis, home of Cardinals.

CHAPTER 84

Hearing from Aretha

I paid another visit to Lisa Ortlieb, over at Oakland County Courthouse. I had known for a while now about a set of photographs she had in her files—pictures of Bob Seaman taken after the discovery of his body in the back of the Explorer. The photographs had been entered into evidence at the trial of Nancy Seaman. The jurors had studied them, and I decided that I should too, but I had been putting it off. Now, as I prepared for my return to California, I told Lisa I was ready to look at them.

I had never met Bob Seaman in life, of course, and now here I was, studying the most intimate kind of images of him, in death. Because his body had been left in the garage and then in the car for several days before it was discovered, his face was discolored and swollen, and the places where the hatchet had cleaved deeply into his skull and a part of his face left a horrifying gash. It was a strange and terrible sight, and though these were images Julie Dumbleton and her family had never laid eyes on—by choice—I knew they must all have been haunted by imagining them.

Once you see the image of a murdered man, it's in your brain forever. I guessed this before I opened up the folder containing the pictures, and after I studied them, I knew I was right about that. Maybe I wished I hadn't looked at the pictures. Or maybe what I wished was simply that I'd never come to Michigan.

It was around this time that I read in the *Free Press* that there was going to be a five-day gospel revival in Detroit, sponsored in part by Aretha Franklin, who would be singing. Aretha was also flying in a gospel choir from Tennessee to join the gospel choir of the Greater Emmanuel Baptist Church. The paper reported that a man named Bobby Jones would be preaching, and though I didn't know his name, the way it was presented in the paper I got the feeling that many others would; there were other great preachers coming, too, and other gospel singers. The event was even free. All of which convinced me that if you were going to be in Metro Detroit during the days in question, there was no better place to be than at that church.

So I headed down Woodward Avenue again and down 7 Mile Road into Detroit, and after getting lost a few times, in neighborhoods where some would suggest that a person should keep her car doors locked at night and the windows rolled up, I found the church—thanks to the assistance of more than one individual next to whom I pulled over to ask directions, all of whom were friendly and helpful.

Once again—as had been true at the funeral of Obie Benson—I found myself one of only a handful of white people in the church. (There were four of us this time, in a crowd of five or six hundred.) Although this was not a funeral, the crowd was dressed well—the men in suits, the women in high heels and colorful dresses, many with hats. Once again, the nurses were in evidence, and the ushers passed out fans to cool ourselves off. Because there weren't enough to go around, the woman next to me on the pew shared hers.

"You in for a powerful treat with Brother Jones and his preaching," she told me. "Say good-bye to sin, sister."

We got to talking. She knew one of the preachers from Christian television, and another from the radio. The way some people follow rock bands or rappers, Shirley followed preachers. Several of those we'd be hearing from today were favorites of hers, she told me, and when they started preaching I began to understand the appeal.

"You are a person who has made mistakes," one of the preachers told us in a rhythmic, high-pitched voice. "But you . . . are . . . not . . . a . . . mistaken person."

"God is ready to give you a new future. Are you ready, children, to accept it?"

Oh yes, brother. Oh yes. We are ready. Thank you, Lord.

"Some people here, they have lowered their expectations. I tell you, brothers and sisters, raise them high. Decide the life you want and ask the Lord. He will listen. He will provide it."

Praise the Lord. Praise Jesus.

I looked around the room, at the rows of worshippers waving their hands and calling out assent to the words of the preachers. There were no churches like this where I came from. If there were, I might have been a churchgoer.

Between preachers, the singers took the microphone—not just standing there, either, but pacing the stage, waving at us, making sounds you might not have supposed could emanate from a human body. Below, in the pews where I sat with the others in the crowd, people were getting up into the aisles and dancing. A woman in the pew just beyond mine was shaking and spinning so violently that I understood now why the nurses were here. Her husband stood to one side, fanning her. Several times over the course of the evening, someone would remind us of the generosity of Sister Aretha Franklin, who had made this gospel festival possible by underwriting the event, even paying for the refreshments. *Praise Sister Aretha,* we called out, taking to our feet.

Now came the moment we were waiting for, when Sister Aretha took the microphone, though I felt from the first note that her voice could have filled the hall unamplified.

Times I'd seen her perform on television, she was wearing fancy gowns—show business getups—but here at Greater Emmanuel, she was dressed like a woman of the church, in a blue suit, modestly covering, though hardly concealing, a physique (never slim) substantially thickened with age. When she started singing, her whole body seemed to vibrate, and so did mine, listening. I had loved the old hits— "R.E.S.P.E.C.T." top of my list—but it was a whole different experience, being in the same space with that voice of hers.

She was singing a song about heaven—"Packing Up, Getting Ready to Go."

"Got my shoes," she called out, as the choir answered her. *Got my shoes. Oh Lord. Yes I do.*

"And I'm ready." *Are you ready?* "Yes I'm ready." *Are you ready?* "Yes I'm ready." *Oh Lord. Oh Lord. Oh Lord.*

She might have been in a trance now. Possibly we all were. I know we were waving our arms in the air, calling out our answers. We were ready, all right. The hand of God could have swung down over the whole lot of us at that moment and lifted up one entire pew full of sinners, and I'm not sure there would have been any sound but rejoicing. We were packed up. *Ready to go.*

Last up (and there appeared to be a kind of batting order) was Bobby Jones. Maybe it was the music, the heat of the night, and the wild dancing of a skinny woman in an orange dress who'd stepped out in the aisle beside my seat, but everything Bobby Jones said suddenly applied to my life.

"I am continuing to encounter people who cause me stress," he said. "But I am a soldier.

"Some of you may be at rock bottom, but let me tell you what I know about rock bottom. It's a good place to begin a new foundation. A . . . new . . . foundation."

I was moved by it all—partly by Bobby Jones himself, and partly too by the experience of being in this place. The women on either side had welcomed me. The singers looked overcome with joy. The woman with whom I had been sharing my fan was patting my leg. I was filled with the spirit.

"Your arrival on the planet is not an accident," Reverend Pearson reminded the congregation. "If you are here, it's because God wants you to be here."

I thought about this. In fact, I had been asking myself why I was here—here in Metro Detroit, spending whole months of my life in pursuit of a story so relentlessly grim and dark that I had not been able to locate, in the whole mess, any glimmer of hope or redemption. Why did anybody need to spend time thinking about the Seaman family? Why did I feel compelled to come to this place, to know their story? For months now, I realized, I'd been asking myself that question, and no answer had appeared.

They were taking the collection now—money to assist Sister Aretha in paying for all the wonderful music and preaching we'd been fortunate enough to partake of at this gospel revival that Sister Aretha's abundant generosity had made possible. I reached into my purse and, recognizing a shortness of funds, pulled out a $5 bill. I folded the bill up to make its denomination a little less obvious.

"Now don't you fold that bill up, brothers and sisters," the voice at the microphone called out to us, as if the speaker were standing at my shoulder.

"Unfold that bill, brothers and sisters, and hold it high over your head. And though I know we are poor people here, and times are hard for many of us, I ask you to reach into your hearts and give as generously as you are able. Let's take out those $20 bills. Let's show our $100 bills. Let's trust the Lord, that if we take care of this house of God, he will take care of us."

I exchanged my five for a twenty and—as instructed—held the bill over my head. Now the voice was telling us to march, one row at a time, right down the center aisle and past Sister Aretha, and wave that bill as we were marching.

"Wave that bill like a flag, before you lay it in the basket," the voice told us, and there we were, half marching, half dancing, displaying our money as we made our way to the front of Greater Emanuel Baptist and handed it over to the spot where Sister Aretha, in her blue church suit, watched over us. It was nothing like how they took collection back at the Unitarian church in New Hampshire, where I come from. That was the good news.

"Forget the past," Bobby Jones exhorted us. "Look to the future. Stop looking in the rearview mirror. Get rid of that thing. I SAID, GET RID OF THAT REARVIEW MIRROR!"

How did he know? That very afternoon, driving the Pontiac down Telegraph Road in the ninety-degree heat of my no-longer-air-conditioned vehicle, the rearview mirror had dropped onto the seat. It was tempting now to take that as a message, and I did.

The service lasted a full three hours—during the last thirty minutes of which we could smell the food (courtesy of Sister Aretha) set out for us to share afterward: fried chicken and collard greens and black-eyed peas and biscuits. I wanted to stay, but it was late, and I had a long drive back to Potter Lake. But it felt like the most natural thing in the world, before leaving the church, to follow the instructions we'd been given and turn to my neighbors on each side in the pew, shake their hand, and let them know Jesus loved them. Never mind that I was Jewish. That night in Detroit, I was a child of God, period.

CHAPTER 85

An Unequivocal No

I n a few weeks I was leaving Michigan, going home to California. I made one final effort to reach Nancy Seaman, and I FedEx'ed her one last letter.

I wrote that I still longed to understand what had happened, and to know the full truth, with all its complexities. What I didn't say in my letter was that I no longer believed that either Nancy or Greg Seaman would tell me anything that would assist me in that pursuit. Having studied, for hours, not only the tapes of Nancy Seaman's phone conversations but also her trial testimony and the tapes from Court TV, and having listened to her remarks to the reporter on *48 Hours,* it seemed unlikely that even if she agreed to talk with me, she would be give me anything more than the familiar list of reasons why Bob Seaman had made her kill him.

Unless her time in prison had brought about a depth of introspection singularly absent in the eight months leading up to her statements after the sentencing, this woman was not inclined to explore any aspect of her story but the injustice of it, or recognize that anyone might bear responsibility for what had taken place other than Jeff Seaman, Dennis Seaman, Lisa Ortlieb, Chief Dwyer, and the Dumbletons.

Julie Dumbleton, in her ceaseless crusade to do battle with everyone who was part of Nancy Seaman's world—TV producers, defense attorneys, "good acquaintances" of Nancy, and Nancy herself—had prepared endless e-mails full of questions she hoped I'd put to those individuals who had done violence to Bob Seaman and Bob Seaman's memory. Julie wanted to pin them down, go after them with examples of inaccuracies in their testimony, statements they had made that contradicted evidence and fact. She compiled lists of questions she longed to put to all of those people who, in her view, had in some way participated in the brutalizing of Bob Seaman and his memory. Chief among them, of course, Nancy herself.

As for me: after months of unrest in my pursuit of Nancy Seaman, I had arrived at a point of clarity on this aspect of the story, at least. I no longer believed that Nancy Seaman, if she spoke with me, would answer any questions in a way that could offer enlightenment. Not only did I strongly doubt she'd tell me the truth, I doubted she'd told it to herself. But there was a more basic reason for my reluctance to enter into any relationship with Nancy: to do so, I would have to feign sympathy or suggest that a kinship might exist between us. And it had become clear to me now: none did.

Maybe Joe McGinniss could befriend a murderer, then portray him in a book as a monster; and Truman Capote could send poems to Perry Smith, then curse because the delay of Smith's execution was holding up the completion of *In Cold Blood*. But I wasn't cut out for that stuff.

I remembered, many years back, when I'd attended the arraignment of Pamela Smart, the young New Hampshire woman who had been charged and would ultimately be found guilty of conspiring with her teenage lover to commit the murder of her husband. I remembered looking at her in the courtroom that day and running into her angry and embittered sister in the ladies' room afterwards. At the time, I remember thinking that although it was dimly possible that I could win the trust of these people and elicit a story from them, to do so would require me to enter into a kind of relationship with them that—though hardly murder—would make me guilty of some form of deception and complicity myself.

I had gone home, instead, to write the story as a work of fiction, never speaking with Pamela Smart or the members of her family, who even now, fifteen years later, continued to offer justifications for her crime. I had never regretted that choice. Now, again, I realized I didn't want to be in a room with Nancy Seaman, or with Greg, for that matter.

Shortly after sending that last letter to Nancy Seaman, I placed a call again to Rick Cox, at his office at the Waterwheel Building—a piece of real estate of which he had now become full owner, thanks to the terms of the buyout agreement made with Bob Seaman back in 1996, when they formed their partnership in the property.

I told Rick, over the phone, that I would be leaving Michigan soon, expressing my regret that he had chosen never to meet with me over my many months of work in Oakland County. I wanted to make sure he understood something. (Here came that part a journalist tries hard to avoid, the card you save for last, because it's nothing less than a threat, really, and the other person knows that.) With or without his participation in an interview, I told him, he remained a character in Bob Seaman's story. With or without his say so, I would be writing about him.

Up until now, the thinnest veneer of civility had existed in our communication. Now it evaporated.

"Nancy will never speak with you," he said. "Greg will not be speaking with you either. The family has made it known to their friends not to communicate with you."

This time, I made no expressions of regret. I did not pursue the issue further. I knew that what I felt, as I heard Rick Cox's words, was a sense of utter relief.

CHAPTER 86

A Trip Downriver

So I was writing a book about this family, and of the four people who were part of it, one was dead, and the other three weren't talking to me.

I had told myself and others, when I embarked on this project, that I would pursue it only if the family would talk with me. One by one, they'd said no. The odd thing was, as I'd been realizing, you could find out a great deal without the assistance of the principals themselves. More, sometimes, than they'd tell you themselves. More, sometimes, than they themselves might understand or acknowledge.

A picture of Nancy Seaman had in fact begun to take shape in my brain some time back, made clearer and more terrible when I first heard the tapes of her telephone conversations from jail—and it was a deeply disturbing one. But where Julie Dumbleton saw her as the personification of evil, I was not inclined to believe that such a thing existed, except in the rarest of circumstances, and I doubted this was one.

Unlike Lisa Ortlieb—a woman I liked, but one whose politics and attitude toward criminal behavior differed markedly from my own—I was not inclined to believe that a fifteen-year-old boy like the one she was currently preparing to prosecute for the undeniably hideous murder of his mother should be tried as an adult. I tended to believe that if you looked deeply enough into the life of virtually anyone who had committed a crime, you would discover experiences that might not excuse the behavior, but could at least explain it.

People who hurt other people had usually been badly hurt themselves, I believed—freely acknowledging that my attitudes on this subject qualified me as a total bleeding heart. And so, as much revulsion as I had come to feel about what Nancy Seaman had done, not only to her husband but to her sons, I searched now for the source of the injury I thought must have occurred in her life, to leave her as disturbed an individual as she now appeared to me.

As one who believes that an understanding of virtually all human behavior begins with an examination of a person's childhood—her parents, where she grew up, and the circumstances in which she was raised—I knew what I needed to do.

So I paid a visit to Lincoln Park, Michigan (downriver, as it's known), where Nancy Seaman—then D'Onofrio—had spent the first eighteen years of her life.

As it happened, this was also the town where Lori Brasier's husband Mike Benczik had grown up—though he'd been a few years behind Nancy at school. Saturday nights at Potter Lake, he told me stories about what it was like in Lincoln Park then—the glory days of the high-paying assembly line jobs for the men who could get them (not that they were likely to live particularly long lives if they did; it was brutal work). Mike had described to me the easy, socially acceptable racism of those downriver communities, intensified by the 1967 Detroit race riots and the mass exodus that had followed, leaving Detroit little more than a bombed-out war zone. The fires that were first lit back in 1967 still burned in the city for years after, every summer, Mike said—an event that came to be known as "Devil's Night." Lincoln Park was close enough that from certain streets you could smell the smoke and, some nights, even see the flames. "The burning," they called it. If there was a single image that had stayed with him from his youth, Mike told me, it was that one.

The trip from Farmington Hills to Lincoln Park took about forty-five minutes, but the place I ended up in was another world from the one where I'd started out my journey that morning. Traveling M39 heading east, the houses got noticeably smaller and more closely spaced, interspersed with heavily industrial areas. I passed alongside a tangle of freeways and bridges and then, in Novi, the stark sight of a water tower painted to resemble a Pistons' basketball—a rare spot of playfulness and color in an increasingly gray landscape.

This was Ford country, as I knew when I hit Dearborn—where the instantly identifiable insignia at the top of Ford World Headquarters loomed as the highest point on the horizon, with clusters of Ford plants (including the one where Jeff Seaman performed his calibration work on the Explorer) and the Henry Ford Museum and shopping center just across the highway, and streets named after Ford vehicles.

Some people in Lincoln Park worked for Chrysler and GM, and a few may even have worked outside the industry, but it was obvious, driving the streets of this town, which of the Big Three was biggest here. Until I visited Lincoln Park, I had never imagined that a town might exist in which virtually every citizen drove a single make of automobile, where the car in nearly every driveway and outside every home (smaller homes, more economical models of car) was a Ford.

Cars mattered a lot to kids of Lincoln Park. Cars put food on the table, and cars got you out of town, at least as far as Woodward Avenue.

"That's what we did, as kids," said Brent Hunt, who had graduated with Nancy D'Onofrio in 1970, from Lincoln Park High, and was now an attorney in nearby Allen Park. Though he didn't know Nancy personally, he said—she was a quiet girl—I had stopped in to meet him, regardless, just to hear his reminiscences of growing up in this town.

"We drove around, got into fights with kids from other schools, turned their car over, drove someplace else. Back in those days, cars were everything."

For the girls in his high school class—even one like Nancy Seaman, a class valedictorian and president of the Future Secretaries of America—college was unlikely, Brent told me. I had asked Jeff Seaman, when we spoke, why his mother never pursued a college scholarship though she was a top student.

"She would have had to write on the application that her father was a school custodian," he said. "She could never have done that."

"The best thing a girl like Nancy could do," Brent added, "was to marry a guy with a good job at Ford and prospects for advancement in the industry."

Which she had done, of course.

Now I passed down the main street: past the Masons and the Moose Lodge, the trophy store, the roller rink, the bridal shop featuring a mannequin in the window that looked to be a size fourteen, the bowling alley and the billiard parlor, the Krispy Kreme and the dialysis center. It was a town that made Lapeer look prosperous, a town from which the move to a place like Pontiac or Flint could be viewed as a step up the ladder.

There had been a time when this town prospered, I knew—back in the heyday of the American automobile industry. Then came the Japanese cars, the outsourcing of automotive production to places outside of Michigan, downsizing, layoffs. Nobody visiting Lincoln Park today would call it a thriving place.

I drove over to 821 Merrill Street, where Nancy D'Onofrio had grown up, and found a "For Sale" sign out front. I pulled up alongside the curb of the house, a brick bungalow, and except for the minor variations of wrought iron fences and trim, nearly identical to every other house on the block.

I studied the sale circular in the plastic case attached to the realtor's sign: "*A Sparkling Diamond Ready for a New Family*," it said. "*Three bedrooms, two and a half baths, all in the space of 1200 square feet, with a two car detached garage off to the die and composite asphalt roofing. $141,900.*" I walked up to the door and knocked.

The young mother who answered—one baby on her hip, a toddler on the floor—was friendly, and invited me in even after she learned I wasn't a prospective buyer. She had been dimly aware that someone convicted of some type of crime had grown up in this house, but she wasn't losing sleep over it. She cheerfully gave me the tour of the place, which took about a minute. Considering the size of the bedrooms, it was a good thing the children were as small as they were.

I asked her where she and her family were planning to move when they sold the house. She laughed. "Everybody's got their house on the market here," she said. "That doesn't mean anyone's buying."

A Dozen Krispy Kreme Donuts

A dozen years back, Eugene D'Onofrio had sold the house on Merrill Avenue where he and his wife had raised their children, Nancy and John. The house where he lived now—a neat, well-maintained property in a neighborhood of similarly tidy homes—sat on a corner lot in the town of Woodhaven, fifteen minutes from Lincoln Park and no more than a mile from the King's Crossing development where the condo was, whose purchase had been made possible by Eugene D'Onofrio's loan of $10,000 to his daughter.

When I heard about the loan, I was surprised that a woman like Nancy Seaman—living in Farmington Hills, holding down a reasonably well-paying job, and married, however unhappily, to a man with sizable assets—would have borrowed a sum of money like that from her elderly father, a retired school custodian.

The extremely modest home in which Nancy had grown up, on Merrill Street in Lincoln Park, gave little indication that Eugene D'Onofrio possessed a great deal in the way of assets. But now, pulling up in front of the place he and his wife, Lenore, had purchased when he retired a dozen or so years back, I was surprised. This wasn't a gated community or anything close, but it was a nice-looking neighborhood.

One added feature of Eugene D'Onofrio's house was a fine redwood deck out in back, with bird feeders and garden furniture. A sign next to the front door announced that the house was protected from theft by a professional alarm system.

Lori Brasier's friend Lillian—one of the weekend gang from Potter Lake—had a theory about how to approach Eugene D'Onofrio, and because she was herself a Detroit-area native and a daughter of working-class parents of a similar age to Eugene, I took her advice. "Bring a dozen Krispy Kreme donuts," she told me.

A dozen? Eugene D'Onofrio was a small man, living alone.

"They have to be Krispy Kreme," Lori added. "There's a store in Lincoln Park that has the complete range of choices." So now, as I headed up the walk to Eugene D'Onofrio's door, it was with a large box in my hands. The full assortment.

I rang the bell and waited. From inside the house, no sign of life, and no way to know if anyone was home, since the garage door was closed. No sound of television. No lights on, but it was daytime, after all. The grass had recently been mowed. On the ground, not one leaf or stick.

I was just about to leave when I heard footsteps inside the house. Then, through the glass, I saw the small, thin, anxious face of an old and frightened-looking man, just about my height, wiry as a bantam.

He studied me, looked down at the box of doughnuts, then back into my eyes. I tried to imagine how it must have seemed to him, to observe an unfamiliar woman (just the age of his own daughter) standing there in her summer dress, with a notebook. Maybe he sized up my car too—as people tended to in these parts. If he had—particularly now, with the Pontiac's large, recently acquired dent on the driver's side door facing his entryway—he might have thought I was looking for money or selling magazine subscriptions.

He opened the door just a crack. "What do you want?"

I told him my name, said I was writing a book. I hoped he would let me in, I said. I wanted to talk with him.

"I know about you people," he told me. "I don't have nothing to say to you."

"I know you've gone through a terrible time," I said. "This must be so hard for you. A lot has been said about your daughter. Maybe you'd want people to hear your side."

"Nobody listened at the trial. Every time I tried to tell them what was what, they cut me off. They never let me tell how it was."

"I would," I told him. "I've come to listen."

This was true. I would do that. But I also knew that just as Lisa Ortlieb had led Eugene D'Onofrio into dangerous territory by doing nothing more than asking him to tell what happened—letting him open up, only to do further damage to his daughter's case—so might I. I held no ill will toward this heartbroken old man, but I strongly suspected that if I were thinking as a daughter, not as a writer, I'd tell him to keep his door shut to a person like me.

"That lawyer woman. Double talking. Twists your words," he said, spitting his sentences out. "She kept cutting me off. And that jury. All they cared about was getting home to finish their Christmas shopping."

"So tell me," I said. "I'd listen."

"My daughter said not to talk to nobody."

"You've been through a lot," I said. "Nobody seemed to remember, but I know you'd just lost your wife when all this happened."

A look came over him then. There it was. His wife of fifty-five years was gone. What was a man to do?

"I'm so sorry," I told him.

He opened the door. I handed him the box of doughnuts. No small talk. We made our way to the living room.

It was a modest house, but immaculately kept, not that much was likely to disrupt the order here. Eugene D'Onofrio lived alone now and, apart from his sister, had few visitors. There was a television set and a glass case with figurines and special china inside—the sort of thing a woman would have collected over the years. On the mantel, family photographs (Nancy in a red Christmas sweater), images of the American West. A cowboy. A sunset. A woodworking magazine. A tray table.

"My wife and I got together in '48," he said. He'd been stationed in California, but after the war, he'd come home, and they got together. They were married fifty-five years, he told me.

"We got along real good. She was a strong-minded woman, all right. But we worked it out. I minded my own business. We raised two nice kids. Thirty-two years, I worked in an electronics factory. Then they up and moved the operation to Puerto Rico, and I went to work for the schools as a custodian. I'd repair telephones, clocks, lights. Any little thing that had to be done. It was a good enough life. I never thought something like this would happen."

He was sitting in a La-Z-Boy as we talked. His TV chair, from the looks of it. I sat on the couch, embroidered doilies on the arms. Between us were the doughnuts, but they went untouched.

"Nancy was always a good girl. Got along with everyone. Used to ride alongside me in the truck when I went on errands."

I asked him about boyfriends in high school. She'd been such a pretty girl, I said, with that beautiful long hair.

"My daughter only had one boyfriend ever, before him," said Eugene, referring to Bob, whose name he evidently preferred not to mention. "But my wife chased the first one away. Then came this joker. I was never too enthused about him, but what are you going to do?"

Jeff Seaman had told me, that time we'd met, that Bob Seaman always got along well with Lenore D'Onofrio, but Eugene told another story.

"My wife never liked him," he said.

Eugene focused on the recent years then. There was a time, he told me, when Bob Seaman had hired him to oversee a roofing job over at the Waterwheel Building. Eugene was supposed to monitor the workers Bob had hired—to make sure they weren't screwing him.

"One time when I was up on the roof and the contractors had left," he said, "he just started yelling at me. I didn't do this. I didn't do that. He had booze in his hand. The man was intoxicated."

He still couldn't say Bob Seaman's name, I noticed. As he spoke, he seemed barely to look at me. It was as if he were speaking to himself.

"I looked around, and behind me there was a long-handled shovel. I may not be a young man, but I was ready for him. I say to myself, 'If he comes after me, I'm going to let him have it.' I can take care of myself."

I remembered Julie Dumbleton telling me that for years, the Shelby and the Boss had been stored in Eugene and Lenore D'Onofrio's garage, and knowing how Bob felt about those cars, it seemed unlikely he'd leave them with anyone he didn't like and trust. But whatever good feeling might have existed in the past between the two families, recent events now left room for only one picture of Bob in Eugene D'Onofrio's eyes, and the negative view extended to Jeff.

"Jeff was always a bad apple. Thought he knew everything. Didn't even have the courtesy to call and tell me when the police arrested my daughter."

Although there was no question in his mind now that Bob had abused Nancy, he didn't appear to possess any firsthand memories to confirm that. His daughter had told him so, after her arrest, and that was good enough for him.

One thing he did know, firsthand, was that Bob Seaman had been in money trouble, he told me. "In debt up to his ass."

His evidence spoke to the thinking of a man of his generation, a man who still remembered the Depression—and had suffered long and hard back in those days. To Eugene D'Onofrio, a hefty mortgage was evidence of financial instability, irresponsibility even. A sign of failure. The same kind of debt that in the state of California served as an indication of big-thinking prosperity and vision, here in Woodhaven, to a man like Eugene, signified reckless foolishness.

"That house they lived in wasn't paid for, you know," he told me now, by way of evidence. (This would be the $60,000 mortgage on the house on Briarwood Court.) "He owed money on the Upper Deck too."

This was the reason, Eugene told me, why he'd given Nancy the $10,000 for the condo down payment. His daughter had explained it all to him: Bob was broke. Oh sure, he had bought her a Lincoln Town Car, but who ended up driving it? He did.

"It was a Ford product," he added.

"You know another thing?" he told me. "After my wife died, this husband of hers, my son-in-law, he tells my daughter he's glad my wife was dead." This news, too, had come from Nancy.

"He tried to burn the house down twice," Eugene told me. (This would be the time Bob left a pot on the stove to boil an egg, and forgot about it. The second incident, too, was an attempt at basic meal preparation gone awry.)

"And that son of his," he said, with disgust. (This was Jeff he was talking about again.) "You know he tried to break into my house?"

I hadn't heard about this, I told him.

"You know that sign I got on the front of my house?" he said.

"Welcome?"

Not that one, he told me. The one announcing the security system. He got that thing set up after Jeff broke in one time and tried to take a bunch of things out of his basement.

"What things?" I asked.

"Boxes of her clothes that I've been storing for her for when she gets out. He came and tried to take them. Messed everything up, but

I guess he got scared and ran off. Now I'm all set up with security if he tries to break in again."

One thing people didn't understand, he said, was that Nancy was going to bring the body to the police, if only they hadn't arrested her like they did. That was her plan, she'd told Eugene. That afternoon they came and got her, she'd been planning to drive over to his house in Woodhaven, pick him up, and drive straight over to the police station. She just wanted to have her father at her side when she did it, and who could blame a girl for feeling that way?

Talking with Eugene D'Onofrio this way, I felt a terrible wave of sadness come over me. A substantial portion of what he reported to me—the idea of his son-in-law's abuse of his daughter, the notion that Bob Seaman had been a spendthrift who'd gone through all his money, the picture of Bob trying to burn down his house and having an affair with Julie Dumbleton, his daughter's reported plan of taking him with her to bring the body to the Woodhaven Police Department—had come to Eugene entirely through his daughter. Whatever the truth might be, Nancy's portrayal of what had happened remained real to him. To question what she had told him, he would have to consider a story far darker than the one she had conveyed to him.

I was again reminded of that, as Eugene recounted to me what his daughter had told him her husband said to her as he came at her in the garage with the knife.

"He told her that once he finished with her, he was coming over to my house. He said he was going to kill me and take everything I owned."

The notion that Bob Seaman—in the aftermath of murdering his wife—would drive an hour west to Woodhaven for the purpose of stealing a TV set and Mr. Coffee may have been far-fetched, but at least one person was buying it: Eugene D'Onofrio. And it made him plenty mad, too.

"I says, let him try and come after me. He could come to my house, but one thing I'm telling you, he wouldn't come out of it. I have my ways of taking care of a guy like him."

Jeff too. "I wanted to slug him," Eugene added, suggesting (as he did with surprising frequency) physical violence as the remedy for maddening behavior on the part of someone in your life. Perhaps it was a familial trait. "That was Jeff for you," he went on. "Getting his father all riled up like that, about the condo. Then what does he do? Talks to the prosecution. I'm telling you, they put the wrong person in jail on that one. If I was that Becka, I'd be plenty worried right about now. They say if a person's father abused them, they're going to abuse somebody someday too. She's sitting in the hot seat right about now, married to that one."

There was one good thing, anyway, Eugene reflected. His wife, Lenore, hadn't lived to see any of this. If she had, it would have killed her for sure.

He spoke now of that December back in 2003. His wife had been sick, so he'd taken her to the doctor. She'd recently been diagnosed with diabetes, and now the doctor was telling them she needed to be admitted to the hospital, on the double.

The doctor had wanted her to ride over in an ambulance, but Lenore said no. She wanted her husband to drive her. Well, OK, said Eugene. So they set out for Henry Ford Medical Center. An hour's drive, give or take.

"Partway there," he said, "she falls over in the front seat. She's got her head on my lap, and she's not saying nothing, but all I can think is I better keep on driving, so I do."

He had driven the rest of the way with his wife lying in his lap like that. A half hour maybe? When he pulled up at the hospital—the emergency entrance—he called out for someone to come help him, and a couple of attendants had come out with a stretcher. That's when he knew it was bad. The looks on their faces.

They wheeled her in, took her away, while Eugene waited. Finally someone came out. "'I'm sorry to have to tell you this,' the doctor said, 'but your wife died on the way to the hospital.' They couldn't get her heart started back up."

Just telling the story now, Eugene D'Onofrio got very quiet and still. "That whole time I was driving," he said, "she was already dead. She was dead in the car."

It was an awful story, all right. If Eugene D'Onofrio's nights were haunted now by the thought of how it might have been if only his wife had ridden in that ambulance, he didn't share that with me, and I didn't pursue it. There was plenty more, these days, to haunt the days and nights of Eugene D'Onofrio.

"That was when everything started to go wrong," Eugene reflected. The day his wife died.

Now Nancy was off in that place up north, and all he cared about was seeing her get parole. "She can come home and live here with me," he said. "I need her home with me."

Meanwhile, they talked on the phone once a week or so. (Tonight he was due to get a call, in fact. She would not be happy when she heard he'd entertained a visitor—me.)

Nancy didn't want him to come see her, he told me. So he hadn't actually been up to that place, the prison those bums had her in. He hadn't actually seen her in many months now. But she sent him letters. He had one in his pocket now. He didn't care to show me.

I knew already that he had no more use for Jeff in his life, but now I asked about Greg. It was a source of comfort for him, probably, to see his grandson, I suggested. I asked if he came by a lot to visit.

"Not so much," he said. "He's real busy."

CHAPTER 88

In AA Circles, They Have a Name for It

M y visit with Eugene D'Onofrio had left me with an uneasy feeling, but once again no clear, hard answers to the question I'd been living with for months now: How did Nancy Seaman come to kill her husband? It was surprising enough that this old man had opened his door to me—a total stranger with nothing to offer but a dozen Krispy Kremes and the possibility (not that he fully recognized this) that what he said would only reinforce for the world the picture of Nancy as an unbalanced and dangerous woman and a liar.

No doubt it was naive to have supposed that nearly four decades since he'd last lived under the same roof with his daughter, Eugene D'Onofrio could tell me things about how she grew up and what their family was like that would explain her murderous act that Mother's Day weekend—or all the strange and paranoid behavior leading up to it. And of course, he hadn't done that.

Maybe he knew a dark secret that would have explained everything. If he'd known the answers, he wouldn't have told them to me. But very possibly, he no longer knew them himself, if he ever did.

So I was left—as had been true so often that summer (at the wheel of my Pontiac, generally, on some stretch of Michigan freeway)—to speculate. Everything I believed about human behavior suggested that when an individual behaves in pathological ways, as an adult, the origin of that behavior is likely to be found in his or her childhood. But whatever it was that may or may not have taken place in the D'Onofrio household, decades earlier, I could only guess at it.

As I had before my visit to Woodhaven, but more strongly now, I considered the possibility that the D'Onofrios had been a household in which some kind of violence existed. I wished I could have talked with or even heard more about Nancy's mother, whose death had preceded the murder by just over four months.

I thought about what Jeff and others had told me: that his maternal grandmother was the powerhouse of the family, a strong and forceful woman whose death had devastated her husband and daughter.

"If my grandmother hadn't died, none of this would've happened," Jeff had told me that night at Chevy's before he stopped talking to me. "It was her dying that made my mom fall apart."

Picturing Jeff—a young man so like his father that his mother seemed to have transferred her hatred of her husband onto the son— I thought now about Bob, and who it was who had shaped his outlook and character. What experiences in life had brought him to that night (or morning) in the garage, with a hatchet in Nancy's hand? If part of who Nancy had become might be explained by whatever had gone on in that tiny brick house on Merrill Street in Lincoln Park, maybe two people one state over, in Missouri, might offer me some glimmer of understanding into the other player in that terrible and deadly drama: Bob.

It was high summer now. The Dream Cruise was over. The tomatoes were coming in, corn nearing shoulder height. Over in Lapeer, men had even started talking about duck hunting season. Softball season was winding down, and parents were taking kids back-to-school shopping. The natural order of the season was one of completion and new beginnings, but as for me, I felt unsettled.

When I first came to Michigan, it had been with the goal of understanding how a seemingly successful, high-functioning family like the Seamans could self-destruct as they had. Even phrasing it that way, I could hear the voice of Julie Dumbleton in my head, pointing out that it wasn't her beloved friend Bob Seaman who'd brought about any destruction, only Nancy. But to me, the story was more complicated: Bob had chosen to remain in that deeply troubled marriage, rather than get out. What did that say about him?

As one acquainted with the dynamics of a different kind of troubled family—the alcoholic kind—I knew that when one person in a
family is engaged in dysfunctional behavior, everyone living with that
person is similarly affected, and anyone who does not extricate himself becomes part of the system. Regardless of Bob Seaman's culpabil-
ity or innocence where domestic violence was concerned, the term
enabler came to mind when considering his relationship with Nancy.
Here was a man who would never have run a car without making sure
the fluid levels were where they should be and the belts in good order,
yet on the floor of that three-car garage of his, with its neat black-and-
white tile, he had let the garbage pile up (not only figuratively, but literally) around the same vehicles he so meticulously restored. He once
drove a thousand miles to pick up a Ford F150 truck in Tennessee, but
never went to a marriage counselor.

When I first came to Michigan, my mind was open to the possibility that Bob Seaman had abused Nancy Seaman and threatened her
life, to the point where she had picked up that hatchet. Back in December, when I met Greg Seaman at the trial, I had seen him as a sensitive, heartbroken young man standing lovingly by the side of his
mother. Nine months later, a far darker picture had formed, of a
young man whose very existence, perhaps, depended on the belief that
his mother was a blameless victim and his father (assisted by the
Dumbletons) responsible for everything that had ever gone wrong in
his mother's life.

In the name of keeping that picture intact, he had reconfigured the
entire universe, demonizing his brother in the process. As the jailhouse
tapes revealed, he had not only been lied to; he had also lied himself.
And still, despite the ugliness of his behavior (to his father, his brother,
Jake Dumbleton), Greg Seaman now looked to me like a second victim of Nancy Seaman—the only difference being that his father was
dead, where Greg still walked the earth.

I had learned some things over the course of my time in Michigan:
I no longer believed that Bob Seaman had come after Nancy with a
knife that night. (And I believed it was the night of Mother's Day that
Nancy had killed him and not, as she claimed, the morning after, before school.) I did not believe that Bob Seaman had been having an
affair with Julie Dumbleton or that there had been anything inappropriate in his attitude and behavior toward the softball players he

coached or toward Jenna Dumbleton. I did not believe that Nancy Seaman ever intended to turn herself in to the police voluntarily, as she claimed. And despite her purchase of the condo and her claim that she was ready to give up on her marriage, I believed this was a woman who—regardless of her anger toward him—could never have let go of her husband, a woman who believed that without Bob Seaman around as the object of her rage and the reason for every disappointment she experienced, she would, as she put it, "cease to exist."

But her bitterness toward her husband had been real. The intensity of rage required of a person to take a hatchet to another human being's skull was something I had never experienced. To some involved with the case, the only way to make sense of Nancy Seaman's actions had been to assume that Bob Seaman must have been some kind of monster, to bring such violence on himself. But if that weren't the answer, one was left to ask: what was? Nancy Seaman's rage and aggression had to come from someplace. After all this time, I still didn't understand: What had produced it?

CHAPTER 89

The Family You Wish Were Yours

A troubling phenomenon occurs when an individual expresses so much anger toward another: we tend to assume that the object of the anger must have in some way inspired it. Rage doesn't breed in a vacuum, surely. A loving, openhearted, reasonable husband does not get murdered by his wife. So what had Bob Seaman done that was so bad? What crime had he committed, so terrible as to drive his wife to murder?

It wasn't fair to blame the victim for the crime perpetrated against him, yet (like so many citizens of Oakland County, when the news had broken of his murder) I had that impulse where Bob Seaman was concerned. It had been impossible not to entertain the thought that some dark, secret sickness in him might have driven his wife over the edge.

By this point, I had assembled a collection of images of Bob—many of them revealing, some surprising: he listened to Rush Limbaugh, but went to bat at Borg Warner in the defense of a black colleague he believed to have been unfairly treated. He kicked his son out of the house when they'd argued. But he also drove all over the state of

Michigan looking for parts for that son's car. He ran a batting cage, and traveled to India for Hyundai.

Still trying to make sense of the picture, I listed what stood out for me about Bob Seaman: he was a highly accomplished man, a man who had a patent on a five-speed manual transmission and oversaw a division of a major engineering corporation.

But he was also something of a cowboy. He had taken up guitar at age fifty. As a high school boy, he'd been a trampoline champion. As a man, he loved off-road truck driving. He had learned to speak a little Korean and had sampled monkey brains in India, but he also loved hanging out in the Dumbletons' family room, eating pizza with the kids and watching movies with Mustangs in them.

He was a man who, when trying to get across to his ballplayers the concept of whole-body follow-through, had chosen to demonstrate it by going directly from a fast pitch into a somersault. He made a lot of money on occasion, but seemed not all that prudent in how he'd managed it—invested in a 49 percent partnership with a man he didn't like or respect much (and one who, for all appearances, had not held him in particularly high regard). He had spent hundreds of hours rebuilding Mustangs with his sons, but he had been willing to watch his marriage fall into extreme disrepair and do virtually nothing about it besides move to the basement and keep out of his wife's way as much as possible. (This was perhaps not so rare or surprising in the world of middle-class dysfunctional marriages.)

He had told Julie Dumbleton, when she asked him why he'd married Nancy, that there were three things about her that filled the bill: she was smart, single, and short (shorter than him). Not a whole lot to build a marriage on. If there had been more to it at one point, that time appeared to be long gone. And yet he'd stayed on. In Nancy's case, I could see the marriage having provided a sense of identity she had been unprepared to forfeit. They were "a handsome couple." People admired the Seamans. So what if things were rotten inside? They looked good.

It came to me, as the summer drew to a close, that in spite of all the data I'd assembled, a crucial piece of information about Bob Seaman eluded me. Why did he stay?

Up until now, I had focused my attention primarily on how things had been for Bob and Nancy during the years they'd spent together.

But it occurred to me now that to find my answer—if there was one—I would have to look farther back, to the place where Bob Seaman had been raised and the people who'd raised him.

The common wisdom, in understanding the origins of a murder, is to examine the pathology of the murderer, of course—in this case, Nancy Seaman. Maybe—as I now believed—she was a borderline personality, an out-of-control woman, a woman who had struggled up from the working classes to an affluent middle-class lifestyle and was then profoundly threatened by the dissolution and separation from the attachment that had made it possible.

But if that were so, what did it say about Bob Seaman, that he had remained married to her for thirty-two years? As I had done in my pursuit of answers about Nancy Seaman, I looked again to the previous generation in hope of finding a few answers.

Ward and Helen Seaman were eighty-nine and eighty-seven years old now. I knew from their son Dennis that they lived in a small apartment in Ballwin, Missouri, on the outskirts of St. Louis, where they'd raised their four children. Helen suffered from Alzheimer's (to the point where her family remained unclear as to whether or not she'd even grasped that Bob was dead), but Ward was going strong, still active at church and weekly bowling, and serving in the Loyal Order of the Masons.

I asked Dennis to put the question to his father: would he and his wife be willing to meet me? I said I'd make the trip at a time when Dennis and his sister, Margie, were out there with them, so they might feel more comfortable about such a visit.

The word came back: OK. I booked my trip then—with the plan of flying into St. Louis, renting a car, spending a few hours with Ward and Helen Seaman, and flying back to Detroit that same afternoon. I figured that given their ages and what they'd gone through, it wouldn't be fair to strain them with a longer visit.

It was just after eight-thirty in the morning when I pulled up to the modest apartment complex where the elder Seamans made their home. Dennis greeted me at the door, then led me in to the living room.

Ward Seaman was not a particularly tall man, yet he gave the impression of being one, probably in part because even now, nearing the close of his ninth decade of life, he stood surprisingly straight, and his gait, like his gaze, was so steady. He extended his hand to shake mine, and I felt the absence of that pointer finger, lost so long ago in the factory accident, like its mate on his other hand. This was the accident about which he had stayed home for exactly one day before returning to work. He had given the $2,000 settlement from the company that had employed him to one of his sisters, for cancer treatment for a child who'd later died.

The four of us (Dennis, Margie, Ward, and I) shared a cup of midwestern-style coffee then—a little weaker than I tend to drink it. I gathered that Helen was in the bedroom, and sometimes we'd hear her cry out softly or sigh, but otherwise she was quiet. All around us were photographs—of Ward and Helen with their children in their younger days. (She a pretty woman, in her no-nonsense dress; he looked, as his wife and now his daughter liked to say, like Tyrone Power.) On the sideboard, a lineup of photographs of their sisters and brothers and their spouses. Ward ran through the names: Thelma, Floretta, Iva, Ralph . . . several of them dead now, though a surprising number were still living, into their eighties. This appeared to be a family that, under normal circumstances, had been blessed with the gift of longevity.

Sitting on the easy chair across from Ward Seaman as I was now, here in Missouri—with the family pictures all around, the glass case with Helen's collection of Hummel figurines, and a plaque from the Masons on display—I felt no impulse to ask about the murder of Ward's oldest son. What could possibly be learned by asking the question, "How did you feel when you heard your son's wife murdered him?"

We talked about the farm where Ward grew up, in Mattoon, Illinois: 180 acres on which his father had grown winter wheat, except when the chinch bugs came and they had to drive a horse up and down the rows, pulling a log and pouring out creosote, to kill them. When the bugs got real bad, he told me, you switched to another crop: hay maybe, or clover.

They kept horses too, and cattle. Made butter. Made cheese. His father, though he didn't have much education, had been a "scientific farmer," rare for those times. He used to take soil samples from the farm all the way to Champaign-Urbana to get tested. He was a curious person. Always ready to learn something new, as Ward had been himself, and later, Bob.

When Ward's parents were young (Dust Bowl days), they'd headed to California one time, for a better life. His dad worked as a projectionist at a movie theater. His mother played the piano for the silent movies. They'd come home after a while (no gold in Califor-ni-ay after all), but as a boy he could remember lying in bed, hearing his mother play that old movie music, imagining the pictures that might have gone with it. Bad guys chasing the good ones. Galloping horses. Beautiful women.

Not that he had a lot of time for it, but as a boy he loved playing baseball.

"Our backstop was willow trees," he said. "Sometimes you had to get a shovel and clear the manure off the field before you could play. Share a glove. But I could run all right. It was a mile and a half to school in those days. I liked to race there with my pals. Running backwards, just for a good time, and to build up my strength."

Those were Depression years—turnips for dinner, cardboard in their shoes. Times got so tough his dad had to take a job in town, doing carpentry work, and his brother got a job with the Civilian Conservation Corps for $18 a month and room and board. (That's when FDR had made Democrats of them all. And Ward still was one.) With two crops in the ground and two head of stock per acre, a harrow to run, and a tractor in need of constant tinkering to make it go, they still had to let go of the hired hand, so Ward left school to take care of the farm. He was nine.

"Now they'd call it child abuse," he told me, about those days. "Back then, my dad just bragged on what a good job I did, and I felt proud."

He'd always been a learning type of person, and he missed school. Sometimes he'd try to drop in for a few weeks, pick up a little know-how, but there wasn't much in the way of spare time. He carried around a dictionary called a Jumbo, to learn words, and worked on math problems he made up.

Helen was the little sister of his friend, a few farms over from theirs, "a spunky gal." When he'd write her a love letter, he'd wish he'd stayed in school longer so he could spell better, but she forgave his ignorance. Sixty-nine years ago, when he was nineteen and she was seventeen— or close enough, anyway—they'd tied the knot on a Fourth of July— she in a wedding dress bought for $11, which represented the better part of her summer's earnings. They'd set the date for Fourth of July because that gave them the day off for the honeymoon night before getting back to the haying.

Early on during my visit, Dennis had to take off for an errand, and Margie got occupied taking care of her mother, but Ward went on with his story. I might have thought, listening to him, that it didn't have a lot to do with what I'd come all the way from Detroit (all the way from California, really) to hear about. I might have looked at my watch and noted that in just three hours I was due to get on a plane. Still, when Ward offered me a second cup of coffee, I said thanks, and we carried on.

He and Helen lived in a tourist court for a while there, he told me. Helen got a job peeling potatoes. There was no heater, and when a rat skittered across the floor, she just threw her knife at it and carried on. That was the kind of life you lived, he said.

They'd worked his uncle's farm a while—Helen too, until the baby came. That would be Margie, in 1938. A bad dry spell then, and still he worked those clods, waiting for rain, only it didn't come. They lost the crop.

"That's when I said it: 'I'm not farming no more.'"

The family up and moved to St. Louis then. Got a little shacky place so cold there was snow on the blanket when they woke up in the morning, but they papered it inside for insulation, and Ward fixed it up till it was pretty.

He got two jobs, at Century Electric and at L and M appliance, repairing motors: went to work at four-thirty in the morning, came home at midnight, and in between, he studied those service manuals, to learn all he could. When people threw out a motor, thinking it was done for, he'd take that thing apart and make it go, then sell it. This was how a person made ends meet in those days.

Or more than that. Ward had fixed up that first little place they had and sold it for a profit. Did the same a second time—"wheeling and dealing." By the time Bob came along, nine years after Margie, the Seaman family was finally getting someplace.

"We was a couple of hicks, no doubt about it," Ward said. "But we could still put on our good duds on a Saturday night and make time for a barn dance."

The story continued to unfold. A job at the Buster Brown Shoe Company. Then a job (these were war years now) at a munitions factory. That was where Ward's aptitude for machinery really came in handy. He loved that machine shop. He had a knack.

"I'd get loaned out to help the engineers," he said—Ward, with his elementary school education, with a dictionary in his pocket for self-improvement, making the parts that made the ammunition, making the dies.

It was in the machine shop—working too fast, trying to get too much done, and not using the safety—that he'd cut off those two fingers, the pointer on each hand. After it happened, with his hands in his armpits to stop the bleeding, he'd stepped out into the parking lot so he could cuss freely.

Ward and Helen had four kids by now: Margie and Bob, Dave and Dennis. There wasn't much in the way of spare time, but he made sure to be around those children enough that they knew who their father was. He didn't know all that much about sports, on account of having had to work the farm when he was baseball-playing age, but he took the family to Cardinals games at Sportsman's Park, where they'd get stuff like a pen in the shape of a baseball bat and cheer for Stan the Man. That would be Musial.

The fact that he'd never played the game didn't stop him from taking charge of the Valley Park boys' basketball team, one of the worst there was. But he knew how to keep those boys under control. When they gave awards that year, his team took first place in good behavior, if not athletic talent.

Ward's other favorite pastime with his kids was making slot cars. "You'd buy the kit, but the first thing we'd do was take 'em apart and modify 'em," he told me.

"Change around the magnets, sand down the metal to cut down on friction. Put different tires on."

Nights after work, Ward brought his boys to the slot car races. They were big winners. And later—not a whole lot later, actually—they moved on from those to real cars. Ward had Bob working on his first V-8 engine before he was thirteen. A Nash.

Telling me about those days, Ward shifted into the language of an engineer. He was using his hands now—all six fingers and two thumbs—to demonstrate the concept of a wrist pin inside a mold, the hollow skirt of a piston, a strut. I didn't have a clue what he was talking about. For Ward, though (and no doubt for his sons, if not his daughter), the inside of an engine was as familiar as the street where they lived.

He was "tickled to death," he said, when Bob got accepted to University of Missouri-Rolla, in the engineering program (and "doing extry good" once he was there), and again after he graduated, when he got hired by Ford. All his life, Ward had been an engineer without a degree. Now his son had one, and from the looks of things, he was going someplace big. Then he married Nancy, and if anyone was ambitious, it was that girl.

"She didn't go to college," he said, "but the way she talked about that job of hers, she would be owning the Ford Motor Company before you knew it."

When Bob and Nancy visited in Ballwin, Ward and his wife noted the way Nancy had chosen to retreat to an upstairs bedroom with Jeff and Greg, away from the rest of the family, including the many cousins right around Jeff and Greg's own age. But neither Ward nor Helen was inclined to judge. When a person married into this family, that was it. You accepted them.

Bob never complained about his wife or his marriage. He just stayed away from Ballwin, more and more, as the years passed, and the family's visits to Farmington Hills were even more infrequent. Once, Margie said, when they'd flown in to see Bob and the family, it was only after they'd spent a few hours in the kitchen visiting with Bob that they discovered Nancy had been home the whole time, upstairs in the master bedroom. Another time, she'd lost her temper at Bob over his failure to purchase a certain kind of coffee cake for their visit.

We talked this way for a few hours, and though I had worried before coming to Ballwin that my visit might be hard on Ward Seaman, he showed no sign of wearing out. He had a mind and a memory as sharp as the fan blade on a crank shaft.

It was getting on one o'clock, and my flight, an hour's drive away, was set for three-thirty. Ward was reminiscing about a visit Bob had made, just a couple of years ago, when he'd traveled back to Mattoon with his folks to the old farm, where his Aunts Thelma and Iva and Floretta still lived. They still had the land there, though it was leased to a farmer now. With all that newfangled farm equipment. No more horse-drawn harrow, that's for sure.

"I wish I could see that place," I said to him, taking a sip of my third cup of coffee.

"Well, we could up and go," he said. It was a four-hour drive from Ballwin, Missouri, to Matoon, Illinois. If we were going to get there before dark, we'd best not dillydally.

Half an hour later, the four of us were climbing into my subcompact car: Margie, Ward, and I, and Helen—who had emerged from the bedroom partway through the morning to sit beside her husband on the couch, her hand in his. She didn't say a lot, though now and then she nodded or smiled. I had known people with Alzheimer's who turned bitter and angry, and that was surely understandable, but it wasn't Helen Seaman's way. She had a sweetness about her, as she contributed her occasional observations. At one point in the morning, she described a skit she used to perform with her Eastern Star group—the women's side of the Masonic lodge. "I was the fifth point in the star," she told me, beginning to recite one of her lines.

We headed north on the highway then, beyond St. Louis, toward Illinois, then eastward toward Mattoon. As we drove, Helen reminisced a bit herself, about her people back in Indiana. More than once, the mention of a city or state or geographical feature would touch off a song, and Helen would begin to sing it. "Meet Me in St. Louis," of course. Helen would launch into some fragment, "I'm going back to Kansas City."

"What song does this remind you of?" I asked Helen as we crossed the Mississippi River (for the first time ever, in my case). Not missing a beat, she started in on "Ol' Man River." Now and then she looked over at me.

"I don't know who you are," she said sweetly, "but I like you."

She didn't sing about the corn being as high as an elephant's eye, but it was, in Illinois. Not as high, however, as the cross that had been erected in the middle of a field on the outside of town, as we reached Mattoon, round about supper time. (Supper time, Mattoon time, anyway: five o'clock.)

The terrain here was astonishingly flat and largely treeless, though there was no shortage of grain growing here; off in the distance, in some of the fields, there was the unexpected sight of oil derricks. (There were some on Ward Seaman's land, in fact—not that they'd produced any sizable gusher. But it was not unusual for farmers in these parts to lease oil rights to their land.)

We passed Spanky's Sports Bar and a couple of feed stores, a tractor dealership and another tractor dealership. We passed a couple of tanning parlors and an electrolysis establishment and a pool hall, which looked to be one of the few places in town a person might go for a good time after five in Mattoon. The Cornerstone Christian Bookstore had a sign out front: Sizzling Summer Sale. Bly's Donuts was advertising fried pies.

Then we were at Aunt Thelma's—home to Helen's younger sister. Just a year back, she'd lost her beloved husband, Ralph, and only a few weeks before, her son Michael had died of diabetes. He'd been preceded by his brother Ralphie, who'd headed out to Hawaii to perform in musical shows and died young. I studied his photograph on the wall now: an eight-by-ten glossy of a man handsome enough to be a soap opera star.

Margie walked me through the house, showing me the photographs of each of Helen's siblings alongside his or her spouse, displayed on the mantel: Ralph and Thelma, Margie and Joe, George and Mary, Iva and Kimmery, Lucille and Jimmy, Glenn and Dorothy, and Ward and Helen, naturally. Of all the Shriver spouses, she told me, only Ward was still alive.

This family had not escaped tragedy, either. Jimmy had died young, on the steps of a hospital. There was a child who'd been raped and murdered and one horribly disfigured in a fire, and another child was dead of leukemia (the one whose hospital bills—or part of them— had been paid for with the settlement for the loss of Ward's two fingers). There'd been a suicide (Ward's brother) and money problems, of course. A bad apple of a husband. A daughter who turned out a little crazy. Still, Ward had told me that morning what good fortune he had known in life. What a lucky family theirs had been.

We made an early night of it, on account of the long drive we'd taken. I checked into the Budget Motel on the outskirts of town—a low, drab line of rooms with a swimming pool out back that looked as if it hadn't held water in years. The next morning, rising early for coffee at Bly's Donuts before heading back over to Thelma's, I flipped through that day's *Mattoon Gazette*. I was surprised to see the name of my motel prominently featured in a front page story: a year or so back, there'd been a big fire at the Budget Motel, touched off by the activities of a couple of occupants who'd been running a crystal meth lab there. One of them was now in jail. The other would be, if he ever got out of the burn center. That had been the other thing people did after hours in Mattoon, I guessed. Besides playing billiards.

Over at Thelma's, it was a different story. There was breakfast of course, and more coffee. Then we took our places around the organ in the living room (as the family always liked to do, Margie explained, when they got together this way, and as Thelma did on a daily basis, even when alone). We all sang a hymn.

We visited Aunt Iva next—Helen's older sister, a tiny woman, perfectly dressed, with her hair in a tidy net. She kept the TV on all the time, she said, because she didn't know how to work that goshdarned remote control. She took me down to the basement to show me her canning kitchen, full of enough provisions that a family of four could probably live off the contents for the better part of a year.

We moved on then to Aunt Floretta's, where we visited some more and talked about the old times. After that it was time to head back to Ballwin, with a stop at McDonald's somewhere between Illinois and Missouri, where I had to excuse myself for a few minutes to make a call on my cell phone, explaining my late return to Detroit to my friends at Potter Lake. When I came back to our table, Helen looked up at me sweetly as usual and said, "I was worried about you, dear. I didn't want to lose you."

On the plane back to Michigan, I started to cry a little, thinking about Helen Seaman and how she had stood in the hallway of the couple's little apartment in Ballwin to say good-bye to me, holding on to a piece of her Eastern Star costume. I thought about how Ward had spoken of Lynn, the former wife of Dennis, from whom he'd been divorced for going on twenty years, and Linda, former wife of Dave, same story.

"They're still our family," he said, though the divorce between Linda and Dave, when it happened, had been an awful one, and in the end, it had been Ward and Helen themselves, though they were in their sixties at this point, who'd stepped in to raise Dave and Linda's two sons through their teenage years.

This was the family Nancy Seaman had married into and chosen to keep her distance from on visits with her husband and sons, all those years. As a person somewhat short on relatives herself, I imagined what it would have been like to be a daughter-in-law in this family—thought about what it would have been like for my children to have had Ward and Helen Seaman for grandparents and to celebrate Thanksgiving around Thelma's table, or Iva's, with canned beans and beets and corn from the summer garden, and afterwards singing around the organ, probably. It was true, I had a tendency to romanticize families like the one with whom I had just unexpectedly spent the last thirty-six hours. Still, it was impossible not to feel, as the plane lifted off and the broad, flat Missouri landscape disappeared behind the clouds, that I had just been in the presence of a kind of goodness and purity of spirit that represented everything that household on Briarwood Court had lacked.

As for what in his upbringing might have led Bob Seaman to stay in his own disastrous marriage, I had discerned no trace of pathology in the household of Ward and Helen Seaman, but there was this, perhaps: Bob had grown up in a family where people made things work, no matter what. It had been loving and forgiving, but the message was, you did the best you could, and you didn't complain. Chinch bugs might take your crop, a machine might cut off your fingers—you carried on. True, every one of his siblings (Margie, Dennis, and Dave) had gone through divorces, but maybe Bob had decided he was going to be the one who stuck it out to the bitter end. Which in a way he had.

I thought about this on the flight back. But what I thought of most of all was how, in all that time, all that talk, I had not heard Ward Seaman or Helen or any of the aunts speak a single angry word about Nancy Seaman. She had destroyed one of the family, in the most brutal way, and no doubt they never wanted to lay eyes on her again. But it wasn't their way to express bitterness or hatred.

"She was an odd girl," Helen had said.

"She wasn't my favorite," Ward told me. And left it at that.

CHAPTER 90

Breakdown on Telegraph

I
t was time to go home. I hadn't found out everything
I wanted, but the summer was drawing to a close, and I needed to step
back from the world of Nancy and Bob Seaman. As much as I was loving my time at the cottage on Potter Lake and my weekends with Lori
and Mike, I wanted to sleep in my own bed again.

In fact, I was still having trouble sleeping at the lake. Hearing me
talk about what was going on, my friends back home and my children
said it sounded as if I was becoming obsessed with Nancy Seaman.

"It's kind of a depressing thing to be thinking about every day, isn't
it?" my daughter asked me, and I agreed it was.

On my last morning in Michigan, I woke earlier than usual, because
I had a plan. Although I had swum almost every morning that summer, I had never yet swum clear across Potter Lake to the other side.
That day I did, and back again. I was halfway across the lake when I
saw a police car pull up beside the cottage. A man in uniform got out.
He stood there on the edge of the water, watching, as I swam back to
shore. Seeing him there, I observed something almost like panic in
myself. *What was he doing there? What had I done?*

Nothing, it turned out. He had been driving by, noticed me swimming far out, and thought he'd just make sure I got in safely. Now he took off. But the anxiety I'd felt, seeing him, stayed with me.

I had made the plan to spend that day at the Ford Motor Company, touring a part of the assembly line. Given what an important role Ford, and its cars, had played in the life of the family that had so consumed my attention all these months, it seemed like a good idea to see what the factory was like, to observe an actual automobile under construction here in the Motor City.

Heading north on Telegraph Road toward Interstate 696 toward the Ford plant at Dearborn, I felt a grinding underneath my Pontiac and then a terrible snapping sound. I just managed to pull off the road into the breakdown lane, where I called AAA. When the AAA tow truck operator looked under my vehicle, he shook his head.

"Chassis's rusted clear through," he said. "I hope you weren't planning on driving this baby again."

As it happened, I was flying out the next morning. Once AAA took off with the car, I called Lori's husband, Mike, who came to pick me up and brought me back to their house. So I never did make it out to the Ford assembly line, but that night, in Lori's SUV, I took Lori and Mike's kids, Ben and Alex, out to Red Lobster (their favorite restaurant) for dinner and then to see *March of the Penguins*. Next morning before dawn, I flew home to California.

CHAPTER 91

A Surprising Development

⟳ In late August, a hearing was scheduled in the case of
Nancy Seaman. I was home now, and felt no need to return for this,
having heard that the proceedings would be strictly a routine matter:
an automatic motion on the part of Michael Farraone, the appeals attorney for Nancy Seaman, to vacate the guilty verdict the jury had
handed down six months earlier. It would not be Lisa Ortlieb representing the prosecution this time but the appeals prosecutor, John
Pallas, a serious young man who had now taken over the case.

Nancy Seaman was not present, of course. Neither were either of
the Seaman brothers or most of those who had sat through the trial
itself, though Eugene D'Onofrio was present, as well as his son, John.
The judge, John McDonald, was the same one who had presided over
Nancy Seaman's original trial.

My friend Lori, though she would normally have covered this event
for the *Free Press,* also missed this hearing, having been on vacation.
But later that day, I managed to track down a young freelance reporter,
Jon Irwin, who had been in attendance. It was from Jon that I learned
what had transpired in the hearing.

The defense had met with the judge to inform him of an affidavit (not yet in hand, but in the works) to be submitted by Rick Cox, business partner of the deceased, alleging that Bob Seaman had been "destitute" and in failing heath at the time of the murder. Michael Farraone had submitted to the judge the view that this new evidence—none of which had been a part of the original trial—would support the defense claim that Bob Seaman had attacked his wife in a bitter rage, out of fear that she was leaving him. Among other motives for such an attack, cited by Farraone, was the information that as a teacher in the school district, Nancy provided Bob Seaman's health insurance, which he was not prepared to forfeit.

Also submitted by Michael Farraone that day was a letter written on behalf of Nancy Seaman by Dr. Lenore Walker. Now, she reiterated her extensive credentials and asserted that the psychological tests her colleague Dr. Abramsky had administered to Nancy Seaman "showed that Mrs. Seaman's psychological state of mind" was in keeping with that of a trauma victim.

"Despite the older son's denial of abuse in the family, . . . she never stopped loving and trying to protect him," Dr. Walker had written.

"The testimony all fit into the cycle of violence which would support Nancy Seaman's growing fears of imminent danger from Bob Seaman. Had I been permitted to so testify, I would have drawn a chart of Nancy Seaman's cycle of violence and compared it to the average battered woman's cycle, demonstrating the changes in tension building and perceptions of danger through the years of living with Robert Seaman.

"Testimony supports the initial purchase of the hatchet as not connected to its subsequent use as a weapon. Mrs. Seaman's behavior in returning the hatchet can be explained by her typical behavior in denying the violence, manipulating and covering it up. This is also true for her denials to the police and hiding the body for several days."

After presenting Judge McDonald with the documents supporting his motion for a reconsideration, Farraone further argued that Larry Kaluzny had been "too nice" to defend Nancy Seaman adequately. The jury was going to do anything to convict her, he said, adding, "It's not too late for Your Honor to see justice done."

Then the judge himself weighed in. Over the insistent objections of appeals prosecutor John Pallas, he cited Nancy Seaman's small size relative to that of her husband, combined with Bob Seaman's alleged reputation as "a brawler," as leaving him in a state of "disbelief" that she could have acted with premeditation. He spoke about the proximity of the stab wounds to one another, as indicative of rage and fear.

Having expressed his disbelief that a woman like Nancy Seaman would plan a murder of this nature, Judge McDonald then made an extraordinary move. For reasons that were arguably without any legal precedent (and despite acknowledging that it was not within the bounds of judicial oversight for him to do what he was about to), the judge now changed the guilty verdict of Nancy Seaman from first-degree murder—the original unanimous finding of the jury in the case—to second degree. With the change of verdict, Nancy Seaman could now entertain the possibility that her sentence might be reduced from life without the possibility of parole to as little as ten years.

It was, courthouse observers asserted when they heard the news, an extraordinary move on the part of the judge, to take this kind of material into account (now, with the trial over and no rebuttal from the prosecution, which argued not only that it could rebut all of these statements but also that it was in any case not within legal bounds to submit new "evidence" after the trial in this manner).

But the judge had spoken. A resentencing would take place in a month, he told the court—though experienced courthouse insiders knew already the new parameters delineated by the reduced charges. Nancy Seaman could be out on parole in as little as seven years, by age sixty-three.

CHAPTER 92

The Boss

J udge McDonald's astonishing reversal of the jury's verdict—though inspiring jubilation among Nancy's supporters—set off a storm in Oakland County and beyond. Although he was an unusually soft-spoken and mild-mannered individual, John Pallas, the prosecutor for the appeals stage of the Seaman case, called the judge's actions "outrageous" and "out of bounds."

"In my seventeen years as a prosecutor," he said, "this may be the most stunning act on the part of a judge that I've ever personally witnessed."

In Arizona, Dennis Seaman was furious, of course. His father, Ward, in Missouri, took the news in much the way he had taken every other hard thing that had occurred in his nearly ninety years of life on earth: you put your hands under your armpits to stop the bleeding, go out to the parking lot a minute to cuss, then carry on the best you can. Ward and Helen's granddaughter Dawn, Margie's daughter, observed that she could never feel all right about serving on a jury after this.

"What's the point of going through all that?" she said. "If the judge just throws out everything you decided after it's over?"

For Julie Dumbleton and her family, the news of what had tran-spired confirmed her worst fears. "The b****" (as she now routinely referred to Nancy, in her e-mails) was getting the last laugh. Julie and her family would never be free of this woman.

I called Julie the day I heard the news, knowing how upset she'd be. I pointed out to her (as Lisa Ortlieb and John Pallas had, as well) that the judge's action would now be appealed—first in the circuit court and, if it weren't shot down there, in the Michigan State Supreme Court. In our conversation about the downgrade of the charges to sec-ond degree, John Pallas had expressed extreme optimism that these other courts would overturn the judge's action, but pointed out too that in a worst-case scenario, in which Nancy Seaman might face the parole board in another ten years, it was highly unlikely (virtually unimaginable, he said) that her application would be looked on fa-vorably. She could spend the next thirty-five years endlessly reapply-ing for parole and getting her hopes dashed every time.

None of this seemed to do much for Julie or her husband and chil-dren, Jake in particular.

"I feel betrayed," Julie cried. Nothing I could tell her seemed to change that.

One good thing, for me at least, came out of the judge's actions. When I called Dennis Seaman to hear his thoughts about what had happened (not too hard to guess what those might be), he told me that in light of what had just taken place, his nephew Jeff was recon-sidering the idea of speaking with me.

In his remarks, both on the day of Nancy Seaman's sentencing and again at the most recent proceedings, the judge had specifically ques-tioned Jeff's credibility (after first acknowledging—strangely enough—that it was not his place to do so). It was on the basis of his belief that Jeff had lied in court (and that despite abundant evidence to the con-trary, Greg had told the truth) that the judge had overturned the jury's decision and ruled as he did.

"I think Jeff might be ready to talk to you now," Dennis told me. "After what happened, he wants to be sure his father's side of the story gets told."

So once again, but from California now, I dialed Jeff Seaman's num-ber and heard the familiar recording. With a certain sense of déjà vu, I once again left a message—a whole series of them, in fact. Finally—not right away, but a couple of weeks later, as the month of September drew to a close, Jeff called me back to say he'd meet with me.

Not at his house. His wife wasn't interested in being part of this. He did not plan on showing me the family videos in which I had expressed repeated interest, or pictures from the old days with his parents and brother. He would meet me someplace for coffee the following weekend, he said. This time, when Jeff suggested that I call him when I got to town, I told him (with a memory of previous attempts to connect with him) that I'd like to pin down the place and time now.

OK, he said. Starbucks in Dearborn, 9 A.M.

I had never gone so far out of my way to visit a Starbucks, but now I did.

He walked in the door at 9:25. Though he knew I'd traveled two thousand miles the night before to see him (flown all night, actually) and knew that our meeting had been preceded by months of phone calls and letters, he walked in with the air of someone who wanted nothing but a cup of coffee.

Vente frappuccino, actually. There was a CD for sale at the cash register—early recordings of Bob Dylan, from his acoustic days. "My dad liked him," he said.

Although it had been Judge McDonald's downgrading of the verdict that inspired Jeff to meet with me, we didn't talk about that. Remembering how busy he'd been, last time we'd spoken (Fourth of July, from the cell phone store), I asked him how things were coming along with the 2007 Explorer, whose engine had been giving him problems.

They'd got the problem solved, finally, he told me. (Not that there wouldn't be a whole new set of problems with whatever model they gave him next to calibrate.) "Launching a car," he said, "is one of the hardest things a person can do. But I live for problems. I only exist in the realm of chaos.

"Somebody that raised a troubled kid would understand what it's like to do my job," he said. "A *really* troubled kid—autistic or something. Only imagine if your kid went from being born to age eighteen in two years, and all the issues you had to deal with got packed into that narrow time frame. That's what it's like, getting a car into production.

"In all of Ford Motor Company," he said, "there's only a handful of people who do what I do." Of all of them, he was the youngest.

He talked about the Explorer then. "We had a durability issue," he said, and then he went on to explain what that meant, as if I might actually understand. To Jeff, at least, the implications had been huge.

"This was bad," he said. "This was a quality issue. The world was ending. This was 'evacuate the women and children' time. Only we solved it.

"The solution was dramatic," he told me, adding cryptically, "Let's just say, if you're really cold, you don't set your drapes on fire."

We weren't just talking about a model of Ford, of course. We were talking about what it meant to be an engineer, and a car person. Who Jeff was, more than that, was an almost endlessly curious, can-do type of individual from a long line of similarly minded men, beginning with his grandfather Ward, but very possibly (though Jeff didn't mention him), Ward's father too—the movie projectionist and scientific farmer. And certainly Bob Seaman: owner of a patent, proprietor of the best batting-cage operation the state of Michigan had ever seen, former trampoline champion, master of five-speed manual shifting, cheerful consumer of monkey brains, tireless coach to twelve-year-old fastpitch softball players, and loving restorer of vintage Mustangs.

"If you want to describe us—me, my grandfather, my dad," he said, "we're all the type that only really exist if there's a hundred things going on all the time, and they're all difficult. I thrive on drama and so did my dad. I don't mind working really hard. I like it. I like to fix problems."

That was the appeal of an engine, of course. It was fixable. As other things in life were not.

"My dad could do anything with a car," Jeff told me. "In the realm of personal relationships, it was a little different."

The best thing for a person like that, of course, was taking a car, and building a personal relationship around it. Bob Seaman had done that with Jeff—with great success, from all appearances, when the two of them had tackled the project of rebuilding the Boss, back when Jeff was a kid—in much same way that Ward had done, with Bob, so many years before, with those slot cars, and then with the old Nash, in the garage back in St. Louis.

His dad hadn't given him the title to the car, and that was OK with Jeff. "He did something better," Jeff said. "He taught me how to fix up my own Mustang."

Jeff was ready for another frappuccino now. When he came back to the table, I asked about his brother. In Greg's case, we both knew, the project of fixing up a Mustang together as Bob and Jeff had done had touched off a disaster.

I asked him about the incident Greg had described to Marsha Low in the *Free Press* interview, in which he claimed his father had hit him so hard when he was a kid that Bob had split his lip. In the article, Greg made a point of saying he'd taken a Polaroid photograph of his injury, in case he needed proof later—but had thrown it away at some point in the intervening years.

"This is pretty ironic," said Jeff. "That instant camera was mine. It was a gift from my parents, only it wasn't a Polaroid. It was a competing brand, and not long after I got it, the company that made it got sued by Polaroid for infringement of their patent or something, so they took the film off the market. There was no way to use that camera after that. It was basically a paperweight. No way my brother could have taken that picture he talked about. We didn't have film."

For all these months, Jeff had remained silent. Now, though, it was as if everything he hadn't said over the course of the last year had to come out, like the steam from an overheated engine.

"Rick Cox," he said, laughing in the manner that had succeeded in alienating the judge and no doubt others in the courtroom, when he testified at his mother's trial.

"Rick's the kind of guy that's easy to like, if you don't know him too well. He'd make a great neighbor—maybe not right next door, but kitty-corner to your house. You know those women who fall in love with men on death row? Rick's a little like that. He loves rescuing lost souls, or people he thinks are lost souls. My mom being one, at the moment. Like it's going to get him into heaven or something."

For Jeff, the clearest way to assess an individual, if he came from the world of engineering, as Rick did, was to speak of how his career had gone since attending Rolla, where Jeff had gone to school and also where Bob Seaman had met Rick in the first place.

"Rick's one of the two-thirds that didn't graduate," he said. "And the funny thing is, the guy has no mechanical skills. Any time anything went wrong at that Waterwheel Building, he called my dad in to fix it. *Toilet clogged? Call Bob.* It was a pretty good deal for him, getting my dad on board as an investor, because he got a full-time handyman in the bargain. Along with a major cash bailout, just when he was in trouble financially."

One thing that mattered a lot to Rick right now, over at the Waterwheel Building, Jeff said, was getting the old waterwheel to turn again. He'd spent $10,000 on some kind of "magic bearings" that were meant to fix it once and for all, but they hadn't worked, so Bob had been constantly tinkering with that thing. Since Bob's death, Jeff said, the wheel no longer turned.

"You know why? My dad isn't there anymore."

Saying this, a look came over him. His speech might be humorous and brittle, his delivery jocular and tinged with a certain wry cynicism, but his blue eyes, under their long lashes, gave him away. For a moment, it was as if a cloud passed over. Then it was gone.

If it was baffling to me why Bob Seaman would have chosen to go into business with Rick Cox in the first place back in 1995, when he bought that 49 percent share in the Waterwheel Building, it was less so to Jeff.

"My dad was sitting on around $3 million in cash at the time, as a result of the buyout from Borg Warner," he said. "But the truth is, he was never all that sharp about money. He was more interested in projects. And even though Rick was a little lame, he was part of that old Rolla mafia, along with Dennis Schleuter and Ron Schoenbach, and my dad was real loyal about that. He'd drag anyone up the corporate ladder that he could, if they'd been at Rolla with him."

"I'll tell you how it was with my dad," Jeff told me, surprisingly serious now. "He was never some grade-point jock. He wasn't top of the class. I'm not even all that sure if he was incredibly smart. But he had this will. He wouldn't quit. He was able to brute force his way through things. He also had this unique ability to inspire other people to do things they'd never achieved before. That's where his success came from."

Jeff was on his third frappuccino. We'd been sitting in this Starbucks for a few hours. Lunchtime had come and gone.

"My dad's career as an engineer was a lot like my baseball playing," he told me.

How so, I asked?

"I have zero talent. I don't look like a baseball player. I'm the shortest guy. I'm definitely not the skinniest. I don't run. I don't field. I don't do anything but hit.

"But I always got the heart awards, back when I played in Little League and high school," he went on. "Because I do everything at a 110 percent, same as my dad. You know how few people slide into bases? Nobody cares enough. But he did."

On his wooden bat team the year before, Jeff told me, he hit .400. At age twenty-five, he already had bone chips in his shoulder. He could feel them every time he swung a bat. He ran, he said, "with cloddishness"—unlike his brother Greg, who had "a swanlike grace" in baseball, but who never deeply cared about the game.

Of course I asked him what he thought of his mother's allegations of abuse by his father. The tone of those Post-it notes from Bob to Nancy had revealed little—no, nothing—in the way of tenderness or love for her, just as her messages had given evidence of nothing but profound anger, hostility, and disappointment.

"Did my dad yell at my mom?" he asked. "Sure he did. Did my mom yell at my dad? Definitely. They were ugly together. It was sickening. Becka and I didn't want to be around them. That's all true.

"But if my mother was being physically abused by my father," he continued, "I would definitely have gone to the police. I would have lost all respect for him. You know what I hate the most? I hate it that she got my grandfather to lie for her. To put an eighty-year-old man on the stand and tell him to lie."

I asked him if he ever thought there might have been abuse in his mother's family. He looked into his cup.

"You remember what my grandfather said at the trial?" he told me. "When Lisa Ortlieb asked him if he knew what spousal abuse was? He said 'It's when one spouse kills the other one.' To my grandpa, I guess, someone had to die before it even qualified."

We sat there for a moment. I was just waiting.

"Look at my uncle," he said. "The guy went to Vietnam . . . I mean, he enlisted for god's sake, right at the very end of the whole damn mess. What's that about? All I can tell you is, both him and my mom, they got out of that house the minute they graduated from high school.

"My dad was always nice to my grandpa. When Grandpa needed money for that house in Woodhaven, my dad helped him out.

"Did you see that deck out in back of the house?" he asked me. "Over at Grandpa's? My father built that deck. He spent his weekends, all one summer, working on that project. I bet my grandpa didn't tell you that."

He had one more observation of Eugene D'Onofrio, a memory that stuck in his mind, he said. It was an odd one.

"He used to get psycho about the birds on the telephone wire, when they'd crap on his driveway," Jeff said. "He got a gun and shot them all down. This was a populated neighborhood, mind you. Houses and people all up and down the street. And still he takes out his gun and bam bam bam. Blows them away."

"My brother? What can I tell you? People tell me I must be devastated that my brother and I never talk anymore, but the fact is, we never really did. He called me up a few months back actually. He couldn't get the Shelby started. I told him what to do. Another time he called to ask where to get a particular kind of bumper for the Shelby, and I told him. That was the sum total of our communication."

It might not be that hard to track down a Shelby bumper, I said. I was guessing that, thanks to the Internet, even a person like me could find one. Jeff agreed that this would be so.

"My brother cares what things are worth," he said. "He measures stuff by what it cost. When we divided up the stuff in my dad's office, it wasn't hard, because all he wanted was the fax machine and the computer, the printer. You know one of the biggest fights we had over all that? The tools. I wanted them because I love to work on cars. My brother wanted them because they're worth a lot of money.

"The fact that he wanted the Explorer," Jeff said, meaning the Explorer that had held his father's dead body. "That disturbed me on such a deep level. But the Ferrari and the Shelby? He can have those."

I had gone on eBay recently to look up prices on Shelby Mustangs of the vintage of Greg's. There was one for $100,000. Another for $120,000. A 1970 Boss for $22,000.

And still, Jeff said, he'd never trade the Boss for the Shelby.

We had been sitting at Starbucks for almost seven hours by now, longer than I had ever sat in any restaurant. Never mind that neither one of us had consumed a bite of food. His initial wariness and brashness had long since worn off.

I saw in Jeff Seaman, now, a young man who loved his wife, and his friends, his home-renovation projects, his tools, his job I think, the boys he coached in baseball. He also loved the Boss, and because the story of the Boss was all tied up with the story of Jeff's relationship with his father, I asked him the question now that I'd been holding onto a long time.

"Can you take me to see the Boss? Could we go for a ride in that car?"

His answer was not unkind, or angry, but it was firm, and came without a moment's hesitation.

"You won't ever see the Boss," Jeff told me. The Boss was personal.

"I would never trade my Boss for fifty Bosses," he went on. As he spoke now, he had the air of a man delivering a poem, though with utterly no awareness that he was sounding that way, I knew. His voice had changed register, however, and his eyes looked different, too.

"You can look at all the Bosses you want on the Internet. Just not *my* Boss.

"It's a very symbolic thing," he said. "It's the first thing my dad and I worked on together that I contributed to without it being completely my dad, and to me, that is priceless. I could talk about the Boss for five days and never talk about anything automotive. It's on a higher plane. It's not about the car. And I can tell you now, whatever Greg feels about owning the Shelby, he will never understand that.

"Anyone with half a brain and a key could start the Shelby, but the Boss is different that way. The Boss takes a certain touch. I don't let other people work on this car. My dad touched this car. The only other person that's going to work on this car is me."

He drives it, though. He doesn't believe a car like the Boss is meant to sit in some garage, or a museum, or for that matter, sail down Woodward Avenue on some bright or rainy August afternoon, when the crowds are out for the Dream Cruise. Sometimes, on weekends, Jeff and Becka go for a ride in the Boss. It might be all a person needed to know about his marriage to hear Jeff say that Becka understood this car.

It was getting on midafternoon now, and Becka was home waiting for him. They were working on a basement renovation project together and they needed to get over to the hardware store. I didn't ask which one.

As we were parting, I mentioned something I imagined that he must know already, even estranged from his brother as he was. Today, at a church in Indianapolis, his brother was getting married to Kristen Sears. She would be changing her name, but not to Seaman, as it turned out, because Greg had officially changed his name to D'Onofrio. The young couple would be living not far from Farmington Hills, in Troy, Michigan, where Greg was embarked on a promising career in the automotive industry.

Jeff hadn't known about the wedding, evidently. Now, hearing the news, he smiled in that same oddly incongruous fashion that had won him few friends at his mother's trial.

"My brother," he said. "He always had a short attention span."

CHAPTER 93

Leaving the Motor City

S o I was back in Marin County.

Over the months that followed, I continued to communicate with many of the people who had been part of my story, and part of my summer in Michigan.

Sometimes now, after pouring my coffee in the morning, I'd dial Lori Brasier's number at the courthouse, and when she'd answer, "Courthouse bureau," I'd answer back, "Mill Valley bureau," and then she'd fill me in on the latest grisly or bizarre or simply heartbreaking case that she was covering that week. She had also sold her first book: a detective novel called *Go Fish*, finished while her husband, Mike, was off duck hunting with his friend Ken up at the lake. During one of these calls (on break from covering the trial of three members of the Albanian mafia), she told me about a conversation she'd had with a deputy from over at the jail—a black woman—who had volunteered to Lori, unsolicited, the news that while incarcerated there, Nancy Seaman had ignored completely the presence of the black deputies, speaking only to those who were white.

I did hear one surprising piece of information about Nancy Seaman during this time: she was not receiving visitors. I had already learned that she had told her teacher friends not to come see her—the

same word she'd given to Rick Cox and the Schleuters and the Schoen-
bachs—but now it turned out she wasn't even letting her father and
brother come to the prison. Or—this was most surprising—her son
Greg. No one.

One of the people I sought out in the months following my return
from Michigan was Dr. Lenore Walker, the expert witness on Battered
Woman Syndrome. It wasn't easy to track her down, because she spent
so much time traveling around providing expert testimony, but eventually I located her at her home in Florida. She was very busy, but had
a few minutes, she said, to speak with me about the case and the syndrome she herself had identified and named, and about the extremely
frustrating situation she had faced testifying in the state of Michigan,
where the law prohibited her from actually examining the defendant
about whose mental state she had been asked to testify.

"Dr. Abramsky administered the TSI [Trauma Symptom Inventory]
test," she told me. "I studied the results of the test. But I was not allowed to divulge the specific findings—though there was no question
in my mind that Nancy Seaman suffered from Posttraumatic Stress
Disorder and Battered Woman Syndrome, as a result of the beatings
she experienced in her marriage to Robert Seaman."

I asked Dr. Walker if she had actually met Nancy Seaman. No, she
had not. Had she heard Nancy Seaman's testimony during the trial?
No again. Similarly, she had not heard Jeff's testimony, or Greg's, or
that of any of the other witnesses in the case, though of course she had
studied the evidence extensively.

"And this would be the evidence provided by Larry Kaluzny?"

"I also spoke with the prosecutor," she said. "I reviewed the entire
case."

"In the months following the trial, then, perhaps you saw the Court
TV broadcast of Nancy Seaman's testimony?" I asked. I assumed, I
said, that she had now studied the trial transcript, given that she had
submitted a letter to the judge recommending the reduction of charges
from first degree to second degree—a letter in which she specifically
referred to and relied on her familiarity with the evidence in the case.

"I didn't have an opportunity to do that," she said, reminding me
how busy she was assessing other cases.

"Those tapes of Nancy Seaman's conversations with her son Greg,
when she was in jail," I said. "They were something, weren't they?"

"She was a mother who loved her sons very much and wanted to
protect them," Dr. Walker noted, a little distractedly.

"You did hear the tapes?" I asked.

Actually, perhaps she hadn't. It had been a long time.

"And what did you make of Nancy Seaman's affidavit to the court, seeking the personal protection order against Julie Dumbleton?" I asked her now. "Some of the things she wrote in that struck me as a little disturbing . . ."

This, too, Dr. Walker had not reviewed. Then she told me that it appeared our time had just about run out. Perhaps I could track her down another day, after she'd had a chance to review her files on this matter. But she was going to be very busy, she reminded me. She had a trial coming up next week, and another one after that.

"Just one more thing," I asked her. "If I were charged with murder and looking to get off on a Battered Woman defense, I would do my darnedest to make those psychological tests indicate that I'd been a battered woman." No doubt Dr. Walker had encountered individuals who'd tried this in the past?

"Absolutely," she agreed. "That's why only highly trained experts are equipped to assess the test findings. I know how to spot that kind of thing."

Still working on the Seaman story, as usual, I placed a call to the man who serviced my car over in Berkeley, Russ McClure, who had most recently come to my rescue when I neglected to put water in the radiator and destroyed my head gasket. I had a quick question for him, for research purposes, concerning the engine on a Mustang, but we got to talking after that, about Bob Seaman's cars and therefore about Bob Seaman.

"You know what his son told me, when I asked what kind of music Bob listened to when he drove the Shelby?" I asked Russ.

Always a polite man, my mechanic friend interrupted me now. "I doubt he listened to music," Russ answered. "He would have wanted to listen to the engine."

How did he know, I asked?

"There was something about that car," Russ told me. "The engine on a Shelby doesn't sound like any other engine."

What came over the telephone then was a soliloquy, off the cuff, on the nature of the Mustang and what it meant to men.

"Not any Mustang," he said. "We're talking about the great ones— 1970 and earlier. Before fuel injection. This was a nearly perfect car in its simplicity. The 289 engine. One of the best Ford ever made.

"Take a look under the hood of a Jaguar, and it's a labyrinth," he went on, "but the Mustang was something anyone could understand.

A man could work on a Mustang. Maybe his life was out of control, but his car was something he could understand.

"The name says it all," said Russ, his voice rising, and still in the same state of heightened agitation, particularly dramatic in an individual I had always known as soft spoken, thoughtful, contemplative. "Raw horsepower! We're talking here about a volatile thing, a killing machine. And still, what goes on with the engine may be more controllable than a man's life."

He paused for a moment then, to breathe. "You have to understand men and their cars, Joyce," he told me. "It can be a relationship like no other."

From Lori Brazier I learned that Larry Kaluzny had lost two more big cases, and that Lisa Ortlieb had won a couple more. More significant for Lisa, though (much as she loved to see justice done), was the news that she was pregnant.

I asked about the case of the fifteen-year-old who'd killed his mother, the one I knew Lisa had been prosecuting. Interestingly, to me—given her hard-line approach to crime and the fact that Lisa had pushed to have the boy tried as an adult—she had put forth a petition to the court that would have allowed the boy to seek parole at the age of thirty-seven (though no earlier than that).

Despite the urging of Ortlieb, and of the boy's grandmother (mother of the murdered woman), the judge presiding over the case had ruled against this petition, arguing that twenty-two years was not sufficient time for the boy to serve in such a crime. This ruling had been handed down, Lisa now told me, by none other than Judge John McDonald— the same man who had overturned the verdict of the jurors in the Nancy Seaman trial and reduced Nancy's conviction from first degree to second degree.

Jake Dumbleton—the young man who had kept as far away from me as possible for much of the summer—dropped me an e-mail that fall to say he'd written a paper for English class. Would I proofread it? When (happy to assist) I opened the document, I saw that it was a story about the day he'd come home from baseball practice to learn of Bob Seaman's death. Perhaps he wanted me to read it for reasons that went beyond checking the punctuation and spelling.

He told me now, when he called me back from Albion College, that he was taking a psychology course.

"Would that have been the kind of thing you'd have pictured your-self studying, a couple of years ago?" I asked him.

Definitely not, he told me.

I was hearing regularly from Julie Dumbleton too, and like her son, she said she was doing better, though I had learned not to bring up certain topics when we communicated—*48 Hours* being one. (I had tried repeatedly to reach Nancy Kramer, the producer of the seg-ment about the Seaman murder, but she had not returned my calls, and when I finally got her on the phone, she explained she was not at liberty to discuss with me the process by which CBS produced its programming.)

In the spring of 2006, Jenna Dumbleton celebrated her sixteenth birthday and got her driver's license—a day (like so many others around the Dumbleton household) that brought Bob to mind, of course. Jenna was doing well at school, Julie told me, but there were other pressures in her life. The shoulder injury that had been giving her trouble, during the summer I spent in Michigan, attending fast-pitch softball games, had now flared up, worse than before. A story in the local Northville paper that ran the morning after opening day of softball season reported that Jenna—star pitcher on her team, the Mustangs—would have to stay off the mound for at least part of the season, while she waited for the shoulder to repair. For a family like the Dumbletons, this was a bad blow.

One day when we spoke, Julie told me she had recently been cruis-ing the Internet looking up "Women Killers" with a search engine (she couldn't help herself), when she came upon the name of a professor in California who was writing an article on the subject. After reading her letter to him about Nancy Seaman, he'd decided to include what had happened to Bob in a textbook he was writing. This had given Julie a wonderful feeling of empowerment, she told me.

"Now Nancy's going to be in a textbook, as a nut case," she said.

As always, when I talked with Julie, I was unsettled by the obvious pain that had stayed with her, almost two full years after Bob Seaman's murder. Of course, it had been more than the murder itself that trau-matized Julie.

I think it was the way something which was, to her, so simple and pure had been transformed in the eyes of the media into something "creepy" and even immoral that had so utterly disheartened Julie Dum-bleton. It would be like Ward Seaman, being accused of tampering illegally with those slot cars, or Helen, absconding with funds from her Eastern Star Ladies' Society.

Specifically because her sense of violation was so great, however, Julie now saw me, and the book I was writing, as her "last hope" of undoing all the damage incurred by the media coverage of the case to date and, more than that, restoring Bob Seaman's reputation. She offered to proofread my manuscript for me and check the facts (reminding me, as she did so, of all the trouble that other author had gotten into recently, the one who wrote the Oprah book about his experiences in drug rehab).

It was a heavy responsibility, having Julie Dumbleton's whole sense of well-being depend on something I wrote, and I had a sinking feeling, as I read her e-mails and heard her voice on the phone, that nothing I could do was likely to provide what she sought.

Still, I liked her and did my best to stay in touch. When she wrote me, one day around Christmas, to ask once more how my work was going, I shot back a quick note: "I'm still trying to understand why Nancy Seaman did it."

"I can tell you right now," Julie responded, and though she was too polite to say it, I could feel, under the surface of her words, a certain small impatience. *Was that my problem? Why hadn't I asked sooner?*

"Hell hath no fury like a woman scorned," she fired back.

For Dick Dumbleton, the focus remained on his children, he told me: making sure they stayed on the right track in life and didn't let this terrible and disillusioning experience turn them into angry or cynical human beings. He told me the advice he'd given Jake, and Jenna too, that he hoped would serve them well when they were feeling lost—a variation, actually, on the acronym *WWJD* adopted by young people in the Christian fundamentalist world, to keep Jesus in mind. The letters Dick suggested that his son and daughter refer to for guidance were *WWBD: What would Bob do?*

Whether in response to that question or simply as a way of honoring the man he continued to grieve, Jake Dumbleton announced that winter his intention to get a tattoo on his back. It would be the letters *RLS,* and beside them, the word "family" in Korean.

"I wish you wouldn't do that," Julie had told him. "Every time you see the tattoo, it's going to be a reminder."

"How can I be reminded?" Jake pointed out. "It's going to be on my back."

But the truth was, with or without a tattoo, Jake Dumbleton would remember Bob Seaman.

Margie Palmer—eldest child of Ward and Helen Seaman—had been occupied, over the last months, with the task of moving her parents, Ward and Helen, from their apartment in Ballwin, Missouri, to Riley, Kansas, where she lived, down the block from her daughter Dawn and her grandchildren. As always, she reported that her father was doing well, and going on regular bowling outings with his great-grandson. Nothing stopped that man.

Dennis Seaman continued to show signs of wariness where he and I were concerned—never having been fully convinced, evidently, that my alleged feminism wouldn't get in the way of my reporting his brother's story without tilting the scales heavily in favor of Nancy Seaman.

Jeff—after our intense one-day meeting at Starbucks—once again ceased to return my calls. Despite the friendliness of our handshake at the coffee place that day, subsequent calls to Jeff's cell phone yielded only the same familiar message, though somewhere along the line I heard he and Becka had gotten a puppy: a Jack Russell terrier they'd named "Torque."

About Greg Seaman, I heard nothing. But of course, there was no Greg Seaman anymore, only a Greg D'Onofrio. Long ago, in her application for the PPO against Julie Dumbleton, Nancy Seaman had expressed the fear that if Bob abandoned her, she might "cease to exist." How odd it was, I thought, that in the end the one who'd disappeared was Greg.

I went to a party in San Francisco. Hearing what I'd been up to—and that I'd spent the summer in Michigan—a number of my fellow guests expressed the view that I must be happy to be home again.

"Michigan's a red state, right?" someone said. "Vegetables overcooked enough for you?"

Truthfully, I missed the state of Michigan, and not just for the lakes and the swimming. I missed my friends there. I missed the heat of summer nights. I even missed seeing all the great old cars lined up in parking lots, on Friday nights, with their hoods up, so car lovers cruising by could study the engines.

Driving past the high school in my town of Mill Valley, I looked at a bunch of teenagers—Goth clothing, heavy on the piercings—and thought about the Compuware girls' fastpitch softball team, icing their rotator cuffs and traveling, weekends, to unglamorous places like Ohio and Kentucky for tournaments, in the company of their parents. Their hero: Cat Osterman, a nineteen-year-old left-handed pitcher from Houston, Texas, member of the 2004 gold medal–winning Olympic women's softball team and U.S. Softball Collegiate Player of the Year for 2005.

There were worse people to emulate, that was for sure.

I went to see the movie *Capote* the night it opened, almost writhing in my seat as I watched the spectacle of another writer—now long dead—who had obsessively immersed himself in the story of a murder and its perpetrators. Unlike me, that writer had gotten into bed with the killers, and ultimately betrayed them in ways that may even (as some speculated) have hastened his own decline and death. As brilliant as the book—that his efforts and subterfuge produced—had been (and in fact it sat on my desk all that year, just to the right of my computer), I felt grateful, again, that I had not come close to befriending Nancy Seaman.

I found myself following the auto industry with a new vigilance, noting the absence of American cars on the freeways of Northern California, listening for news reports about the loss of jobs. In January of 2006 came the announcement from Ford Motor Company: as many as ten plants, out of forty-three, would be closed down. Twenty-five thousand workers were to be laid off, a fifth of the company's workforce. Although there were no gale-force winds, no breaking of a levee, it was a disaster for that city on the scale of a hurricane. A different kind of conflagration for Detroit than what took place in 1967, but no less destructive.

In the city of Detroit, Martha Reeves (formerly of Motown's superstar megasuccessful group Martha and the Vandellas) was elected to the city council. One of the first projects she hoped to put before the council, she announced, was the installation (long overdue) of a statue commemorating Aretha Franklin, godmother of soul. In Holly-

wood, I learned, the director John Waters was developing a television
series, inspired by real court cases, with the first episode set to feature
the Seaman murder. It was going to be a comedy. No role for Chief
Bill Dwyer in that one, probably.

I had hoped that my return to sunny California—land of foreign
cars and heirloom tomatoes—might put some distance between myself and Nancy Seaman, but the story came home with me.

"So why did she do it?" more than one friend asked me, knowing
I'd been gone all summer, working all year. I must know by now.

"Her marriage wasn't all she'd dreamed it could be," I said, lamely.
"I think her husband disappointed her."

He hadn't been her knight in shining armor after all. He took her
away from Lincoln Park, all right, but Briarwood Court hadn't turned
out to be the promised land, and maybe for reasons that went beyond
the one her son Jeff had mentioned to me (confirming Julie Dumbleton's report): that Nancy had been shocked and disgusted by how
many nonwhite families were living on their very street.

The list was long, of things that had left Nancy Seaman dissatisfied
and angry. Her husband hadn't fixed the step out in front of the house.
Her husband didn't bring home the right kind of coffee cake. Her husband hadn't become president of Borg Warner.

The freezer in her neighbors' barn made a humming sound that
distracted her. Her in-laws had failed to give her a present the first time
Bob brought her home for a visit. The school system where she taught
celebrated Martin Luther King Day but not Veterans' Day. A little boy
broke a window on her car. Julie Dumbleton's dog was scary (never
mind Julie Dumbleton herself).

Nancy Seaman was a woman who had substituted the appearance
of having a happy marriage for the experience of actually having one.
She measured the performance of her husband against that of her acquaintances' and coworkers' husbands, and found him forever coming up short. To her, the only way Bob Seaman should be happy was
with her. And if he couldn't be happy with her, he should at least stick
around to be miserable with her. The one thing that was totally unac-
ceptable: leaving.

As close as I could guess, that was what angered Nancy Seaman
the most. She had bought the condo and packed up her belongings,
and maybe she would even have moved there eventually if things had
worked out differently. But the one thing that she would never allow

was for Bob to leave her first. And that's what he'd told her he was doing.

She was a woman who could not picture herself without a man— a woman who could write, in that PPO application, that without Bob she might cease to exist. In that way, I now knew clearly, she and I bore no resemblance to each other. But in another way, and a deeply upsetting one, the part of Nancy Seaman I recognized within my own self was finally becoming clear.

On a rainy night in winter, I had dinner with a couple of therapist friends, with whom I shared my frustration over coming up with a conclusion to the book I'd been writing.

One of the therapists was named Candis, a woman just about my age and just about the age of Nancy Seaman and Julie Dumbleton.

When I described to her the alarming and seemingly unabating grief of Julie Dumbleton even now, close to two years after the murder, she nodded.

"She feels responsible for Bob Seaman's murder, of course," Candis offered. "So do her children. And in a certain way, it's an understandable conclusion."

It was a lightning bolt for me. As much time as I'd spent meditating on the case, as many hours as I'd lain awake considering the characters involved, this had never occurred to me, but the moment my therapist friend suggested it, I wondered why I'd never seen it before.

While no one could say the tragedy on Briarwood Court had been the Dumbletons' fault, it was also possible that if Bob Seaman had never met the Dumbletons he might be alive today.

It was also possible—highly likely, even—that something else would have come up, some other object to absorb the rage of Nancy Seaman. Still, it had been the Dumbletons who, in Nancy Seaman's view, had ruined her life. Their friendship with her husband had sent her over the edge and led her to kill him.

"No wonder she's so upset," Candis said. "I would be too. Or at least I'd be getting some heavy-duty therapy right about now."

So maybe that was Julie's story, but what of mine?

"What was it that drew you to this story?" Candis asked me. It was a question I had asked myself plenty of times, of course. Only this time, she followed up with an observation of her own.

"Every family has a murder, you know," she said to me. "Not literally in most cases. But someone in the family feels a need to kill somebody else. So where was the murder in your family?"

The picture came to me then, not of the man I was once married to, but of the children we shared. He and I had parted long ago, but they had stayed around, absorbing the rage and sorrow the death of our marriage had created. Unlike Nancy Seaman, I had never marched my children to the closet where their father's clothing hung, to say, "See, you may not feel you have a father, but really you do." I didn't take them along with me to confront some lover of his on her front lawn, and I didn't roll up the sleeve of my blouse to show them bruises and say he'd given them to me. No such issues had arisen, in our lives.

But this much was true: like Nancy Seaman, at times I had asked my children to choose me over their father. I had attempted to enlist their ultimate loyalty. I didn't want to kill him, but I wanted them to behave as if he were dead.

That first morning I learned about the Seaman family, I thought that I wanted to explore the story of a marriage gone horribly wrong, and over the course of many trips to Michigan in the months that followed, I did that.

But really, the story that haunted me and wrecked my sleep that year, was not so much the part about the Seamans' marriage. It was the part about the Seamans' children. The violence they endured and the deaths it produced began long before that Mother's Day night in the garage, and it was still going on, almost a year later (and a year after that). And although I had taken in the story with the complacence of a woman who said, "I'd never do something like that. I'd never commit murder," a terrible realization came to me. In some ways, I had done that.

Madame Bovary, c'est moi.

What I got wrong, for a time—what provided me with false assurance and what led me off course from a clear view of the truth—was imagining that Nancy Seaman's only victim was her husband and that the only act of homicide in her story took place when she lowered her hatchet into her husband's skull.

Killing Bob Seaman was only one act of violence perpetrated by Nancy Seaman. The other was asking—requiring—her younger son to choose her over his father. In some ways, it could be said, she asked her son to kill his father, to save her life.

And he said yes.

I didn't know it at the time, but I think now that it was this similarity between my story and the Seamans' that drove me to get on a plane to Michigan that December. There was a time when I had asked the same thing of my children that Nancy Seaman asked of hers. There was a time in the history of my own family when seeing my children, the people I loved most in the world, offering up their love and loyalty to the person who had inflicted the greatest pain I'd known felt like an act of abandonment and betrayal, and I told them so. I asked them to engage in mutiny, come over to my ship, sink his. With great wisdom and a surprising degree of compassion, they refused. They even forgave me.

The truth is, a kind of violence lurks under the surface in some of the most civilized-seeming families, and though, most likely, it won't lead to murder, small deaths occur in families every day. They did in mine.

I traveled to New York that winter—the city where my son Charlie lives. At age twenty-three, he was out of college now, living in Brooklyn, making music and painting, and running an after-school arts program for kids. He had a sweet and loving girlfriend—a teacher of yoga, herself a child of divorced parents. Though they were young, these two did not look for additional drama in their lives. They'd seen enough of it.

I took Charlie out for lunch one day during my visit. Sitting across from him at a little vegetarian restaurant on the Lower East Side, I asked him a question, though I knew his answer might make me sad.

"Did you ever feel afraid, after the divorce?" I asked him. "Did it ever seem to you that I was out of control?"

I was talking about my anger toward his father, I told my son. I was talking about times when, whether I said it or not, I had seen Charlie's love for his father as a threat to his love for me. I was talking about the position I'd placed him in—him, and his brother and sister—of standing, unprotected, in the war zone, with the bullets flying from both directions. No wonder my children had huddled close and clung tight to each other, though Nancy Seaman's had taken the opposite approach and scattered.

Charlie looked at me kindly then, no malice or desire to hurt me present in his voice.

"Yes," he said.

At some point in the discussion, he had picked up his fork and knife, and now, as we spoke, he enacted a little dance across the table-cloth. *His father, fork. Me, knife.*

It was a hard thing to watch, but my water stayed on the table this time, and I felt no impulse, for once, to lift the glass over my head and upend it. I told my son I was sorry, then. Later, I would tell his brother and sister that too.

There was more to be said, and no doubt there were some things that had happened in our lives that no apologies could repair, but mostly that was the end of it.

⌐ᴧᴧᴧ← About the Author

Joyce Maynard has been a reporter for the *New York Times*, a magazine journalist, radio commentator, and syndicated columnist, and is the author of five novels, including *To Die For,* which was based on a true crime and made into a major motion picture starring Nicole Kidman. Her best-selling memoir, *At Home in the World,* has been translated into nine languages. She appears regularly as a storyteller with The Moth in New York City and serves on the faculty of the Stonecoast Writing Program in Maine. Mother of three grown children, she makes her home in Mill Valley, California, and Lake Atitlan, Guatemala.

Her Web site is JoyceMaynard.com.

~~~ Index